BEYOND
REVOLUTION

BEYOND REVOLUTION

A New Theory of Social Movements

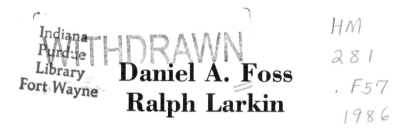

Daniel A. Foss
Ralph Larkin

Introduction by Stanley Aronowitz

Critical Perspectives in Social Theory Series

Bergin & Garvey Publishers, Inc.
MASSACHUSETTS

First published in 1986 by
Bergin & Garvey Publishers, Inc.
670 Amherst Road
South Hadley, Massachusetts 01075

6789   987654321

Printed in the United States of America

LIBRARY OF CONGRESS CATALOGING-IN-PUBLICATION DATA

Foss, Daniel A., 1940–
 Beyond revolution.

 (Critical perspectives in social theory)
 1. Social movements.   2. Radicalism—United States.
I. Larkin, Ralph W., 1940–   . II. Title.
III. Series.
HM281.F57   1986   303.4′84   85-20157
ISBN 0-89789-077-9
ISBN 0-89789-087-6 (pbk.)

*This book is dedicated to
the memory of
William F. O'Donnell,
1939–1973,
sociologist, artist, social activist,
visionary, friend:
Casualty of a failed revolution.*

Contents

ABOUT THE AUTHORS

DANIEL A. FOSS was born in The Bronx, N.Y., on July 26, 1940. He received his B.A. in Sociology at Cornell in 1961; his M.A. and Ph.D. were granted by Brandeis University in 1962 and 1969, respectively. Foss' dissertation was published, in abridged form, as *Freak Culture*. He taught at the School for Critical Studies at the California Institute for the Arts, and at Livingston College and the Newark College of Arts and Sciences, Rutgers University. Upon finding himself unemployable as a sociologist, Foss took courses in data processing at Syracuse University and New York University. He has been employed as a computer programmer and data base manager for academic and government researchers. He continues to have an abiding interest in the historical study of social movements, medieval Europe, and China.

RALPH LARKIN was born in Los Angeles on May 27, 1940. He was graduated from the University of California, Santa Barbara, in 1961, and taught elementary school in California. He received a Master's degree in education at California State University at Northridge in 1966 and a Ph.D. in Sociology of Education at UCLA. Larkin moved to New York in 1970, where he worked as a Research Associate at the Center for Urban Education. In 1973, he became an Assistant Professor of Sociology at Rutgers University, Newark, where he and Daniel Foss met. They collaborated on the study of social privilege, social movements, and post-movement phenomena, which resulted in several articles and this book. The publication of Larkin's controversial *Suburban Youth in Cultural Crisis* by Oxford University Press resulted in the denial of tenure at Rutgers. Larkin presently operates his own research consultancy in New York City. His scholarly interests remain focused on the reproduction of social domination and the various struggles against it.

Preface

This book occurred due to the circumstance that sociologists no longer read history. In a discipline which canonizes those who read history as classical theorists, we succumbed to the delusion that reverence for them had relevance to practice. What is more, history was our pornography in that it dealt with the dirty parts of human life unmentioned and unthought about in polite social discourse. We observed that social conflict is both as old as social privilege as well as ever-recurrent, and that the form in which social movements have become stereotyped within sociology is representative of only a thin time slice in the historical record. To correct the irrational stereotypes, we wrote this book, fully aware that the prevalence of irrational stereotypes and distorted images are no accident and are valid objects in the investigation of sociology itself. Where we find eternalizing or other ahistorical distortions, we so indicate and try to account for their existence, from whatever part of the political spectrum they derive.

The practice of the sociology of social movements and the construction by psychologists of personality profiles of social-movement participants dictate that the object of investigation in the respective disciplines remain both stable and quantifiable (e.g., size of membership rolls, frequency of meeting attendance, conservatism-liberalism). Additionally, on the behavioral level, the procuring of external grant support requiring up to a year for approval, the hiring of the soft-money staff, design of the data set, blocking out of data records, sampling and/or subject recruitment, methodological choices regarding data not collected, and so forth—these concerns are familiar to the reader and constitute a lead time element of up to two years. During which time the object of investigation has transmuted itself beyond anything envisaged in the research design or has completely disappeared, or has, worse, been superceded by phenomena of an avowed, albeit spurious, "social movement" character. The confluence of intellectual dispositions with contracted promises to the funding agency, and personal interest in research outcomes, can create a situation in which funds are returned unspent, papers go unpresented, articles unwritten, and promotions unsought. This can render the object of investigation to the realm of low probability exogenous event and nothing may eventually be studied. *Something* must be studied and the appropriateness of studying it proceeds therefrom.

We are suggesting, nay, committing, an unseemly disruption from the back halls of social science, that the hallmark of the object of investigation as it confronts the would-be investigator is its evasion of, resistance to, or, in the most extreme case, destruction of, the processes whereby it is conventionally objectified. We deny, however, that investigation is impossible: it must proceed from observed patterns of qualitative change in the object of investigation, one of whose defining processes is the emergence of the human subject in history such that in a social movement a huge psychic leap occurs. *Anyone who was there will never be the same and, correspondingly, and dialectically, anyone who was not there is constituted as no longer the same in relation to those who were, however much they deny it*. The investigation of social movements which proceeds from an open-minded alertness to qualitative changes in participants, as well as in their observed behavior, is *decisive—beyond the study of social movements—to the creative formulation of macrosocial theory*. We herein will suggest that the critique of capitalism in its most recent phase requires that one cease fixation on the exploitation of productive labor to focus instead upon wasting time for its own sake and social discipline for its own sake.

Symptomatic of the discontinuity of our thinking with the rest of the profession and the disarray of social-movement theory was our placement at association meetings in paper sessions that included, among other topics, earthquake disasters and pedestrian behavior at intersections. Most of our published work on postmovement phenomena ended up in journals focusing on sociology of religion. With a few exceptions, our work seemed incomprehensible to other sociologists, even when it was appreciated. In 1978 we decided that the remedy to the problem was to write a comprehensive explication of our theory of social movements. This volume is the result of that effort.

While writing this book, we received help from friends and associates who read the manuscript and commented on it, provided resources, and encouragement. We would like to thank and express our appreciation to Maurice Stein, Henry Eskowitz, Mike Brown, Andy and Harriet Lyons, Ray Calluori, Murray Karstadt, and Miriam Fischer for their comments on the manuscript in its various stages. We would especially like to thank Stanley Aronowitz for his support and help in publishing this work. We would also like to thank him and the staff at *Social Text* for publishing what was once an appendix to this work called, "A Lexicon of Folketymology of the 1960s," in their book, *The 60s Without Apology*.

Ralph Larkin would like to single out Peter Freund for his support, encouragement, and careful reading and critique of the manuscript. In addition, I would like to thank my wife Debra, for her support and unfailing confidence in me; my parents Ralph and Edna Larkin; my in-laws Herman (now deceased) and Jennie Douglass; and my children Stephen, Thomas, Andrew, and David for their love and emotional support.

Introduction

Until the 1960s, the study of social movements, particularly in the United States, was safely subsumed within social science as just another field of empirical study. The tendency in American sociology and political science to renounce "grand theory" in favor of theories of the middle range, or no theory at all, effectively limited social movement study to things that could be counted. Although some very good work was done, social movement study became an ethnographic enterprise, a branch of the "participation" subfield of political science. Rarely, if ever, did researchers consider the question of the relation of social movements to the processes of historical change. This relation, like many other issues, was generally considered better dealt with by silence.

Of course, the one exception was marxist social theory. But even here, the subject was confined to the study of working class organizations, trade unions and left-wing parties. Views of other social movements were limited to those in precapitalist societies, in which peasant revolts, middle-class rebellions, and even proletarian movements were discussed, say, in terms of the transition from feudalism to capitalism, or in any event were subsumed under broadly conceived class theories.

Since 1968, investigators and social theorists have elevated the status of social movement research to the level of grand theory. The reason seems quite clear: the May '68 events in France, part of a world-wide student revolt, and the Cuban, Chinese, and other "third-world" revolutions signified the appearance of new social actors on the historical stage. For many writers—Andre Gorz and Alain Touraine in France, Alvin Gouldner in the U.S., Jürgen Habermas in Germany, to name a few of the most important—the marxist problematic of working-class revolution had come to an end; either new classes, such as the intellectuals, or movements whose relationship to class was ambiguous or nonexistent, had entered History without the old parties and their constituents. Peasants, feminists, intellectuals, ecologists, and youth—these social movements prefigured an entirely new historical paradigm. Social movements became the euphemism for the "new" subject.

Today the study of social movements has taken on an intellectual urgency unparalleled since the rise of working-class movements in the nineteenth century. Although the old empiricism has by no means disappeared from the discourse, the entrance of social theory into the consideration of issues surrounding the appearance of new social movements has already replaced the old questions: it is no longer sufficient to study how social movements arise and what the character of their activities is. Now the questions are: What are social movements? What is their relationship to class categories? What is their place in the general and specific processes of social transformation?

Prior to the pivotal decade of the sixties, social research, implicitly or explicitly, understood social transformation almost exclusively in terms of class, i.e. economic, terms. "Collective" action was said to occur at those moments in history when workers, middle classes, and peasants were no longer able to consent to the policies of the state, the "hegemonic" ideologies of ruling classes, or prevailing economic conditions. Although social theory has hotly contested the causal agents of collective action (some attributed its appearance to crisis in the economic sphere, others to the "revolution of rising expectations" identified with better times), the key idea in almost all cases was that strikes, demonstrations, and other disruptive manifestations of mass discontent were the function of class deprivations that were somehow ignored by the forces of social order. Even when this notion was disputed, the underlying agreement among most students of mass movements was that their impetus could be ascribed, generally, to a rational calculation among their subjects that disruptive forms of action were more efficient for achieving certain goals than normal methods of peaceful petition or electoral participation.

Beyond Revolution is perhaps the most sweeping challenge to these theories that has appeared since social movements became an appropriate subject for theory. Foss and Larkin have examined effectively and comprehensively the major variants of theories that explain the appearance of new social movements on the basis of some form of rational calculation, whether "resource deprivation"-driven or motivated by the capacity of social categories to engage in a contest over resource mobilization. Moreover, Foss and Larkin have refused the narrowly construed concept that social movements are invariably class-determined, although they do not deny that class forces remain an important underlying structure in accounting for various types of social struggle. For them, class movements are one important type of social movement, but in analyzing the most recent decades of mass struggle, they find that these movements have involved many other sections of the population. For Foss and Larkin, the youth, race, feminist, and religious movements of the sixties and seventies are not to be understood as the displacements of class struggle but should be engaged on their own terms as valid responses to the historical conjunctures, *including* economic forces, that produced them.

But *Beyond Revolution* is more than critique. It advances its own theory of social movements, one that defines *what they are* (in contrast to much of the recent literature on the subject), and *what they do* in terms of the social reproduction of prevailing social relations. Social movements are not the same as purely cultural movements, such as intellectual tendencies, religious movements, and art trends; they involve a specific form of political intervention. Foss and Larkin argue that social movements disrupt the form of social reproduction, even if temporarily; that they entail, for their adherents, a reinterpretation of social reality; and that they almost always propose a transformation of social relations and of "human nature." So, not every strike, demonstration, or riot is identical with the appearance of a social movement—striking workers belong to bureaucratic unions that have long ceased to possess the characteristics of social movements; counterdissidents may only engage in demonstrations; and riots can take place within the context of a football rally. What the authors have achieved is to place social movement in a specific framework, showing that its appearance, throughout history, is largely unanticipated by ruling groups or social observers because its leading characteristic is the rebellion against the prevailing social structure which is thought by those in control to be a fact of nature.

Second, *Beyond Revolution* is concrete. Throughout the text, four key world-historical events are drawn upon to illustrate their theory: the English revolution of the seventeenth century; the French revolution a century later; the Bolshevik revolution; and the revolts of the 1960s and '70s, which includes much more than the so-called western new left, embracing the Iranian Revolution and other third-world movements. The historical and global character of the examples strengthens the claims of the text. Foss and Larkin boldly have adduced "laws" of social development corresponding to the emergence of new social movements.

Third, *Beyond Revolution* offers not only a theory of entailment but of stages in the rise and decline of these movements. According to the authors, social movements are short-lived and arise only under determinate conditions. In both victory and defeat the tendency to routinization (in winning cases) destroys the institution-shaking quality of the movement, and decadence (in losing cases) produces demoralization among even its most fervent actors, and, consequently, the old order reestablishes itself.

Although Jean-Paul Sartre's monumental *Critique of Dialectical Reason* is not invoked in the text, there are striking parallels with this work. Sartre's philosophy of history can be considered a "marxism of spontaneity." He posits the dialectic between the "practico-inert" (the givens of the social world: the past) and the emergent transformation of seriality (isolated individuals) into groups-in-fusion that are constrained by the practices of the past but can transform social relations. Sartre's is not a theory of history in which parties and elites play the crucial role in changing society; rather, change is seen as the result of the unanticipated formation of rebellious movements in which the mind/body split, the contradiction between the individual and the collective realms, and differences between ideology and conscious intervention are temporarily overcome. Sartre's book (1960) had the immediate impetus of the Algerian revolution, which for him constituted the main case in point for the argument. Needless to say, this work is only now beginning to receive the attention it deserves, for even the French "left" has dissociated itself from Sartre's insistence that movements cannot be "built" according to party edict or bureaucratic plan. Together with Henri Lefebvre, whose work on everyday urban life anticipated the famous student and worker rebellion of May '68, Sartre insists on the primacy of the social to explain the political in the face of the marxist tendency (since Kautsky and Lenin) to privilege the state (the political institutions) and most importantly, the party, as the real arena/agents of social change. So, Foss and Larkin place themselves in a different tradition, a tradition now represented in France most notably by sociologist Alain Touraine, one that insists on the self-production of society. *Beyond Revolution* is not only the best work on social movements since Touraine's important work of 1968–77, deriving from the significance of the May events, but the authors have gone beyond that work by reading back into history the general conditions for the formation of social movements. That is, they have not explained the unanticipated appearance of new social movements as the product of specific late capitalist conditions of, say, post-scarcity; they have shown that the attempt to disrupt social structure is the key to understanding the revolutionary process in any society marked by classes and economic and political hierarchy. For, in concert with Sartre and Lefebvre, Foss and Larkin have insisted that the reproduction of social relations—ideologically, economically, and politically— must be disrupted by movements that constitute themselves as an alternate community in the wide meaning of the term, in order to really make change, and that these changes are not limited and instrumental in character but propose to revolutionize the human condition.

In essence, a social movement is simultaneously utopian and practical: it engages in collective action to make changes, but will not be satisfied by concessions from the ruling group. Feminists demand an end to male domination and patriarchy even as they wrest jobs and social equality within the existing order; the most radical sections of the Black freedom movements in the U.S., U.K., and South Africa demand human rights, including voting rights, at the same time as they propose to transform race and other social relations. These movements are like Halley's comet: they shoot up and light the sky and fall. But it is the stuff of which social transformation is made. Foss and Larkin take their place in the tradition that regards trade unions, socialist parties, organizations of social reform as the *sediment* of failed social movements, the forms in which the future becomes the past.

This perspective locates *Beyond Revolution*. It is clearly influenced by the social movements of the 1960s, most of which regarded their immediate predecessors such as trade unions, left-wing organizations, and single-issue pressure groups as obstacles rather than allies. These institutions, in many cases, were once social movements that felt obliged, in the long periods between upsurges, to function within and not against the state and its bureaus. As many observers have noted, they tend to become bureaucracies themselves and therefore part of the existing order. Their revolutionary and radical phrases are part of their legitimating baggage but have little to do with their practice. When the new social movement period arrives, even against their will, the established liberal and left organizations find themselves defending the arrangements they have made with the existing order, discover they have become agents of social reproduction and condemn the new social movements as irresponsible. In turn, the hostility of the establishment left helps radicalize the new social movements.

For an illustration of the dynamics at play here, consider the birth and fate of Students for a Democratic Society (SDS). It began as a student movement seeking to democratize liberal representative institutions that had evolved into hierarchies excluding ordinary people from processes of decision making. In 1962, SDS felt it was by no means a new social movement in the sense discussed here. It had begun to reinterpret reality in political terms, but was not seeking a "new human individual" or a new definition of social relations. The antagonism of labor and liberal leaders towards these fairly limited goals produced the beginning of radicalization among a generation of students that believed in civil rights and later opposed military intervention in the third world. SDS became part of a social movement when it no longer defined itself in terms of "issues" but demanded nothing less than social transformation. Even as a fairly substantial majority of liberals and a growing minority of labor officials supported the antiwar program of student radicals, the "movement" had already surpassed its own program, which had presupposed working within and not against the prevailing structure. By the late sixties, SDS was proposing a new mode of life in which social, cultural, political, and economic relations would be radically changed and the whole ethos of self-interest and competitive advantage overthrown. The profound radicalization of the youth and student generation was not matched, of course, by a general radicalization among workers, professionals, and others. With the possible exception of the most radical wing of the Black freedom movement, the youth movement found itself politically and ideologically isolated. Foss and Larkin do not discuss the particulars of the ebbing of the world-wide counter politics of the youth movement, but discuss in some detail the results. The seventies are marked by a massive reinstitution of the social order. The disruption is over: radicals carry their fervor in their heart but return to school, most typically, to law school; others enter mainstream reproductive institutions like electoral politics and trade unions; still others raise families in that peculiarly private way that seems unique to America. In short, "life" goes on.

Sociologists and psychologists tend to interpret "normality" as a life-cycle phenomenon. Youth rebel, but the 30s and 40s of a person's life are times for careers and families. So, radicalism turns out to be a generational phenomenon, something that passes with age. Others take a purely conjunctural position: the movement dies when repression breaks its ranks, or factionalism causes damaging splits or economic and political conditions change as reforms are enacted to thwart the radical motion. Foss and Larkin take these historical conjunctures seriously, but by making a transhistorical analysis, they show that as social movements become power groups, as the revolution settles into reform, in *all* social movement periods the dynamic is lost and bureaucracy settles in.

Since *Beyond Revolution* posits the persistence of ineluctable contradictions, the period of calm and order is more or less temporary. New social movements arise as reforms wear thin or promises go unkept. If a new social contract is often able to produce decay in the upsurge, its abrogation by those in power is a built-in feature of the structure. Reforms are a way of preserving hierarchy and exploitation. They contain the "seeds" of their own dismantling: either the power group renounces them in the name of efficiency, law and order, and so on, or they fall of their own weight. Times change, and with them, the demands.

Beyond Revolution constitutes a new standard against which all other books on social movements should be measured. However, since its authors have refused a simple linear causality, many will find its insights more satisfying than its "theory." Those social scientists whose research is still locked into methodologies of the eighteenth century will have a difficult time with the book's multilayered causality. And history will continue to play its tricks on them.

STANLEY ARONOWITZ

Chapter 1

The Guises of Social Movements

The theory in this volume is discontinuous with all prior work concerning social movements. It is not only discontinuous with the analyses of mainstream sociology and political science, it is also at variance with Marxist perspectives, which tend to disavow the social movement perspective for such concepts as "political action," "vanguard party," and "revolution." Because of the broad scope of our project, we have not only developed a theory of social movements, we have also posited metatheories of society and human nature. Societies are historical phenomena every bit as much as they are structural entities. The human subject is also an artifact of historical development and is determined within broad limits by the level of material surplus. Thus, our metatheory is necessarily dialectical and humanistic, in that the human subject is presumed to be part of the material conditions of a given historical period.

To the best of our knowledge, no society exists that does not have some mechanism for the suspension of social structure. It is in this sense that rituals in so-called primitive societies are viewed by anthropologists as universal phenomena. In class societies, the suspension of social structure and normal everyday functioning (in addition to vacations, holidays, and ritual occasions) occurs during periods of social movement in which there is widespread popular insurgency. Members of social categories usually excluded from history begin asserting themselves as historical actors. This forceful assertion of "antistructure" determines the parameters of a social-movement period, which is necessarily shorter than the intervening periods of social quiescence. During the interim between movements, elites reappropriate their positions as controllers of historical development and pursue their own self-interests relatively unfettered by the unwashed masses. This is also true following social revolutions, when new elites have emerged and have taken control of the instruments of domination.

It is the hope of the authors that this work can, in some small way, help enhance the understanding of social movements by analyzing them in historical and comparative perspectives. Only then can we appreciate them in their complexity. Social movements are the collective expression of the highest sensibilities of the species—the desire for freedom, liberation, and self-determination. The ultimate value of our work must be judged on its contributions to understanding the historical development of society, especially during social-movement periods.

What is a Social Movement?

To this end we offer the following definition of a social movement: *A social movement is the developing collective action of a significant portion of the members of a major social category, involving at some point the use of physical force or violence against members of other social categories, their possessions, or their institutionalized instrumentalities, and interfering at least temporarily—whether by design or by unintended consequence—with the political and cultural reproduction of society.*

The preceding is deliberately worded to exclude as irrelevant the issue of whether a given social movement "succeeds" or "fails" to permanently transform the prevailing relations of exploitation and domination. This therewith excludes from further consideration the idealist and economist errors of those who apply this standard of evaluation even to the extent of denying the legitimacy of the appellation "social movement" to episodes in social history marked by dissidence on the part of the "wrong" social categories or by dissidence articulated in terms of the "wrong" ideology. For example, from a 1975 statement of a group affiliated with the Weather Underground: "The New Left of the 1960s failed because it lacked a class analysis and a working-class base." Likewise, the wording is contrived to exclude cultural changes. That is, religion, ideas, art, shamanism (including psychotherapy), and so forth—where these are not accompanied by overt collective forcible conflict (including nonviolence and civil disobedience) with the representatives of established relations of exploitation and domination. The same device is also intended to distinguish between social change and social movements proper. By social change, we mean the quantitative and qualitative changes in the appearances of social relations, which continue throughout periods of dissidence and quiescence alike.

By social category is meant a human aggregate defined by one or more of the lines of cleavage within the social order. In their ensemble, such cleavages give rise to the "normal appearances" (to borrow Goffman's phrase) of society; that is, of society in its routine condition or as encountered by the isolated individual in its everyday-life nomenclature. Social categories that have served as the basis of social movements at one time or another in history have been enormously diverse. They have included status groups (that is, groups ranked hierarchically by prestige deriving from privilege recognized in law or custom, e.g., the medieval titled nobility, knights or gentry, bourgeoisie, free peasants and laborers, villeins, slaves); orders, guilds, and confraternities; castes (that is, occupational categories ranked hierarchically in order of ritual purity); social fractions defined by reference to visible styles or levels of consumption (poor versus rich or sansculottes versus culottes); categories defined by religious or secular ideological belief (believers versus heretics and infidels or socialists versus liberals, conservatives, monarchists, fascists, and so forth, with all of these in times of social quiescence organized into political parties accepting votes and volunteers from all strata); genders; age grade (e.g., youth or students); sexual-orientation categories (homosexual versus heterosexual); "the people" represented as a category antithetical to the state or regime (especially if the state or governing clique is of alien provenance or, as in the Iranian Revolution, because the governing clique has persecuted all rival or potentially rival sources of political initiative impartially and thus lacked a base of support in any major social category); military versus civilians; and ethnic groups. As to the latter, it should be recognized that the operative lines of ethnic cleavage are a good deal more fluid than is asserted by the ideological representations of ethnic "traditions." For example, the Greeks in the sixteenth century supported their "historic" enemy, the Turks, against Italians and Spaniards as the East against the West. Southern Slavs separately rose against common enemies (Turks, later Hungarians) only to give vent to the most ferocious conflict when united in their own state, Yugoslavia. Also, ethnic groups may be either geographically compact or dispersed (e.g., Jews and Zoroastrians), with U.S. Blacks[1] displaying some of the characteristics of the first in the rural South and of the second in the urban North. Ethnic groups may likewise divide (or combine) along lines of language, religion, culture (in the sense of "way of life" other than language or religion), political history (including those instances where ethnic divisions were themselves the outcome of social movements, e.g. the Dutch, the Swiss, or the WASPs of the United States; the latter were themselves divided in the course of social movements and countermovements into Yankee and Dixie versions, which subsequently recombined), appearance (the "prejudice of mark"), and race (the "prejudice of origin"). In short, there are hardly any appearances of society entailing invidious distinctions among humans that have not at one point or another in history constituted the basis or the point of departure for social-movement behavior.

It will be noted that this list omits the word *class*. There is no doubt that class relations, that is, relations of exploitation, underlie or heavily influence the course of all social movements and countermovements. However, it is quite rare that the "appearances" of society, as embedded in the everyday interpretation of social reality, correspond with any precision to class relations. The exceptions occur in those periods in which new axes of exploitation emerge rapidly from older social relations.[2] It is precisely the developing interference with the reproduction of this everyday interpretation of social reality that represents a defining characteristic of any social movement. A dissident social category necessarily begins with the "appearances" of society, including its own; whether or not the reinterpretations of social reality that emerge in the course of the movement embody class analyses is immaterial. The expression "class struggle" will be avoided here because it lends itself so readily to confusion and does not help us understand, historically speaking, the interference with the reproduction of social reality.[3]

Problems of Interpreting Social Movements

A classic example of the problem of the reinterpretation of social reality arises with regard to the English Revolution of 1640. From 1637, England was perturbed by mounting dissidence, to which legitimacy if not leadership was lent by Puritan clergy and professional jurists associated with, protected by, or recruited from the gentry, a leisured, landowning, subaristocratic status group whose distinctive badge of status was the right to display family coats of arms. By 1640, nearly the whole of the gentry—as evidenced by the outcome of the election of the House of Commons in that year—was in opposition to the government of Charles I, in which it was joined by a section of the titled aristocracy, and was at first united in its determination to curb the monarch's pretensions to the continental-style absolutism. Christopher Hill, Lawrence Stone, and Perez Zagorin have emphasized the fact that the whole of the ideological struggle, that is, the reinterpretation of social reality, conducted within and by gentry was couched in the language of religious sectarianism and constitutional legal theory.[4] From Hill, in particular, one may draw the following explanation of why this was necessarily true: The gentry was a status group that displayed considerable homogeneity in its appearances, that is, in its consumption styles and mental life; but it did not constitute a *class* in that the character of the exploitative relationships were subject to considerable variation. Some landlords, especially in the commercially developed south and east, had long since become profit-maximizing capitalists who increased their revenues through rack renting, enclosures, and sensitivity to market conditions. Others, concentrated in the backward and traditionally turbulent north and west, thought in more feudal terms of maximizing military power on the spot and regarded their peasants as potential infantry in time of war; these accordingly adopted a patriarchal policy of restraint in raising rents beyond the traditional level. Between these extremes there were gradations and local peculiarities. (Meanwhile, a minority, resented by the remainder, augmented their landed revenues by access to redistributed surplus in the form of the proceeds of state office and monopolistic privileges "in the king's gift," after the fashion of the continental nobility.)

Secular economic change differentially disturbed the gentry, unsettling some in their rise as others were unsettled in their decline; but the impact of the aggregate of these disturbances upon the gentry as a whole could only have been to focus their attention collectively upon their shared appearances as privileged status group. Specifically, it penetrated their shared differences in political philosophy—founded upon their entrenched position in Parliament and as unpaid local magistrates—with a regime that aimed at despotism yet lacked the revenue and coercive machinery to impose it; and upon their differences in religious faith—Catholic, Puritan, or sectarian—with the same regime that was visibly manipulating the tenets, structure, and ritual of the established church to mold it into an instrumentality of that despotism ("thorough"). The increasingly radical measures adopted by the Long Parliament to secure itself against a resurgence of the royal power, especially the abolition of the church hierarchy, then repolarized the gentry. By the outbreak of war in 1642, the gentry stood against the crown along lines partly ideological (in terms of religious faith, political allegiance, and willingness or reluctance to contemplate mobilizing the multitude for the defense of the revolutionary regime) and partly territorial (in terms of the military situation at the outbreak of war). Hill (1958), in a brilliant article, "The Agrarian Legislation of the Long Parliament," demonstrates most convincingly that the immanent logic of the revolution, expressed in emergency wartime expedients, was the generalization and systematization of bourgeois social relations: (1) Confiscated lands of the crown, the church, and absentee royalists were sold off in large parcels to new owners who moved quickly to recoup their outlays in the shortest possible time by subjecting these properties to profit-maximizing procedures (rack renting, enclosures, etc.), either out of principle or because they feared that the fortunes of war or politics might bring retrocession to the original proprietors. Other royalists were fined and consequently went into debt to preclude confiscation; however patriarchally minded they may have been, they were obliged to become profit maximizers to pay off the principal plus interest. (2) The underbrush of medieval survivals in land law was cleared away for the landlords but not for the peasantry; thus large property was protected by the abolition of the status of tenant-in-chief of the crown. Meanwhile, the "customary tenants" received no parallel proprietorship in their small holdings. (3) The process of redistributing land, as well as the receipt of fines levied upon royalists and the rents from impounded or confiscated but unsold lands—not to mention the whole of the state finance of the revolutionary regime—was concentrated in the hands of the London moneylenders, who were thereby enabled to make a quantum leap toward the development of a centralized, sophisticated, and resourceful money market that could within decades surpass that of Amsterdam. In still other essays, such as those of the conservative parliamentarian James Harrington and the reactionary royalist Earl of Clarendon (both cited in *Puritanism and Revolution*), Hill indicates that by the time the democratic thrust of the Levellers had been smashed in 1649, the awareness of the importance of property interests during and after revolution had come to pervade the propertied class as a whole whether royalist or republican to the point that they depicted such interests if anything more simplistically than the facts of the revolution warranted.[5]

The period in which social movements, especially those of the working class, were permeated by explicitly formulated secular-rationalist doctrines, exhibited acute class consciousness, and lent themselves readily to formal-organizational cohesion was, in the developed (or "core") countries of bourgeois society, peculiar to a period beginning in the early nineteenth century and ending about 1960. At least in the United States, formal organization was accompanied by the emergence of occupational specialties such as those of the organizer, the professional revolutionary, the radical journalist, and the theoretician. (Those who regarded the trends in these directions as inexorable laws of history consequently were called the Old Left during the 1960s.) In retrospect, these trends now appear as logical consequences of the increasingly despotic authority relations embedded within the capitalist labor process. By this is meant not only the arbitrary command exercised through foremen and straw bosses, but increasingly also the fruits of the capitalists' seizing of control of every aspect of the labor process and embodying it via production engineering, first in the assembly line and more recently in the "continuous flow" process.

Consequently, the mythology surrounding bureaucratized dissidence took on the appearance of self-evident validity, culminating in the first four decades of the twentieth century: Workers manifested their dissidence in part by spontaneously joining in the thousands of mass organizations, such as trade unions and political parties, within which bourgeois social relations were systematically reproduced. So, just as in times of social quiescence the "captains of industry" commanded the "labor forces" unhindered, the leaders of working-class organizations in social movements of the first four decades of the twentieth century ordered about "the great army of labor" or the "rank and file" in strategies, tactics, offensives, lines of defense; even individuals and small groups were alluded to as "elements" and "echelons."[6]

In bourgeois society, the subsiding of working-class movements was commonly disguised by the deposit of an imposing mass of bureacratic sediment which continued to call itself "the labor movement" or "the socialist movement" long after overt social conflict had ceased (except for periodic and highly routinized strikes). One curious result has been the institutionalization of the position of the shop steward or "union rep," who notoriously collaborates with management in the suppresion of threats to factory discipline in intervals between contract negotiations. Closer to the concern here, another result has been a thorough obfuscation of sociological analysis of social movements, perhaps worst of all among avowed Marxists who are still characterized by the use of the mixed metaphor "building a movement." We find, therefore, to this very day a strange identity of perspective between the bourgeoisie and avowed subversives of the Marxist persuasion, which denies the capacity of the working class to accomplish anything collectively unless so ordered by trained experts.

The "traditional" working-class movement of the nineteenth and early twentieth centuries is therefore a thing of the past in the developed "core" of bourgeois society and may well be obsolete in parts of the periphery as well, Poland notwithstanding. In those parts of Europe in which "class consciousness" is most rigorously institutionalized, the end was heralded first in France in 1968, when the authority of the Communist party over the working class collapsed at the height of the movement in May 1968 under the impact of the slogan of "autogestion," in effect a demand for the liquidation of the despotic authority relations embedded in the capitalist labor process. This was to some extent replicated in northern Italy in 1969–70. In Britain, first in 1974 and then in 1979, it became apparent that the Labour party and the Trades Union Congress (TUC) hierarchy quite lost the ability to dictate to the working class and consequently became permanently estranged from each other, as the Labour party must appeal to the electorate whereas the TUC must follow their followers since they are their leaders.

In the socialist world, the expropriation of the bourgeoisie, whether by revolution or by military conquest, has everywhere been followed by the emergence of a new exploiting class that has in each instance reinstituted a variant or plain copy of the capitalist labor process. Charles Bettelheim, in his stimulating book, *Class Struggles in the USSR: 1917–1923*, discerns the original sin, so to speak, in errors of policy made by the Bolsheviks in that period. But he is himself guilty of an idealist error, since the institutionalization of collegial relations beyond the social-movement period proper (from the outbreak of political strikes in 1916 to the suppression of the Kronstadt Rising of 1921, or perhaps until the suppression of strikes and peasant revolts against the Bolsheviks lasting up to 1923), would have presupposed a degree of development of the human subject beyond what was historically possible.[7]

Excepting only the socially sanctioned display of the splendor and luxury of the rich and the circumstance that the exploiting class bureaucratically possesses—without formally owning—the means of production, contemporary socialist society is comparable in its stratification of classes and status groups to bourgeois society, though it forswears certain powerful instrumentalities of bourgeois social control: (1) organized religion; (2) parliamentary processes, that is, "working within the system to secure meaningful change through the electoral process"; and (3) escapist fantasies of "striking it rich" coupled with alienated identification—promoted by the media—with big-spending celebrities such as Jackie Onassis and her ilk, mink-clad Rolls-driving athletes, film and video superstars, and fashion models. As a result, it is interesting that collective action by the working class has brought down—temporarily—the regimes of Hungary (1956) and Czechoslovakia (1968) and thrice induced major changes in that of Poland (1956, 1970, 1980–81).

The social movements of the 1960s in the United States witnessed the entire disappearance of "class" as the basis of visible dissident social categories, though certainly not as an underlying reality. The dissidents were drawn from two principal sources: (1) the lower strata of the working class, whose core consists of the racial minorities, together with adjoining strata of the racial-minority population; whence the Black movement and its parallels among Chicanos, Puerto Ricans, and Amerindians; and (2) persons who in times of the social quiesence would have been candidate members of the bourgeoisie, whence the "youth," "students," "counterculture," etc. The women's movement spun off from that, and the gay movement spun off from the latter in its turn. In each case, the principal factor in dissident social cohesion was subculture rather than formal organization. Dissident ideological formulations were of the "subjectivist" type, that is, they emphasized the intensification of inner mental life and the importance of the subculture as the outward shared manifestation of this; reinterpretation of reality was conducted in each case from this standpoint. The dissident categories were each in some sense biologically defined, that is, in terms of race, age grade, gender, and sexual preference.

The entertainment industries in the 1970s reacted to their experience of the previous decade by deliberately overpackaging stylistic fads with the least modicum of rebellious overtones; in the instance of punk rock this postponed the possibilities of commerical success. On the other hand, there has been an unqualified success in transmuting the "ex-counterculture" into elitist and expensive "alternative life-styles," which serve not only as emblems of social privilege but as stimulators of the volatility of household consumption and thus the real possibility of being publicly branded as a "life-style failure" on top of the older penalties attendant to occupational failure.

It would, consequently, be futile to expect that the next round of social movements will resemble those of the 1960s any more than the latter replicated the working-class movement of the 1930s: New contradictions have been piled on top of the older ones and will doubtless be attacked from new directions by new methods; these are as certain to be as incomprehensible to Bobby Seale, Abbie Hoffman, and Robin Morgan as the 1960s were to George Meany. The subcultural cohesion of the movements of the 1960s had, as their precondition, the existence of bourgeois culture which was restrictive and conformist. With the incorporation of "alternative life-styles" into contemporary culture, the presumption that the next social movement will be based on dissident subcultures is highly questionable.

A Brief Restatement

This chapter is titled "The Guises of Social Movements" because they take such varied form. Although they may or may not permanently alter social relations, they are one of the prime mechanisms for doing so. Certainly as important, within a social movement there is *always* an alteration in the development of the human subject, which influences social change beyond the social-movement period.

Although social movements have been engaged in by numerous collectivities, taken on religious, formal-organizational, and subcultural forms, and involved great varieties of strategies and tactics, all social movements are characterized by three mutually reinforcing characteristics: (1) intensifying overt conflict, (2) the reinterpretation of social reality by members of dissident collectivities, and (3) the reappropriation or "disalienation" of human capacities alienated from dissidents as part of their socialization to subordinate positions in the social structure.

It is the manifestation and mutual reinforcement of these three characteristics within a social formation that delimit a social-movement period, during which dissident collectivities engage in conflict with the regime and its instrumentalities, calling their right to dominion into question. By overtly challenging and interfering with the reproduction of the relations of social privilege and participating in forms of mass collegialization themselves, dissident collectivities become agents of antistructure. Statuses are temporarily suspended, role structures are interfered with, and people who once knew their places refuse to accept them. As long as the three characteristics are mutally reinforcing, the social movement is ongoing. When relationships between them attenuate and become fragmented, society has entered into what we have referred to as a postmovement period (Foss and Larkin, 1976), in which social structure is reimposed by dominant elites and movement participants are forced by necessity to accommodate themselves to the return of quiescence.

By concentrating our attention on the internal laws of motion and development of social movements (i.e., the natural history), issues of motivation and success are put into the perspectives of historical and comparative analysis. Conceptualizations in social-movement theory have been so overly concerned with motivation in the search for social-psychological "causes," and success in the analysis of organizational "mobilization," that social-movement theory has been doubly distorted. First has been the psychologization of social movements by those who have operated in the tradition of Gustave LeBon ([1899]1960), currently represented in the work of the relative deprivation school. Second is the work of neo-Weberian resource mobilization theorists, most recently joined by Marxists and New Left theorists, who have taken seriously the Old Left criticism of the 1960s that they "failed" because they had an insufficient organizational base and lacked doctrine. Before proceeding to our own theoretical statement, we will first examine relative deprivation and resource mobilization theories.

Notes

1. The capitalization of "Black": It is technically proper to use the capital "B" to denote USA-born persons of sub-Sahara African descent, since "Black" is the term by which they themselves denote their ethnic group and by which they identify ethnically. The lower-case "b" is technically correct for generic allusions to recent Anglophone and Francophone immigrants (Jamaicans, Trinidadians, Guyanans, Haitians, etc.) from the Caribbean region and to Hispanophone immigrants of sub-Saharan African appear-

ance (such as Dominicans), since these draw ethnic lines among themselves and Blacks, who reciprocate in kind. Sub-Saharan African immigrants should likewise be lower-cased to distinguish them from Blacks. Thus one may for example write, "The Blacks are by far the largest of all black ethnic groups in the United States."

Analogously, the whole of the U.S. population socially defined as of European descent (that is, e.g., Portuguese immigrants regardless of color), should be called "white," with a lower-case "w," since these comprise numerous groups of distinct ethnic identification whose names for their particular ethnic groups should be capitalized (e.g., Poles, Italians, Jews, Irish, Hungarians, Ukrainians, etc.). An exception must be made for the largest white ethnic group, the WASPs, whose members have an unfortunate tendency to call themselves "Americans."

Certain immigrants who, though perhaps of darker color than some Blacks, are not of sub-Saharan African descent, e.g., Dravidians of south India, Melanesians, Australian aboriginals, Yemeni Arabs, etc., should be denoted by their place of origin.

2. See E. P. Thompson (1966) for his remarkable elaboration of the mechanism of capitalist exploitation developed by English factory operatives during the early nine-teenth century.

3. Properly speaking, the concept of "class struggle" includes (1) the fact that ex-ploitative class relations posit as their precondition the possession of the effective means of violence by the exploiting class either as the guarantee of the conditions of exploitation or as part of the mechanism of exploitation or both; (2) everyday pushing and shoving activity within the confines of the exploitative relation between exploiters and exploited; and (3) the actual overt collective resort to force and counterforce, explicable in terms of class relations, observable during social movements.

4. Cf. Christopher Hill, *Puritanism and Revolution*. London: Secker & Warburg, 1958; *The Century of Revolution: 1603–1714*, New York: Norton, 1961; *The World Turned Upside Down*, Harmondsworth, England: Penguin, 1973; Lawrence Stone, *The Crisis of the Aristocracy*, New York: Oxford, 1965; *The Causes of the English Revolution: 1529–1642*. New York: Harper, 1972; and Perez Zagorin, *The Court and the Country*, London, Atheneum, 1970.

5. It was Harrington, by the way, who coined the term "superstructure" in 1651, 200 years before the revelation unto Marx.

6. All this gave an unanticipated advantage to the Fascists, who could supplement the military metaphor with authentic militarism (the socialism of the trenches), and who not only copied their opponents' organizational methods down to the last detail, including the red flag, but vastly surpassed them in fields of street theater and pageantry. What is more, though the fascists were under no obligation to engage in class conflict, they did make free use of the combativeness of all sorts of hooligans whom their opponents spurned as too disreputable and whose antics offended their bourgeois feeling for tidiness and order.

7. If further proof is needed, consider the fate of the Maoist experiment dear to Bettelheim's heart of replacing the "capitalist road" management of industrial production with "revolutionary committees": This has apparently contributed mightily to the im-mense popularity enjoyed in the working class by Teng Hisia-p'ing (Deng Xiaoping), whose program is akin to that of Stalin, that is, a rising standard of living based on rapid industrialization coupled with the development of a military capability comparable to the USSR. (The Chinese regime has an advantage that Stalin lacked: As an ally of the United States against the USSR, it can draw upon foreign capital and need not resort to the "primitive socialist accumulation" associated with Stalin's five-year plans.)

Chapter 2

Relative Deprivation and Resource Mobilization

Relative deprivation (RD) and resource mobilization (RM) theories view movement participants as rational calculators seeking to maximize psychic, social, or material profits and minimize losses. Wheras RD theory centers on motivation, RM theory presupposes it, while examining internal organization, recruitment, and mobilization of forces, including sentiment.

Relative Deprivation Theory

Relative deprivation theory received its impetus from James Davies in his classic article "Toward a Theory of Revolution" (1962), in which he generated a synthesis between Marx and Toqueville on the causes of a social movement. Although he noted that Marx mentioned both "absolute" (i.e., immiseration) and "relative" deprivation in his work, he dismissed the former and accepted the latter, since it conformed more closely to Toqueville's observation that the French Revolution of 1789 occurred following a sharp economic decline preceded by a long period of progress. Davies saw revolutions occurring as a consequence of rising expectations, which, because of an economic downturn, outstripped society's ability to satisfy them. For Davies, psychology was the critical factor: "Political stability and instability are ultimately dependent on a state of mind, a mood, in a society" (1962:6). In Davies's simplistic causal scheme, he was guilty of both economism and psychologism. The reason he saw Marx stating antithetical positions on the causality of revolution is because Marx always focused on social relations; in his "Economic and Philosophical Manuscripts of 1844" (1963), he stated that in periods of economic decline, the working class experiences immiseration as they are called upon to suffer the brunt of the crisis, sometimes being forced to exist below the level of subsistence. In periods of economic expansion, he noted, the bourgeoisie was able to extract increasing amounts of surplus value from the labor of the workers, elevating their relative position vis-à-vis labor. The important fact, ignored by Davies, was that both immiseration and relative deprivation are a consequence

10

of the relations of exploitation between the bourgeoisie and the proletariat. Davies's attempt to focus on the psychological well-being ("mood") of the people and tie it to a specific economic trend eliminated other probable causes of revolutions. Consequently, Davies's conception was recast by Ted Gurr (1970:52-58) as "progressive deprivation" and subsumed under a more comprehensive theory of relative deprivation.

Because of the comprehensiveness, sophistication, and scholarly acclaim he has received, we will center our attention on Gurr's most important theoretical work, *Why Men Rebel*.[1] Gurr's book was presented in the form of a logico-deductive axiomatic theory. The core of the theory is a set of probabilistic hypotheses that relate dependent to independent variables. The major dependent variable is "political violence," which may or may not take the form of a social movement. The issue of political violence and social movements is addressed in Chapter 7, "Social Movements Versus Political Violence and Mobilization."

As evinced by the title of Gurr's work, the major focus is motivation:

> This study proposes some general answers to three basic questions about our occasional disposition to disrupt violently the order we otherwise work so hard to maintain: What are the psychological and social sources of the potential for collective violence? What determines the extent to which that potential is focused on the political system? And what societal conditions affect the magnitude and form, and hence the consequences, of violence? [1970:7-8]

Thus, Gurr set out to establish the conditions under which the propensity to commit violent acts are maximized and those conditions under which such violent acts are politicized, that is, directed at the state. The relative deprivation model posits social conditions as preconditions for violence—they influence the probabilities of the occurrence of violent acts of a collective nature. Though such variables as socialization, tradition, and legitimacy of the system will influence the probability and shape of violence, the critical factor exists in the minds of individuals. Collective violence has as a necessary condition the existence of a gap between the "value expectations," that is, what people feel they are entitled to by virtue of their membership in a collectivity, and their "value capabilities," or what they expect the future to bring to them given past experience. Gurr saw this gap as a continuous variable defined as relative deprivation. It exists in all societies at all times. However, its rapid acceleration signals problems for the maintenance of social order.

RD theory is based on the frustration-aggression hypothesis, which states that when goal-directed behavior is interfered with, subjects who are frustrated in successful achievement will increase their propensity to resort to violence. Gurr saw the frustration-aggression hypothesis as reflecting a basic truth about human nature:

> The frustration-aggression mechanism is . . . analogous to the law of gravity: men who are frustrated have an innate disposition to do violence to its source in proportion to the intensity of their frustration, just as objects are attracted to one another in direct proportion to their relative masses and inverse proportion to their distance. [1970:37]

However, as Gurr noted from the evidence, frustration is not sufficient to produce violence to its source. Anthropological and clinical evidence indicated that frustration could induce many behaviors, only one of which is direct violence against the object of frustration: submission, dependence, avoidance, scapegoating, and self-destruction are equally viable alternatives. The inconclusiveness of the frustration-aggression hypothesis renders it questionable as the basis for a theory of collective political violence, as McPhail (1971) has noted in his review of studies of correlations between frustration-aggression indices and riot participation. The problem becomes magnified when attempts are made to measure and assess indices of frustration at the level of macrostructure. The virtue of such concepts as "value expectations" and "value capabilities" is that they are subject to public opinion survey measurement. If a regime were to assess the variety of collectivities under its control, it is likely to be able to spot centers of ferment. It must, however, be pointed out that these two variables are heuristic and the regime might do just as well, if not better, by employing spies and informants or reading police blotters or newspapers. Gurr's theory is probabilistic, not causal; the reason being that it is a quantitative theory and eliminates those factors (e.g., the collective reinterpretation of social reality on the part of dissident collectivities) that may be more important but are not subject to quantification.[2]

The circulating medium for relative deprivation theory is "values." For Gurr, there are three types of values: Welfare values are concerned with economic and psychological well-being. Power values constellate around the desire to participate in decisions affecting one's life and security. Although Gurr uses the terms "participation" and "security," they seem to be confused with "influence" and "autonomy," which are implied in his definition: *"Power values are those that determine the extent to which men can influence the actions of others and avoid unwanted interference by others in their own actions"* (1970:25). Finally, there are interpersonal values. They include status, community, and ideational coherence. Briefly, although slightly redefined from Gurr, these values are, respectively: the desire to attain a respectable station in life; support, companionship, and affection; and meaning in life.

Each collectivity in the social order can be defined by its value position, value potential, and value opportunities. Its value position is the amount of value it has attained. The value potential of a collectivity is what its members see it as capable of achieving. The value opportunities can be separated into three categories: personal, societal, and political. Personal opportunities are the possibilities for individuals within a collectivity to enhance their value. Societal opportunities are those avenues for a collectivity to become socially mobile. Political opportunities are those that allow a collectivity to "induce" others to provide them with value satisfactions. Each social category, then, can be located in the social order according to its position, potential, and opportunities, given the value structure, values being all those things that "men" want.

Gurr identifies three types of relative deprivation: decrimental, aspirational, and progressive. Decrimental deprivation occurs when the value capabilities of a social order decline and value expectations remain constant. Such can occur when a social category experiences downward mobility. Aspirational deprivation occurs when the value expectations increase without a simultaneous increase in value capabilities. Such a case occurs when people are exposed to societies that have higher standards of living that are not open to them. Progressive deprivation is, as mentioned above, Davies's J-curve form of deprivation, or the revolution of rising expectations as, say, in evidence during the French Revolution of 1789.

Gurr's theory of relative deprivation predicts that revolution can occur when things get better, stay the same, or get worse. By doing so, he is saying that *any* or *no* fluctuation in the economy can generate political violence, since relative deprivation can occur at any time in the economic cycle. Thus, Gurr's simplistic economism is reduced to absurdity. Add to this the political violence in the Western world by the social category of "youth," that is, the candidate members of the bourgeoisie, in the 1960s throughout a period of increasing economic well-being, declining in concomitance with the recession of 1969–70, induced in the United States by the Nixon administration at least partially for the purposes of social control. One begins to question (1) what it is in the macrostructure that leads to relative deprivation, and (2) whether relative deprivation can be assessed prior to violent outbreaks. (We are in no way claiming that the the youth movement of the 1960s declined because of recession.) This leads us to the difficulty that relative deprivation may only be able to be assessed *ex post facto* since it cannot be tied to any quantitative social change, nor can it apparently be inferred prior to social disruption. Additionally, actual participation within a social movement generates an alteration in the locus of motivations of participants, which neither social scientists nor activists could possibly have anticipated.

It seems a truism that people rebel because they are discontented and they are discontented because they feel they are not getting that to which they believe they are entitled. The obvious is being labored over in a social-scientific, logico-deductive, hypothesis-verifying way. The mystique of language, charts, boxes, and arrows covers the overriding simplistic conceptions of Gurr. First, the dependent variables, collective and political violence, are overblown and vague (see Chapter 7 of this book for a complete analysis of the term "political violence"). Second, it is an attempt to prove the obvious, which is obvious because it is resurrected in hindsight. Third, Gurr is attempting to turn what is an explanation after the fact into a predictive theory. In this he fails because of the lack of relationship between relative deprivation and violence directed at the system of exploitation and stratification; it does not concur with fluctuations in the economy; and he stumbles at precisely the same place every theory that attempts to explain social behavior on the basis of espoused or inferred attitudes stumbles—there is very little correlation between the two, be they acts of racial discrimination or of political violence. In Gurr, we have the triumph of form over content.

Resource Mobilization Theory

One of the most recent developments in social movement theory has been the increasing concern of sociologists about the ability of groups in movement to marshal resources to their cause. Useem (1975) saw the problem of mobilization of resources from the perspective of the protest organization. He was concerned with the ability of an organization to exploit issues, generate constituencies, develop programs, build infrastructures, and maintain commitment and solidarity. He saw these as problems that protest organizations must solve if they are to be effective. He was writing for an audience that is interested in forming groups directed at social change. Although Oberschall (1973) took a more "value-free" approach, he shared with Useem the belief that a social movement could not develop unless it was able to exploit a resource base.

Oberschall viewed mobilization from a macrostructural position by analyzing the various features of a society that accelerate or retard and give shape to social conflict. Using a more or less neo-Weberian approach, he classified social systems on a *gemeinschaft-gesellschaft* dimension. Midway between the two ideal types, Oberschall included the category of "weakly or unorganized" collectivity. He cross-tabulated *gemeinschaft-gesellschaft* with a hierarchical dimension. Societies were identified as segmented if they had castelike boundaries between higher and lower social categories. They were termed integrated if such boundaries were somewhat permeable. Thus, in an integrated communal *(gemeinschaft)* society, the probability of collective protest was minimized, since the community had access to the problem-solving centers. However, in a segmented associational *(gesellschaft)* society, collective dissidence would be much more probable. Dissidence would more likely be sustained and intense than in other social formations. Without going into detail, we can view Oberschall as refining Smelser (1964) by differentiating the types of social strain generated by social structures. In addition, he proffered a rough idea of the forms and intensity social movements would take within certain social structures.

Oberschall's resource mobilization (RM) theory posited the same motivational axiom found in relative deprivation theory: that the individual rationally/calculatedly maximizes scarce goods. His point of departure was Mancur Olson, Jr.'s, *The Logic of Collective Action*. Olson presented a model of the formation of interest groups for the purpose of obtaining "collective goods" whose existence for the membership (higher wages for workers, higher prices for farmers) presupposes the existence of a formal organization empowered to discipline individual members. As individuals, they maximize returns not by joining or contributing, but as members maximize returns still more by precluding the isolated action of any of them in the former capacity. For Olson and Oberschall, then, we have a sociological Keynesianism: the assumption of the rational-accumulating egoistic individual is retained, whereas the assumption of the capitalist "free market" is explicitly rejected.

They fixed upon a model of bureaucratic mass organization and pressure-group formation to start with. However, such organizations normally abstain from social conflict except as episodic dissidence. Oberschall, nevertheless, approached the problem of social movements by way of "conflict group formation in large collectivities," for which Olson's theory admittedly is inappropriate:

> Olson's theory would predict that large collectivities deprived of civil liberties and political rights would not develop from within an opposition organization for obtaining these goals if the members of the collectivity pursued their own selfish interests in a calculated, rational way and if they have complete freedom to join or not to join an opposition movement. In effect, each member of a large negatively privileged collectivity might as well wait until others take the risks and pay the price of mobilization and of opposition. But if each member follows this rule, then no opposition

movement is ever likely to be formed. Nevertheless, we know from history and from our own experience that opposition movements and conflict groups are formed quite frequently. Since Olson's theory is basically sound, one is led to question some of his assumptions with a view to modifying and extending his theory for the case of political opposition and conflict groups. [Oberschall, 1973:114]

Oberschall tried to get around this by questioning Olson's "assumption that the members of a large collectivity are unorganized individual decision makers similar to the numerous, small, independent producers in the market of the classical economist" (1973:117). Oberschall consequently pointed to the pre-movement prevalence of established collectivities. Where society is still on the *gemeinschaft* side, dissidents supposedly follow the lead of their traditional leaders. One would ordinarily suppose this to be more appropriate to counter-dissidence, except perhaps for colonial countries where the European powers handed over the state under fairly amicable conditions. Not surprisingly, Oberschall relied on cases such as these, especially in Africa, to the detriment of instances such as Vietnam, Angola, Mozambique, Guinea-Bissau, Algeria, and the like.

Where society has become *gesellschaft*, Oberschall suggested that "[the collectivity's] members might already be partly organized along associational lines for purposes other than opposition" (1973:117). Under such conditions, he posited that the "collectivity" behaves "rationally" in maximizing power. He said:

> The very real theoretical gain achieved is that a theory of mobilization of opposition and conflict groups, social and mass movements, of protest behavior and collective political action, is essentially the same as the theory of mobilization for economic interest groups, and that the simple assumption of rationality in economic theory is sufficient in this theoretical effort. Thus, one need not make assumptions about individual motivation based on alienation or psychopathology, and a single theory spans the entire range of political and social movements, regardless of whether they are designated as extremist, leftist, rightist, centrist, or mass movements by their opponents and detractors. [1973:118]

It is apparent that collectivity is a most central term here; but what is it? Oberschall equates collectivity (1973:118) with "quasi group," a term attributed to Dahrendorf; but this is incorrect. We propose our own definition as follows: Humans may be said to constitute a collectivity to the extent and for whatever reason they act collectively. Multinational corporations and peasant villages of the sort that practice agriculture involving collective technique (e.g., wet rice culture or medieval open fields) constitute *ongoing* collectivities. Trade unions, religious bodies in secular society (excepting the clergy), and friendship groups meeting informally constitute *occasional* collectivities. The military and other total institutions are *enforced* collectivities. Subdivision of these categories and devising of cross-cutting categories is obviously possible ad infinitum. "Women" are not normally a collectivity except of the informal friendship-group type. We prefer on these grounds to use the term "social category" after Poulantzes (1975), to designate commonplace pigeonholes ordinarily employed by everyone in everyday life to depict the appearances of society. Ongoing social-movement collectivities are emergent in the course of social movements themselves. Thus we may have and in several periods have had ongoing women's movement collectivities; and "the working class" or "the industrial proletariat" has constituted itself as an ongoing collectivity on such occasions as Russia from 1917 to 1923; the United States in the 1930s; and France in May and June of 1968. Our objection is not so much to the word itself as to the degree of solidarity—voluntary or compulsory—denoted by it, which renders the usage appropriate in certain contexts and out of place in others. X

Even within social-movement collectivities, the generalized prevalence of cost-benefit accounting procedures remains to be proven: Obviously, where dissidence is highly bureaucratized, as under the leadership of Marxist-Leninist vanguard parties with their accountantlike computations of the "correlation of forces," strenuous efforts in this direction may be inferred, but the substantive rationality of the same—evaluating their policies post facto—may not. For earlier periods when movements were permeated by religious ideology, the idea makes no sense: What "sensible" person, that is, of the rationally calculating bourgeois persuasion, would have joined in Albigensianism at the time of Innocent III, knowing perfectly well that this entailed at best a fight to the death (and otherwise not even the chance to defend oneself)? Would the Jews similarly have taken on the whole Roman Empire in A.D. 66-73? It was much more likely that dissidents in these epochs would appeal to the alienated supernatural, as the Boxers in the China of 1898 depended on spells and incantations for protection from bullets. (The same was done by Native Americans and Africans.)

More recently, where social movement cohesion has depended on culture rather than formal organization, the same assumption has led Oberschall to equal and opposite errors: Where riots and insurrections occur without visible guidance by a rationally calculating entity, he refuses to impute to them any substantive rationality: "The lower-class urban riots of the 1960s by black slum dwellers in the U.S. are an example . . . of collective outbursts devoid of leadership, organization, and explicitly articulated goals that arise in a collectivity that is both segmented from the rest of society and weakly organized within itself" (1973:122-23). To imply that these riots were without achievements—and substantial ones at that—is obviously conterfactual. One dimension of these achievements, in the form of federal programs, was in its content dictated by the selfsame "leaderless" character of the riots, as the preexisting leaders had evidently lost their moral authority over the masses they were supposed to keep in hand. Recall, for example, Governor Spiro Agnew's anger at the Black elite of Baltimore following the eruption of that city's ghetto in April 1968. Moreover, given the control, surveillance, and infiltration capabilities of the state in the present epoch, the very existence of a leadership cadre wielding effective powers of guidance over a Black population regimented in mass organizations would have precluded any possiblility of riots or insurrections taking place. What actually happened was substantively rational. Vide the near extermination of the Black Panther party, whose intentions in this direction were mostly notional and who were substantively more effective as a media myth than as a Marxist-Leninist vanguard party.

The state apparatus tended to persecute most ferociously those entities organized as a mirror image of itself, this having been facilitated by the *eo ipso* susceptibility to infiltration. Consider the thirty-one-year FBI harassment and surveillance of the Socialist Workers party, whose devotion to the forms of legality certainly far exceeded that of J. Edgar Hoover. Consequently, the "mobilization" idealized by Oberschall was not only (1) impossible and (2) contrary to the trend of the times toward cultural rather than formal-organizational solidarity in social movements, but also (3) self-defeating, as it would have rendered a laboriously built organization hostage for the good behavior of its members while rendering potential bribees conspicuous.

Contrarily, where "organizations" appear to have existed, this was accepted at face value:

> [T]he overnight rise of the Free Speech Movement (FSM) at Berkeley in the fall of 1964 was possible only because of the existence of a prior network of political, civil rights, and special interest groups in an already highly politically mobilized and ideologically sophisticated student population. All groups, right and left, felt their interests threatened by the sudden ban on campaigning at the Telegraph-Bancroft entry to the campus during the 1964 national election campaign. The FSM grew out of an overnight merger of these various campus groups. On a campus where most students are social isolates and organizational networks weak, the rapid rise of a student protest movement would have been impossible. [1973:127]

The preceding used as evidence what must rather be proven, specifically (1) that most Berkeley students were not "social isolates" as much as students anywhere; (2) that the various campus "organizations" primarily had in common the ban on political activity; (3) that Right and Left were meaningful designations and the students consequently "ideologically sophisticated," yet somehow the Right, in the midst of the Goldwater campaign, did not fly at the throat of the Left in support of the Board of Regents, of its own political coloration, but concluded an "overnight merger" with the Left to form the FSM; and (4) that the number of "members" of these "organizations" was sufficiently large to warrant the usage of "highly politically mobilized." This is reasoning *ex hypothesi*.

What in our opinion distinguished the Berkeley campus in 1964 from other schools of the same size was the intensity of the development in the South Campus area of a dissident subculture wherein bohemian cultural radicals and political radicals mingled promiscuously (in every sense of that word), for which the corner of Bancroft and Telegraph (and the plaza beyond) constituted a species of agora much like the corner of Lenox Avenue and 125th Street in Harlem at that time. This subculture was already quite visible by 1960. By 1964 its emergence was three to four years in advance of anything comparable with the possible exception of Cambridge, Massachusetts. As we analyzed the situation, if the South Campus subculture was to be taken as the "pond," then the "organizations" were to be understood as "ripples."

In consonance with his emphasis on formal organizations, Oberschall viewed ideologies as concrete givens. He noted:

> It is best to think of protest ideas and opposition ideologies as producing a collective response in conjunction with the presence of real or felt grievances, discontents, and suffering. The ideas serve to explain private

wrongs and sufferings experienced by individuals in terms not of private shortcomings of accidental events, or of eternal, unalterable states, but in terms of shortcomings of the society that can be remedied and of particular groups for the collective welfare. [1973:179]

Here we find that the RM approach tends to conceive of ideology as rationally calculated and in the form of doctrine. Within the natural history framework, a social movement is characterized by a continual reinterpretation of reality. It is only in the advanced stages or in the wake of the movement that such reinterpretations assume the characteristics of an ideology. (See Chapter 5, "The Reinterpretation of Social Reality," for an elaboration of this point.)

With the decline of social movement activity in the United States in the 1970s, social movement theorists of the Left, Center, and Right have concerned themselves with the "causes" of social movement success and failure. This has led to increased emphasis on the formally organized aspects of social movements. For such New Left theorists as Michael Useem and William Gamson, it has meant examining "protest organizations" with history only providing context. The more moderate or centrist theorists have focused more on "resource mobilization," which presupposes the existence of a formal-organizational structure at the core of the movement that must carry on exchange relationships with potential clientele, suppliers of material resources, and other organizations. Whereas the Left, is more given to analyzing the goals and structures of the protest organization (Useem, 1975) and its sociohistorical context (Gamson, 1975), RM theory emphasizes rational calculation on the part of social-movement organizations in interaction with their environments. In all these cases, collective action and even dissident behavior is subordinated to the analysis of behavior within organizations that are identified with social movements. Surprisingly, this sort of analysis has been applied to the movements of the 1960s, when formal-organizational activities were at a minimum, spontaneous collective dissidence was at a maximum, and, the basis of cohesion was the maintenance of a dissident subculture (Foss and Larkin, 1976, 1979). The assumption of bureaucratized dissidence is tied into desires on the part of the Left that the 1970s would be a time of consolidation of the political gains of the 1960s in liberal-reformist directions. In addition, it is a repudiation of cultural dissidence and overt conflict that was characteristic of the period in much the same way Jesus freaks, Hari Krishnas, and Marxist sectarians rejected the validity of their former behaviors within the movement. For the more moderate theorizers, this means focusing on the more "legitimate" or, perhaps, "serious" aspects of agitation for social change.

The work of McCarthy and Zald (1977) is a classic example of this trend. First, they define a social movement (SM) as "a set of opinions and beliefs in a population which represents preferences for changing some elements of the social structure and/or reward distribution of that society" (1977:1217-18). Therefore, social movements need not take on any behavioral attributes at all, since they are defined wholly in terms of public sentiment. Second, within this structure of sentiment exists organizations that are dedicated to promoting changes in line with sentiments. These organizations are called "social movement organizations" (SMOs) by McCarthy and Zald. They are the building blocks of social movements. We emphasize the term "building blocks" because

McCarthy and Zald see social movements as edifices in the body politic. Third, "social movement industries" (SMIs) are the collectivities or organizations that cater to the social movement, the movement being, of course, the sentiment structure. Finally, there is that section of the social order that is organized around social movements.

McCarthy and Zald view social movements as having a continuing existence within the social order. During periods of quiescence, they occupy an extremely minor and narrow sector. The activity that can be attributed to them is relatively small. (We would suspect that McCarthy and Zald would see such organizations as CORE, NOW, Naders Raiders—subsequently known as Public Citizen— and Common Cause as SMOs in the latter half of the 1970s.) The social movement sector competes with other sectors of society for resources in a sort of capitalist-free enterprise market. In this sense, resource mobilization theory maintains the myth of the free enterprise of ideas. Social movement organizations (SMOs) must compete as part of the social movement sector with non-movement organizations for the allegiance and resources of the population. Within the social movement sector (SMS), there is competition between SMIs and SMOs. An example of the former would be the recruitment of Black women by NOW—the women's movement industry would be competing with the Black movement industry. Competition between SMOs would be exemplified by intramovement rivalries, such as the rivalry between Orientalist sects, Jesus freaks, and Marxist sects for the hearts and minds of youth in the early 1970s.

Once the elements of their theory have been explicated, McCarthy and Zald turn their attention to the development of hypotheses concerning the relationships of SMSs, SMIs, and SMOs to societal resources. Their only hypothesis in relation to the development of an SMS (which is their only index of whether or not a social movement is developing) is that it increases with the rise of discretionary income. It is here that we are left with an unresolved theoretical contradiction. Are we to assume that if a social movement sector expands then discontent is increasing? If that is assumed, then McCarthy and Zald are in the position of stating that discontent increases only when things are getting better economically. This is certainly contradicted by the Polish workers movement of the summer of 1980, when the shipyard workers of Gdansk struck over an increase in the price of meat. We might also point out that the French Revolution of 1789 began over the rise of the prices of bread beyond traditional levels. Thus, McCarthy and Zald's hypothesis seems patently absurd. But suppose the expansion of the social movement sector does *not* indicate an increase in discontent. We must then assume SMOs have absolutely no relationship to discontent or social crises; those organizations are nothing more than charities. This problem cannot be solved by adding more hypotheses about the development of SMSs, e.g., "The greater the discontent in a social order the greater the expansion of the SMS." Since the expansion of the SMS would be the prime indicator of the increase of discontent, the hypothesis would be tautological. The problem reverts to defining social movements idealistically in terms of discontent without addressing the question of social action. The authors have reified the concept, rendering it meaningless. Who in American society is not discontented, including the rich? Who doesn't want an alteration in the calculation of rewards (whatever that is, since it covers both the desire for class privilege and an egalitarian society without classes) that increases their benefits? According to such a definition, all of America, with the possible exception of a few eccentrics, mental retardates, and a small minority of self-satisfied fat cats, are members of social movements!

What McCarthy and Zald have attempted, and what resource mobilization theory tries to do in general, is render social movements—which are, by their very nature, disjunctive with normal society—understandable using concepts that apply to the normal appearances of society; which as Levi-Strauss (1966) and Touraine (1977) have pointed out, appear more cohesive than they really are. In so doing, they have distorted the phenomena of social movements to the point of unrecognizability. To McCarthy and Zald, social movements are sectors of the economy relegated to the fringes, dependent on discretionary income for their growth and development. The phenomena of social movements, such as strikes, riots, property destruction, marches, and sit-ins are viewed as epiphenomena and the problem of the relationship of social movements to social relations is not even attempted. By assuming that the core of a social movement is necessarily formal-organizational, which has been refuted by the experience of the 1960s everywhere in the Western world, and focusing on the relationship between those organizations and their "task environments" (to use a term coined by organizational theorist William Dill, [1958]), questions of causality are begged and social-movement phenomena that define them as distinctive are ignored. More insidiously, social-movement behavior is viewed as the consequence of competition between various SMOs as they calculate and execute actions that give themselves notoriety and increase membership in exactly the same way a corporation would engage in advertising campaigns to increase sales and profits: "Treating SMO target goals as products . . . and adherence as demand, we can apply a simple economic model to this competitive process. Demand may be elastic, and its elasticity is likely to be heavily dependent upon SMO advertising" (McCarthy and Zald, 1977:1229). Given the resource mobilization model proffered by McCarthy and Zald, social movements can only mirror social relations in the larger society. Since this is a capitalist society, social movements (presumably even when opposing capitalism) can only adhere to a capitalist model. Even goals are commodities!

McCarthy and Zald tend to take a highly simplistic model based on utilitarian economics and organizational theory; a much more complex approach is taken by Charles Tilly. He is by far the most sophisticated of the resource mobilization theorists. First, he is extremely well read, and second, he knows history, especially that of eighteenth- and nineteenth-century Europe. Tilly's theoretical work has, as its central focus, collective action, which

> . . . consists of people's acting together in pursuit of common interests. Collective action results from changing combinations of interests, organization, mobilization, and opportunity. The most persistent problem we will face in analyzing collective action is its lack of sharp edges: people vary continuously from intensive involvement to passive compliance, interests vary from quite individual to nearly universal. . . . Our chief effort, then, will flow along the lines going from organization to mobilization to collective action to revolution. Especially from mobilization to revolution. [1978:7]

Tilly notes that it is very difficult to build causal models that take into consideration interests, grievances, and aspirations (1978:6). This is indeed true, especially when "collective action" takes on the characteristics of the forcible assertion of antistructure by dissidents. Aspirations skyrocket, grievances multiply, and interests intensify within the process of collective action. Such phenomena are impossible to predict, especially from ahistorical probabilistic models such as relative deprivation. Therefore, Tilly focuses on the processes of organization and mobilization in relation to collective action. Tilly's main concerns are "What are the determinants of collective action?" and "How is collective action transformed into revolution?" We will be more concerned with the former question herein.

Why does collective action become the critical concept for Tilly? Strangely, the reader is not apprised of his reasons. It is assumed, a priori, that collective action is worth studying. We are told, however, that there are risks involved: Everybody's an expert, the subject matter is highly volatile and political, and the concept straddles a chasm between causal and purposive explanations. Causal explanations are those in which an actor's behavior can be predicted by his situation. Purposive explanations attempt to uncover rules that underlie action and constrain alternative behaviors. Tilly, therefore, attempts to achieve the best of all possible worlds through synthesizing the two explananda. The question of "Why study collective action?" has not been satisfactorily answered. Although it has a certain heuristic value—that is, it can be measured—its substantive significance as a sociological or historical concept is quite limited. As Tilly himself admits in the quotation above, it has fuzzy edges. The definition, as in the case of other definitions of social movements (cf. Blumer, 1948; McCarthy and Zald, 1977), is overly inclusive. It includes all political action engaged in by any identifiable social grouping, including the state. Implicit in Tilly's use of the term is the notion of action against the state. Included in the definition is both routine and "nonroutine" action, ballots and bullets, lobbying efforts and revolutions. Though these disparate categories of action may be lumped together for the purposes of counting, the reliability (i.e., internal consistency) of the concept as a variable is highly questionable. Tilly's perspective is problematic in that the focus is collective because it can be treated as a dependent variable in a multivariate analysis. In his section concerning the measurement of collective action, he gives examples of how such collective action as strikes could be assessed on such dimensions as size, duration, and frequency (1978:90-97). This introduces another ambiguity in his scheme. Are strikes, riots, and civil disorders collective action or indicators of collective action? If the former is the case, then the term "collective action" is not a variable at all, but rather a loose category of a whole variety of specific actions, some of which may be unrelated to others, thereby undercutting the unidimensionality that is necessary for variable analysis. If, however, collective action is a set of specific behaviors that can be ranked on a scale in terms of increasing intensity, conflict, or violence, then the issue shifts to what is being measured, collective action or qualities of collective action (e.g., incidence of violence). This may seem to be an exercise in hair splitting, but it has important consequences for the development of theory. Tilly states:

> . . . [T]he accumulating literature of collective action offers an inviting terrain for theoretical exploration. My plan here is to draw on it in proposing general concepts and hypotheses for the study—contemporary or historical—of concrete cases of collective action. We return to some

of the problems posed, but not resolved, by Marx's analyses of nineteenth-century political conflicts: how do big structural changes affect the prevailing patterns of collective action? Among the big changes, I want especially to inquire into the effects of urbanization, industrialization, state making, and the expansion of capitalism. Among prevailing patterns of collective action, I would particularly like to know what kinds of groups gain or lose the capacity to act together effectively, and how the forms of action themselves change. [1978:49]

The central assumption of Tilly's theorizing about collective action is that there is continuity between open conflict and routine collective action. At this point, Tilly is asserting that collective action is a continuous variable. We must ask ourselves if an understanding of collective action is sufficient to answer the questions he poses, especially when he insists on making no qualitative distinction between routine and nonroutine collective action. Although size, duration, and frequency may be indicators that something serious is occurring, we do not know the nature of the process without some sort of historical analysis and awareness of the underlying social relationships that are manifested in the collective action. The notion of collective action may be helpful in understanding the "natural history of a social movement" (Rule and Tilly, 1972), but it is insufficient without sociological and historical analyses, which raises the question of its marginal utility—that is, its sufficiency becomes suspect.

Tilly expressly avoids the social movement perspective because of the underlying assumption of social-movement theorists that the nature of their subject matter is nonroutine, discontinuous behavior. He also notes that the social-movement perspective evolves out of the Weberian's concern for charisma. Though this is only partly true, it provides the basis for the comparison of the collective action and social-movement perspectives.

In its sociological form, the social-movement perspective is something to be avoided because of its lack of a sufficient definition, also a problem with Tilly's perspective. It has been ahistorical and psychologistic. The Weberian conceptualizations have been criticized above as overly concerned with organization and leadership and lacking sufficient definition. Moreover, the issue of discontinuity is central to the problems inherent in Tilly's paradigm. First, there is a qualitative difference between routine and discontinuous collective action that is obliterated in Tilly's perspective. Some collective action leads to further action, some does not. Some alters the consciousness of the participants significantly, some does not. Some collective action is part of an ongoing social force, some is merely episodic. Some is dissident, some is counterdissident. Without an analysis of social relations and historical processes, these important distinctions are washed away. Collective action is torn from its social and historical context and strapped into a stochastic procrustean bed of variable analysis. It is indeed ironic that Tilly can sing the praises of Marx's analyses of the Revolution of 1848—which is a natural history—and claim the red flag of pro-Marxism, while taking a Marxian perspective and forcing it into an overgeneralized positivistic model of relations between variables.

The confusion found in *From Mobilization to Revolution* seems to stem from an internal contradiction in Tilly's theorizing. He tends to waffle from positivistic to historical explanations of collective action. (The term "collective action" itself has a positivistic tinge to it, since it can be considered a variable that can be easily enumerated and subjected to multivariate analysis. It is also devoid of historical context.)

Perhaps this point can be illustrated from his earlier major research efforts. In his exceptionally subtle and complex study of the causes of the counter-revolution in France in 1793, in *The Vendée*, he apprises the reader of his intention to focus on the urbanization process as a causal factor in the counterrevolution. Thus, the reader is braced for Durkheim and anomie theory. Tilly, however, unexpectedly launches into an analysis of the political economy of social relations. Urbanization, it turns out, is the attempt by the Parisian bourgeoisie, fresh from their success of taking over the state, to impose bourgeois social relations in the rural territories. Tilly stated that the opposition took a religious orientation because the revolutionary government removed the *curés* from positions of local power—politically and economically—by substituting a secular officer of the government to oversee political relations, selling off church lands (of which the bourgeoisie was the most prominent buyer), and making *curés* employees of the state. Those *curés* that did not comply with the changes were removed from office and state-approved ones were installed in their places. Thus, local *curés* were subject to control by the newly bourgeois centralized state. Once the bourgeoisie took control of church lands, they subjected them to capitalist "rationalization" and rack renting. Thus the residents of the Mauges were subject to a new, more alien, and harsher form of domination and exploitation than before the revolution. When war broke out between France and Prussia, the Patriots attempted to conscript from the countryside, exempting themselves. This was the precipitating cause of the counterrevolution as residents of the Vendée took up arms against the government, led by local nobility and anti-Patriot clergy. Of course, local nobility and exiled clergy had very good political and economic reasons for struggling against the revolutionary regime. So did the peasants, who were being taxed by the state for an unpopular war and also were called upon to fight it. There was also unrest among the artisans who were dependent on the bourgeoisie for work and were suffering from a crisis in industrial production. Thus Tilly began with Durkheim and ended up with Marx. Urbanization, introduced as the major concept, receded as Tilly examined the underlying social relationships between the major identifiable classes and status groups. Urbanization, then, could not be separated from the political economy of social class relationships, since it became an artifact of class action. The counterrevolution in the Vendée was not a consequence of the breakdown of traditional relationships and a consequent vacuum of leadership, leading to meaninglessness, aimlessness, and anomie, but a reaction against the imposition of a new and alien set of relationships. Marx won, Durkheim lost. The explanation rang of the analysis of the historical development of social relations between classes.

Whereas *The Vendée* is a natural history of a social movement, *Strikes in France*, by Tilly and Edward Shorter, is much more positivistic, inquiring into the alterations in strike behavior from 1830–1968. Tilly introduced his concepts of competitive, reactive, and proactive forms of collective action, noting that strike activity developed from a spontaneous, unorganized activity into that which became less violent and more planned and organized. This work is of less interest to us than Tilly's *The Rebellious Century*, with Richard and Louise Tilly.

The Rebellious Century represents a gearing up for *From Mobilization to Revolution*, which is the most complete statement of Tilly's theory of collective action. *The Rebellious Century* examines the sequence of collective action in three European states—France, Germany, and Italy—between the years 1830 and 1930. The book begins by noting that for the three countries, the hundred-year period studied had high levels of collective action. All three countries—even though Germany and Italy were not unified states at the time—were shaken by the Revolution of 1848, Germany and France were struck by the Revolution of 1830, with Italy having delayed rebellions in 1831. Italy had a particularly violent decade between 1860 and 1870, beginning with revolts in the south in 1860, shifting to the north in 1866. Following the First World War, Italy was again subjected to increasing violence until Mussolini's fascist takeover in 1922. France's history throughout the nineteenth and twentieth centuries has been fraught with insurrectionary violence—in addition to 1830 and 1848, there was unrest in 1871, 1907, 1919–20, and 1936–37. After the Second World War, there were revolts in 1947–48, 1950–52, 1955–56, 1958, and of course 1968. Although Germany has experienced less violence, there was a rash of strikes between 1909 and 1913, mutinies and the Spartacist Revolt in 1918–19 and nearly continual street fighting between 1931 and 1933. The Tillys felt that the countries and the period were quite fruitful for the comparative study of collective action. The analysis was focused on the question "Does collective action occur because of a breakdown in social order or because of the increasing solidarity of dissident elements within the system?" Thus, we are again given a choice between Durkheim and Marx.

In all fairness, the Tillys noted that the answer to the question was fraught with subtle distinctions and could be seen as the same phenomenon viewed from different perspectives. In an attempt to answer the question, they analyzed collective action in terms of who was rebelling against whom, proximate and long-term causes of the conflict, and the nature of the revolt. They concluded that if one must take sides, solidarity theory is a better explanation than the Durkheimian breakdown theory. First, they noted a qualitative change in the nature of collective action over the period studied, which indicated that rebellion began in the form of competitive action in which no political orientation could be discerned and tended to take the form of brawls between youth gangs of neighboring towns. Collective action entered an intermediate phase of reactive behavior, in which spontaneous mobs would rebel against an aggressive action by a dominating group. Rebellions in which tax collectors were ridden out of town were of that order. As the century matured, so did collective action. Dissidents were banning together and organizing in formally constructed associations. In addition to reacting against imposition of authority, they began to hold forth alternative programs, plan strategy, and engage in forms of protest that required discipline and ongoing organization, such as the mass strike. Second, the Tillys noted that there were three basic situations that led to collective action: economic crises, state-building activities, and industrialization. Only economic crises could be associated with the breakdown of social order. The other two are characteristics of the imposition of new social orders. Also, the unique histories of the countries have implications for the onset of collective violence. For example, France and Italy experienced heightened levels of violence during the periods of industrial spurts, whereas Germany was relatively quiescent during its industrialization period, but experienced greater levels of violence prior to industrialization. Collective violence tended to be located in the countryside at the beginning of the century and relocated in the cities at the end. Throughout the period studied, there was increased evidence of the participation of the proletariat in collective violence. The Tillys concluded:

> If we must choose between breakdown and solidarity theories, we have to take solidarity. If we have a chance to revise existing theories, we must build in representations of mobilization, contention for power, and repression. Instead of a direct line from "change" to "protest" through "strain" or "hardship," we discover multiple lines. The rearrangement of everyday life transforms the organization of collective action. [1975:269-70]

Is this to be taken as a victory of Marx over Durkheim? Although there is certainly an attempt to focus on the historical relations between classes, the within-class relations are treated as a black box. That is, what are the *subjective* elements within the experience of the conflict groups that lead to the development of solidarity, or in Marx's terms, when is a class in itself transformed into a class for itself? The reader is given a sense of the historical shifts in class relations. What is not given is how these shifts influence the daily lives of potentially dissident elements within the social order. The treatment of collective violence by the Tillys, when compared to, say, Marx's own analyses of the Revolution of 1848, is bloodless. However, what is even more important is the apparent lack of concern for the subjective elements in collective action. This oversight is apparently responsible for Charles Tilly's movement into the resource mobilization camp in *From Mobilization to Revolution,* in which, in the absence of data, Tilly opted for a utilitarian model of motivation for collective violence. In his introduction to *From Mobilization to Revolution,* he stated that he had produced "stone soup." He was more correct than he thought: utilitarian motivation theory stones in a Marxist soup. The stones are indigestible and the soup is thin. When researchers assume that participants in collective action engage in a calculation of potential costs against potential benefits, they are distorting the reality of social action. It may even be true that certain forms of collective action or violence during a certain historical phase may be characterized by rational calculation on the part of the participants. Is one to assume that the tremendous continent-shattering revolts that shook Europe between 1848 and 1850 were the result of the rational calculation by dissidents who saw that they could achieve short-run gains through their rebellion? The problem with such conceptualizations is that when a social movement is in progress, the locus of motivation is subject to alteration to the point where dissident collectivities see rebellion as the only alternative to capitulation. Rational calculation, which underlies the utilitarian's theory of motivation presupposes that all people adhere to conventional reality at all times. Even Max Weber and Gustave LeBon understood that this was not the case! It is especially true that the domination of the hegemonic ideology loses its potency during times of social upheaval and that during such periods, the rules of the game change (see Chapter 6, "Disalienation"). It is truly disheartening to see such a talented and scholarly researcher as Tilly repudiate the notion of the subjective leap and eschew social-movement theory for collective action theory, lumping qualitatively different types of social action together in a homogeneous whole while relegating social movements to "waves" of collective action. Such recent experiences as the social movements of the 1960s in the West and the Cultural Revolution in China should clue us in to the differences between routine and sporadic collective action and that which constitutes social movement behavior. In 1968, one was either part of the problem or part of the solution. Middle-class youth were "crazies on the loose" experiencing the "reality gap" (see Foss, 1972, for an elaboration of the subjective elements of social-movement behavior). The common threads running through RM theory are the (unproven) assumptions that (1) social-movement behavior is subject to rational calculation on the parts of the participants, (2) the efficacy of a social movement is based on the qualities of leadership and formal organization, and (3) social movements can be understood using concepts that also apply to ongoing social relations. Underlying these assumptions is the presupposition that social movements can be controlled by leadership from within or without. Though they may be popular among sociologists who desire to subject social movements to "rational" or "scientific" analysis and radicals who see themselves as vanguards, they have failed to prove that such analysis provides superior understanding to the historical record. This is especially true of Tilly's work.

Conclusion

There are serious shortcomings associated with RD and RM theories that undermine their ability to apprehend and understand the complex phenomena of social movements. First, they tend to underplay the so-called "spontaneous" aspects of social movement behavior. This is because they tend to analyze social movements using categories and concepts drawn from ongoing social structure, thereby distorting the social reality of social movements to fit into preestablished categories, making them banal, as in the extreme case of McCarthy and Zald (1977). Such trivialization tends to overemphasize formal organizations and their impact on social-movement behavior. Second, hierarchical aspects of social-movement structure are overemphasized, whereby the actions of leadership strata and movement "superstars" are accorded powers they simply do not have. Third, they tend, with the possible exception of Tilly, to ignore historical forces in the generation of social movements. Thus, the models of social movements tend to be static, as in the case of McCarthy and Zald; reductionistic, as in the case of Gurr; or inadequate to differentiate movement periods from periods of social quiescence, as in the case of Tilly. Finally, none of the theorists attempt to examine the problems of the underlying consciousness of social-movement participants as they engage in praxis, deepening their understanding of the social order and calling forth new repetoires of behaviors in line with their new interpretations of how society works. This is because, especially in the cases of resource mobilization and relative deprivation theories, the emphasis has been on studying phenomena that can be measured and subjected to variable analysis, i.e., political violence and collective action. Neither term is sufficient to distinguish routine, normal, and episodic dissidence from that which builds upon itself and takes the form of nonnormal dissidence, that is the hallmark of the social movement.

Notes

1. The title was unfortunate, since it was published at the very time that *women* in the Western world were rebelling against masculine domination and the very sexism implied in Gurr's work.

2. Although Gurr claimed in his introduction that his theory is about as useful for rebels as establishmentarians, we regard this as sophistry. His theory presupposes a large social-scientific establishment to collect and analyze data concerning the potential for violence by a particular collectivity. As we will demonstrate, movements are not "built" but develop on the basis of their own internal laws of motion given the historical conjuncture. Therefore, such information becomes useful only for those who wish to forestall movements.

Chapter 3

The Reproduction of Social Privilege

In our language a herd of sheep is called a flock, a herd of lions is called a pride, a herd of baboons is called a troop, and a herd of humans is called a society. The herds of other species are perpetuated on the level of biological reproduction, including the transmission of genetically encoded instincts and learning capacities whereby subsistence is appropriated, mates found, and danger surmounted or evaded. The reproduction of society, by contrast, involves four levels, each in partial combination and partial contradiction with all the others such that the precise reproduction of the social formation as a whole is inevitably rendered problematic. These levels are:

1. The level of biological reproduction. This includes behavior necessary for the physical subsistence of the members of society, such as eating, excretion, or sleep; the procreation and nurturing of the young; and activities necessary to the maintenance of people in a condition of somatic and psychic health, including shamanistic ministrations, individual and group expressive behavior, play, and most sexual behavior.

2. The level of material reproduction. This includes the making, maintenance, and consumption of products, used or possessed by society as a whole or by any individual, group, or category therein.

3. The level of cultural reproduction. This includes behavioral norms, the techniques of production, shared beliefs about the nature of the universe, social relations, "human nature," etc., or ideology, and shared conceptual categories that define "meaning."

4. The level of political reproduction. This includes, besides the reproduction of the form of the polity itself—where it is differentiated from society as a whole—the reproduction of patterns of domination and authority relations throughout society.

Our purpose in this section is to analyze the reproduction of social privilege in its historical context. We begin with the analysis of the material level of reproduction, since biological reproduction is dependent on the social formations generated by the other levels of social reproduction. Access to the necessities of subsistence and satisfaction of basic human needs depends on the relation of a particular social formation to the physical environment, which is often conditioned by such historical forces as colonization, conquest, and epidemics. Within social formations there is obviously inequality in the accessibility of need-satisfying activities and products. At the material level of social reproduction, we will explore the evolution of exploitation. At the cultural level, we will examine hegemony. At the political level, we will examine the process of domination.

It is herein that we lay the theoretical base for the study of social movements. We assume that the basic etiology of social movements resides in the process of the reproduction of social privilege and that social movements, regardless of the subjective awareness of the participants as to their purpose, are attacks on the maintenance of social privilege.

Society is an organic unit that alternates between periods of social quiescence and social movement. Although our major focus is on social movements, it is our purpose to understand what happens during the longer intervening periods of peace that lead to the forcible assertion of antistructure (cf. Turner, 1969) by dissident collectivities. Our major focus is on the reproduction of social privilege in bourgeois societies, but it is important for us to distinguish between the bases for the maintenance of privilege between bourgeois and prebourgeois societies. By taking the historical and comparative view, we can examine the ways in which problems within the relations of exploitation, domination, legitimation were improved upon by bourgeois elites. In so doing, we are also able to analyze the historical development of capitalist society and the emerging problems within capitalist social formations. By gaining an understanding of the forces of development of contemporary capitalist society and the maturation of contradictions within it, the periodicity, social categories, forms, and "issues" of the next social movement in the capitalist West can be understood.

The Material Reproduction of Society

X A material object becomes a product when it is consciously modified by the direct or indirect (through animal traction or machinery) application of physical human energy (labor) for a preconceived end. Direct appropriation of nature may occur without the use of products, as when fruit is plucked off a tree or a prey animal is killed with a rock found on the spot. Products do, however, enter into the picture when the fruit is sliced off the tree with a sharpened object or the rock is preshaped to render it more lethal. Food itself becomes a product when derived from a domesticated plant or an animal species. Cooked or otherwise prepared food is likewise a product.

Material reproduction requires the simultaneous and continuous operation of the processes of the fabrication and repair of objects. That is, the production and the using up, possession, and accumulation or hoarding of products, subsumed under the term "consumption." Products are obviously consumed in the process of producing other products and must be periodically replaced to ensure continuing production. New production is also called forth by the perception within society or a portion of society that existing products are worn out, depleted, or used to capacity. The definition of "capacity use" or "depletion" may involve levels of social reproduction not yet discussed: A pyramid, for instance, was deemed to be used to capacity when the monarch it commemorated was entombed within it; though the object itself would endure for millennia, it nevertheless devolved upon the succeeding ruler to commence constructing his own. It should be added that the process of production, even under capitalist conditions, presupposes the expectation of consumption. However, capitalism—in contrast to all preceding social formations—presents the recurrence of production outstripping society's ability to consume (cf. Marx, 1973).

Material reproduction does not require that products be consumed by the same people who produce them or even consumed within the same society. Products may be exchanged for other products or for a medium of exchange. They may also be produced consciously and explicitly for sale as commodities to unknown—but necessarily anticipated—ultimate consumers in an anonymous market. Moreover, there are in every society persons who—even if by virtue of infancy—consume products but do not produce them. When an entire section of society systematically consumes products produced by the labor of another section of society, does not produce products by its own labor in exchange, and possesses access to means of dominance sufficient to ensure the regular delivery by the producers, then an exploitative relation is said to exist between social classes.

The difference between the material product required to sustain the entire population at a material standard of living conventionally defined (or historically determined) as mere subsistence and the total product produced by the exploited class or classes is the surplus regardless of by whom it is consumed. By virtue of the vagaries of nature such as weather and soil fertility, their own efforts and ingenuity, or the special favor or slackness of the exploiting class or classes, a portion of the exploited class or classes enjoys a material standard of living above the level of "subsistence" as conventionally understood. The difference between this relative material prosperity and the subsistence level represents the *unappropriated* surplus as well as—if they are indeed fortunate—part of the *redistributed* surplus. The aggregate product consumed by the exploiting class or classes constitutes the *appropriated* surplus, whether consumed in private luxury or in the performance of their public duties. Their hangers-on and minions who ensure the extraction of the same product from its producers in appropriate volume and regularity are compensated out of the appropriated surplus.

Material Reproduction in Prebourgeois Society

Prior to the advent of bourgeois society there was no exploiting class that directly and systematically intervened in the labor process. Exceptions occurred only for relatively brief periods of apparent dearth of productive labor power. The particular appearances of prebourgeois exploiting classes depended rather on two factors: first, the relative magnitude of the appropriated surplus; and second, those activities represented as the occupations peculiar to that class or classes exempt from productive labor, such as war (with an important difference arising here between commanders of soldiers and knightly warriors),[1] civilian administration, religion, law, scholarship, cultivated leisure, pomp and ceremony, and the like. The second factor thus represents the mode of absorption, that is to say, consumption, of the appropriated surplus. Different prebourgeois exploiting classes supported by the same relative magnitude of appropriated surplus could and did adopt quite various styles of life and occupational specialties. A classic case is that of Egypt, where the labor process involved irrigated flood-plain agriculture, which had been substantially developed by the second millennium B.C. This form persisted until the incorporation of the Nile Valley into the capitalist world market in the nineteenth century, when the large-scale cash-crop cultivation of cotton was introduced. During this long period the exploiting class was altered in its appearances—and this was the "coloration" imparted to society as a whole. This occurred many times under successive native regimes and those of assorted conquerors, including Asiatic and Libyan nomads, Nubians, Assyrians, Persians, Hellenistic Greeks, Romans, Byzantines, Arabs, Mamluks, and Ottomans. Where these regimes—especially the latter two—intervened in the labor process at all, the result was disruptive. In Roman times Egypt supported 7.5 million people, a figure not reached again until the last century.

Prebourgeois exploiting classes were essentially parasitic. Their primary need was for elite consumption, including the means of violence. As the latter guaranteed the production and hence the consumption of all other varieties of elite products, the thrust of their ambition was toward the maximization of military power, either through the incumbency of key offices in state-type polities or through the accumlation of military might on the spot in feudal-type polities. It might be conjectured that the easiest and most immediately rewarding policy for any prebourgeois exploiting class faced with the ever-present threat of an absolute or relative decline in the magnitude of the surplus was precisely the perfection of the means of violence and the social relations of violence: Absolute declines occurred through demographic disasters such as famine, natural calamities, epidemics, or invasions causing gaps in the ranks of subsistence-level producers subject to exploitation. Prebourgeois exploiting classes were rarely capable of innovation in either labor-saving technology or in the labor processes with which existing technology was used, though they were quite capable of systematizing labor processes and the machinery of surplus extraction. Thus the Romans generated treatises on estate management in addition to their achievements in the spheres of administration and law, but were quite unable to find practical applications for Hellenistic science. Meanwhile, fundamental innovations in iron production and agricultural technology were being made by German and Slav "barbarians." The means of violence could be used and were in fact used to tie the scarce laborers to the spot; labor-saving devices were most commonly introduced when these were not only ready at hand, but also when the machinery for the coercion of scarce laborers had broken down or become ineffectual.[2]

The alternative predicament was the tendency of the relative magnitude of the surplus to decline due to population increase once the basic forms of the means of production, the labor processes associated with them, and the level of development of the human subject, the ensemble of these comprising the "forces of production," had attained a relatively fixed or final pitch of apparent perfection. The human subject includes every possible manifestation of human individuality, especially the capacity to innovate in any sphere of activity. It must never be forgotten that the level of development of the human subject is itself part of the "objective conditions" in any social order; however, the degree of this development is determined—not precisely, but within certain broad limits—by the relative magnitude of the surplus, both appropriated and unappropriated. Under these conditions it was normal for prebourgeois exploiting classes to employ the means of violence to not only maintain but actually *increase* the absolute magnitude of the appropriated product: Apparent superfluities of labor were turned to the advantage of the exploiting classes by compelling the exploited to accept more abject servitude in preference to starvation or hopeless revolt. Pools of unappropriated surplus were mopped up; material living standards of large sectors of the exploited class were pushed below *absolute* subsistence levels, that is, to the point of interference with the biological reproduction of society; and the politico-military apparatus of the exploiters was streamlined to facilitate the preceding.

Moreover, for any prebourgeois exploiting class the use where practicable of military force for accumulation through annexation, plunder, or levying of tribute constituted an attractive supplement or alternative to exploitation. The latter is most evident in those types of feudal polities in which the effective means of violence are widely distributed through various hierarchical levels of subpolities, since society as a whole was under such conditions. A home front was maintained in a perpetual state of mobilization for a war of all against all. Peasants had to be relied upon for emergency corvée labor in transport, fortification, and so forth. The exploited could even under favorable conditions be used as troops and thus hope for mobility into the exploiting class. Thus it may be noted that until the fourteenth century—when the legitimacy of the Catholic hierarchy first became seriously eroded—the clergy had long been more conspicuous than the lay lords in maximizing the revenue from their estates. Most notable among these were the monasteries, from the Benedictines in the sixth and seventh centuries to the Cistercians in the twelfth and thirteenth.

To repeat, the material reproduction of prebourgeois class societies was characterized by the primacy of the needs of consumption in calling forth production; that is, there were no "laws of motion" intrinsic to the processes of production that required perpetual activity on the part of the exploiting classes to dispose of an ever-growing volume of products. Rather, it was production, not consumption, that was problematic. Exploited classes produced their own subsistence and were additionally made to produce the upkeep of essentially parasitic exploiting classes as well as that of various apparatuses of enforcers, collectors, overseers, and ideological specialists who ensured the production and delivery of the appropriated surplus. Relations governing the appropriation of the surplus were thus relations of surplus absorption, that is, of the consumption of part of what was produced, and not "relations of production," since the exploiting classes did not continuously intervene in the labor processes. Indeed, it was entirely characteristic of these societies that the absolute magnitude of the appropriated surplus tended to remain fixed for long periods without reference to productive capacity or labor supply, to the advantage of those—especially peasants—who managed to raise output or install labor-saving contrivances or otherwise produce unappropriated surplus. Of course it was greatly to their disadvantage in times of crop failure, famine, flood, or invasion.

Material Reproduction in Bourgeois Society

If prebourgeois exploiting classes are comparable to parasitic organisms (see William McNeil, 1976; McNeil calls them "macroprasites" by contrast to organisms causing infectious disease, or "microparasites"), then the bourgeoisie is a *carcinogenic agent*. Marx (1967) aptly remarked, in volume 1 of *Capital*, that when viewed from the outside capitalism appears as "a system of production for production's sake." By virtue of the "laws of motion" of the capitalist "mode of production"—bourgeois society's peculiar arrangement for getting products produced—the material reproduction of society is interfered with unless it takes place on an ever-expanding scale. The particular form in which the surplus is appropriated is the value of the surplus product produced by laborers over and above the value of the product necessary to reproduce their labor power at a level of subsistence appropriate for the time and place. The objective of the bourgeoisie as a class and as individuals, in fact the very purpose of life in bourgeois society, is "the endless accumulation of abstract exchange-value" (Marx, 1973:409-410), that is, the limitless piling up of claims on society's ability to consume or, vulgarly, getting rich.[3] If the system is in that condition which the bourgeoisie has traditionally called "sound," this may be most predictably accomplished by the consumption of the appropriated surplus in the expansion of productive capacity, including the purchase of additional labor power, but in such a way that the savings of the bourgeoisie increase faster than does the wage income of the proletariat. The resulting chronic imbalance between society's ability to produce products and its ability to consume them leads not only to periodic crises—whether in the form of the old-fashioned "trade cycle" or in the more contemporary guise of "belt tightening" contrived and administered by the state—but additionally to ferocious marketing pressure on the part of the bourgeoisie. This includes the progressive dominance of marketing considerations over product design (extending in our times even to military weaponry), ever more sophisticated marketing techniques, and systematic inducements to consume new products and new models of existing products before the products already sold have been fully used up (see Baran and Sweezy, 1966).

Capitalism is the first true "mode of production." The "dominant relation" of bourgeois society—the capital-labor relation—is in fact integral to the labor process: Since labor power, the source of the surplus appropriated in the process of production, is bought and sold as a pseudocommodity—"pseudo" because however much the laborers may self-consciously develop "marketable skills" or are regarded as "hands" by the bourgeoisie, the labor power is not really separable from the living beings of the laborers—it follows that, from the standpoint of capital, the cost of labor is always too high. This represents the equivalent of a permanent dearth of labor even in the presence of substantial numbers of "unemployed" persons, thereby inducing the bourgeoisie to, first, continuously intervene in the labor process, and then, ultimately, to seize control of the labor process in every detail (see Braverman, 1974).

The mode of production is thus in a sense society's relatively self-contained device for getting products produced in ever-growing mass; "relatively," because it must among other things rely on the state—ultimately on the means of violence—to guarantee the conditions of accumulation. It tends to focus new needs and capacities—which emerge with the increasing development of the human subject—rather narrowly in terms of products. By its example it induces socialist societies that emerge from revolution against it to define their *raison d'être* in terms of catching up with it. Possibly most disturbing, and as Marx (1973:410) foresaw, every hitherto autonomous domain of social life becomes coerced into conformity with the dictates of the mode of production.

A condition of the existence—or reproduction—of the capitalist mode of production is the reproduction of the bourgeoisie as a class. But this in turn requires the reproduction of the bifurcation of this class into entrepreneurs—who are themselves increasingly reproduced in the subcategories of owners and employee managers—and politico-military specialists. The latter guarantee the conditions of the accumulation carried on by the former.

The reproduction of their division of labor derives from the unprecedented character of capitalism as a mode of production. Marxian theory has traditionally concentrated on the role of the state in securing the conditions of accumulation by ensuring exploitation through the forcible suppression of the proletariat and championing the "right of poverty" generally. Some writers, like Gramsci (1977; and, more recently, Miliband (1969), have considered the role of the state in reproducing the cultural and ideological hegemony of the bourgeoisie. O'Connor's recent works (1973, 1974) deal largely with the significance of state subsidies—"indirect surplus value"—and redistributions of income in the performance of the "accumulation function" and the "legitimation function" of the state in bourgeois society. What is thus far lacking in Marxian theory, however, is a comprehensive analysis of the process of the capitalist mode of production, the inner logic of which is "production for production's sake," the using up of the products produced, that is, consumption. Capitalism has never, at any time, relied exclusively on the combination of the household consuming retail merchandise and the capitalist consuming the means of production. It has always depended heavily on elite extravagance—especially in the earlier phases of bourgeois society, when this was marvelously effective in concentrating hordes of parasitic consumers around courts and aristocratic establishments. Commodity production was stimulated and market relations were developed. Later capitalism depended even more on collectivized military (comprising war, preparation for war, and colonial expansion) and civilian consumption by the state. This is apart from the importance of war as an alternative to the trade crisis in accomplishing the massive devalorization of capital through military devastation: From the standpoint of the capitalist system as a whole, World War I was a lousy war in that the territory subject to devastation was negligible. Technological advances made during the war were, moreover, not readily usable in civilian industry in part because too much existing plant remained undestroyed. A major European state had been knocked out of the world market yet was manifestly too weak to represent a plausible excuse for continued "preparedness." This should be borne in mind when pondering the magnitude and persistence of the slump of the 1930s. World War II was by contrast a wonderful war from the same point of view; even for Germany it was more economical. It pulverized a much vaster area into ruins thereby both requiring and permitting several major states to reconstruct their heavy-industrial base almost ex nihilo—prompting some representatives of the British bourgeoisie to regret publicly in later times that the Luftwaffe had not done as thorough a job on their own country as the Allied forces subsequently wreaked upon the Germans—making room for enormous new civilian industries. As a bonus the political results of the war legitimated a high level of pump-priming militarization ever since.

The process of capitalist consumption necessarily involves many things that the rationally accumulating entrepreneurs might never countenance if left to their own devices. The entrepreneurs, from their own perspective, denounce them an egregious waste out of hand; nevertheless, should they come to savor the accumulation-promoting fruits of these policies—be they war or "do-good" social reform—they inevitably adapt themselves. Accordingly, overall political direction—including custody of the means of violence—in bourgeois society is systematically entrusted to what might be called *consumption formations*, which are typically distinct in style and mentality from the entrepreneurs themselves, however much they are, together with the entrepreneurs, integrally part of the bourgeoisie. The consumption formations retain their distinctiveness apart from the entrepreneurs although individuals may pass from the entrepreneurial category to enter electoral politics and career military men may become corporate officers. The division is reproduced with the reproduction of the bourgeoisie as a class.

Beginning with Marx himself, the Marxian tradition has been bedazzled by the twin manias of the entrepreneurial category for production and accumulation. Consequently, it has long been handicapped in the analysis of consumption formations and the process of capitalist consumption as a whole. Marx, for example, was faced by the persistence of the British "landed gentry" in control of the state apparatus of the world's leading industrial power in his day. The landed gentry, moreover, often lacked pecuniary wealth commensurate with their prestige, social status, and access to the leading posts in the state. Were they capitalists specializing in the agricultural branch of production? A precapitalist survival? A class unto themselves? In the famous chapter 52, "Classes," of volume 3 of *Capital* (1967:885-86), Marx gave his last word on that subject (or any other, for that matter). He decided that they were indeed a class, with their own unique relationship to the means of production, that is, they lived off the rents accruing from landownership. But he apparently decided almost immediately that this was silly and stopped writing altogether. "Here the manuscript breaks off," Engels noted.

Another case concerns the millions of people found in every corner of bourgeois society working in offices. They are remunerated out of *redistributed surplus*, that is, out of profit as understood by Marx. They proliferate in part because it is impossible to determine with any precision their quantitative relation to the cost of doing business or to the performance of any administrative services; on the other hand, it is perfectly clear that their employment involves the consumption, rather than the production, of products. Their role in the material reproduction of society, both on and off the job, is in consumption, hence we choose to call them "the surplus-absorbing strata" and "dependent consumption formations." The main Marxist schools of thought, however, perversely choose to quibble about their "relation to the means of production," and hence whether they represent a "new working class," the position of the

French Communist party, or a "new petite bourgeoisie," the position of Poulantzes (1975), or a heterogeneous category occupying a variety of contradictory
positions in the class structure (Wright, 1978).

In bourgeois society the labor process and the techniques of production tend
everywhere toward uniformity and differ only as to the degree of introduction
of the latest and most advanced labor-saving productive processes. Among the
countries of the capitalist core area, however, aside from differences in relative
magnitude of output, there are striking differences in the appearances of society
traceable to the process of capitalist consumption, which subsumes the uses
to which appropriated, unappropriated, and redistributed surplus are put. The
preceding does not refer to the so-called "distribution of income" as much,
since this is only an appearance of the overall process of capitalist consumption.
The major variants are:

1. *Export-led growth*. This version, currently exemplified by Japan (as previously by the United States in the 1920s and by Britain in the nineteenth
century) requires that a major part of the appropriated surplus in the form of
products be used up in other countries, whether as means of production or as
household-consumption goods. (The Japanese will sell you a $1 billion cement
plant as easily as an $80 TV set.) Such exports may be only marginally prof-
itable, but they do make possible the continuity of a high level of production
while the remainder of the appropriated surplus is consumed as yet more
advanced means of production, which makes possible a still larger volume of
production of even cheaper products for export, and so on. The domestic working
class is meanwhile spared not only the difficulties of periodic layoffs, but also
the corrosive effects of excessively high living standards upon industriousness
and subservience.

2. *Household-consumption-led growth*. This was to some extent characteristic
of the United States in the 1950s and much of the 1960s; it is today perhaps
best exemplified by West Germany. This variant requires that much of the
appropriated surplus product be used up by a substantial fraction of the mass
of the population. This in turn implies the retention of a substantial amount
of unappropriated surplus—as income exchanged for the surplus product consumed—by the upper stratum of the working class, to the intense displeasure
of the local entrepreneurs. Even more, it implies a massive reliance on dependent consumption formations, including office workers and administrators,
servants (who reappear, e.g., as waiters and cab drivers, as "service industry
employees," lumped together with altogether different types of labor), sales
personnel, professionals, semiprofessionals, etc., all of whom are supported
out of redistributed surplus. The profitability of this variant appears at some
points to be integrally related to ever-rising material standards of living; but
if these should rise too high too fast for too many it has been demonstrated by
the experience of recent history that the cultural and political reproduction of
society (see later in this chapter) is interfered with. Another difficulty arises
when the surplus redistributed to the dependent consumption formations is
rising faster—by reason of the mounting systemic pressure for ever-higher levels
of consumption—than it can be appropriated from the direct producers and
consequently appears to threaten the nominal rate of profit (as defined by the
entrepreneurs), thus promoting a general rise in prices—or "inflation"—and
inroads upon sales by imports.

3. Military-collectivized-consumption-led growth. The clearest historical example of this was Nazi Germany in the 1930s and 1940s, but the United States during the Civil War and World War II also illustrates this variant quite well. Moreover, it represents a built-in feature of capitalist accumulation in the "advanced countries"—exclusive of Japan—of the capitalist world as well as the socialist world) as a whole at this time. Its essential feature is the reliance on the state to superintend the consumption of a major part of the surplus product in the form of military goods, related equipment, and means of production for manufacturing the same. This may take the form of consumption in war, storage of the products in question until they become obsolete and more elaborate products then built, providing free military assistance to client states, or even furnishing foreign aid to a newly defeated enemy to repair the damage recently wrought as it is to the advantage of capitalism as a whole—as opposed to any particular state—that the late foe consume the means of production required to restore the war-ravaged economy as quickly as possible.

4. Civilian-collectivized-consumption-led growth. Historically, the Swedish road to capitalism, it is now characteristic of the United States and increasingly of Europe. In the United States it evolved out of variant 2, possibly as a response to the threat to the social order represented by excessively high material standards of living for too much of the population. Accordingly, it differs from variant 2 in that consumption within bureaucratic apparatuses continues to increase or increases at a faster rate, whereas household consumption is held constant or either declines or is maintained on credit. An obvious drawback is that this variant is no less "inflationary" than variant 2. Also, since the leadership in the expansion of collectivized consumption passes from "private enterprise" to the "public sector," the entrepreneurs chafe at the exactions of the "politician" fraction of the bourgeoisie and rouse popular support against their colleagues.

5. Luxury-consumption-led growth. Historically, this has been the French Road to capitalism. This variant is now obsolete, but traces remain in France, which boasts a distribution of income that would make the United States look egalitarian.

Bourgeois society, dependent as it is for stability on an expanding level of production, has developed and expanded consumption formations that consume the surplus product. Central consumption formations are the household, the entrepreneurial strata (including corporations), and the state. The extravagant consumption of the bourgeoisie is insufficient to maintain an expanding economy. Therefore, greater sectors of the population are employed in consuming the surplus. The upper middle class is the most obvious social category that composes the constituency of consumption formations, consuming on the job as well as off in their roles as volatile consumers.

The Level of Cultural Reproduction

Cultural reproduction involves the inculcation, perpetuation, and transmission of, first, that body of shared or stored things done and made in society, that is, behavioral norms and the prevailing *techniques* for appropriating nature (as opposed to the *process* of material reproduction). Second, it involves shared ideas, beliefs, notions, theories, and narratives concerning the origins and history of the universe (comprising both the extrasocial—"nature"—and social components, with the latter definable as including the dead, the unborn, the reincarnated, the good and evil spirits, the divinities, the manipulable cosmic forces, etc.). This includes the significance of customary behavior and technique, the quality and sources of right and wrong (or health and sickness, success and failure, etc.), how the universe (including the social universe however understood) operates both ideally and actually, why some people in society are better than others, why other societies are different and inferior, and so on, all of which may be subsumed under the term *ideology*. Third, cultural reproduction involves shared conceptual categorizations of the universe, which give rise to thought forms characteristic of the culture and which unite individual, social unit, society as a whole, and nature in a "totalization" (cf. Levi-Strauss, 1966) whereby social life, individual life, and the universe as a whole are all implicitly understood as what is in common parlance called "meaningful." This third dimension of culture listed here is most elusive to cultural insiders, who in times of the failure of its reproduction seek out "meaningful work," "meaningful relationships," and persons who may be hired to "put meaning back" into their lives. It is most difficult for them to apprehend that "meaning"—whatever is meant by that—is implicit within the thought forms that the collectivity imposes upon itself, and that said imposition is efficacious to the extent that there is scant evidence of people "looking for meaning."

Cultural reproduction systematically reproduces the conditions for the disruption of its own continuity. First, culture is objectified in social structure. In primitive societies the social structure is routinely subject to disruption from without (cf. Levi-Strauss, 1966, "diachronic discontinuity," and Douglas, 1966) by perils of natural and human origin. They are also subject to disruption from within by contradictions within the social structure. Douglas points out that pollution taboos, rituals, and myths tend to coagulate at points where the social structure is exposed to external threat and where it is subject to internal contradiction. An example of such disruption is illustrated by Turner (1969) in his analysis of Ndembu ritual. The Ndembu exists in social units in which there is a contradiction between rules of residence and rules of descent. Within the ritual, they symbolically harmonize the contradictory principles of matrilineality and virilocality. Second, the products of primitive societies, being nonstandardized, each in part represent the objectification of the direct producers' esthetics and are subject to incessant change in style, form, and even level of technique. Language, in its form as a shared system of behavioral norms, changes at a rate that is fairly constant; this makes possible the science of glottochronology.

False Consciousness and Alienation

To Levi-Strauss the necessity for "synchronic systematization" requires an incessant struggle against the consequence of "diachronic discontinuity" by calling upon the sphere of ideology as myth, to which—in accordance with Mary Douglas (1966) and Victor Turner (1969)—could be added rituals, pollution taboos, and the interpretation of these things formulated by the primitives themselves. The result is the imposition by the collectivity upon itself of an ideological assertion of a greater degree of solidarity, continuity, and absence of contradiction that in fact prevails, or at least is deducible from the analysis of the inner logic of the social structure. This is, therefore, *false consciousness*, which is, accordingly, a component of the ideological formulation generally accepted within even primitive societies and not limited to those characterized by relations of class exploitation.

The same may be said for *alienation*, which inevitably accompanies domination even though exploitative class relations may not necessarily be present. Alienation is the appropriation of certain human capabilities as the exclusive possessions of a social category and their denial to the dominated, who, correspondingly, render psychic tribute to the dominators for possessing what has been appropriated. Alienation is literally a reward paid by the victim to a successful rip-off artist. Alienation permeates not only the ideological sphere but also the system of conceptual categories according to which the perceived universe is organized; that is to say, the sphere of "reality" and meaning. Say that, in a sentient sexually dimorphic species, in the absence of domination, reality may be either male or female. Yet by virtue of domination he makes what makes sense to him make sense to her. The species is named "man," implying that he is normal and she is deviant to pathological. The masculine principle is given pride of place over the feminine in the categorization of the universe. But, as Mary Douglas points out, with the exception of empirically very rare societies where the social structure is such as to render patriarchy unmitigatedly absolute, the abstract dominion of the masculine principle will be disconfirmed by actual social life and the system of categorization is consequently "at war with itself." Reality leaks. Ideology is called into play (as myth, ritual, taboo, rationalization, etc.) when the organizing principles of "reality" contradict one another, leave things out, or leave loose ends hanging.

The ramifications of false consciousness and alienation obviously become much more pervasive in societies characterized by exploitative class relations. The exploited class is made to produce the material support of a specific ideological apparatus—or of ideological specialists who overlap here with the polity, there with organized religion, or even with both—which explicitly and systematically affirms the nonexistence of a class contradiction. Their existence reinforces the self-evident, eternal, and categorical character of the lodgement of alienated human capacities within the exploiting class in general and within themselves in particular.

In prebourgeois society the principal visible role of the ideological specialists was not the legitimation of exploitation—although this was occasionally done—but the personification of reifications (abstractions regarded by the collectivity as if they had independent, that is, thinglike, existence), which are themselves expressions of alienation, such as "the arts," "spirituality," "thought," "learning," "law," "philosophy," "ideas," "perfection," "virtue," and so forth ad infinitum, and even those ultimate reifications, Faith, Truth, and Tradition. As the embodiments of such things, living or dead (and often the longer dead they were, the greater their importance), they served the exploiting classes implicitly by imbuing them with conviction and confidence. This occurred to the extent to which exploiting classes were enabled to reproduce within themselves the explicit conviction—or even better, the unconscious assumption—that class society had a "higher purpose" outside the material reproduction of society, which made it a "civilization." The ideological specialists (in material terms parasitic off the exploiting class) thus facilitated that class's own parasitism by inverting it into a resolve to defend civilization, uphold civilized standards, or some such mystique. The latter was of course invariably propagated to the exploited classes whether or not it was likely to be plausible to *them*.

One of the consequences of the reproduction of the ideological specialists was, accordingly, the reproduction of the distinction between them and the exploiting class itself. A little distance was functional from the perspective of the long- or even medium-run interests of the exploiting class (and derivatively of the ideological specialists themselves) since this was conducive to the evolution of a code of conduct for the class as a whole. Thus, exploitation could be limited short of the point where it led to class suicide by way of revolution, interference with the biological reproduction of the laboring population or its flight and dispersal elsewhere, or the incitement of foreign aggression by the conspicuous display of indolent luxury. Generally speaking, the more gruesome the exploitation the greater was the distance. The Confucian scholar, for instance, displayed his integrity in retiring from public life during the corrupt and declining phase of a dynasty, but would rush to serve the state when a peasant revolutionary or crude general seized the throne and required assistance in promoting reform. When the exploiting class comprised savage Dark Age warriors, the ideological specialists were found exclusively in Benedictine monasteries. The perpetration of aristocratic hedonism in famine-ridden societies such as India or the Roman Empire practically dictated the emergence of the most extreme asceticism. Occasionally, ideological specialists served the exploiting classes best by getting into trouble or getting killed: Their fates served to develop or invigorate standards of class conduct and restraint. Almost the last thing they contemplated was the end of exploitation, which implied the end of the redistributed surplus that supported them. In any case, only a very select few ever attempted to appeal to the mass of the exploited directly, and if they did so the message was one of justice, compassion, righteousness, humility, saintliness, goodness, peace, love, brotherhood, patience, conscience, charity, benevolence, enlightenment, and so forth. In short, they legitimated exploitation by proclaiming its cosmic irrelevance, by formulating an idealized representation of it, by advocating limits to it wholly dependent on the goodwill of exploiters, and by inducing the exploited to believe that— in modern parlance—"the system still works."

The formulations of the ideological specialists, at least during periods of social peace, entered by a "trickling-down" process into the sphere of the hegemonic ideology. The term "hegemonic ideology" was evolved by Gramsci (1973) to comprise the interpretations of society imparted to the social order as a whole, which reflected the predominance of the exploiting class by way of the polity, organized religion, and other apparatuses that are at its disposal or that it subsumes. These ideas are not, in any class society, even bourgeois society, found in a state of formulation reflecting any intellectual sophistication or profundity and orderliness of thought. This was true even among typical members of the exploiting class. Yet they constitute a set of commonplaces shared by all classes about how social life is carried on both ideally and practically. This could change dramatically during social movement periods when these formulations were vehicles of ethnic and/or class conflict. We therefore see in the Roman Empire the Monophysite heresy expressing the resentment of Syrians and Egyptians against the ruling apparatus; Donatism that of the Africans; Pelagianism of the British; and Arianism the manifestation of the exclusivism of most of the Germanic tribes while fighting Rome and, subsequently, as rulers of the conquered Romano-provincials.

Hegemony in Prebourgeois Society

The hegemonic ideologies of prebourgeois class societies differed widely from place to place and period to period in their detailed elaboration, but were essentially similar in those features bound up with the reproduction of false consciousness and alienation:

First, the ordained purpose of the producers of the surplus was to make possible the mode of absorbing the surplus practiced by the exploiting class. The cake, in other words, existed to support the icing, which, in its decorative splendor, represented what the cake was all about. It was understood that the consumption of the surplus animated the social collectivity as a whole. This principle was normally so self-evident that its overt statement was necessitated only by the possible failure of the reproduction of exploitative relations. The Confucian sage Mencius, who lived in the fourth century B.C., during the "Warring States" period, wrote, "...[I]t is said, 'Some labour with their hands, and some labour with their minds. Those who labour with their minds govern others. Those who labour with their hands are governed by others. Those who are governed provide food for others. Those who govern are provided with food by others.' This is universally regarded as just" (Dobson, 1963:117). But this was said in a context in which the ruler was admonished to rule with "benevolence," that is, to restrain his greed for troops and taxes, lest the cultivators desert his territory for his enemy's or revolt against him. The Roman historian Livy (1962:92-93) recounted a legend associated with an episode in 493 B.C., when the debt serfs of early Rome defied their masters by collectively refusing to supply the produce due to them. The Senate, according to the story, thereupon sent an orator who likened the nobility to the stomach of a body and the laborers to the limbs. If the limbs did not continue to supply nourishment to be digested by the stomach, they would themselves cease to move.

Second, the exploiting classes were everywhere understood as qualitatively superior beings set apart from the exploited by a distinction that invoked the alienated supernatural, whether by direct descent from the deities (preconquest Mexico, the aristocracies of the pre-Christian Germans, Homeric Greece); by association with clergy entrusted with the study, ritual invocation of, or direct experience of the supernatural, or merely suited by character, intelligence, and skill to serve the Divine Ruler (pharaonic Egypt, Hellenistic monarchies, the Roman Empire of the third century); the Successor of the Prophet (Arab Empire); the Lord's Annointed (late Roman/Byzantine Empire, Carolingian Empire); the Son of Heaven, who holds the Mandate of Heaven by right of a successful uprising led by himself, or an ancestor (China). In other words, everywhere prebourgeois societies fall under the sway of territorial states or feudal polities there was to be found nobility.

Third, again following Gramsci, there was a pervasive tendency in pre-bourgeois society toward the autonomy of the reified sphere of "the law" or "positive law." The legendary—even if historical—Great Lawgiver was a recurrent figure: Hammurabi, Moses, Solon, Manu, Huang Ti, Yao, Shun, Yu, Wen, Wu, the Duke of Chou, Justinian, Muhammad, Alfred the Great. By projecting "the law" as a reified entity outside of and "above" the exploitative class relation, the exploiting class sacrificed some gains accruing from indiscriminate predation, but secured long-term strategic advantages: (1) It collectively protected itself against mutual predation and expropriation by its own members who, as individuals, might lose sight of the class interest. (2) It had custody of "the law" in written form, which is no small advantage where most are illiterate and the script consists of pictograms, ideograms, hieroglyphs, cuneiform, complex syllabary, or Inca quipu. When the script was alphabetical it might turn out that legal proceedings were kept in a dead language, such as church Latin for the canon law and "legal French" for the English common law. (3) It collectively acquired, via the mediation of the polity, the ability to legislate. Custom is notoriously more conservative of the interests of the exploited than is legislation, even where the exploited are nominally represented within the polity. (4) Most important, as Gramsci pointed out, awareness of the existence of legal protection—as opposed to knowledge of the content and specific applicability of this protection—enforced by a judicial machinery that is apparently impersonal and that does not present itself in class terms (at least in theory), serves within the hegemonic ideology to convince the exploited that society is just, fair, and reducible to orderly and logical principles; that there is a limit to the exactions of the exploiters the transgression of which is in principle remediable; and that which they possess is somehow safeguarded and cannot be taken from them "lawfully."

Fourth, religious beliefs propagated within the sphere of the hegemonic ideology tended to include at some point the claims of the exploited if the latter were exceptionally harshly treated. Unstinted divine benevolence did not shine upon the exploiting class once it had gone too far, though this might be very far indeed. There was consolation for the poor not only in the transmigration of souls or in life everlasting, but also in tales of mighty sinners, evildoers, and wicked oppressors brought low by the wrath of the gods. Those faiths that did not accomplish this (such as the cults of the Greco-Roman gods, the Teutonic gods, and the Shinto gods) tended to make way for those that did. Religious beliefs redefined excessively in favor of the exploiters would periodically be corrected by subcults, schisms, and heresies—often first popularized within the exploiting class itself—which worked in the opposite direction.

Fifth, the hegemonic ideologies of prebourgeois society, in considerable relative contrast to those of bourgeois society, tended to be upheld with great rigor at points manifestly quite remote from questions touching on the legitimacy of exploitative class relations or of the polity. This rigor can perhaps be interpreted as reflecting a need, deriving from the level of the material reproduction of society, for maintaining the integrity of culture hardly less strong than that found in preclass "primitive" societies: (1) Given the absence of standardized production, every product necessarily represented an immediate objectification of culture on the part of the cultivators and fabricators, much as in primitive society. (2) Again, as in primitive society, the domains of the interpretation of "social reality" and the categorization of "cosmological reality" were very closely mapped onto each other. (3) The exploiting class was most imprecisely depicted and legitimated within the hegemonic ideology as a hereditary or otherwise privileged status group (e.g., the medieval order of celibate clergy) understood as intrinsically superior, with this superiority reflected in its mode of consumption of the appropriated or redistributed surplus.

Therein lay precisely what was problematical in the hegemonic ideology of prebourgeois society: In the event of social conflict the exploiting class qua privileged status group was invariably held up to its own idealized standard. Its claims to intrinsic superiority and to privilege as a hereditary or otherwise closed order were vitiated by evidence of its members' contemptible personal character and their incapacity for their high station; and, moreover, this evidence tended to accumulate the more the dissidents were motivated to look for it. The latter might then either insist that the exploiting class enforce upon itself a nobler or holier manner of consumption or conclude that the class as a whole was superfluous, i.e., "When Adam delved and Eve span/Who then was a gentleman" (Cohen, 1961), so that the issue had to be settled by violence.

Within the sphere of the hegemonic ideology, however, potential dissidence could normally be fended off by ideological outworks, permeating the everyday lives of the mass of the exploited, which focused the attention of the latter upon their own moral and characterological deficiencies and upon their own invidious distinctions whereby they were split into a multitude of fragments along lines of legal categories, ritual purity and other forms of petty hereditary privilege, petty relations of exploitation, longstanding kin-group quarrels, and minute gradations of wealth and status. The exploiting class, contrarily, was observed in distorted perspective, normally in the context of spectacles, rituals, and the performance of ceremonial courtesies; quite often a foreign or dead language was spoken or intoned or else a class-specific dialect or accent was used. The exploited would have no a priori knowledge of what was frivolous or corrupt. Consequently, only the most serenely confident—or suicidal—of prebourgeois exploiting classes would have countenanced untrammeled speculation within its own ranks—let alone its inferiors—as to the necessity of its rituals, manners, theology, esthetic style, or monumental consumption (that is, edifices such as tombs, palaces, fortified residences, statuary, cathedrals, frontier fortifications, which were built by the labor and or at the expense of the exploited class to the greater glory and eternal memory of the exploiting class. The beginning and end of prebourgeois hegemonic ideologies is the reproduction of the mode of consuming the surplus.

Hegemony in Bourgeois Society

Of all historic exploiting classes the bourgeoisie alone is continuously present in the labor process. This class, initially finding the labor process in its "naturelike" condition and subjecting it to the capital-labor relation, proceeded to incorporate into itself the sole power—appearing as the sole *capacity*—to make innovations in productive technique and to set the labor process in motion. (Consider the likelihood, given the sway of bourgeois relations of production, that the members of a United Auto Workers local would believe that they are capable of operating the factory without the presence of management, let alone introduce automated productive technique, which would eliminate their own jobs.) Consequently, the bourgeoisie, in contrast to all its predecessors, has legitimated itself and has induced the reproduction of this legitimation within the hegemonic ideology of bourgeois society as *productive* on two principal counts: (1) It calls attention to the tremendous productive forces it has unleashed, both in terms of ever-more advanced technique (progress) and in terms of the ever-mounting magnitude of products that it orders produced for sale (delivering the goods). (2) It emphasizes the terrible burdens (responsibility) of administering the labor process (management) and ensuring the realization of surplus value (hustling, meeting the payroll, the bottom line). The illusion is that because the bourgeoisie (or at least part of it) is a hardworking, that is, a *busyness* class, it is also a *productive* class. But historically, the reproduction of this illusion has taken different guises. Through Marx's day and perhaps into the early twentieth century, the specific reward of capital, personified as the owner, was represented as taking the specific form of profit, whereas that of the laborers was understood as taking the specific form of the wage, that is, a given quantity of money per time units worked. The whole of the profit, less the relatively minuscule expenses of doing business, was quite visibly at the disposal of the owner for accumulation less luxury consumption.

In any case, it is clear that the classical entrepreneurs were visibly privileged in that they were conspicuously exempted from the discipline of the labor process. Aside from the characteristic monumental architecture of this epoch, the ornate railroad station, the bourgeois of the Gilded Age comported themselves much as had their predecessors: They spent vast sums on town houses, country seats, vacation villas, private railroad coaches, lavish formal entertainment, art collections, bejeweled women of exquisitely delicate complexion and refined manners whose obligatory frailty required them to be prone to fainting spells, sumptuous yachts expensive beyond price ("If you have to ask what one costs," said J. P. Morgan, "then you can't afford one"), and, of course, armies and hordes of servants.

The second epoch has witnessed the emergence of a bourgeoisie of dual character, that is, as "investors," or owners of capital, and as employee managers, that is, as administrators of capital. Some entrepreneurs are exclusively the first, that is, rentiers, speculators, and idle rich; some are exclusively the second, that is, executives headed for the top whose salaries are not yet high enough to permit them to invest; but most combine both functions. The increasing specializaton of the managerial function corresponds to the share of the profit, i.e., redistributed surplus, received for the exercise of this function disguised as a *pseudowage*. For this pseudowage the top executive must not only work long hours but must also *appear* to do so. This is epitomized in the monumental architecture characteristic of the epoch of monopoly capitalism, the corporate headquarters and other office buildings. Here the bourgeoisie conspicuously consumes the services not privately of domestics but rather collectively of subaltern bureaucrats and clerical workers whose total consumption on and off the job derives from redistributed surplus. These expenditures are "necessary" to the cost of doing business in much the same way as domestics were "necessary" to the "proper" style of life of the Victorian bourgeoisie. The contemporary bourgeoisie is, therefore, at least in *appearance*, subject to the discipline of the work place; the older image of the idle-rich squanderer has been ideologically downgraded. So thorough is this change that the Prince of Wales and future Charles III of England has been taken to task in the British news media for lacking "a career" or even "a steady job."

Unlike the historic predecessors of the bourgeoisie, who asserted claims to privilege as hereditary or otherwise closed status groups, the bourgeoisie denies that it is one even though it is. More correctly, the denial of the existence of hereditary privileged (or disprivileged) status groups within bourgeois society, except possibly as anonymous vestiges, is systematically reproduced within the hegemonic ideology of bourgeois society. The privilege of saving an increasing portion of income—once that income exceeds a certain determinate point—and thereby accumulating sizable wealth plus the additional right to transmit said wealth to posterity intact are guaranteed by law (if only by way of subterfuges and loopholes) in every capitalist core state. Also, whereas in former times there was no precise correspondence of privileged status and the exploitative relation, it is most difficult to "have money" in bourgeois society without owning, however indirectly, some entitlement to surplus value. In the ideological sphere, however, the question of hereditary privilege is never broached directly, barring a systemic crisis. Instead, the principal consumption formation (the state) is given considerable autonomy in objectifying the abstract principle of "equality" in protective legislation replete with administrative apparatuses to enforce it. "Equality" is thus successively redefined: first, negatively, as "equality of rights," by the suppression of the special privileges of the former aristocracy and established church; second, "equal justice under law," or the protection of rights in property equally for great owners, small owners, and owners of none at all; third, "democracy," or the extension of nominal rights of representation in the polity to all adults, at least in principle; fourth, "equal protection of the laws," the abrogation of the formal persecution of certain categories of citizens by means of legislation; fifth, "equality of opportunity," or the abrogation of the right of private citizens to persecute others de jure; finally, "affirmative action," the symbolic effort to provide certain limited advantages to select numbers of those groups or categories whose persecution in the past has been found irremediable in the present.

The concept of equality is never systematically reproduced within the hegemonic ideology so as to signify or imply "equality of result." It is objectified and operationalized so as to systematically reproduce all the material inequalities that are officially deplored. Nevertheless, it does facilitate the mobility of highly talented individuals into the bourgeoisie, which is thereby strengthened, from the dependent consumption formations ("the middle classes," "the consumers") and into the latter from the working class. In the latter case, the position of the dependent consumption formations is strengthened as an *employed* status group interposed between the employed bourgeoisie and the working class, thankful that it is employed. This is no small factor in the protection of the bourgeoisie from the working class, though the bourgeoisie may not necessarily be protected from the dependent consumption formations themselves. Bourgeois society has displayed a historic tendency to emancipate itself from behavioral norms and institutional patterns not immediately derived from the capitalist mode of production itself, as are industriousness (the work ethic, which Marx considered an artifact of the system of commodity production) and, simultaneously, hedonism (the American standard of living, which he interpreted as an artifact of the incessant pressure to expand markets for products). Also tied to the mode of production is the reproduction of the segregation by class of the rearing of the young as well as the segregation of mental life in general. (For instance, the top 1-2 percent of U.S. households by income, that is, the bourgeoisie proper, watch television the least; cf. Mander, 1978.) In institutional patterns not integral to the mode of production but dependent on it, capitalism has, for example, demonstrated the capacity to revolutionize the form of the family—the conditions of biological reproduction—not once but twice: It first generated the substitution of the nuclear for the extended family, accompanied by a sharp increase in birth and fertility rates; it is presently engaged in the substitution of the modular[4] for the nuclear family, accompanied by an even sharper drop in these same rates.

The entire domain of mental life in bourgeois society is likewise dependent, and increasingly so, on the mode of production proper. This is associated with the objectification of the reproduction of mental life in mass-produced products, upon which depend the vast industries of music recording, consumer electronics, publishing, broadcasting, photography, cinema, art (galleries, supplies, appraisals, auctions, criticism), "live" entertainment, and so forth. The reproduction, including the initial or "original" production, or vulgarly the "creation" of mental life, is consequently increasingly subsumed by "reproduction" in the narrow sense of the word (recordings, copies, etc., along with playback equipment), which is subject to the market forces and "laws of motion" governing the circulation of commodities and the accumulation of capital. The difference between these and "pure" commodities is that the use value of the product for the consumer inheres not in the product itself but in the musical performance or literary composition or set of ideas objectified in it.

The rise of the sheer bulk of the industrialized means of the reproduction of mental life has been concurrent with a secular decline of commitment by bourgeois society to the reproduction within the hegemonic ideology of specific ideas, doctrines, theologies, moralities, esthetic traditions, artistic forms, and other aspects of cultural expression. In this bourgeois society differs markedly from its predecessors, wherein states would routinely wage war using such matters as ostensible grounds, and entire classes might occasionally go down to irreversible defeat. (Thus, for example, the Byzantine Empire was extinguished by refusing to accept as the price of military assistance the doctrines of papal supremacy and the double procession of the Holy Spirit.) To sustain the extended reproduction of the products objectifying mental life, as well as that of products in general through the development of new human needs in strict association with products corresponding to them, it is necessary to periodically smash and recycle all sorts of cultural forms and ideologies, including the "end of ideology" ideology. Stagnant pools resisting cultural change are mopped up. Whole peoples are stripped of ancient traditions, which may then be repackaged and resold; thus the Jews are first assimilated so that their descendants may consume neoorthodoxy as an "alternative life-style." Marxism emerges as a tool for career mobility and even dominates the intellectual life of major countries such as France, Italy, and Japan without the slightest evidence of any adverse effect on the reproduction of the bourgeoisie as a class. (Marx [1973:410ff] foresaw much of this. It may be doubted that he could have predicted that his picture would adorn a parlor game called Class Struggle.) The specific representation of the above in the bourgeois hegemonic ideology is the notion of "freedom" (or human rights), wherefrom the United States named its world order "the free world." Like "equality," "freedom" has proved susceptible to broadening as new "freedoms" are defined. Thus, to the traditional "four freedoms" (of speech and religion, from want and fear) have in recent times been added, e.g., "academic freedom" (the right to advance one's career by advocating the subversion of the state by which one is employed), "freedom of expression" (the right to profit by the publication, exhibition, or display of quondam "pornography"), "freedom of sexual orientation" (the right to participate in homosexuality without loss of social privilege), and possibly even "freedom of life-style experimentation" (the right to be publicly intoxicated on substances other than alcohol). "Intellectual freedom" is of course welcomed under the conditions of the "free marketplace of ideas." The only ideological use of the word free that is categorically suppressed is in the sense of "without pecuniary cost," i.e., freedom from bourgeois society itself. (Hence the absurdity of the militaristic advertisement calling for greater military expenditure that was painted on bus-stop benches in Los Angeles, a center of U.S. armaments production: *"Freedom is not free!"*)

Unlike its predecessors, bourgeois society does not reproduce a single, relatively compact community of ideological specialists committed to the intellectual and stylistic integrity of "civilization." C. P. Snow's notion of the *Two Cultures* vastly understates the situation, for there are several: (1) the academic "hard" scientists; (2) the extra-academic "hard" scientists and engineers; (3) the academic humanist-generalists; (4) the extra-academic humanist-generalists, including the "literary world" and cinema critics; (5) the academic humanist-specialists, subdivided by discipline; (6) the political intellectuals, including social scientists who write and lawyers; (7) the psychologist intellectuals; (8) the Marxist intellectuals, subdivided by profession and orientation; (9) the feminist intellectuals; (10) the "art world"; (11) the assorted devotees of "serious music," subdivided by the period of its composition; (12) the theologian-moralists; and so forth. In most of the foregoing, careerism dictates a quest for controversy or at least the appearance of originality. Even the professional critics of the various arts are essentially paid to disagree with each other, thereby collectively inducing their readership to resonate to the issues over which they debate. Moreover, the former "folk culture," which had subsisted in a "naturelike" state prior to its liquidation at the hands of the industrialized reproduction of mental life (cf. Ewen, 1976) (or its subtle transformation from within by the invention of a major-label recording contract and other forms of availability to extra-folk marketing), now becomes the domain of critics and connoisseurs within the cultural elite. Even the most commodified and industrialized cultural products, such as comic books and bubble-gum cards, in part precisely because they had previously been "low culture" now become the objects of sophisticated analysis, with elaborate esthetic systems devised to apply to them by professional critics. But this proliferation of cultural elites coincides with a new departure in bourgeois cultural reproduction.

Historically, the reproduction of the bourgeoisie as a class had always been accompanied by the systematic reproduction of a formation that might be called the cultural counterbouregoisie, and that is perhaps best remembered as "bohemianism." Comprising a mixture of political and esthetic dissidents, highly stratified by wealth and fame (or notoriety), this formation was united by its location in a metropolitan zone such as the Rive Gauche or Greenwich Village, but even more by its overt contempt for whatever in mental life appeared to be labeled officially bourgeois by virtue of its respectability. If the bourgeoisie fancied classicism, the bohemian became romantic. When that caught on, the counterbourgeoisie affected realism. With the prevalence of that style, the opposition tried impressionism, cubism, anything to *épater le bourgeois*.

During periods of social upheaval the cultural counterbourgeoisie tended to tag along behind the crowds or to run for cover: Their intention was to shock and scandalize in an individualistic fashion, not to engage in overt conflict and certainly not to submerge their individuality dictated by the emergent pattern of class and bureaucratized dissidence. Nevertheless, in times and places of especially stifling cultural conformity or ideological censorship, they appeared from the outside—and even from the inside—to be fully merged with the whole of the political opposition and were persecuted accordingly.

The cultural counterbourgeoisie was thus systematically reproduced through the 1950s—the beat generation in the United States, the angry young men in Britain, etc.—until, during the social upheaval of the 1960s, the bohemians became the new masses, recruiting millions of people. In the 1970s—through devices discussed at length elsewhere—the boundary setting off the counterbourgeoisie was liquidated, whereas all sorts of cultural and ideological diffuseness were introduced into the bourgeoisie itself as well as its subaltern strata: "We have no intellectuals in the Bay Area," said the editor of the *Yoga Journal*, "only creative people."

The upheaval of the 1960s did represent, while it lasted, the conscious interference, on the part of diverse and mutually hostile cultural oppositions, with the systematic reproduction of cultural and ideational patterns understood as characteristically bourgeois, even if in such vague and nonsensical language as "middle-class conformity." Yet in earlier social movement periods parallel developments occurred—e.g., in the 1930s, when a substantial part of the cultural counterbourgeoisie espoused one or another variant of Marxist doctrine—only to be reversed in the ensuing conservative periods. This time the change appears permanent. Whether this represents the culmination or logical conclusion of a secular trend in bourgeois society, or else whether it represents some emergent failure in the reproduction of the bourgeoisie as a class due to underlying structural contradictions of capitalism, or even, possibly, whether it represents *both*, must await clarification by events yet to come.

Political Reproduction

The Forms of Political Relations

Regardless of whether power exists in its "raw" form, with the means of violence openly displayed, or as so-called legitimate authority (classified by Weber into traditional, charismatic, and legal-rational variants), there are in class society three basic styles of wielding it outside the household:

1. The patriarchal. In this type of relation one party is unmediatedly, that is, personally and directly, dependent on the other for subsistence or possibly future reward or both, and the dominant party is meanwhile reciprocally dependent on the subordinate for labor, military service, or other contribution; the relation may actually involve real, adoptive, or fictive kinship. A distinction should perhaps be made between patriarchy as an institutionalized authority relation and patriarchy as an ideological representation: The latter is a convention of hierarchical systems where the topmost levels are unseen and remote from the bottom, as when the traditional Russian peasant alluded to the faraway tsar as *batyushka*, little father, although the local administrators of the state exercised despotic control over him. Likewise, exploiting classes habituated to the command of forced labor affected a guise of patriarchal relations unless, of course, they encountered insubordination, at which time the despotic essence of the relation became manifest (at least to the laborer).

Patriarchal relations are commonly found in association with petty exploitative relations in societies where the main axis of exploitation lies elsewhere; that is, for example, between rich peasant and poor peasant, or between master craftsman and journeyman, or between ward heeler (or the "Godfather") and recent immigrant. They are also typical of exploiting classes organized into great households competing for power: The Roman aristocrat thus employed his dependents and hangers-on upon whom he relied for political support. The Germanic chieftain was accompanied by his following of armed warriors who anticipated reward in the form of landed property.

2. The despotic. This type of relation implies the ability of the dominant party to command the subordinate party under the threat of summary forcible sanctions in case of refusal. It is commonly accompanied by arbitrary acts of force and violence—ranging from insults to destruction of possessions, mutilations, lynchings, and massacres—against members of the subordinate category or specially targeted fraction thereof, which have the effect of reminding the subordinates of the irremediable character of their subjection.

Despotic relations must enter at some point into any system of class exploitation, either as part of the process of appropriating the surplus or as the guarantee of the conditions of exploitation or both. In state-type polities despotic relations are, moreover, the essence of the social organization of the effective means of violence.

3. The collegial. In relations of this type a body of individuals, defined for this purpose as peers, collectively render a decision by some procedure whether personally, as in a meeting, or impersonally, as in an election or in the classical market mechanism, which is to be accepted as binding upon all. Collegial relations should not be confused with "democracy," especially in prebourgeois society, when they were invariably expressions of privilege: The members of the electoral college of the Holy Roman Empire, for example, were despotic rulers in their own principalities. The imposition of collegial relations upon an exploited class could moreover represent the intensification of subjugation for the purposes of more ruthless exploitation; hence, Russian landowners imposed the redistribution of lands upon village communes to preclude the emergence of a rich-peasant leadership in their villages (cf. Blum, 1961).

Of all forms of class society only bourgeois society possesses a genuine "mode of production." Within that mode of production, as Marx (1973:239-75) understood, the capitalist labor process itself involves despotic relations, which appear to be entered into voluntarily by the laborers in accordance with collegial processes that determine the price of labor impersonally by the supposedly competitive actions of capitalists and laborers alike. The realization of surplus value likewise occurs via the market mechanism involving the appearance of impersonal collegial relations among manufacturers and consumers whereby the prices of commodities are determined.

These authority relations are paralleled in the idealized image of the polity, whereby the social collectivity, through its representatives elected by collegial procedures, that is, by "equal" citizens, governs a centralized administrative apparatus whose means of enforcement are ultimately despotic in character.

The actualities of authority relations underlying the appearances of both the economy and polity, however, are, in general, the prevalence of a combination of collegial and patriarchal relations within the bourgeoisie and its subaltern strata, and the exercise of despotic relations by the bourgeoisie over the working class as a whole, which single out the most submerged and marginal strata of the working class for exemplary treatment.

The perpetuation of the political reproduction of society, which requires the continued reproduction of manual toil, must be taken into consideration when, during the past decade, the bourgeoisie responded to the rise of energy costs not by a still faster introduction of capital-intensive technique, which might have led to the technically feasible possibility of permitting the whole of society to engage in office work; but rather, to a switch to *labor*-intensive technique (see Rothschild, 1981, for data). From the standpoint of the level of the political reproduction of society it is no more possible for the bourgeoisie to imagine life without a working class than it was for a debt-ridden antebellum Virginia planter to imagine life without slaves.

Bureaucracy is the contemporary mode of social discipline within bourgeois society. The idealization of bureaucracy represents it as applying uniformly to all ranks, strata, and classes, uniting them all in either a Parsonian or a Marcusean totality; but this misrepresents the difference within the bureaucratic edifice in those authority relations that prevail for the bourgeoisie on the dependent consumption formations (i.e., the "middle class," whose labor consumes rather than produces material objects) on one side and those that apply to the working class on the other. It is after all the production workers, of all the bureaucratic strata, who alone are excluded from the corporate headquarters office building. One might hazard the guess that one of the most important, if not the paramount, aspect of the social privilege enjoyed by the surplus-absorbing strata, that is, the dependent consumption formations, consists of their exemption from the rigors of the authority relations imposed on the working class. What is more, given that it was perhaps the extremely rapid numerical and income growth of these surplus absorbers relative to that of the working class that emboldened the younger ones to rebel in the 1960s, one might ponder the possibility that the technically—and even, possibly, economically—irrational perpetuation of manual toil at its present levels is in part dictated by the necessity for the reproduction of the awareness within this stratum of its social privileges, thereby precluding it from similar adventures in the future.

The State as Alienated Authority

Alienation on the level of material reproduction is above all *exploitation*, that is, the alienation of the human capacity to labor in the working up of material. Alienation on the level of cultural reproduction is above all *false consciousness*, the alienation of the human capacity to interpret society subsuming the individual in society. Alienation on the level of political reproduction is above all *domination*, the alienation of the human capacity for government.

(Alienation on the level of biological reproduction is subsumed in the whole of patriarchal relations such that the species is understood as Man.) Government is the capacity of society to take care of itself. The caring function implies a limited despotic relation for its exercise: parent-child, shaman-patient, professional-client, defenders-defended, and so on. Where government becomes alienated, it is by consequence of the concentration of the means of violence in the polity. In preclass society such concentration may be wholly subsumed in the level of biological reproduction. In class society the polity is found either as the state, an organization that monopolizes the effective means of violence in a given territory, or as feudalism, in which the means of violence are accumulated by all levels of subpolities locally and wherein the hierarchical levels of subpolities are mutually dependent such that effective coercive power is not deductible in a logical and determinate fashion from rank.

The state, which in class society may be commonly called "the government," tends to maximize the accumulation of the means of violence at its disposal and therewith the generalization of despotic relations both within itself and in society as a whole; thus it is the ultimate guarantee of all relations of superordination and subordination. At the same time it tends to minimize the caring functions that it proffers. The alienation of government eventuates in a double-edged fetishism: First, the state and reified notions of power and dominion are worshipped so as to imply the diminution of the remainder of society on which the state is materially parasitic. Second, there is propagated a fear of chaos, invasion and plunder at the hands of criminals or subversives in the absence of the coercive power of the state and the despotic relations upon which this is founded and which it presupposes—as in the labor process—which are summed up in the overtones of the word *anarchy*.

In prebourgeois society the characteristic or ideal vocation of members of the exploiting class is that of the politico-military specialists. The maximization of wealth is subordinated to the means of the acquisition of the means of violence or access to the control of the means of violence. This is true despite the fact that exploitation is a presupposition of domination. Prebourgeois society lacked a "mode of production," that is, a relatively self-contained set of relations whereby it was ensured that products got produced. There was instead a situation of, materially speaking, large scale consumers producing nothing, for whom production was problematic and had to be ensured by some threat of force on the spot. This in turn fostered an effort to cast the exploitative relation with an aura of patriarchalism however despotic its actual conditions. It likewise fostered an effort to represent the proper sphere of life of the exploiting class to be rulership or the tendering of spiritual guidance or administrative services to the same. For prebourgeois exploiting classes solvency was never the critical virtue; lavish and magnificent consumption and redistribution were instruments for maximizing politico-military power. The very transition to capitalism was itself marked by a historically unprecedented preference for pecuniary income over territorial power or state office.

The bourgeoisie as a class is reproduced as entrepreneurs (combining the owning with the managerial functions) and politico-military specialists. This bifurcation is preserved such that in appearance there is continuous tension between these two sectors of the bourgeoisie. One manifestation of this tendency is the perpetual reluctance of the entrepreneurial sector to sanction the expenditure of funds upon the upkeep of the politico-military specialists. In classical early-nineteenth-century bourgeois ideology there was an animus against a large and expensive state apparatus (however much it may actually have been growing in size and cost at the time). The state was to be the mere guarantor of property, that is, of the exploitative relation, the "night watchman" as the famous metaphor has it. Characteristically, the state was stripped of such caring functions as had survived from the Old Regime; assistance to the poor or unemployed was to be withheld except by way of persecution (cf. Polanyi, 1961). Caring functions were readopted by the politico-military specialists in the course of their exercise of the caring function on behalf of the bourgeoisie as a class: So-called "social reforms," such as measures for the protection of labor or the sanctioning of trade unionization, were always forced upon reluctant entrepreneurs (to refrains of "creeping socialism," "incentive sapping," or "bleeding-heart programs") by political specialists. This was carried out in the performance of their functions in, to use O'Connor's (1973) terms, *legitimation*, or the enhancement of the ideological respectability or plausibility of bourgeois society in terms of "freedom," "democracy," "equality," "opportunity," or individual judgment according to just and fair desserts; or *accumulation*, that is, the intervention of the state in the economy so as to promote the accumulation of capital. Thus an intervention to promote an increase in wages may be an exercise of the legitimation function in that it fosters content of the workers for the regime, and of the accumulation function, whereby the market for articles of household consumption is expanded to the further general welfare of business, whereas the workers on their own may have lacked the strength to prevent the share of profits increasing faster than wages and thus to a slump. Latterly, the state has appeared as the consumer of last resort, performing the accumulation function by collectivizing consumption; and performing the legitimation function, however perversely, by precluding the subversion of capitalism by excessive household consumer affluence;[5] this we call the *scarcity-simulation* function.

The politico-military specialists exercise a caring function for the bourgeoisie as a whole not only by saving the entrepreneurial sector from political, economic, and social disasters that would otherwise be logical consequences of its inclinations; but also in military affairs, external relations, and all activities associated with these. In so doing they discipline the entrepreneurs to think of the class as a whole in terms of this or that country, which, if only for reasons of geography, has this or that national interest not reducible entirely to those dictated by the accumulation of capital. The politico-military specialists may use this understanding of national interests to influence the level of expenditure on the means of violence, which progressively influences the accumulation of capital as a whole. The sophistication of the means of violence in terms of the training of soldiers and the cost and complexity of weaponry rises in tandem with the level of scientific technique. Due to the position of the state as a monopsonist (monopoly consumer), it is not subject to the same degree to the cost-cutting imperative imposed on industries producing goods for household consumption or means of production. The military establishment itself fosters the temptation—understood as the *duty*—of the politico-military specialists to act on their interpretation of these national interests to involve the entrepreneur in military adventures that they would rather have avoided as unpopular or unprofitable (or restrained them from popular or profitable wars that were "not in the national interest"). At times the politico-military specialists may see fit to impose a dictatorship or lesser restraints on the bourgeoisie as a whole in order to carry out a war policy or to preclude the abandonment of one already embarked upon. In so doing it may also promote the plausibility of the motive of pecuniary gain as a human ideal by requiring at least the appearance of the suspension of that ideal for a "higher" or "patriotic" interest; promote unwittingly the function of war in the devalorization of fixed capital through destruction, conversion, reconversion, or obsolescence of military equipment and the means of production used in producing it (or accomplishing the same thing without war as in Japan by the devalorization of fixed capital by administrative decision); and promote the hegemony of the bourgeoisie of one country over that of others.

The entrepreneurial sector of the bourgeoisie, in short, cannot take care of itself. It is required from time to time and sometimes decisively to hand over its destiny to the politco-military sector, which is under some ideological inhibition in understanding or at least in publicly defending its mission in crassly economic terms. It may act in contradiction to the accumulation of capital (e.g., in 1975–76, when Gulf Oil was trying to do business with a regime that the CIA was trying to overthrow in Angola). Alternatively, the politico-military sector may promote the accumulation of capital pervasively, over the long term, and in a fashion not fully understood by either sector, as in the fostering of military Keynesianism or the women's movement.[6]

The geographical units wherein capital was accumulated were historically smaller or larger than the territorial units governed by states; the latter have at times developed national markets out of local ones or at other times competed for hegemony in a single multinational market. Yet it remains that the control of the effective means of violence has been distributed in territorial-state "national" units in the bourgeois core, whereas the countries of the periphery and semiperiphery have come to rely wholly or in part (and in some cases not at all) for their internal as well as external security on the states of the core. It is this pattern of the distribution of the means of violence that ultimately guarantees bourgeois social relations in all their ramifications on all four levels of social reproduction and that must inevitably become the focus of social conflict. That is, efforts at the collective forcible assertion of antistructure interfere with the political reproduction of society. Where relations of domination—authority relations—are interfered with momentarily in the street, in the university, in the household, or in the factory, the resumption of their routine reproduction must be enforced by the state, failing which the interference with political reproduction tends to become generalized. Ultimately, the question may be posed of the interference with the reproduction of the polity as a whole and, most concretely, the reproduction of the means of violence themselves.

Where interference occurs with the reproduction of the means of violence themselves, as when troops refuse to fire on a crowd and instead join it, the generalization of interference with the political reproduction of society as a whole occurs much more rapidly and thoroughly than it does when the political reproduction of society is interfered with in "everyday life," that is to say, outside the polity and specifically outside the military. This represents the difference between what is merely a social-movement period and a period fraught with what is called "social revolution."

The Provenance of Social Movements: State and Society; Core and Periphery

Social movements always focus on geographical units defined by states (leaving feudal polities aside), as these ultimately guarantee the whole of social relations pertaining to the material cultural, and political levels of social reproduction and thereby, indirectly or even directly, exert influence on the biological level of social reproduction as well (in terms of the birth rate, life expectancy, and general somato-psychic well-being of the population). States, as organizations wielding monopolies of the effective means of violence in their respective geographical units, are inevitably the foci of attention in social movements in that the latters' development entails the forcible assertion of antistructure. This may involve the failure of the regime to employ the means of violence contrary to prevailing assumptions as to the nature and workings of "social reality"; or, conversely, a precipitate resort to their employ contrary to the same sort of assumptions. A temporary local defeat of, or successful resistance to, the employ of the means of violence may generalize resistance. In rare cases, the apparatus by which the political regime wields the means of violence is destroyed and therewith the state itself.

Yet forms of society do not coincide with geographical frontiers: A given polity such as Nigeria may embrace several, ranging from the preclass to the peripheral-capitalist; the Roman Empire may have been still more diverse. Alternatively, medieval society—or "Christendom," as it was locally known—could display considerable homogeneity of technique throughout its agricultural and industrial core area, though with considerable local variation in the character of the exploitative relation and the degree to which the polity was more of the state type or of the feudal type. Similarly, bourgeois society, core or peripheral, embraces two-thirds of the human species and still decisively determines the character of the development of the socialist countries.

It should therefore not surprise us that social movements appear to come in waves which transcend political frontiers however they may be focused on particular states. In some periods this was attributable to structural conditions common to regions much larger than political frontiers: For example, in the upheavals of the early fourteenth century, especially in the period 1333–43, there was as a common background of rural overpopulation and soil exhaustion; stagnating markets for urban products partly attributable to limited rural purchasing power and partly to the onset of the Hundred Years' War; and state building accompanied by mounting elite consumption—including that of the church, despite its waning political influence—at the expense of rural and urban producing classes. In the late fourteenth century and through the period of the Hussite Wars, social movements had as their structural background a generalized labor shortage caused initially by the bubonic plagues and subsequently abetted by predatory interstate and civil wars induced by the urge and ability of the greater magnates to resort to plunder to compensate for revenues unobtainable through exploitation of scarce labor power. A cultural crisis centering on the declining ideological hegemony of the church and the demoralization of the great feudal magnates (for the latter, cf. J. Huizinga, *The Waning of the Middle Ages*); and the obsolescence of the feudal cavalry corresponding to the revival of the infantry arm, such that Swiss or Czech peasants could prevail against the German chivalry.

In modern bourgeois society the rule is that upheavals in capitalist core countries rapidly spread to other core countries and to the periphery, though immense social movements in the periphery do not necessarily find echoes in the core countries if these are in a period of social quiescence. A dramatic illustration of this occurred in 1848, when the February Revolution in France was imitated throughout Germany beginning with the key states, Prussia and the Hapsburg monarchy; and then in non-German Hapsburg-dominated areas including Italy and Hungary; with lesser degrees of social conflict becoming manifest in Rumania, Scandinavia, and even the United States (as a recrudescence of antislavery agitation, albeit short-lived, 1848–50).

A contrast between the 1960s and the 1970s should establish the point: The former decade was one of social movements in the core countries practically without exception. The events of 1968, partly inspired by events in the core, included the overthrow of a political regime in Czechoslovakia and the occupation of university buildings by students in Turkey, Poland, and South Korea; student dissidence in Mexico was bloodily suppressed in the Plaza of Three Cultures; the toll exacted by the Mexican military has been variously estimated from 500 to 3,000. By the end of the decade there were "Black Panthers" in Israel protesting discrimination against Jews of non-European descent; and untouchables *(dalits)* in Bombay, India, were organizing the Dalit Panthers.

The decade of the 1970s was quite turbulent in the periphery and semiperiphery (Portugal, Spain, Greece, and Turkey). To take the semiperiphery first: There was a complex political and social upheaval triggered by a military coup in Portugal, which lasted through most of 1974 until late 1975. Basque nationalism has been rife in Spain, with less intense working-class dissidence. In Greece, passive resistance among ordinary soldiers contributed to the fall of the regime of the Colonels (1967–74). Religio-political dissidence and counterdissidence in Turkey culminated in pogroms perpetrated by Sunnis on Shi'ites from December 1978 through January 1979. To consider the periphery: There was a full-scale revolution of the "classical" type—as reproduced within the military—commencing in February 1974. Protracted wars came to victorious conclusions in 1975 in Cambodia, Vietnam, and the counties of the former Portuguese Africa. Guerrilla warfare steadily intensified for several years in Zimbabwe, until the negotiated settlement establishing the Black-dominated Mugabe regime. In 1979, there were revolutions in Iran and Nicaragua. These are merely some of the more dramatic events.

Contrast this with the capitalist core in the same period, where the picture is one of social somnolence tending toward political reaction: Elections in France, Italy, Great Britain, Canada, and even Sweden gave victory to the Right. In the United States, the manifest and growing incapacity of successive heads of state, partly personal and partly political in origin (since presidents structurally lack the capacity to do very much about domestic issues of concern to the electorate, though they wield vast power in the international politico-military sphere), have thus far not led the citizenry to question the iron necessity of staggering or lurching through the day one way or another. But this might change, as part of the periphery is so situated geographically that its upheavals have the capability to cause the American way of life to run out of gas.

Notes

1. This represented a difference in vocational outlook of the most profound importance in terms of the *appearances* of prebourgeois society, which, e.g., was easily appreciated by a monk chronicling the deeds of William the Conqueror at Hastings: "But it would have seemed shameful and slack to William to take on the role of general in that conflict in which he crushed the English if he had not also done his duty as a knight, as had been his custom in earlier wars" (Lyon, 1967:98). Where a prebourgeois exploiting class legitimated its existence in part by its monopoly of the martial arts, it sometimes paradoxically maximized its military power by consigning itself to permanent weakness vis-à-vis external enemies rather than countenance changes in military technique, which might have involved the arming of the exploited class. Hence the suicidal behavior of the French nobility in the Hundred Years' War (until divine intervention appeared in the suitably incongruous guise of Joan of Arc); the disarmament of the Hungarian peasantry by the nobility following the revolt of 1514 and the refusal of the nobility to rearm them at the time of the German Peasant War (1525) and on the eve of the Turkish conquest at Mohacs (1526); and the preference of the Japanese nobility to seal the country off after 1600 rather than permit the introduction of firearms to change the rules of samurai warfare.

2. This in fact was precisely the difference between the late Roman Empire following the demographic catastrophe brought on by epidemics of smallpox and measles in the third century and Merovingian Gaul following the equally horrendous epidemics— principally of bubonic plague—in the sixth century and afterward.

3. A funny thing happened to the word *rich* on the way to capitalism: It is derived from the Old English *rice*, meaning kingdom or rulership; thus a *cyning*, that is, a member of the divinely descended lineage eligible to rule, was said to "feng to rice"— come into the kingdom or take power—when his reign commenced. Similarly, French *riche*, German *reiche*, and Spanish *rico* all derive from cognate words in Teutonic languages akin to German *reich* and Old Norse *riki*, both meaning state or dominion (Sweden/Sverige = Sve + Riki). These in turn appear to descend from an ancient Indo-European root with the most widespread distribution of cognates, e.g., Old Irish *ri*, genitive *rig*, king; Latin *rex, regis*; Sanskritic *raja*; and possibly Russian *ruka*, arm.

The point of this is that it was not until relatively recent centuries that it occurred to an exploiting class to conceptually separate the process of amassing material wealth by exploitation from the process of the consumption of the same in the accumulation of the means of exercising dominion, whether as magistrates and military commanders in state-type politics or on the spot in feudal-type politics. Making this point with regard to medieval society, Edward P. Cheyney (1936) translates *ricos hombres*, the appellation of the feudal-magnate stratum of medieval Aragon, as "the ruling class."

One of hallmarks of capitalism is precisely the preoccupation of the exploiters with the accumulation of capital—as means of production and as tokens of abstract exchange (value)—to the neglect of wielding the means of violence whether in person or mediated through an apparatus by virtue of holding a magistracy of state. Yet a curious paradox emerges when bourgeois society is contrasted with its predecessors: In Roman times the agricultural core of classical society lay in Egypt with secondary cores emerging in Sicily and Africa (Tunisia); its commercial and manufacturing core lay in Egypt, Syria, and Asia Minor; but its politico-military core migrated successively to Italy, Spain, Gaul, and Illyricum (Yugoslavia). The agricultural core of medieval society was in northern France, southern England, and western Germany; its primary industrial core was in the low countries, with secondary cores in Italy and the Rhineland; its commercial and financial core was in Italy; but its politico-military core—depending on the fortunes of state building, war, and hereditary succession—could be found in various times in Germany, England, France, or briefly even in the papacy. In bourgeois society, contrarily, it has been that the rise of a new center of developed production in a state previously peripheral had not been followed within a few years or at the most decades by an effort on the part of the state in question to elbow or shove its way into the politico-military core of the state system.

4. By modular family (easy disassembly, easy reassembly), we mean the form that is supplanting the nuclear family in which minimally one partner has been married at least twice, having had progeny from the former marriage. As divorce *and* marriage rates increase per capita, the modular family emerges as the characteristic type among certain sectors of the surplus absorbing strata. Between 1960 and 1973, marriage rates rose from 8.5 to 10.9 per 1,000 (an increase of 22 percent) and divorce rates doubled from 2.2 per 1,000 to 4.4.

5. By this we mean that as the level of the aggregate surplus swelled in the post-World War II period, it was more or less democratized in the form of increasing household consumption, especially in the surplus-absorbing strata, interfering with the reproduction of the rational accumulator. In the minds of a significant sector of the surplus absorbers—youth—it became evident that material scarcity was at an end. This meant, to them, that society could relax, life no longer needed to be harnessed to the market mechanism, and the species could turn its attention to concerns of a "higher" order, namely subjective development and self-actualization. Bourgeois relations were attacked as a fetter on such development.

6. By sponsoring a denatured corporate feminism, creating opporunities and increasing aspirations of women, capital increases competition in the labor market, effectively cutting the price of white-collar labor.

Chapter 4

The Intensification of Conflict

Morales said to me, "It is strange—isn't it?—the process of the Revolution." El proceso de la Revolucion is a phrase constantly on people's lips, one which usually makes them pause, for it makes it possible for them to stand off and look at what has happened to them in a few years. "In 1958, I told a fellow student in the Movement that I expected our Movement would establish a decent constitutional government and he said to me, Is that all you think this enormous effort will accomplish? It was then I got my first suspicion of the process set in motion. Who would have thought that it would take us to socialism and me to the Party!" (From a 1967 conversation with a Cuban doctor in José Yglesias, *In the Fist of the Revolution*, p. 68)

According to the anthropologist Victor Turner (1969), just as there is an evident human need for social structure whereby the reproduction of society, in particular the level of material reproduction, is promoted, there is also a universal need to periodically express—or indulge in—an antistructure whereby the social structure is periodically suspended such that the statuses of the workaday world are abolished or reversed, and the collectivity experiences a moment of exaltation that he calls "communitas." He illustrates this in his analysis of the rituals of the Ndembu, a people thus far denied the blessings of class exploitation. The level of cultural reproduction, in effect, provides for the suspension of the levels of material, cultural, and political reproduction on ritual occasions, thus having the contrary effect of reinvigorating the social structure between ritual occasions. Turner points out obvious parallels in the class societies of the Mediterranean and India: the Mardi Gras and Holi festivals. He evidently intends his model to apply to social movements in class societies, though his examples are drawn from religious movements that explicitly renounced overt social conflict. There is, nevertheless, no denying the element of celebratory euphoria associated with social upheavals: In July 1967, for example, Governor Hughes of New Jersey, having denounced Newark as "a city in open rebellion," proceeded to deplore the "carnival atmosphere" in the streets. It was difficult to tell whether he was more shocked by the breakdown of order or by the festivity of the rioters. However, "communitas" need not assume the guise of shared grim determination or sacrifice; so it is probably idle speculation to distinguish between "instrumental" and "expressive" social movements. Indeed, there is in all authentic contemporary revolutions, no matter how serious their style, euphoria at the decisive moment, as in Portugal in April 1974 and Iran in January 1979, when the troops of the regime stuck red carnations in their guns.

If social structure is *eo ipso* painful among preclass societies such as the Ndembu, it must be doubly painful in class society, where, after all, the exploited pay the upkeep of the group that does the "civilization," a second group that ensures the continuity of the payment, and a third that explains why all this is desirable and inevitable. Excellent reasons for social dissidence are always present, which will not be set aside by Mardi Gras playacting. After all, there is no evidence that the material well-being of the average human anywhere was improved by class society before 1800 (cf. Braudel, 1973), and there is plentiful evidence that since that date the material improvement in the capitalist core countries—which of course does not correspond with any precision to nonmaterial improvement—systematically entailed the deterioration of material conditions for the vast majority of humans in the periphery (cf. Amin, 1974).

Hypotheses as to macroeconomic conditions that instigate social movements have led to no definitive conclusions, perhaps because these generalize from a few "great revolutions" while ignoring dissidence with less spectacular consequences. The old-fashioned "immiserationist" perspective once looked to economic depressions and declining living standards as especially conducive to revolt. More recent notions look to periods of prosperity as more likely to generate upheaval because of "revolutions of rising expectations," or "relative deprivation." That is, an illusion of perspective on the part of people on the rise, who believe that they should be rising even faster, and consequently feel that they are declining. Other recent explanations include "social strain," or the dislocations and antagonisms among the various social categories due to unaccustomed affluence, and "status inconsistency," or the unease of long-established status groups at the prospect of the newly affluent rising above their station. Sophisticated wrinkles include attributing movements to long periods of improvement followed by sharp declines, as may have been true of the French Revolution; or, contrarily, to long depressions followed by sharp upswings, as may have been true of the revolutions of 1848. One cannot rule out the possibility that any sort of macroeconomic change or even no change at all—in effect, prolonged boredom—may serve as the background to social upheaval. Focus on political and ideological trends, that is, on "legitimacy," has led to no more clear-cut results except insofar as it clarifies the situation leading to the initial demands (the developments Professor Stone [1965] calls the "precipitants" and "triggers").

We may consequently generalize about the development of social movements only once they have emerged. They display the development of the three ongoing, simultaneous, and mutually reinforcing processes mentioned in Chapter 1, "The Guises of Social Movements." We will now examine the phenomenon of the *intensification of social conflict*. This refers to progressive departures from the routine of "politics," under the customary rules, as well as to departures from formally sanctioned types of conflict, such as strikes for higher wages or lawsuits. It is necessary to stress that the period in which these innovative departures occur and develop, followed by the usually much briefer period during which they subside, together define the temporal extent of the movement, and that this is the case irrespective of the institutionalized consequences, if any, of the movement. That is, the movement must be understood as temporally limited to the conflict period whether it eventuates in the total transformation of social relations, palliative reforms supplemented by modest reshuffling of the governing circles, no change at all, or a counterrevolutionary regime that is more oppressive than the initial situation.

We understand social movements, on the basis of all the historical evidence known to us, as limited temporally to periods of a few months or years, and that the duration of such periods may be delimited in terms of ongoing and intensifying *overt social conflict*. Without this pivotal criterion, all distinctions among social movements, general social change, and cultural, intellectual, or artistic movements would be—as we find they generally are in the sociological literature—hopelessly muddled.

Social-movement periods have *always* alternated throughout history with periods of social quiescence, which are usually longer in duration. In the analysis of preindustrial social movements there is substantial agreement among historians and other social scientists as to the length of social-movement periods. With the development of bureaucratized dissidence (i.e., social movements characterized by formal-organizational cohesion) in the nineteenth century, the analytic problems became more formidable for social scientists principally because of the persistence of bureaucratic entities such as political parties and trade unions, which continued to call themselves "the movement" despite the absence of indices of true social movement activity such as rapid increases in membership and escalating turmoil in the form of strikes, riots, demonstrations, insurrections, and so forth. The movements of the 1960s were, moreover, fertile ground for still other analytical errors because of their characteristic *subcultural cohesion*. Some social scientists denied them the status of social movements altogether because of the relative absence of the familiar type of bureaucratized dissidence recalled from the past, e.g., the 1930s. Others on this same ground subjected these movements to simplistic analyses. Still others, identifying with these same movements, were led astray by the fact that the subcultures of the dissident groups persisted after the overt social conflict itself had become sublimated either into general change or into routinized "radical" intellectual activity or both.

These departures from social quiescence include innovations in conflict behavior, in the social categories appearing autonomously in the arena of conflict, and in the location of the terrain of conflict. We see the development of conflict within social movements as following three laws: (1) the Law of Mounting Stakes, (2) the Law of Emergent Contradiction, and (3) the Law of Shifting Terrain. The remainder of this chapter will analyze these laws in detail.

Innovation in Conflict Behavior, or the Law of Mounting Stakes

This level of development is most clearly visible in situations wherein a certain modicum of low-level routinized dissidence is tolerated or sanctioned by law. When the possibilities of open and secret negotiation, as well as whatever is meant in practice by the freedoms of speech, press, petition, and assembly have all been exhausted, then some act of forcible defiance elicits a mass response by way of support and imitation. Forcible defiance means, at minimum, placing one's body in some spot where by law or custom it does not belong, whether spontaneous (as in Rosa Parks's action of sitting on a whites-only seat in a crowded Montgomery, Alabama, bus in 1955 because she was "tired") or contrived (as in the first "sit-in," February 1, 1960, in Greensboro, North Carolina, when four Black college students, impeccably dressed in conservative suits and ties and reading Bibles, vainly awaited service at a whites-only lunch counter until beaten up and arrested). Both sides may then proceed to the use of mounting levels of force in response to each other's raising of the stakes, culminating in "political" strikes, riots, arson, looting, and ultimately insurrection on the one side and employment of the effective means of violence, such as the standing army, on the other. One variant proceeds along lines of rising levels of "nonviolent" force employed by the dissidents, e.g., from hunger strikes to self-immolation to efforts at disrupting the regime by such means as masses of people lying across the railroad tracks, in accordance with Mohandas K. Gandhi's doctrine of *satyagraha*. This, however, presupposes not only traditional religious self-discipline among the dissidents, but also either self-restraint on the part of the regime deriving from a tradition of "fair play" that limits the ferocity of its response or an equivalent restraint in the guise of adverse media coverage of repressive measures taken openly. The absence of such restraints on either side can lead to the immediate transition to violent forms of force.

The historian Flavius Josephus (1970) in recounting the historical background of the revolt of A.D. 66–73 against Roman rule, recounted a quite sophisticated use of nonviolent resistance against the Roman governor Pontius Pilate in A.D. 32: When the latter sought to comply with an order to install Roman eagles in Jerusalem (a sacrilege to the Jews), a crowd said to number 30,000 converged on the governor's residence at Caesarea and in unison presented their necks as if for decapitation, maintaining that death was preferable to tolerating the presence of the heathen eagles; Pilate had them removed. However, Pilate next confiscated the sacred Temple treasure to finance an aqueduct to improve the Jerusalem water supply. A peaceful protest took place outside the Roman garrison in Jerusalem, but Pilate secreted in the crowd a number of soldiers in disguise armed with leaden truncheons; on Pilate's signal they proceeded to break heads. One Jew, who appears in the Gospel of Mark under the name of Barabbas (literally, "son of his father," or "Joe Blow"), under sentence of death for "sedition," managed to kill a Roman soldier. Consequently, when the next preacher of nonviolence came to town and got into trouble with the regime, the Jews of all classes preferred Barabbas.

In much the same way, when neither the nonviolent disruptions inspired by the teachings of Dr. Martin Luther King, Jr., nor adverse media coverage had much impact on the ferocity of the repressive measures employed by the Birmingham, Alabama, Police Chief, Eugene "Bull" Connor, in May–June 1963, a riot broke out in the Black ghetto of the city, where much of the populace was not under the discipline of traditional Black Christianity. In this riot, which set a precedent for those of 1964–68 in the North, the police were driven off the streets by missiles thrown by the crowds at their vehicles. It was in fact this event that was decisive in prompting the Kennedy administration to force a settlement, for which Dr. King was given full credit.

In another variant, the regime is so repressive that the most modest act of dissidence, even if formally legal, is punished with immediate repression to the point of summary execution. The regime may err on the side of stringent repression to the point of summarily executing persons suspected of dissident ideas or those thought to be friends or acquaintances of suspected dissidents or, indeed, for no specific reasons at all. The late Iranian monarchy provides an example. In such a situation, dissidence, if it is to emerge at all, must begin at an advanced stage of the use of force, as the only basis of confidence for the dissidents is the certainty that there are too many of them to all be summarily executed. In a variant of this variant, the regime is apparently wholly successful in stifling any possible dissidence within civil society, but reproduces within the effective means of violence on which it relies the same contradictions that exist between itself and civil society. In such situations revolutionary forces may be unleashed when crowd action suddenly manifests itself and intensifies in tandem with the progressive disintegration of the armed forces (Russia, March 8–12, 1917). Alternatively, a spontaneous crowd action signals a military coup on the part of a section of the armed forces (e.g., Addis Ababa, Ethiopia, February 14, 1974, when a taxi driver, protesting a state-imposed increase in the price of gasoline, drew a spontaneously riotous crowd, which in turn prompted a military coup, which overthrew the monarchy). The emergent contradictions within civil society are then reflected in a succession of military coups and revolts (as in Ethiopia, 1974–77). Yet another possibility is that a section of the armed forces, detached for a prolonged period from the political and ideological ambience of civil society, constitutes itself as a dissident social category, and overthrows the regime (Lisbon, Portugal, April 1974); subsequently the emergent contradictions within civil society are strictly harnessed to the polarizations within the military itself (whence the Portuguese revolutionary slogan "Army and People!"), and the ultimate social and political settlement in civil society is a reflection of the outcome of a succession of coups and countercoups along political and ideological lines. In the Portuguese case, the ultimate coup led to the dictatorship of the conservative General Eanes from late 1975. This personage became the duly elected president of a bourgeois constitutional republic whose parliament was initially numerically dominated by a coalition of socialists and populists. In late 1978, General Eanes finally dispensed with Soares, his socialist prime minister, and replaced him with a man of his own political persuasion, Nobre de Costa, a conservative described as a "nonpolitical technocrat." The Portuguese revolution was somewhat exceptional in that the armed forces were throughout to the left of the fascist regime they overthrew and continued to move to the left through the initial series of coups. Perhaps more "normal" was the behavior of the French army in Algeria, which in 1958 replaced a conservative republic with a reactionary but pragmatic dictatorship and then in 1962 sought to replace that with a fascistic regime.

As part of the intensification of social conflict, participants in a social movement as a rule innovate new channels of lateral (that is, interdissident) communicaton as well as vertical (that is, between themselves and the leaders of the movement) communication whereby they supplement the usual channels of communication flowing downward from the regime or the exploiting class as a whole. This may involve the innovation of wholly original media (alternative or "underground" presses, *Samizdat*, wall posters, graffiti, etc.) and interpersonal contact (telephone trees, networks, cells, affinity groups, consciousness-raising groups, "soul sessions," ad hoc meetings, periodically assembling groups with the most rudimentary formal structure). In addition, dissidents may divert to social-movement uses communications techniques never before employed in this way: In Iran, for example, we have the instance of a country in which the whole of the press and broadcasting industries were a cartel monopoly of the royal family and the state. Iran was plentifully supplied with the household luxury consumer goods of the advanced countries. Consequently, ingenious use was made of the cassette recorder. In the first place, it was used to copy inspirational messages and calls to arms from the exiled symbolic leader of the revolution, Ayatollah Ruhollah Khomeini, who perhaps was the logical leader of the diverse opposition precisely because he was in exile, his social program was nebulous, and he was head of the faith that embraced nearly the whole of the population and that by tradition accorded at best conditional legitimacy to the secular ruler (since the latter was not of the house of the Caliph Ali, assassinated A.D. 661, and his son, Sharif Husain, assassinated A.D. 680). Khomeini's voice could be taken as the closest thing to a direct revelation from God (*ayatollah*—reflection of God), and as the movement gained in momentum, ever-greater numbers were moved to take his equation of the regime with Satan, a being of Persian invention, quite literally. During the actual street demonstrations, moreover, cassette recordings were made of gunshot noises and, following the dispersal of the demonstrations, these tapes were played back through high-wattage stereo systems to confuse and disorient the armed forces.

As conflict intensifies, dissident collectivities develop innovative modes of collective action. Additionally, new social categories are called into the conflict. This, we call the Law of Emergent Contradiction.

Innovation in the Players of the Game, or the Law of Emergent Contradiction

It is a well-known feature of social movements, most conspicuous in revolutions, that as the intensity of dissidence rises there occurs a simultaneous development of the autonomous identity of social categories, which, usually of lower social rank than the original champions of the movement and at first subsumed in the united opposition under their leadership, come to articulate their own demands and interests in contradiction to policies pursued by their social betters or in rejection of settlements these had previously regarded as final. One commonly finds that the emergent categories are structured in an exploitative class relation with the earlier dissident vanguard, or that they are otherwise subject to neglect, injury, contempt, or persecution at the hands of the "natural leaders" of the "people." What is more, their appearance as *historical subjects* is unprecedented and had not been entertained as a serious possibility during the preceding period of social quiescence. Indeed there is a pattern in social movements, repetitive to the point of monotony, whereby the initial dissidents assert the universal validity of collegiate relations (that is, "participatory" or "democratic" procedures) in wielding power, but understand tacitly that this applies to themselves alone or to relations between themselves and the embattled regime; simultaneously, they insist on the reproduction of exploitative relations at the level of material reproduction, despotic or patriarchal authority relations throughout civil society, and the continued exclusion of the lower orders from the blessings of collegial procedures that they have achieved within the polity as their pride and joy. The contradiction between abstractions and everyday practice readily conduces to suspicions among the multitude that their superiors are not merely prisoners of ideological self-deception, but are positively hypocritical, and that their manifest caution in prosecuting the common cause reflects not mere pragmatism, but treason and accommodation with the enemy (which often proves to be the case). Hence we find those successions of movements within movements and revolutions within revolutions that, as in Crane Brinton's *Anatomy of Revolution*, are often perceived by outsiders as transitions from the "moderates" to the "radicals" or "extremists."

As a case in point we may consider the English Revolution, whose initial leadership was described previously in the context of its placing itself at the head of society in opposition to an unpopular regime: Recall that the united opposition had initially envisaged little more than denying to the monarch the fiscal and political means for the erection of a continental-style autocratic despotism. Charles I oscillated wildly between inconclusive concessions and inept repression, leading the gentry opposition in Parliament to make political demands beyond its original intentions, including the claims of exclusive control over the armed forces (which could not be reconciled with the original ideological posture of defending the traditional English constitution). These events took place under the noses of the inhabitants of the City of London. As vividly described by Zagorin (1976), these swept aside the entrenched oligarchical government of the municipality, with its intimate financial ties to the crown, replacing it with a more broadly based local government, with effective control of the streets and the local militia vested in a provisional Committee of Public Safety. (Revolutions are notoriously traditional in their nomenclature, whence the reappearance of this appellation in the French Revolution to designate the Robespierrist regime of the Year II.) The aroused populace, under the leadership of the London bourgeoisie, was then able to throw its weight behind the gentry opposition in the crisis that brought about the execution of Strafford (political pillar of the regime and organizer of the remaining armed forces prepared to fight for Charles I against Parliament) and subsequently in the civil war itself. Zagorin emphasizes that the open appearance of the urban bourgeoisie as a political force was quite contrary to the custom of the period (except, of course, for those of its members who as individuals had acquired the landed property, style, and outlook of the gentry).

With the outbreak of the civil war, the command of the armed forces of Parliament was given to titled noblemen, and political leadership as a whole was vested in a landed faction sometimes known to history by reason of their religious views as the Presbyterians. (That is, they favored the Scottish system of church governance, whereby the church officials were selected by collegial procedures among the clergy and important laymen, but the clergy themselves were appointed; the right of appointing the parish clergy was in many places an attribute of landed property at this time.) This faction, which was quite comparable in its social conservatism to the enemy it was fighting on the battlefield, was charged with considerable justification of being loath to bring the war to a victorious conclusion. Consequently, there occurred the episode of the "purge," whereby the more vigorous commanders and organizers of the New Model Army, whose leader was Cromwell, expelled the earlier leaders from their army commands and from Parliament itself. Power was now vested in the Independents, a coalition of the more radical gentry and the urban bourgeoisie, whose religious policy was "Congregationalist." (That is, the validation of the claims of the clergy to inclusion among the saints by reason of the inspiration by divine grace was to be determined by collegial procedures within the congregations.) This power was henceforth exercised through the army command.

Social movements, in accordance with the Law of Emergent Contradiction, display the developing *vertical* spread of collegial relations in society, that is, downwards to more exploited and dominated social categories, and their *horizontal* spread, that is, to wider and more encompassing functional areas of social life (as opposed, say, to their confinement to episodic encounters with the formal procedures of the polity as on Election Day). But revolutions, or at least all historic revolutions to date, are defended by despotic relations, specifically those authority relations implanted in the hierarchical structure of the armed forces loyal to the revolutionary regime and implicit in the organization of support activities associated with a war effort of any complexity and sophistication. (For possible exceptions to this generalization one might have to go back, say, to fourteenth-century Switzerland.) There consequently comes a point in the development of a social movement that has eventuated in revolution where the means of violence at the disposal of the revolutionary regime, whether of its own creation or the preexisting but undismantled military apparatus, arrests the momentum of collegialization and reverses the process. In the English Revolution this moment had come by 1649: The Levellers, based socially on rich peasants—who as a status group were known as "yeomen" and urban artisans, were as numerous as ordinary soldiers in the ranks of the New Model Army (moreover having, while fighting the civil war, been systematically defrauded by their officers of their claims to purchase confiscated lands [cf. C. Hill, "The Agrarian Legislation . . . " 1958]). They had come to suspect (rightly) that Charles I was plotting further civil war and, by implication, the motives of Cromwell and the other senior officers in refraining from abolishing the monarchy. The "agitators" (this word, like purge, dates from this period) therefore called for the abolition of the monarchy and the extension of the parliamentary suffrage to male holders of small property (though not universal manhood suffrage). As many belonged to the multitudinous competing small Puritan sects beyond the fringe of "respectable" religious life, they made a case for religious toleration (for Protestants only, of course). Their mutiny at Putney was suppressed by General Ireton. This event still more completely doomed the movement of the Diggers, landless laborers who squatted on uncultivated land and simply dug in. Nor was Cromwell's militaristic regime conducive to the development of incipient feminism. (For feminism in this period, cf. Sheila Rowbotham, 1972.) Paradoxically, with the various propertied groups split along complicated ideological and political cleavages, the only possible center of power was Cromwell and the army command, who spent several years vainly seeking to create a durable source of legitimacy and a base of popular support for themselves. Meanwhile, the propertied groups found themselves under the yoke and the taxation imposed by the very thing for which in theory they had originally opposed: that is, a centralized, despotic, militaristic, and expensive state.

Less dramatic examples of emergent contradiction may be adduced from social movements in the United States in the 1930s and 1960s. In the former period the trade unionization of the working class was initially promoted by the state in Section 7a of the National Industrial Recovery Act (1933), which by establishing the National Recovery Administration to regiment the economy along the lines of the Italian Corporate State (and itself copied by Nazi financial wizard Hjalmar Schacht) sought to eradicate judicial definitions of unions as "monopolies in restraint of trade" to procure labor representation in industrial cartels. A spontaneous popular upsurge was manifest by 1934 in the form of receptivity to unionization and mass adhesion to unions that already existed; but the existing AFL leadership, traumatized by successive defeats and a dwindling base during the period 1920–23 was unable or unwilling to respond. It clung to the obsolete policy of unionization by craft and trade, which not only precluded the unionization of heavy industry but moreover corresponded to the stratification of the working class itself into status groups related to ethnicity. (That is, the elite or skilled workers had an overrepresentation of Irish and German Catholics, Scandinavians, and Jews; ordinary workers in manufacturing, especially heavy industry, had a similar disproportion of southern and eastern European immigrants; and Blacks were assigned to the hardest and lowest-paid work or to none at all.) In the second phase, 1936–39, the "industrial unions," which had broken away from the AFL to form the more visibly class-conscious CIO, successfully penetrated such previously impregnable industries as steel and automobiles. In 1936 the UAW imitated the French device of factory occupation ("sit-down strike") in Flint, Michigan, and in 1938 fought the equally symbolic "battle of the overpass" at the Ford works in Dearborn. A simultaneous Black movement was under way, but its course was more difficult to chart: Black political action and collective-conflict action since the 1840s at the latest has displayed the alternating and sometimes concurrent—but mutually contradictory on the ideological plane—thrusts of assimilationism (the demand for the color-blind society) and nationalism (of varying content but exhibiting the recurrent feature of a suspicion of the prospects for a satisfactory alliance with any groups of whites). The assimilationist tendency was represented by the efforts of trade union leaders is such as A. Philip Randolph (for decades leader of the Brotherhood of Sleeping Car Porters; subsequently the most conservative of Black leaders in the 1960s) and Bayard Rustin (discredited as an Administration stooge in 1964) and supported by the Communist Party which was fairly successful in recruiting Black intellectuals during this period. By 1942, after the overt entry of the United States into World War II, the autonomy of the Black working-class movement was such that Randolph was able to pressure President Roosevelt—by threatening a mass protest march on Washington—into signing an executive order that banned, however ineffectually, racial discrimination in war industry. The nationalist thrust was present also, as displayed in the Harlem riots of 1935 and 1943—

the prototypes for the "long hot summers" of the middle and late 1960s—and as perhaps articulated on the ideological plane by the late Honorable Elijah Muhammad, whose Nation of Islam (now Bilalian Nation) was founded in Detroit (1931) and Chicago in the period, spreading to other northern cities.

The Black movement of the 1960s was initially led by the southern Black elite of clergy, lawyers, teachers, and entrepreneurs who had the support of that section of the urban Black working class under the sway of the pulpit and were abetted by northern white money and propaganda as well as volunteers from among intellectuals and students both Black and white. The initial objectives were wholly assimilationist in appearance, with rival groups ranging on the conservative-to-radical spectrum according to the degree of nonviolent force to which they were prepared to resort. Students and young intellectuals supplied leadership to the rural Black working-class (soon to develop its own leaders) areas of the Deep South where the Black elite was feebly developed. The assimilationist or "civil rights" phase of the movement faded out in disorientation during 1964–66, in part because the initial assimilationist objectives had been enacted into legislation, which, however, had no impact on more fundamental structural inequalities; but primarily because the leading edge of the movement had visibly passed to the Black ghettos of the northern cities, where the most depressed strata of the working class in the United States were largely concentrated. Young Black intellectuals at this time adopted nationalist postures and symbolism; this included those still operating in the South, where they developed the Black Panther symbol (in Alabama) and the "Black power" slogan (in Mississippi) and renounced cooperation with former white allies. Northern Black elites, lacking the moral authority conferred by traditional religion and having lost the political initiative, were confined to playing games of "extremists and moderates" with the state on various levels. (This is a game common to many social movements undergoing the development of emergent contradiction: "If you don't deal with me, you'll have to deal with them!" Subsequently, the visible leadership comprised young intellectuals of wholly mythic significance. That is, their authority was symbolic and derived from acts, rhetoric, style, and slogans that procured Black admiration in part by frightening whites, but whose ability and direct collective dissidence was insignificant. One might even argue that the efficacy of the often spectacular dissidence that did occur derived precisely from its insusceptibility to manipulation and prediction from within and from the absence of an organizational structure that might have been held hostage.

The movement based on white candidate members of the bourgeoisie ("youth") in the 1960s was no less of a novelty in recent history than the Black movement, but like the latter its similarities to preceding movements, including its manifestations of the laws of social-movement development, often appeared in guises equally unprecedented, if not more so. For example: There is a tendency for social movements in bourgeois society to reproduce the division of the bourgeoisie itself into entrepreneurs and politico-military specialists by developing dual and contradictory thrusts of "economic" and "political" character. (In the stereotyped working class movements of the first half of the twentieth century, this took the form of debates over the priority to be given to strikes for wage increases by the trade unions relative to that accorded pressure on the state by the party. This debate resounded with charges of "naive economism" or "parliamentary cretinism.") Thus the specific form of the economic thrust of the youth movement—during the period of greatest intensity in 1967–70—was toward the maximum possible renunciation of bourgeois social relations ("dropping out") in favor of the promotion of communist (not socialist) social relations, including demands for collegial ("participatory" or "tribal") authority relations in organizational structures impinging on everyday life or else the removal of everyday life to remote rural regions, and the production, exchange, or simple appropriation (including "ripping off") of use values. The "political" thrust took the form of confrontation with the state over, e.g., the Vietnam War, racism, and educational policy. For purposes of protest solidarity this required the dissidents' presence in the vicinity of if not necessarily enrollment in a college or university (that was *not* necessitated by the economic thrust). These contradictory thrusts were reproduced at the level of leadership as acrimonious debates between "politicos" and "druggies," though such distinctions were far less acute among ordinary participants whose solidarity rested on a common subculture and who might by turns emphasize politics, then drugs, sex, or communal living, then politics again. The distinction was certainly not made by counterdissidents, who lumped both thrusts together under the vulgar "3 P's" slogan ("Peace Pot Pussy"). And most interesting, it was the "street people"—that amorphous aggregation, so despised by the politicos, of dropouts, "spare change" beggars, drug dealers, speed freaks, burnt-out cases, hangers-out and hangers-around, and teenage runaways increasingly recruited from the white working class—who perpetrated some of the most dramatic acts of collective violence of the youth movement, e.g., in Berkeley, June 28–30, 1968.

It was precisely the subculture, with its emphases on "rediscovery of the body," "consciousness," and the intense scrutiny and forceful experience of the minute details of everyday life ("bringing it all back home"), that facilitated the emergence of a separate feminist movement in 1967–68. The story that has been handed down recounts that women in SDS chapters at that time were restive over consignment to menial tasks, whereas the male "heavies" monopolized discussions of policy and "analysis." Consequently, they formed their own groups wherein the enemy was redefined from "the straights," "the system," "the ruling class," or "establishment" to "men" or "patriarchy."

Innovation in the Definition of the Problem, or the Law of Shifting Terrain

Routine politics is conducted in terms of "issues." That is, from the perspective of the exploiting class in its day-to-day practice of formulating policies and making decisions, there appear certain options of rather narrow scope wherein the ideological premises that limit that scope are never questioned and indeed even brought to the level of awareness; much less are the structural conditions underlying the ideological restrictions ever considered. This set of options, at least in bourgeois society, is "public opinion," which unless quantitative survey research is specifically indicated, usually connotes the opinions of those strata sufficiently educated and sophisticated that they can articulate the technicalities involved in the process of the acquisition of education and sophistication: Public opinion is divided into that which is "responsible" and that which is dismissed as "irresponsible," "muddle-headed," "wooly-minded," at best "bleeding-heart," and at worst "the wild-eyed crackpot lunatic fringe." With its options "clarified"—whether by public opinion or by secret deliberation—the regime then yields, and in fact believes itself to be yielding, to obvious necessity; survey research is resorted to in the determination of whether the obvious necessity is *popular*. Routine politics in periods of social quiescence most often resembles the radio commercial wherein the consumer debates with him or herself, "Should I take something strong but effective? Or something gentle but safe?" The underlying message is that he or she must at all costs take *something*, specifically an acceptable compromise in the form of the advertised product. Occasionally, it is true, politics *does* resemble the TV deodorant commercial featuring rival crowds, one noisily championing "The stick! The stick!" while the other shouts for "The spray! The spray!" until one courageous independent-thinking leadership type pronounces for "the roll-on"; the crackpots who believe that daily baths with soap suffice are unrepresented. Advertisers are deliberate brainwashers; however, the stuff of politics is the appearances of society that accomplish their own brainwashing in the course of the routine living of everyday life.

Consider this contemporary issue: The regime has pronounced that of two wicked alternatives—either more inflation or more employment coupled with cutbacks in "social programs"—it has chosen the latter. A "conservative" opposition announces that the regime does not go far enough (although it is more conservative on this issue than the conservatives when they were last in office) and a "liberal" opposition says that it has gone too far. Yet the differences in policy represented by the rhetorical differences of all three positions can only be marginal, since both the "rate of inflation" and the "rate of unemployment" are structurally determined and reflect a contradiction between capitalist relations of production and the necessity to maintain social discipline (see Chapter 9, "Conclusion," for details). The prices of products rise because the productivity of labor does not. Consequently, to support the growing numbers of office workers and other consumption formations who must be hired to use up the products society produces, society must charge itself extra; the state appears as the consumer of last resort, since it may go into debt indefinitely. Productivity does not increase because capitalists do not invest in new productive technique. They cannot do so because they must thereby drastically reduce the size of the working class. Although they could easily hire the laid-off workers to push pencils in offices and still make money through increased exports reflecting the declining real cost of production, they will not do so because this would contradict the authority relations intrinsic to the capitalist labor process, by virtue of which the whole of the strata superior in social status to the working class understand themselves as privileged. But unemployment neither may fall too low, lest the whole of the "employed" category lose their sense of privilege with respect to that category called "unemployed," nor rise too high, lest it no longer appear plausible to most of society that a normal human being, that is, a person genuinely in search of employment, will surely find it with a little persistence. The dictates of a capitalist economy contradict those of bourgeois society as a specific form of society. The practice of the bourgeoisie is here conditioned by its experience of the decay of social discipline in the 1960s, most painfully among candidate members of the bourgeoisie themselves.

During the course of social-movement development such issues, hitherto apparently isolated, discrete, and unrelated, are generalized. That is, connections and patterns are found among them and are understood increasingly as manifestations of conflict between major social categories, the boundaries and character of which will also appear to shift in accordance with the development of conflict and consciousness. An example of the generalization of issues in the 1960s might be found in the reconceptualization of the 1960 election issues of economic growth, unemployment, and civil rights into, first, structural unemployment, poverty, and cultural deprivation, and ultimately into the issue of racism defined in social-structural rather than attitudinal terms. Another example was the generalization of numerous foreign-policy questions—including the Vietnam War, the Dominican intervention, Cuba, colonial wars in Africa, the China policy, the Middle East, etc.—into those of "the military-industrial complex," the United States as "world policeman," or "imperialism" vis-à-vis the "Third World." New "issues" appear, that is, whole new areas of social life are redefined as problematic and grounds for conflict. Examples of such new issues in the 1960s were environmental pollution, legalization of abortion and marijuana, rights of Selective Service registrants in evading induction, rights of conscripts within the military, hair and dress codes in schools, the work place, and the military, rights of defendants in the structurally racist criminal-justice system, the definitions of "pornography" and "obscenity," teenagers' rights of access to contraceptives and contraceptive information, the right of academics in the employ of the state to favor in the classroom the victory of the enemy in time of war, the right of state employees to steal state secrets in a time of war for dissemination to the public in order to undermine the war effort and the right of the press to publish the same, the rights of welfare recipients, the legitimacy of discrimination in employment on political and ideological grounds, the lengths to which the state is obliged to go to suppress or even reverse discrimination on ethnic or gender grounds that it had previously condoned, and so forth. Finally, new and previously unconsidered options are introduced into the debate on certain issues: Thus, in the opposition to the Vietnam War, grounds for opposition shifted from the pragmatic ("a mistake") to the moral ("inhuman killing") to the radical (assertion of the right of revolution against the United States) to the revolutionary ("Bring the war home!"). "Pragmatic" perspectives yielded support for policy options such as a negotiated peace short of victory or the end of the bombing of North Vietnam on the grounds that it was ineffectual. Moral opposition promoted options implying the recognition of the defeat of the United States, such as calling for the withdrawal of the U.S. troops from Vietnam to preclude their further perpetration of genocidal acts or dying in the commission of genocidal acts implicit in the pursuit of military victory; or else calling for the cessation of the most genocidal acts—such as the bombardment of North and South Vietnam, Laos, and Cambodia—which logically implied a negotiated surrender. Radical opposition called successively for (1) victory for the NLF/PRG in the belief that it was an independent force desiring and capable of sustaining a separate socialist-neutralist regime in South Vietnam; and (2) victory for the DRV regime in Hanoi. Revolutionary opposition, of course, called for imitation of the actions of the enemy on the battlefield "in the belly of the beast" to destroy the systematic promotion of "imperialism" at its source (e.g., the position of the Weathermen, subsequently the Weather Underground). The entire landscape of political categories thus, during social movements, is transformed until it becomes entirely or at least partially incomprehensible in terms of the political language and categories prevailing in the immediate premovement period. But this shifting terrain is itself closely tied to the development of consciousness, which subsumes the reinterpretation of social reality and the human being.

Summary

We began this chapter by noting that inherent in the human being is both the need for structure and antistructure; that in so-called primitive societies this latter human need is satisfied through the ritual suspension of structure. In class-based societies the suspension of social structure takes the form of social movements that alternate between usually longer periods of social quiescence.

Our focal point has been the primary evidence that a social movement has occurred: the intensification of conflict, which delimits the boundaries of a social-movement period. We maintain that the intensification of conflict occurs according to three basic laws:

1. The Law of Mounting Stakes. Once the routinized modes of dissidence have been exhausted, social-movement participants will engage in innovative modes of conflict that elicit mass support and imitation by other potentially dissident collectivities. It forces the regime to resort to increasing levels of force, and ultimately to violence, to maintain control, which in turn demands new tactics.

2. The Law of Emergent Contradiction. Social movements often begin with conflict between categories of elites. As the intensity of conflict increases, the autonomous identity of the social categories emerge, the usual case of which members of ranks lower than the original leaders articulate demands of their own. Either through conflict or within daily life the abstract ideological interpretation of what is right and correct are undermined by actual practice. This is reflected in the normal course of revolutions as they move from the moderate to the radical stage.

3. The Law of Shifting Terrain. Social movements begin with the routine issues that evolve around with the appearance of social relations. As conflict intensifies, issues heretofore seen as isolated, discrete, and unrelated are generalized into a comprehensive analysis of the relations between major social categories. This phenomenon will be considered in greater detail in the next chapter, in which we will analyze the process of the reinterpretation of social reality.

Chapter 5

The Reinterpretation of Social Reality

In all social movements we find an ongoing process of the reinterpretation of social reality, comprising the interference with the reproduction of the "hegemonic ideology" (see Chapter 3, "The Reproduction of Social Privilege,") and its increasing replacement among dissidents by new formulations as social conflict intensifies. At the outset of a social-movement period, society is pervaded by a conventional interpretation of reality imposed on all classes (which are themselves mediated by the appearances of other systems of social categorization at best only vaguely corresponding to classes) by routine practice within the confines of relations of exploitation and prevailing authority relations. The formulations of the hegemonic ideology are conducive to the reproduction of the exploiting class, the regime, and the apparatuses of exploitation and domination, and fortified by the possibility of the preceding resorting to force in defense of what is seemingly inevitable, right, and proper.

The hegemonic ideology (or conventional interpretation of social reality) may in part be formulated into abstract theories or idealizations of the practice of the exploiting class or the regime (e.g., Social Darwinism for nineteenth-century capitalists or Official Nationality for the regime of Nicholas I in Russia), but, more important, it is found at the level of commonsensical assumptions and folk wisdom about how society works, how and why it was put there, what the functions of the appearances of society in the various groupings and social types are supposed to be, the legitimate, that is, the idealized bounds of exploitation and domination, the nature and source of reward for virtue and chastisement of wickedness throughout society, and the appropriateness of the prevailing appearances of the exploiting class as status groups (e.g., warriors, leisured landowners, clergy, managers, and experts) for the proper running of things. The hegemonic ideology (or the conventional interpretation of social reality) need not possess the coherence and order of formal logic, so long as the exploited and dominated are content to "make sense" of society and of themselves in the language and from the perspective of the exploiters and dominators.

When collective dissidence arises, the participants come to reject ever-larger portions of the hegemonic ideology. Social relations previously accepted as reasonable, inflexible, inexorable, and primordial now appear as contrived, unnatural, substantively irrational, parasitic, and senseless. Their own subsumption within relations of exploitation and domination, formerly accepted as part of the natural order of things, is repudiated as unjust, arbitrarily imposed and void of moral sanction. The panoply—that is, the trappings, pageantry, and other badges of status, self-serving rationalizations, snobbery, and the various apparatuses of the exploiting class and the regime—is denounced as illegitimate, and even the idea of the necessity for social hierarchy yields to progressively more egalitarian notions. As conflict intensifies and their numbers swell, dissidents discern that the very nomenclature and linguistic structure of common speech embody assumptions about their innate inferiority, inevitable subordination, and social invisibility. Thus, for example, the French Jacobins transformed the nomenclature of dates and places; the Russian Bolsheviks abolished the obsequious form of address, the "-s" suffix; and U.S. feminists promoted the replacement of the element "-man" in titles and job designations by that of "-person" and rendered problematical the generic "he" without any definitively correct usage having yet replaced it.

The dissidents simultaneously reinterpret social reality such that their own insurgency "makes sense" to them. This may involve, at first, a mere modification of the hegemonic ideology; but as social conflict intensifies and their numbers and self-confidence (individual and collective) grow, the reinterpretation of social reality tends to become more sweeping. Thus the positions taken by the New Left in 1962 appear in retrospect as a humanistic gloss on the New Frontier liberalism of the time, whereas, the condemnation of bourgeois social relations in 1969 by youth-culture "freaks" (including the overlapping categories of drug dropouts and New Left politicos) were infinitely more far-reaching.

In the most intense phase of a social movement the reinterpretation of social reality may have proceeded to the point at which, to the movement participants, the wider society appears to make no sense at all or, at best, a wholly negative sort of sense—as a vast and malign conspiracy. For example, the "underground" newspapers published by "freaks" during 1967–70 portray all conventional social relations with a mixture of surrealism and disgust.

Nonsocial Movement Reinterpretations

This social-movement reinterpretation must be distinguished, first, from ideological changes imposed by new regimes that nevertheless leave the exploitative relation and indeed the contours of the social structure as a whole unscathed. Under this heading we may certainly place the substitution of Christianity for paganism by Constantine the Great in the fourth century and possibly also the substitution by Arab conquerors of Islam for variants of Eastern Christianity (Orthodox, Monophysite, Nestorian, Monothelete), Zoroastrianism, and Buddhism in the seventh and eighth centuries. In recent times parts of bourgeois society have been dressed up in assorted officially imposed doctrinal guises, both in the core (National Socialism, fascism) and, more often, in the periphery as for example, African Socialism (Kenya), Arab Socialism (UAR/Egypt), Peronismo (Argentina), Personalism (Diem's regime in South Vietnam),

National Populism or "Sun Yat-senism" (China under Chiang Kai-shek), the "socialism" of Lee Kuan Yew in Singapore, and of course the late and unlamented "White Revolution" of the Iranian monarchy.

Second, it is necessary, as noted in Chapter 1, "The Guises of Social Movements," to distinguish this process from recurrent cultural, artistic, religious, and intellectual movements, even where these, as in the French Enlightenment, may be demonstrated to have furnished ideological ammunition for subsequent collective dissidence. Such movements are part of the normal process of cultural reproduction in all forms of class society and even perhaps in preclass society. Their association with social movements proper is not determinate, that is, they may be confined exclusively to the level of cultural reproduction or even to the froth and foam of the intellectual stratosphere that is today the quarry mined by graduate students and professors. As stated in Chapter 3, "The Reproduction of Social Privilege," it was in a sense the duty of prebourgeois ideological specialists, and still more of the "intellectuals" at the summit of the former cultural counterbourgeoisie, to stand somewhat apart from the hegemonic ideology in its most conventional guise.[1] Thus Socrates was condemned to death by the Athenian landowning class collectively for teaching doctrines that overtly cast doubt on the existence of the gods. Probably few if any of the 500 jurors were sincerely pious, but it was nevertheless reproduced within their hegemonic ideology that faith in the gods (especially by their social inferiors and slaves) was inseparable from the stability of society and the security of the state; the naivete and obsolescence of this proposition obliged Socrates to courageously repudiate it openly. Similarly but even more, the "intellectuals" of bourgeois society were routinely expected to criticize the abuses of the bourgeoisie (especially of its politico-military sector). As noted above, provision for this was made in the bourgeois hegemonic ideology as manifesting the "freedom" of society. Of course, some of the "intellectuals" did, and still do, idealize and extol the bourgeoisie and bourgeois society to an even greater extent than prevails in the hegemonic ideology itself, e.g., "neoconservatism," but then, that is implicit in "intellectual life." Nevertheless, movements on the purely cultural level, whatever their content, *eo ipso* affect the structural foundations of society only in the reproduction of alienation and false consciousness. That is, there is always an implicit claim advanced for the innate superiority of spiritual guides, "thinkers," and "creators" over workaday people and for at least a modicum of social privilege wherein this alleged superiority is objectified. By implication, this argues for the entire system of social relations in which the elite realms of cultural reproduction are embedded and by which they are supported, since these are understood as the adornment of the social order, the "higher things in life," even though the content of particular "creations" may disgust "decent people," thereby reinforcing the faith in the "ultimate significance" of these things by their proponents.

Social Movement Reinterpretations

In our characterization of the reinterpretation of social reality, we intend to emphasize the mental life of ordinary participants in social movements. This can *never* be identified with the ideological statements made by intellectuals, whether as oratory and recorded by scribes or tape recorders on the spot, or as written or otherwise recorded documents; it cannot be easily identified with the recollections in the form of oral history subsequently taken from participants who have lovingly recounted their experiences and actions in great detail. The introduction of new conceptualizations of social reality into the mental life of the dissidents may, for example, arise from ordinary participants who thereby become intellectuals. But these new conceptualizations may themselves reflect the structured conservatism of the thought forms underlying the everyday use of language, and may consequently understate the degree to which the mental life of the dissidents has already been transformed by new *expectations* and *understandings* that dissidents cannot yet verbalize but of which they are conscious as subtle emotional states. In such situations "objective" and "scientific" outside observers—including professional revolutionaries and counterrevolutionary intelligence agencies, as well as experts in the social sciences—can make and have made serious errors in evaluating the vehemence and determination with which dissidents will act on the basis of "hard empirical evidence" elicited verbally. Consider the following examples:

1. L. D. Trotsky, in his *History of the Russian Revolution*, demonstrated— on the basis of documentary evidence such as leaflets, as well as oral accounts taken from participants in the street action—that the Petrograd Bolshevik organization systematically sought to *restrain* the insurrection of March 8–12, 1917 (the "February Revolution," which overthrew the monarchy) for fear of official repression, refusing for instance to distribute weapons after the point at which victory was probable. All that Trotsky could say on behalf of the Bolsheviks on the spot was that the organizations of the other opposition parties gave an even worse account of themselves. Far from seeking to cast aspersions on the "revolutionary vanguard" theory, Trotsky was merely villifying his subsequent political enemies such as the "mere college boy" Molotov; but he was nevertheless obliged to resort to a strained and tortuous explanation *ex hypothesi*, not supported by historical evidence well known to himself, whereby the Bolsheviks could be given credit for the February Revolution on the basis of the preceding period in which they were supposedly leading and indoctrinating the masses (of which there is no evidence given), despite the failure of the local committee in its mission of scientifically determining the balance of forces at the critical moment.

2. The great proving ground of applied social science in the contemporary period is the U.S. intelligence apparatus, especially the CIA, which has at its disposal far greater and more sophisticated means to forestall social upheaval than those available to professional revolutionaries to foment it. The apparent failure of the CIA even in its intelligence-gathering function, whereby it has time after time failed to give advance warning of the intensity of dissidence in various countries (notoriously, for example, in Cuba, 1957–61), has consequently been blamed on the error, incompetence, and careerism of operatives on the spot or upon the mismanagement of the CIA Director. This recurrent pattern was repeated once again in connection with the Iranian Revolution.[2] Thus: "In August, months after the first riots had broken out, the CIA in a top-secret intelligence assessment advised the White House that 'Iran is not in a revolutionary or even a pre-revolutionary situation' " (*Newsweek*, January 29, 1979).

Although Marxist-Leninists are presumably biased in favor of what it is the mission of the CIA to oppose, we have an interesting specimen from that quarter of a failure of equal magnitude in predicting the Iranian Revolution: Fred

Halliday's *Iran: Dictatorship and Development*. Halliday was in Iran as late as September 1978 and, though calling the situation a "crisis" for the regime, located it in the historical perspective of five prior crises since World War II that the shah had withstood without a scratch if not with enhanced power. In any case, he was grossly mistaken as to the outcome, possibly due to the Marxist-Leninist proclivity to rationally calculate the "correlation of forces": On the one hand he was impressed by the bulk and ferocity of the repressive apparatus, that is, SAVAK and the military, it having not yet been revealed that the latter would not fire on anything capable of firing back. On the other, the Marxist-Leninist bookkeeping showed a glaring deficit of anything that could be taken for a serious vanguard party of the working class. And, of course, atheists tend to expect little of revolutionary consequence from the clergy.

Halliday belittled the Ayatollah Khomeini, whose "intransigent demands" he saw as playing into the hands of the shah. Similarly, he belittled the Mujaheddin and Khalq-e-Fedayin guerrillas, subsequently major political forces, for their "restricted cultural level." The author's "realistic" speculations as to the final crisis of the regime indicated its advent as no sooner than the early 1980s, with its most likely scenarios being military coups either outright or in the name of Crown Prince Reza.

3. In late 1966, the eminent sociologist Seymour Martin Lipset announced to an audience of 2,000 at Syracuse University that, according to the most recent and authoritative surveys of U.S. students' political attitudes, there was no evidence of any significant change in the results of such surveys between the late 1950s and mid-1966. Does our knowledge of subsequent history invalidate this conclusion? Yes and no: Attitude surveys presuppose the persistence of ideological conceptualizations and underlying thought forms characteristic of a period of social quiescence. They are, moreover, conducted by persons who adopt the "objective" mind-set, wherein the assumptions reproduced within the hegemonic ideology as to the limits of the possible are embedded. The respondent must assume the mind-set in order to communicate; that is, the respondent must adopt "realistic" notions of the limits of the possible. If the respondent's understandings of the limits of the possible are undergoing change, but such understandings are perceptible only as subtle feeling states whose implications are not understood by the respondent, who is, in addition, unsure as to whether these are at all widespread in their distribution, the respondent is left with no alternative to replying in "realistic" terms. If the survey is, furthermore, taken in a period of "sociocharacterological revolution" (which was exemplified by the 1960s in the United States, with certain striking parallels to early-seventeenth-century England), the breakdown in assumptions as to the limits of the possible may not be confined to the rather restricted terrain of policy issues on which "liberal" or "conservative" responses may be rendered.

Consider the folk-ideological usage of the term "bullshit" in the youth movement of the 1960s. There was, first, the traditional meaning of "lies" or "duplicity." Second, "bullshit" could denote statements that, taken individually, may be demonstrably true, but that lack substantive importance even if true, while in the aggregate amounting to ideological deception. Hence, "Everything you learn in school is just bullshit brainwashing." Third, "bullshit" denoted something understood as substantively irrational whose substantive irrationality the speaker lacks the conceptual apparatus and thought forms to articulate. Hence, "a bullshit nine-to-five job." Fourth, "bullshit" denoted contradictions between intellectual articulations of "radicalism" and the condition of being behaviorally enmeshed in bourgeois social relations. Therefore, for example, a professor who was an avowed Marxist revolutionary, yet who upheld academic discipline and standards while condemning drugs and untidiness, was accused of "Old Left bullshit." Similarly, in 1968, the "action faction" in an SDS chapter (as at Columbia or the University of Michigan) would accuse the entrenched leaders, who argued for the importance of "analysis," of "rhetorical bullshit." In short, "radicalization" implied an *emotional* rejection of the conventional interpretation of social reality as "bullshit"—with this rejection manifested through behavior or "action," i.e., "putting your body on the line"— rather than in subscribing to a fully conceptualized reinterpretation whose forthcoming was, in any case, not all that crucial. The "movement" subculture in fact relied heavily on the intensification of feeling states from whose perspective bourgeois social relations could be critiqued as "bullshit"; for this reason we have used the term "subjectivist ideology" in connection with it. The prevalence of subjectivist ideologies in the social movements of the 1960s was in part dictated by the diffuseness of specific ideational content in the bourgeois hegemonic ideology deriving in turn from the conditions of cultural reproduction in contemporary bourgeois society.

The reconstruction of the reinterpretation of social reality from oral histories taken from participants after the fact is also fraught with possible sources of error, such as: (1) the owl-of-Minerva syndrome, (2) illusions of nonparticipants and counterdissidents, and (3) postmovement adaptation illusions.

1. The owl-of-Minerva syndrome. This is named after Hegel's maxim "The owl of Minerva takes wing after the shades of dusk have already fallen," in other words, the development of consciousness receives its definitive theoretical formulation only after its possibilities for further development have already been exhausted. Thus, where the reinterpretation of social reality is formulated as abstract theories or doctrines bearing something of an "official" stamp, that is, endorsed by recognized leaders and intellectuals of the movement, former dissidents may be tempted to read this back into their own recollections of what they did, felt, and thought during the actual events. Hence, they may claim for themselves a precocious apprehension of and subscription to the "official" version of the reinterpretation of social reality as stated in the form that has been handed down to history. Otherwise, or additionally, they may simplistically reconstruct the process of the reinterpretation of social reality so as to delineate with spurious clarity the stages of individual or collective experience and development that culminated in the official version while bypassing or downplaying the complex currents and cross-currents of mental life that were actually present though in retrospect are inadmissible.

The Puritans of the English Revolution have come down to history as a stolid, abstemious, and self-disciplined lot, fighting for godly virtue against sin in church and state. According to Hill, this stereotype ignores the orgiastic side of the movement associated with the Ranters:

"Religion is now become the common discourse and table-talk in every tavern and ale-house," men were complaining as early as 1641. "Ale-

houses generally are . . . the meeting places of malignats and sectaries,"
a preacher told the House of Commons in 1646. . . . "Eat of Christ,
therefore, the tree of life, at supper, and drink his blood, and make you
merry, John Eacherd, a Suffolk parson who spoke up for the common
soldiers in 1645 . . . Thomas Edwards reported an "antinomian preacher
in London, who stated that 'on a fast day it was better for Christians to
be drinking in an ale-house, or to be in a whore-house, than to be keeping
fasts legally.' . . .

The analogy of modern drug-taking should enable us to understand
that—in addition to the element of communal love-feast in such gath-
erings—the use of tobacco and alcohol was intended to heighten spiritual
vision. Some years later the millenarian John Mason was excessively
addicted to smoking, and "generally while he smoked he was in a kind
of ecstasy." (Tobacco was still a novel and rather naughty stimulant,
though by 1640 it had risen to first place among London's imports.) In
New England, Captain Underhill told Governor Winthrop "the Spirit had
sent into him the witness of free grace, while he was in the moderate
enjoyment of the creature called tobacco." Was it in a tavern, or at a
religious meeting, that Captain Freeman declared that he saw God in the
tableboard and the candlestick? . . .

At one Ranter meeting of which we have a (hostile) report, the mixed
company met at a tavern, sang blasphemous songs to the well-known
tunes of metrical psalms and partook of a communal feast. One of them
tore off a piece of beef, saying "This is the flesh of Christ, take and eat."
Another threw a cup of ale into the chimney corner, saying "There is the
blood of Christ." Clarkson called a tavern the house of God; sack was
divinity. Even a Puritan enemy expresses what is almost a grudging
admiration for the high spirits of the Ranters' dionysiac orgies: "they are
the merriest of all devils for extempore lascivious songs . . . for healths,
music, downright bawdry and dancing." One of the accusations against
Captain Francis Freeman was that he sang bawdy songs. . . .

"Unity with the creation," tobacco "a good creature," parodying holy
communion: we should never fail to look for symbolism in what appear
the extravagant gestures of seventeenth-century radicals. Ranter advocacy
of blasphemy, it has been well said, was a symbolic expression of freedom
from moral restraints. Abiezer Coppe was alleged on one occasion to have
sworn for an hour on end in the pulpit: "a pox of God take all your
prayers." An obsessive desire to swear had possessed him early in life,
but he resisted it for twenty-seven years. Then he made up for lost time.
He would rather, he declared, "hear a mighty angel (in man) swearing
a full-mouthed oath" than hear an orthodox minister preach. "One hint
more: there's swearing ignorantly, i'th dark, and there's swearing i'th
light, gloriously." Even Joseph Salmon, from the mystical and quietist
wing of the Ranters, was also in the habit of using "many desperate
oaths." [Hill, 1973:198-202]

For recent parallels in restrospective oversimplification one need only reflect
on the aftermath of the 1960s youth movement: Those who, in the 1970s,
continued to regard themselves as "radicals" detected as the central thread of
the movement's reinterpretation of social reality the development of the awareness of the implications of anti-imperialist and antiracist struggle among "serious" people, that is, those not wholly taken in by the drug-crazed spirit of
the times, whereby many of them were drawn to variants of Marxism. For those

who, alternatively, identified with the New Age subculture, which comprises Eastern spiritual disciplines, new psychotherapies, "holistic" medicine, natural foods, environmental concerns, and "alternative" uses of technology (e.g., in the fields of architecture, energy, and computer software), there is a tendency to identify the 1960s as the beginnings of a *cultural* movement of consciousness exploration and development of alternative social relations, whereby the social-conflict dimension of the youth movement is deemphasized or disowned (cf. Satin, 1978). This division represents the prolongation of the reproduction within the movement itself of the bourgeois categories of the "political" and the "economic," as noted in Chapter 1, "The Guises of Social Movements." The same process is evident in feminist recollections of the youth movement, especially in its sexual aspects, as a sexist plot promoted by males to devalorize women in the sexual marketplace by increasing the supply relative to the demand, thereby precipitating the feminist revolt.

Another example of the owl-of-Minerva syndrome may be suggested but not proven (since any documentary evidence that might tend to support it has either been destroyed or is kept top secret by the USSR regime): It is an article of faith in all variants of Marxism-Leninism that the Bolshevik party had forged an organic bond between itself and the Russian working class by, at the very latest, the period between the February and October revolutions in 1917. The empirical evidence for this assertion is usually provided in the form of a citation of a tenfold increase in party membership during that period (that is, from 25,000 to a quarter million), but a breakdown by occupation is not provided—though this could easily be done from the CPSU archives—so there is no telling how many of these were workers and how many were intelligentsiya, that is, nonmanual employees and professionals. What is certain is that they did enjoy limited popular support prior to the July Days (a popular insurrection in Petrograd aimed at the overthrow of the provisional government and the Menshevik-SR leadership of the soviets) because of their posture of resolute opposition to the regime's policy of fidelity to the Allies. This they apparently lost when, because of their ambivalence over whether or not to lead the manifestly futile revolt, they compromised themselves with both sides. It is equally certain that there was no mass street action during the October Revolution (November 7)—the work of the numerically insignificant party militia—such as that of February (March 8–13). There is no convincing evidence that the working class was under the guidance of *any* political party between "July" and "October": The substitution of Bolsheviks for Mensheviks in elections to the soviets in this period may be plausibly attributed to the well-known preference for the "lesser evil." Trotsky, in his *History* (1957), indicates that during the period of waffling prior to the October Revolution the workers were paying increasing attention to "anarchists," but these are not described as a party. The working class was in any case acting on its own account in class-conscious but "anarchically" antiauthoritarian actions such as food riots and the takeovers of factories from employers. Evidence for *real* mass popularity in the working class for the Bolsheviks comes only with Lenin's legalization of the factory takeovers *after* the October Revolution and during the ensuing civil war (1918–21). With the end of the civil war came popular chafing at the rigors of the Bolshevik revolutionary dictatorship: This was expressed in antiauthoritarian terms (e.g., "Soviets without Communists!")—generically stigmatized as anarchist—during the Kronstadt Rising of 1921 and the wave of strikes during 1921–22; but such traces died out with the return of social quiescence and the onset of the New Economic Program (NEP) period. After this time foreign observers sympathetic to the revolution ceased to report any disagreement with the version of the history of the revolutionary period promoted by the victorious regime on the part of ordinary members of the working class. (In 1918, Emma Goldman had been shocked by the Cheka's extermination of nests of anarchists in Petrograd on grounds of debauchery and armed hooliganism; but there is no telling whether such people were in any way representative of ordinary members of the working class.)

2. *Illusions of the nonparticipants and counterdissidents.* Nobody in society is *entirely* unaffected by a social movement, which everywhere promotes both a subtle psychic disorientation and a corrosion of social control. The degree to which a social movement thus affects the thought and actions of nonpartic-ipants, especially those outside the visibly dissident social categories, is almost by definition beyond their awareness at the time, and may be at best partially reconstructible later only with the assistance of diaries, documentary records, and statistical evidence.

One obvious and historically recurrent form of this is the disorientation of the *regime*. The latter, albeit the real threat to itself and the social order as a whole may be minimal, may overreact and panic itself into persecution. In this it may either orchestrate or be swept along by the hysteria of counterdissidents, whose fears are equally exaggerated or misdirected. At the other extreme, and typical of the onset of major social upheavals, the regime underreacts; indeed it appears that the whole of ruling circles have gone into a species of hibernation born of either fatalism or fatuity or both. Thus, for example, Charles I of England was described in 1637 as "the happiest king in Christendom" (Wedge-wood, 1955). Similar dream worlds at the top are associated with the French, Russian, and Iranian revolutions.

Another aspect takes the form of acts of omission or commission, usually of the petty sort, involving breaches of social discipline but not consciously ar-ticulated by the perpetrators as motivated by broader social conflict. Such acts may be widespread within social categories apparently characterized by non-dissidence or counterdissidence as well as within the dissident categories. For the former, however, these acts do not lend themselves easily to ideological interpretation, for example, Jerry Rubin's statements in 1968 that "drugs *are* political" and "long hair is the most emotional political issue in America today"; or the Livingston College student's excuse for tardiness in handing in his term paper in May 1970: "I was too busy fighting the revolution." These actions will rather be explained in terms of situational, intrapsychic, interpersonal, or perhaps even meteorological ("a lousy day" or "too nice a day") factors.

Working-class and lower-surplus-absorbing strata ("lower middle-class") whites, for instance, were associated in popular stereotypes in the United States in the 1960s with nondissidence (e.g., support by the trade unions, both leaders and members alike for the Vietnam War) or counterdissidence (e.g., "hard-hats" roughing up antiwar demonstrators or making lewd or provocative gestures at suspected feminists; the "white ethnic" racism of Imperiale in Newark and Rizzo in Philadelphia). Obviously, it was these whites who constituted the backbone of the forces of repression—the local police and the National Guard—

deployed by the authorities on the front lines of social conflict. Nevertheless, in industry the 1960s were notoriously a period of worker absenteeism, especially where the union provided a modicum of protection against summary dismissals. Hence it became a commonplace at this time that one should preferably buy a car assembled on a Wednesday and under no circumstances purchase one put together on a Monday or a Friday.

Absenteeism was the fundamental form of white working-class indiscipline in the U.S. armed forces as well: According to Lawrence Baskir and William Straus, senior officials of the Ford administration's Clemency Board, for the 7,575,000 "Vietnam-era active force troops" there were recorded 550,000 "desertion incidents," that is, cases of "administrative desertion" defined as AWOL of thirty days or more (1978:115). (These figures may represent an underestimate, since some cases were probably covered up and never recorded.) The authors' social profile of army perpetrators leaves no doubt of the overwhelmingly white working-class character of this offense (though Blacks and Hispanics were twice as likely to commit it):

> If there is such a thing as a "prototype" Army deserter of the Vietnam era, he lived in a small town and grew up in the South. He came from a low-income family, often with only one parent in the home. He had an IQ of 90, and dropped out of high school in the tenth grade. He enlisted to get away from problems back home, to learn a skill, or just to find something to do. He finished advanced training and had almost two years of "good time," which often included a full tour in Vietnam. However, he rarely progressed beyond the lowest ranks. He was arrested at least once by civilian police, and he frequently committed other minor infractions against military discipline. After going AWOL once or twice, he went home to stay, usually because of family problems. Two years later, he was arrested and given an undesirable discharge in lieu of court-martial. He entered the service at age eighteen, committed his first serious offense at nineteen, and was discharged at twenty-one. [1978:120]

"Family problems": The bulk of the incidence of administrative desertion was consciously motivated neither by ideological opposition to the Vietnam War nor by fear of the battlefield:

> Every official analysis of Vietnam-era deserters has found the same thing—that the overwhelming majority were neither conscientious nor cowardly. They were men who decided simply to put their own interests over the day-to-day needs of the military.
> Personal and family problems accounted for almost half of all absence offenses. For most enlisted men, military life was their first experience away from home. When their grandmothers died, their mothers fell ill, or their girl friends dropped them, they often wanted to go home as quickly as they could. Frequently, the problem was financial. The military pay scales were so low—starting at $115 per month—that married soldiers sometimes had to go home just to keep their families off welfare. [1978:116]

Yet the same "personal" or "family" motives were presumably also operative in previous wars waged by the United States in periods of social quiescence but not characterized by comparable rates of long-term absenteeism:

Pentagon officials claim . . . that the rate of Vietnam-era AWOLs was no higher than that of World War II or the Korean War. They claim that there was nothing unique or extraordinary about these offenses; only about 10 percent were motivated by opposition to the war, and the rest were no different from the AWOLs that the military has always experienced.

The statistics are correct, but they vastly understate the impact of Vietnam. Only the rate of short-term AWOL (less than thirty days) was comparable to that of earlier wars, and short-term AWOL almost always involved petty misbehavior that bore little relationship to the war. The statistics for long-term absence offenses tell a much different story. Absences of more than thirty days, administratively called "desertion," increased to an unprecedented level. In 1966, the Army and Marines reported about fifteen desertion cases per thousand troops. The rates climbed to more than fifty per thousand in 1969, and about seventy per thousand in 1972. By contrast, long-term absence rates during the Korean War were about twenty-five per thousand troops.

During the entire period of the Vietnam War, there were approximately 1,500,000 AWOL incidents and 500,000 desertion incidents. At the peak of the war, an American soldier was going AWOL every two minutes, and deserting every six minutes. This had an enormous impact on the ability of the armed forces to function. Absence offenses caused a total loss of roughly one million man-years of military service, almost half the total number of man-years American troops spent in Vietnam. The Senate Armed Services Committee estimated that in 1968 alone, well before AWOL and desertion reached their peak, absenteeism was costing the military the equivalent of ten combat divisions of fifteen thousand men each. While few of these young men were consciously voting against the war with their feet, their behavior was unmistakably connected with the unusual stress which they and the armed forces experienced during the Vietnam era. [1978:121-22]

Barring the theoretical possibility that the same cosmic "historical forces" that induced the United States to fight the war also generated the social movements that, simultaneously, impeded its ability to fight, it would appear likely that the same war (i.e., fought in the same place with the same methods under the same ideological representations by troops recruited from the same strata by the same draft) fought in a period of *social quiescence* would have yielded a pattern of military absenteeism closer to that of the Korean War than that which actually occurred (though not identical because of the impact upon morale of military conditions specific to Vietnam). It should then be in this light that one must interpret accounts of motives for desertion given by individuals at the time (or subsequently in exile, since exiles are insulated from the "post-movement adaptations" of consciousness that prevail in the domestic society; that is, they are ideologically—and perhaps, more broadly, psychically "mental museum pieces"). From this perspective, the account of a chain of incidents by a white working-class soldier that prompted his desertion for "personal" reasons, or an analogous account by a soldier of working-class Black origins of a similar train of incidents prompting similar action possibly in addition accompanied by the sudden illumination of "radicalization," should be understood as having made perfect subjective sense to such an individual at the time and in the context of a social movement period in which the threshold of insubordination is lowered. However, this may not be understood as strictly comparable to what might be required to precipitate the same action on the part of a socially similar individual during a period of social quiescence when the threshold of insubordination has once more risen to something like its former level.

3. Postmovement adaptation illusions. All social movements come to an end after a few years at most, giving way to periods of social quiescence; the fever pitch of emotional intensity and the physical dangers of social conflict—to say nothing of the more elemental problem of the regular acquisition of the means of subsistence—cannot be sustained by masses of people indefinitely. Movements that eventuate in social revolution are no exceptions to this, since weariness with social upheaval facilitates the consolidation of revolutionary regimes whose rise had been made possible by popular passion and spontaneity. In the more normal instances, which fall far short of social revolution, social life proceeds much as it had prior to the upheaval.

When a movement comes to an end, the reinterpretation of social reality—as it had been formulated by the dissidents and counterposed to the conventional interpretation at the height of the movement—becomes an incubus to most former movement participants. It has embodied visions of possibilities that could only have been actualized by social transformations that had not occurred, these visions now having become insupportably painful to people who must now return to conventional lives they had rejected. They resort to a number of options, ranging from total obliteration of their reinterpretation to efforts to preserve it in a state of unsullied purity:

a. RETREAT INTO PRIVATIZED CONCERNS. Some degree of reacceptance of the conventional interpretation of social reality as amended by consequence of the movement (especially in postrevolutionary periods) is almost inevitable; the other guys, after all, had won, and in emotional terms, *might* always makes a certain amount of *right*. (Especially poignant in postrevolutionary periods is the circumstance that some of "the other guys" were formerly "us.") The most common manifestation of this is sullen apathy in the public arena, i.e., a "realistic" acceptance of "what is," coupled with a narrowing of focus to domestic, intrapsychic, careerist, and suchlike preoccupations. Hence, following the restoration of the English monarchy in 1660, former revolutionaries ceased to believe in the possibility of objectifying Christ's kingdom in earthly society, transposing it to a wholly spiritual realm:

> "The rich will rule the world," sighed the well-to-do Richard Baxter philosophically; "and few rich men will be saints. . . . We shall have what we would, but not in this world." Not in this world: the words were often heard now. . . . After the restoration. . .Edward Burrough told Friends, "Our kingdom and victory is not of this world, nor earthly." [Hill, 1973:283]

b. DISSIPATION. This is the compulsive obliteration of social and political awareness. The succession of periods of intense social conflict by those in which political and social reaction is combined with a climate of cultural "permissiveness" are a recurrent social phenomenon: Thus the stern asceticism of the English or Puritan Revolution (1640–49) and the Commonwealth (1649–60) was followed by the indulgent escapism of the Restoration period whose tone was set by the "merry monarch," Charles II (1660–85).

Dissipation appeared in the aftermath of the youth movement of the 1960s, although in relation to a social movement in which disreputable appearance, untidy living, psychedelic drug use, and sexual openness were frequently credentials of participation, this statement may appear superficially incongruous. Yet the drug preferences of many turned to barbiturates, soporifics, tranquilizers, heroin, and alcohol, that is, drugs of "consciousness contraction." Sexual faddism flourished, divested of oppositional content.

c. ATTENUATED OPPOSITION. This is the shrinkage of the reinterpretation of social reality to the dimensions of vague notions of, for example, "change." In our example of the English Revolution, the ex-parliamentarian gentry thus became the prototypes of what subsequently—by the late 1670s—became the Whig party.

d. DISSOCIATION OF CONSCIOUSNESS AND BEHAVIOR. This adaptation is popular among privileged dissidents, whereby the conventional interpretation of social reality is accepted to the extent that the individual pursues a conventional career, especially in the professions, and settles down into a "normal life." Meanwhile, the reinterpretation of social reality is retained in a fossilized, petrified, "academic" form, and the individual may engage in "radical" activities of a routine, perfunctory, or faddish character.

e. REPENTANCE. This is the systematic and hyperconformist adoption of the perspective of one's former enemies, often accompanied by accusations of betrayal against those whom one now betrays. A classic case is that of the "professional anti-Communists" in the United States in the 1940s and 1950s, some of whom made lucrative careers out of exposing their ex-comrades of the 1930s.

f. ENCAPSULATION. For those who hold fast to the reinterpretation of social reality with all its visions of possibility and who reject "normal life" there remains this option, since an ongoing and developing social movement no longer exists; the material possibilities for social transformation are absent; and those capable of resisting the appeals of normal life are few. This may take the form, for example, of rusticated isolation or an "underground" existence possibly associated with terrorism. Alternatively, former dissidents may physically remove themselves from the scene of defeat or anticipated persecution and go into exile. In the latter case, exiled dissidents may reproduce arcane ideological divisions on foreign shores, even to the point of establishing entire communities under the guidance of dogmatic orthodoxies whose origins lay in protest against social conditions and associated ruling orthodoxies in other times and places.

We are all familiar with the story of the emigration to New England of the "Pilgrim Fathers" (1620) and the Puritans of Massachusetts Bay (1630), whose passage brackets the social movement in England in the 1620s, culminating in the Petition of Right (1629), which in a sense was the precursor of the English Revolution of the 1640s. Less well known is the emigration of Presbyterians to New Jersey following the restoration of the English monarchy in 1660.

The Presbyterians had been the most conservative (excepting of course, the ultraroyalist Roman Catholics) of all the sects opposed to the established church during the revolution. With the return of Charles II, they expected to "work within the system," as we would say, that is, obtain toleration of their creed in return for tolerating the king. The Cavalier Parliament (1661–67) was, however, packed with fanatical Anglicans who were determined to root out

Presbyterianism with stringent, repressive legislations: the Act of Uniformity (1661), the Test Act (1662), the Conventicles Act (1664), and the Five-Mile Act (1665). Consequently, in 1666, a shipload of Presbyterians left England and settled in New Jersey, naming their community Newark after the English town where the wicked King John had died 450 years before (1216), hence a possible code for "Death to tyrants!" Newark, New Jersey, remained a theocratic state under the "temporal rule" of the First Presbyterian Church until 1745.

g. CULTURAL INVERSION. This final adaptation consists of the readoption of the conventional interpretation of social reality in an unconventional setting while perhaps retaining elements of the social-movement reinterpretation in a fragmented or dissociated form. Such "cultural inversions" of reformist or radical impulses into repressive-reactionary caricatures of themselves are quite common in the wake of social conflict. Christopher Hill, for example, vividly describes the inversion of two cultural strains in the reinterpretation of social reality during the English Revolution of the 1640s, enthusiastic religion and rationalist skepticism as to the validity of received tradition, into reactionary superstition and elitist rationalism:

> Rude plebian soldiers had referred to their royal prisoner as "Stroker," "in relation to that gift which God had given him" of being able to cure the King's evil. Leveller journalists had mocked a story that Charles I's spittle had cured a sick child. But now plebian soldiers and Levellers were silenced. The tremendous ceremonial of the coronation was accompanied by a revival of "touching" on a grand scale. Charles II is alleged to have "touched" over ninety-two thousand persons during his reign, though I do not know who counted. On one occasion half a dozen of those hoping for a cure were trampled to death in the press.
> . . . There was a considerable literature denouncing "vulgar prophecies" among other suspect forms of enthusiasm. Thomas Sprat claimed it as the job of science and the Royal Society "to shake off the shadows and to scatter the mists which fill the minds of men with a vain consternation." Prodigies and prophecies could be self-validating by breaking men's courage and preparing them for disasters "which they fondly imagined were inevitably threatened them from heaven." This had been "one of the most considerable causes of those spiritual distractions of which our country has long been the theatre." The ending of belief in day-to-day divine intervention in politics helped to produce an atmosphere in which science could develop freely; elevation of the mechanical philosophy above the dialectical science of radical "enthusiasts" reciprocally helped to undermine such beliefs.
> "Fanaticism" and "enthusiasm" were the bugbears of polite and scholarly restoration society. The carefully cultivated classicism of the age of Dryden and Pope was (among other things) the literary form of this social reaction. For the radicals Latin and Greek had been the languages of Antichrist, as were the languages the universities, law, medicine, the three intellectual elites. [1973:353,355]

Similarly, the inverse relationship between antislavery and anti-Catholic sentiment in the antebellum era in the United States is pointed out by Ray Allen Billington (1964).

The aftermath of the progressive era offers another instance. Progressivism began as a liberal reform movement within the nonmonopoly bourgeoisie (i.e., the groups whose status and cultural dominance were immediately threatened by the rise of monopoly capital; cf. Richard Hofstadter, 1955). The progressive era, although a cultural unity, comprised two distinct social movements each—in conformity with the Law of Emergent Contradiction—culminating in a working-class movement: 1904–1907, possibly terminated by the Panic of 1907; and 1912–14, subsiding with the onset of the war boom. (The first period witnessed the initial prominence of the Socialist party and the IWW and the second their emergence as major working-class organizations; both were suppressed in 1917 for opposition to the entry of the United States into World War I.) Culturally and ideologically, bourgeois progressivism had been characterized by efforts toward the moral purification of government (drives against corruption; women's suffrage; technical modifications of the political process such as initiative, recall, referendum, and primary) and of business practices (antitrust legislation, regulation of child labor, consumer protection, creation of a central bank, conservation, etc.); contemporary historians now interpret the underlying dynamics of this reform at the federal level as the paradoxical consolidation of the grip of monopoly capital in the guise of regulation (cf. Kolko, 1963; and Weinstein, 1968). Simultaneously, the bourgeois progressives sought to extend to the immigrants the benefits of the dominant culture (by means of the diffusion of education, settlement houses and social work, and the beginnings of empirical sociology—among whose practitioners the Protestant clergy were heavily represented). With the end of World War I these themes emerged in the repressive-reactionary guises of Prohibitionism and nativism. Andrew Sinclair (1964) analyzed Prohibition as the pseudoreform that represented a distortion of the characteristic moral uplift purificatory thrust of progressivism. John Higham (1955) likewise chronicled the shift in emphasis from the paternalistic effort to "Americanize" the immigrants to racist and xenophobic measures to exclude them and to terrorize those already here along with racial minorities, as exemplified by the recrudescence of the KKK and its growth to 5 million members by 1925.

During the 1970s, such cultural themes of the youth movement of the 1960s, as consciousness exploration, voluntary poverty, "community," and generational revolt were inverted in some of the patriarchal or mock-bureaucratic "new religions" and some of the more authoritarian of the new psychotherapies such as Synanon, Scientology, and—to some extent—est, whereas New Leftism was inverted into neo-Leninism. The former dissident thus mimiced the social patterns in the wider society, above all in the last decade the reproduction of conventional authority relations in unconventional form, which he or she formerly rejected, while maintaining a posture of nonconflictual estrangement toward that society.

Now that the caveats have been issued and the problems of assessing the development of the reinterpretation of reality within the social movement—which are complex and manifold—we will turn our attention to the thought forms generated within the social movement.

The Thought Forms of Antistructure

The English theorist and social historian Sheila Rowbotham points out, in *Woman's Consciousness, Man's World*, that social categories victimized by the social structure are also victimized by the linguistic structure; they are handicapped in periods of social quiescence in articulating their own variant of the hegemonic ideology, since their use of their own idiomatic speech reproduces the mark of their inferior status. The "working class" is consequently "represented"—for the purpose of utilizing those narrow channels to which "politics" is ordinarily confined in bourgeois society—by persons of higher status than their own who are adept in the "standard" dialect to which "respectable" speech on "serious" matters is confined. The surrogates, also, are closer in their thought forms to those they ostensibly oppose than to those they supposedly represent, reflecting the differences in everyday-life practice between the classes. Any introductory textbook in sociolinguistics will in fact devote at least a chapter to illustrations of the general law whereby, in any stratified society, the speech of the higher strata is always defined as "better" or more "correct" than that of the lower.

Linguistic stigma only scratches the surface of the problem, since the "deep" linguistic structure, that is, the immanent cosmology at the core of society's mental life, is mapped in a complex and subtle fashion onto the social structure (see Chapter 3, "The Reproduction of Social Privilege"). Thus the terms "worker" and "working class" (though not quite as much as the obsolescent "hands" and the obsolete "mechanicks") denote both *intrinsic limitations* and *destiny*. Workers work. That is what, by nature, they do. That they also drink, swear, fornicate, and watch ball games is peripheral and comprehensible in that no better can be expected of persons properly consigned to that station. The mental life of bourgeois society thereby reproduced the mind-body dichotomy found in all class societies in the usual relations of relative prestige, with its characteristic twist: Those whose bodies were used—*employed*—by others in factories (or prostitution: High bourgeois civilization, c. 1914, was the golden age of prostitution) for pecuniary "compensation" (the latter usage positing as its presupposition that surplus value is *not* extracted) were *eo ipso* inferior to the bourgeoisie, who alternatively (1) symbolized status by their physical underdevelopment, e.g., women indoctrinated in the arts of frailty and fainting spells and men whose grotesque obesity by contemporary standards was not held against them even as candidates for the presidency of the United States (this tradition reaching its logical conclusion and termination in the person of William Howard Taft, 1909–13 whose predecessor, patron, and ultimate nemesis was an exemplar of the next alternative); or (2) did the same by spending lavishly on elite sports such as mountain climbing, sailing and yachting, horsy sports—fox hunting, polo, racing, etc.—subsuming horse breeding, training in fisticuffs ("the manly art of self-defense"), provided one did not enter the prize ring and reserved such skills for the proper occasions (e.g., defending milady's honor or smiting a socialist agitator), and sports requiring the expert handling of firearms and other weaponry, e.g., hunting, dueling, and war ("the sport of kings").

At that, "workers" in lands where the English tongue prevails are, linguistically speaking, comparatively lucky: "Work," like "toil" or "labor," is negatively loaded, but at least the same word is also used to denote a "high-culture" artifact (except in music, where the Latin singular equivalent, *opus*, is used unless the production is extroadinarily elaborate and takes the plural form *opera*). But French *ouvriers* or *travailleurs* do *travail* in producing *biens;* an *oeuvre* is something Louis Althusser may write on the subject. Likewise,

German proletarians do *Arbeit* within the *Werke*, albeit the latter word may adorn the cover of Marx's collected writings. They may, however, aspire to linguistic upward mobility by organizing a *Gewerkschaft* (trade union). In this respect the Russian *Rabochiy Klass* is in a most unenviable condition, as both *rabota* (n.f., work; obs., forced labor, from *rab*, slave; cognate to Czech *robot*, servile toil) and *trud* (n.m., toil) are so negatively loaded that neither can be confounded with the writer's *sochineniye*, the painter's *obraz*, or other *tvor'chestvo* (creation); but collectively their prospects are spectacular for they then become a *professional'niy soyuz* (trade union; *profsoyuz* for short). And this particular aspect of the classless society in Russia had already been achieved under tsarism!

Rowbotham was herself sensitized to the magnitude of the issue thanks to her early acquisition of a thick coating of Marxist theory employed in polemics among Trotskyist splinter groups during the early 1960s; as she tells it, this coating cracked apart under the impact of rock music, sex, and marijuana, whereby she arrived at the preliminary synthesis of subjectivist New Leftism; she then followed a common course of development to subjectivist feminism; and by the time of writing the aforementioned book, her first, had begun to reintegrate this with Marxist theory critiqued for patriarchal bias. Her case goes far beyond the still intractable generic third-person-pronoun problem to assert that patriarchal bias ensconced throughtout common speech systematically denies objective reality as encountered by women in everyday life, subsuming the same in patriarchal ideology represented as reality, such that everything identifiable as biologically female or culturally feminine is overcast with a patina of abnormality or inferiority.

The foregoing is by way of introducing the problem, that is, of empirically detecting and describing "the collective development of the thought forms of 'antistructure.' " As the ideological structure of the hegemonic ideology is reproduced first and foremost at the level of common speech, it is first and foremost at this level that the thought forms that posit as their presupposition the suspension by way of progressive repudiation of this hegemonic ideology must proceed: There are, first of all, "countercultures" of resistance, however unconscious; of explicit collective self-differentiation; and, obviously, of "deviance"—however this be defined by theorists in this area—or "marginality" in times of social quiescence. These each have a particular idiom, shop talk, jargon, argot, dialect (U.S. Blacks), or wholly distinctive language (European Jews); these may be supplemented in social-movement periods by wholly new subcultures, which either dissipate afterward or become encapsulated as subcultural enclaves having undergone a subtle vetting of the social-conflict dimension. Thus, whether the basis of movement solidarity is religious, ethnic-communal, formal-organizational, or exclusively cultural, a social-movement subculture is always associated with it: A preexisting subculture merely undergoes a "flowering" of its existing lingo, which is accelerated once the social category with which the subculture is associated undertakes innovative collective social-conflict action. Wholly new subcultures must collectively create a wholly new lingo, subsuming bits and pieces scrounged from the diverse origins of its members into a distinctive creative synthesis. Thus, for example, the white youth movement of the 1960s scavenged lingo from Black speech, sociological jargon, Marxist rhetoric, "folk" music, Black-based rock music,

Yiddish, and its own practice in some areas (sex, drugs, overt "politics") or vicarious admiration in others (motorcycles, guerrilla warfare). This list no doubt could be easily expanded.

Shades of meaning subtly or even drastically changed over the course of a few months or years (q.v. *relevant*). Semantics was not standardized from place to place or even person to person. New lingo succeeded the old, which thereupon became unfashionable, taboo, or even reversed in its loading (q.v. *masturbation*), requiring those aspiring to appear culturally "in" to sensitize themselves to fine changes in meaning, the introduction of new vocabulary, the discarding of "old" words due to overextension of their meanings (q.v. *freak out*, or more broadly to shifts in emphasis of the subculture as a whole (as from the *groovy*" ethic to the *together* ethic to the *mellow* ethic, which all took a maximum of three years, 1967–70).[3]

As antistructure is forcibly asserted by members of dissident collectivities, hierarchical barriers that normally separate them and call for ritualized forms of interaction are breached, allowing for this creative synthesis. One logical consequence of this breaching is that members of the more privileged sectors of the dissident subcultures begin defining their position in terms provided by members of less privileged social categories thus radicalizing their consciousness. For example, in the 1960s, hippies became the "new niggers" and students began defining themselves as "niggers" as evidenced by the popularity of Jerry Farber's book, *The Student as Nigger*, on college campuses. This intermingling of subcultures, the building (however tenuous) of solidarity between them, becomes the crucible for the fashioning of new forms of consciousness. E. P. Thompson (1966) demonstrated that the flowering of Luddism was preceded by the growth of "Societies of Correspondence" among workers of London and several places in the Midlands. The Correspondence Societies were the first working-class organizations by virtue of the fact that they broke away from the old patterns of guild organization and included workers from several types of labor (e.g., weavers, potters, stockingers, dyers, etc.). The Luddites were the first truly proletarian social movement, complete with demands that reverberated through the next 120 years of workers struggles, such as a legal minimum wage, protection for women and children, and the right to organize unions.

Along with the "democratization" of social relations among dissident collectivities comes the impulse to define society from the bottom up rather than from top down, as occurs during periods of social quiescence. There is the tendency to give primacy to "experience" over received interpretations of reality. That is, dissidents become less amenable to interpreting their experience in the social order in categories provided for in the hegemonic ideology; but instead prefer to reinterpret them in terms of the currently evolving counterreality. The reinterpretation, because of its temporal and transient nature, is capable of rapid shifts and is extremely sensitive to alterations in the conjuncture. One only has to look as far as the Iranian Revolution to note that within a few days the enemy of the Revolution changed from the shah to American imperialism, which consequently led to the sacking of the U.S. Embassy and the taking of hostages. Not only is the reinterpretation constructed out of the borrowings of the dissident subcultures and from "experience," which is the result of a new praxis and becomes nonnormal and subject to interpretation from different coordinates (e.g., theft becomes "liberation"), but is built from oppositions to the dominant ideology, as in the case of Black dissidents changing the color symbolism (black is good; white is evil).

The new praxis, whatever form it may take—and it does take new forms during social-movement periods—is fundamentally opposition to the set of social relations that pervade the social order. Thus, as dissidents struggle to alter those social relations, to which, prior to the social movement, most had acquiesced, the conception of reality is changed as a consequence of entry into the struggle. It is one thing to be a passive recipient of one's social subordination and quite another to struggle against it as part of a collectivity. Therefore, the "communitas" that is experienced by dissidents during social-movement periods provides a context in which not only new social realities can be constructed, but also offer a theraputic function in that it becomes a means whereby dissidents are able to retrieve aspects of human consciousness that were alienated from them as part of their socialization to positions of social subordination.

It has been observed that in periods of social quiescence members of subordinated social categories more or less accept their subordination, and problems of alienation and stratification are seen as "personal." During periods of social movement, they are reinterpreted as political. In the former is the internalization of the belief that institutions are objective and stand outside the individual. We might also see this process as reification—that is, that the social order seems suprahuman, having a life unto itself, and is relatively impervious to intervention by mere mortals ("The system runs itself"). During social-movement periods, a subjectivization of the social structure takes place, whereby the institutionalization is redefined as "interests." Structures are seen as serving the interest of certain sectors of society and working against the interests of others. Within the social-movement reinterpretations, then, we find the process of delegitimization.

Though many theorists of social movements claim that social movements must have an ideology, our point is that ideologies are not generally social-movement phenomena, but are reconstructed post hoc when the movement has exhausted its capacity for innovation. What social movements *do* produce, as they evolve, are visions of alternatives to conventional living, normal existence, or the quotidian, and changes in the locus of motivation of social-movement participants, which diffuse into the larger population. Sometimes these changes in motivation are so radical that we have referred to them as "sociocharacterological revolutions," since they portend the emergence of a new kind of human being, such as rise of the "rational calculator" as an important social type in the seventeenth century. Perhaps a more mundane example can be drawn from the populist movement in the United States in the 1880s and 90s, whereby dispossessed small landholders and tenant farmers banded together in the Farmer's Alliance in an attempt to battle credit merchants locally and the newly emerging corporate capitalism nationally. Says Goodwyn of the movement "culture":

> It encouraged individuals to have significant aspirations in their own lives, it generated a plan of purpose and a method of mass recruitment, it created its own symbols of politics and democracy in place of inherited hierarchical symbols, and it armed its participants against being intimidated by the corporate culture. The vision and hope embedded in the

cooperative crusade held the agrarian ranks together while these things took place and created the autonomous political outlook that was Populism. [1978:178]

Thus it was possible for people who had perhaps never been more than 20 miles from home in their life to participate in Alliance wagon trains and attend Alliance conventions hundreds of miles from their residence.

Another aspect of the reinterpretation of reality is what we will call—after Willis (1977)—penetrations. We have noted elsewhere that a social movement begins with a critique of the manifest appearances of social relations and, as it develops, engenders more penetrating critiques and proffers interpretations of society that include aspects that were formerly hidden, obfuscated, or unseen. Again, the populist movement is instructive. It had its origins in Lampasas, Texas, in 1877 and was concerned with freeing farmers from the crop-lien system that had reduced millions of independent farmers to the peonage of tenantry. They developed their own cooperatives, giving them leverage over the local credit merchants. By 1892, they had formed the People's party, attempted to forge an alliance with industrial workers, developed the concept of the "productive classes" on which solidarity could be built in a struggle against the eastern banking establishment. The banks had created the conditions for the tenant farmer's immiseration by making sure the government paid them the debts for the Civil War on the gold standard, creating a deflation that was disastrous to the producers of wealth. The Alliance sponsored a widespread educational program with lecturers fanning out all over the South and West. They were able to tie the miseries of local farmers to national policy and the social relations of capitalist exploitation.

Perhaps another example of penetrations can be gathered from the working-class insurgencies in early-nineteenth-century England. English workers' presses published a tract by the French Jacobin Volney, originally entitled *Ruins of Empire*. An excerpt was published in a cheap paperback edition, entitled *The Laws of Nature*, in which the following dialogue occurs [Thompson 1966:99]:

People: What labor do you perform in the society?
Privileged class: None: we are not made to labor.
People: How then have you acquired your wealth?
Privileged class: By taking the pains to govern you.
People: To govern us! . . . We toil, and you enjoy; we produce and you dissipate; wealth flows from us, and you absorb it. Privileged men, class distinct from the people, form a nation apart and govern yourselves.

Thompson also reported that the recruitment to Methodism tended to be most successful in the wake of political action (1966:389). As a matter of fact, Methodist chiliasm diffused with the greatest success among the working class when their situation was most desperate, such as during the Napoleanic wars. In 1819, a year of expanding worker insurgency leading to Peterloo, the Methodist Committee of Privileges issued a circular

. . . expressing "strong and decided disapprobation of certain tumultuous assemblies which have lately been witnessed in several parts of the country; in which large masses of people have been irregularly collected (often under banners bearing the most shocking and impious inscriptions) . . . calculated, both from the infidel principles, the wild and delusive political theories, and the violent and inflammatory declamations . . . to bring all government into contempt, and to introduce universal discontent, insubordination, and anarchy." [Thompson, 1966:353]

Here we are able to glimpse at the penetration process from both sides of the barricade, so to speak. As the working class forged its own identity through its struggles with the "privileged class"—in which the clergy was included— they were villified as crazy, deluded, "anarchists," and, of course, infidels and blasphemers. As mentioned above, conventional reality is enforced. The rampaging of a peaceably assembled crowd of men, women, and children by the defenders of the order at Peterloo, was, according to Thompson, class war, with the yeomanry on mounts doing the greatest damage. Peterloo effectively ended this period of working-class insurgency.

The thought forms of antistructure are, above all, a consciousness of kind. As we have seen from historical examples, they can take on such forms as religious doctrines as in the case of Thomas Munzer and the Anabaptists or the Heresy of the Free Spirit; class consciousness; ethnic and racial consciousness; feminine consciousness; and even youth consciousness. Within the stratification system of any given society, a consciousness of kind can develop among members of any given identifiable social category based on their common position in the social relations of domination. These thought forms are subversive of the given set of social relations in which they exist. From the outside, they are viewed as sinister and dangerous. Although the reinterpretation of social reality within the context of a social movement may be extremely difficult to assess, not only because of its volatility and ephemerality, but also because dissidents use terms from common parlance that are loaded with different meanings, it may be the single most important indicator of the existence of a social movement, since it provides the basis of, and continuity between actions. Additionally, the development of the consciousness of dissidents also provides the legitimations for intensification and innovation in the means of conflict.

Notes

1. The use of quotation marks—"intellectuals"—designates members of a publicly recognized and mutually defined (that is, an "intellectual" must be accepted by other "intellectuals" as included within this category, which should on no account be identified with more inclusive categories such as writers or academics) status group that stood at the summit of the cultural counterbourgeoisie in the socially quiescent state of bourgeois society. As noted in Chapter 3, the cultural counterbourgeoisie was systematically reproduced as a distinct formation until the 1960s. The *absence* of quotation marks— intellectuals—denotes persons addressing ideological statements to dissident audiences in social-movement contexts and accepted by them as ideological formulators.

2. Seymour M. Hersh, reporting in the *New York Times*, December 21, 1978, attributed the optimistic slant of intelligence out of Iran to the agents' fears of defying the pro-shah line of National Security Adviser Brzezinski, since the careers of at least two of them had been blighted by reports of their contacts with opposition politicians by SAVAK—the Iranian secret police—to Brzezinski over the heads of their superiors.

Nevertheless, according to the same logic, one must assume that at some point the careerist motive would work in the opposite direction, that is, the operatives who failed to correctly assess what was happening under their noses would not be assured of the most brilliant prospects either.

3. A lexicon of terminology has been published by the authors in Sayres, et al., *The 60s Without Apology*, which may give some insight into the thought forms that pervaded the social movements of the 1960s in the United States. The authors' names were inadvertently reversed by the editors. Our names should be listed in alphabetical order in all our collaborative works.

Chapter 6

Disalienation

If I were a carpenter
And you were a Lady
Would you marry me anyway
Would you have my baby?

—Tim Hardin (1966)

Some are mathematicians
Others are carpenters' wives
I don't know where they're all at now
Or what they're doing with their lives.

—Bob Dylan (1976)

As we have attempted to demonstrate, one of the inevitable consequences of exploitation and domination is the alienation of individual capacity. Within the hegemonic ideology, it is self-evident that those at the top of society are in some way inherently superior to those below. That is, they present themselves to the lower social orders as superior by virtue of the intervention of the alienated supernatural into human affairs, such as the Brahmin caste in India characterizing itself as in a second incarnation as human beings, distinguishing themselves from "firstborn" castes by their superior level of consciousness, ritual purity, and material circumstances; alternatively, dominators can idealize themselves as superior by achievement (which may also be characterized as evidence of being God's chosen or possessing superior intellect) as the bourgeoisie has presented itself; or, most recently, as resources seem increasingly scarce, elites legitimate their domination by virtue of their access to scarce institutional resources, such as a high-quality education, information, life-enriching privileges such as trips abroad or increased leisure time, and so forth. It is this very alienation of personal capacity that, given the *appearances* of the social order, serve as prima facie evidence of the innate or structured inferiority of those of the lower social strata. In periods of social movement, dissidents attempt to reappropriate those capacities alienated from themselves as a consequence of their position in the social order. In this chapter, we will examine this process.

Learning as an Alienated Capacity

The forcible assertion of antistructure necessarily implies interference with the political reproduction of society. It therefore makes problematical the role of the polity and prevailing authority relations ultimately guaranteed by the polity in confining the self-interference of cultural reproduction to that level. In the absence of antistructure, advocacy in principle of "the unity of theory and practice" predictably has the impact of the Boy Scout oath; whereas, in the presence of antistructure its advocacy is superfluous. In the late 1960s, dissidents in the various social-movement collectivities of the time were setting about assimilating complex abstract ideas—most often, it is true, not even to the extent designated by the expression "half-baked"—in the spheres of politics, Oriental philosophy, psychology, Marxist theory, poetry, and anthropology *without* the rewards proffered by bourgeois social relations in the guise of the (ultimate) prospect for enhanced material wealth or status. Curiously, the same people might simultaneously resist the inculcation of the same ideas and subject matter in the context of bourgeois social relations as, say, by a teacher standing in front of a class, lecturing for fifty minutes, giving midterms and finals, and dispensing grades. Though an acceptable compromise might involve the same teacher adopting informal attire, bidding everyone to sit in a circle on the floor, yielding to the "group process," and promising everyone a grade of A in advance (unless the school had gone over to a gradeless system).

The relativistic attitude of the students of the late 1960s, whereby the validity of any abstract idea was inseparable from the context of social relations wherein it was presented, is an example of what we have earlier called disalienation. To elucidate slightly: When a human capacity, such as the capacity to learn, has been developed as part of the totality of the development of the human subject in history in such a way that it is represented to its bearers as having been appropriated—*ripped-off*, so to speak—by an external agency, which in turn brandishes it against its bearers as a hostile potency or weapon, as in the implicit assumption underlying the whole of the educational industry to the effect that, "you cannot learn except under circumstances wherein we teach," this was to Marx (1964) and is to us "alienation" (cf. Chapter 3, "The Reproduction of Social Privilege"). Alienation everywhere and at all times has the effect of demonstrating the inferiority of some and the superiority of others, not least to the satisfaction of those whose destiny it is to be accepted in due course into the midst of those understood as "superior." The capacity to learn by exploring the environment and the capacity to "think" are biologically determined (or "hard-wired," as the sociobiologists say), and it is just as natural for "consciousness" to become more complex as it is for striated muscle tissue to get thicker. However, it is not to "nature" or biology but to history that we owe the specific extent of the development of the capacity to learn possible for an individual in a particular social order. History determines as well the forms and constraints under which that development proceeds.

Alienation is invariably found in conjunction with false consciousness, with false consciousness positing alienation's nonexistence: One goes to school to be educated. This is not to say that utter passivity is enjoined; but rather that the education industry rewards you to the extent that your ambition, initiative, curiosity, and "creativity" motivate you in the direction in which it would otherwise push you. Those who proceed thusly are smart, intelligent, bright; those who cannot even be pushed are stupid. The categories "smart" and "stupid" are accepted in bourgeois society as self-evidently real, and not least by privileged (that is, educated) persons who have no idea what illiterate garage mechanics are doing to their cars and could not possibly figure it out. "Intelligence," as measured quantitatively, boils down to something called "cognitive skills," which in turn are those mental capacities that, all other things being equal, should result in high achievement in school, the latter by universal agreement the sole satisfactory legitimation of entry into privileged status groups below the level of the bourgeoisie and increasingly into the bourgeoisie itself by way of the increasingly fashionable masters in business administration degree. The precise relationship between the "skills" allegedly imparted by "the educational process" to the concrete practice of the privileged groups in question is never spelled out, nor is it even closely scrutinized. And this is not all: As it is increasingly accepted among psychologists that "cognitive skills" are lateralized in the left cerebral hemisphere, one wonders whether a definition of "intelligence" could be constructed around functions lateralized in the right hemisphere (in that it has been determined by the research done by TenHouten [1971] and others that certain victimized social categories, including Native Americans and Blacks, display a lesser degree of left-hemisphere dominance than that found among affluent male whites); this would go beyond the question of "cultural bias" in testing, which normally involves nothing more than testing the same left-hemisphere-lateralized functions measured by the "standard" instruments only in subcultural argot. Beyond that, one asks whether it is no more than sheer ideology that "intelligence" be identified as a property of discrete individuals competing against other discrete individuals for status places whose relative importance is normally comparable in quantifiable, that is, pecuniary terms. May we not, perhaps, posit a dialectical relationship between collective and individual learning? In this way "intelligence" would be associated with collective and cooperative practice in which mutual teaching occurs; individual learning and practice would here constitute the basis of personal contributions to mutual education.

This is not merely utopian; it is impossible, as it presupposes a situation in which what is to be learned is determined by collective and individual practice built upon what has been previously learned, which was itself freely chosen in a similar fashion, and so on. It posits as its presupposition, in other words, the suspension of the social structure such that the content as well as the proper forms, e.g., "methodology," of "knowledge" and the system of credentialing it are not dictated by the exigency of a structure of a particular kind to impose a determinate "reality" upon society as a whole. Insofar as there is a human need for structure, there is a corresponding readiness to accept the imposition of a "reality" that must be taken seriously.

Antistructure and Disalienation

But there is also—as we have posited following Turner (1966)—a human need for antistructure, though necessarily for relatively short periods (at least until such a time as production of the basic necessities is carried on by automated machinery while a prolonged vacation from social order is called). In the context of antistructure our little fantasy of disalienated learning can and has taken place. Consider, for example, one of the famous French student graffiti of 1968: "There is neither smart nor stupid. There is only free and unfree." This is about as concise a demystification of the ideology of individual intelligence as one can hope to find. There were also indications in the United States in the same period that collective mutual education could (that is, normally did not but still *could)* be vastly more efficacious in imparting social-science-type information and modes of reasoning. However, such mutual education was for the purpose of fostering the collective forcible assertion of antistructure rather than upholding the structure of bourgeois social relations. There was no reason to doubt a student in those days who, having spent a fairly brief period participating in an intense investigation by a "collective" of the workings of the Selective Service System, the bureaucratic vested interests served by it, and its relation to class, status, and ethnic stratification in society as a whole; or in tracing organizational and personal connections between university officials, trustees, and certain senior faculty to local, national, and international "power structures" announced: "I learned more in six weeks of doing this than in four years of college."

As the degree of disalienation varies in accordance with the intensity of a social movement as a whole, and as vestiges of antecedent social relations are not fully liquidated by even the most thoroughgoing of social transformations, it is hardly surprising that most students, to the extent that they approved of the slackening of the bureaucratic rigor of the "educational process" in the late 1960s, did not educate themselves in any sense, individually or collectively, except in that they further immersed themselves in the more hedonistic aspects of the "youth" culture. Sectoral ideologies asserting the self-evident inevitablility of the alienation of particular human capacities—all subsumed under the overarching hegemonic ideology positing as its presupposition the indubitable necessity for alienation-in-general—are so thoroughly inculcated in the practice of everyday life that they are *assumed,* taken for granted, and not even worth mentioning. If ever overtly stated, it is as commonplace truisms: Without the church you cannot be religious. Without the fear of hunger you will never work. You will cease working if we do not watch you. Only labor power expended in exchange for money is work; otherwise it is a hobby or housework. Without grades you will not study. Without the display of armed force on the streets there will be chaos. Without the state you will not be safe. The army makes a man of you. An unmarried woman is nothing. (This is a free country but) you can't fight City Hall. A fair day's work for a fair day's pay. Anyone who wants to work can get a job. The price of liberty is eternal vigilance.

The lessons inculcated thusly, that is, that whatever is not managed, watched, disciplined, or guarded by force of arms is dangerous; that society consists of selfish, isolated individuals who cannot be trusted; that nonhierarchical cooperative or collective activity for purposes other than getting drunk and meeting potential sex partners is a priori impossible; that invidious distinctions are eternal ("It's still the same old story/The fight for love and glory/On that you can rely/As time goes by"); that those who are not in it for the money are fools or insane; that one cannot do anything about anything except strive for upward mobility; that the human animal is fundamentally wicked, with the questionable exception of oneself; that one's hierarchical superiors *must* know what they are doing since one perforce relies upon them for what little security and sustenance there is. All these were implicit in bourgeois culture and the bourgeois hegemonic ideology and were self-fulfilling prophecies. People did steal, cheat, and fornicate when the back of Authority was turned, though by the standards prevailing since the assault upon bourgeois culture "from below" in the 1960s and "from above" in the 1970s it is remarkable how little they did so. Logically implicit was the positing of a person who, insofar as he or she was a rational calculator, played it safe and took no risks except in habitual gambling dictated by get-rich-quick fantasies and self-destructive tendencies; this person yet represented a formidable human advance over the dependent peasantries of earlier class societies. Upon the reproduction of the human being as here depicted rested the entire edifice of high bourgeois civilization and subsequent developments in the core of bourgeois society through the 1950s: This person produced with his or her life energies the surplus value by which capital was accumulated, the means of violence kept up, and the standards of decorum of the wealthy maintained. This was for Marx (1964) the most fundamental and essential alienation: The proletarian shrank as a human being *in the very act* of producing the aggrandizement of the bourgeois as the representation, the embodiment, the personification of the generalized development of human capacities and the highest level hitherto reached in the emergence of the human subject in history. To this was added further payment for the upkeep of organized religion, the entertainment industries, and other vehicles of bourgeois ideology wherewith the proletarian was comforted with the thought that life was yet "worth it," which, in objective reality quantified in pecuniary terms, it was not.

Marx (1973) foresaw that the emergence of new human capacities, which bourgeois society relentlessly fostered, was to be associated with the marketing of particular commodities or particular skills until a stage of "universal prostitution" was reached and no further human capacities could be developed without subverting bourgeois society as a whole. Then somebody—his guess that it would be the proletariat was wishful thinking—would reappropriate everything that had been sold out and thereby reconstitute the human being as a whole and on a higher level. The only sign of the imminence of such times is the fact that the concept of *together* (see Chapter 5, "The Reinterpretation of Social Reality") was developed by people who had not read Marx (who was not to become popular again until a few years later). But more of this later.

Disalienation is always partial in that one reproduces alienation in the very process of disalienation. For instance, one may engage in the process of disalienation by acting collectively for the elimination of that guise of alienation represented by exploitation. But in doing so one delegates one's capacity to reason and analyze on the level of collective action to a leadership that, however well founded its pretentions to scientific knowledge, has still appropriated this capacity unto itself and cannot be expected to shrink from wielding it as a weapon to perpetuate its dominion over the "rank and file." Along the same lines, if one rebels collectively against the appropriation of one's sexual capacities by prudish Authority, which has brandished them against one as sin, guilt, fear, taboo, and superstitious ignorance, one, in the process, submits to the verdict of socially determined invidious comparisons as to how "good" one's sexual practice is in terms of "experience," performance, frequency and variety of sexual acts, desirability and quantity of one's partners, and so forth. This might be regarded as tantamount to sanctioning the reappropriation of the same capacities by Authority concealed as a sexual marketplace in whose hands one's sexual capacities once more are manifested as an alien power: this time, by inducing feelings of inferiority; and this new and "higher" alienation is suitably disguised by the traditional bougeois marketplace conundrums of "free will" and "free choice."

We will conclude the discussion of this point by asserting that, generally speaking, only in the context of ongoing social movements, that is, presupposing the forcible assertion of antistructure, does disalienation of human capacities outpace the realienation of the same capacities or the more intensified alienation of other capacities.

Consequences of Disalienation: Mobility and Psychic Healing

The two most conspicuous effects of disalienation, most marked in times of thoroughgoing social transformation, are (1) upward mobility or otherwise-enhanced occupational diversity for a certain minority of dissidents, usually those still fairly young; and (2) psychic healing whose effects may resemble the idealized objectives of psychotherapy.

It should not really be surprising that social movements entailing the collective dissidence of exploited classes should as a rule draw their identifiable leadership from the ranks of the exploiting classes or from occupational and status groups dependent on or associated with the exploiting classes. In rarer cases this leadership may derive from the more privileged strata of the exploited classes; but hardly ever does it derive from the most depressed strata until that point in the development of the movement at which, in accordance with the Law of Emergent Contradiction, society has been stirred to its very depths. Initially, though, it might be anticipated at least statistically that the alienation of capacities to articulate, inspire, lead, organize, plan, negotiate, learn from history (usually but not necessarily implying literacy), establish a favorable image for the movement in the minds of diplomats, journalists, or domestic liberals, command on the battlefield, or generally speaking capacities that may be appropriate to visible leadership in the particular context would be least in the higher strata normally accustomed to command, manage, and be served. Such alienation would be greatest in the lower strata, normally accustomed to groveling servility to their "betters," however much the latter might permit them to brutalize each other (which constitutes additional prima facie evidence of their inferiority). It is in keeping with this that either dissidence commences in the higher strata, which subsequently passes into counterdissidence with the insurgency of the lower; or renegades from the higher strata attempt to instigate dissidence in the lower, sometimes with catastrophic results (as in the instance of the Russian Narodniki of the 1870s, whose initial strategy was to "go to the peasants" but were turned in by those they proposed to liberate); or, alternatively, to present themselves as candidates for leadership at the sign of incipient dissidence stirring in the lower depths (e.g., some of the organizers of the CIO in the 1930s, in particular those who were Communists, derived from strata privileged with respect to the working class—though hardly wealthy—and either volunteered their services as organizers or were trained for the purpose by the Communist party and "went into industry"). The latter, for their part, may initially prefer leaders with "class" or at least a presentable modicum of respectability for much the same reasons; once the enemy's aura of incomprehensible political magic and seeming invulnerability has worn through, the issue of the plebian birth or styles of the leadership may diminish.

With the advance of social transformation, large portions of the former exploiting class and high state officials die, go into exile, or undergo an enforced diminution of status; with the exception of those posts requiring elaborate technical-scientific training, their places are rather more easily taken by the lowborn than outside observers such as foreign journalists and social scientists anticipate. It is thus far easier to recruit a military officer than an engineer insofar as the most crucial part of the training of the former is of the on-the-job variety; the same holds for civil state or party officials wherein their posts do not require lengthy training in the use of sophisticated technical equipment. If relative deprivation and resource mobilization theorists posit that frustrated ambition promotes the impulse to revolutionary social transformation, it might well be posited with at least equal plausibility that the revolution *awakens* ambition in those for whom it would have only a few months ago been inconceivable and would moreover have elicited—had it been manifested anyway—the chiding of peers for presumptuousness. This may be the case in that the revolution promotes disalienation not least among those sufficiently young, adventurous, and insubordinate that they have not yet accommodated themselves to a lifetime in the lowly station of their ancestors. For similar reasons, others who might have succumbed except for the revolution to lives of cretinizing toil become cultural creators under the new order.

The practice of extensive and deliberate downward mobility for the purpose of disalienating capacities in the spheres of manual dexterity, physical strength, grace of movement, and so forth, as transpired among white youth in the 1960s, is far less common and is anyway readily reversible for most who try it following the end of the movement. In the 1970s, the disalienation of such alienated capacities became possible in the alienated form of the physical-fitness industry.

The effects of social movements resembling those touted for so-called psychotherapy have been widely noted by participants at the time and afterward; intrapsychic disalienation may perhaps be credited as the underlying reality making possible the developments we have alluded to as the Law of Emergent Contradiction. It also represents the sort of "color" more likely to be preserved in folk song, oratory, and post-facto musings of the sort collected by Gornick (1977) in her study of American Communists who participated in the labor movement of the 1930s than in the documentary sources consulted by historians or in social statistics compiled by sociologists and political scientists. There is, for example, a Russian folk song called "Dubinushka" (My Oaken Club) in which a worker sings a hymn to this weapon, which, one assumes, he once used in street fighting: "The day came and the people arose,/They straightened out the crooked spines of centuries." More exaltedly, the following aphorism was attributed to the late Mao Zedong by the Chinese People's Army newspaper *Hung Ji* by way of somewhat tortuously establishing scriptural justification for the silencing of critics of the Chinese invasion of Vietnam in February-March 1979: "Revolutionary war is an anti-toxin which not only eliminates the enemy's poison but also purges us of our own filth" (*Economist*, March 13, 1979).

The psychotherapeutic literature, whether psychiatric (Kardiner and Ovesey, 1951; Grier and Cobbs, 1968; Sachs, 1947) or Freudian-sociological (Mannoni, 1964; Dollard, 1957), had either diagnosed "powerlessness" as a mental disease or attributed to powerlessness assorted mental problems such as identification with the agressor, internalized self-hatred, crippled ego, impared identity, and similar diagnoses along those lines. These works, with the exception of Grier and Cobbs, antedate the 1960s; their focus was as a rule upon racially defined victim categories, especially U.S. Blacks, black Africans, or other colonials (e.g., Tunisian Arabs in another work by Mannoni, who, as a native Tunisian Jew, asserted his objectivity as between French and Arabs). With the fragmentary and qualified exception of Wilhelm Reich (cf. the essays in *Sex-Pol*, 1971), who was a far better sociologist than mind healer, influenced as he was by the Frankfurt School perspective on the impact of domination in everyday-life practice upon working-class folk ideology. There was no effort at the therapy of a victim category defined by class and the exploitative relation. In the late 1960s, the analysis of the diseases of "powerlessness" was resurrected by the feminists; explicit analogies between racism and sexism ensued. During the 1960s, a minor intellectual upheaval was precipitated by the dissemination of the works of Frantz Fanon (*Studies in a Dying Colonialism, Black Skin, White Masks, The Wretched of the Earth*). A black man born on Martinique, Fanon became a psychiatrist and was employed in the French colonial administration in Algeria, where he diagnosed diseases attributable to despotic power among the French as well as those attributable to the condition of objects of despotic power among the Arabs. In the last work listed, Fanon—who died in 1961 in the service of the FLN (Front Liberation Nationale) guerrillas—expounded a psycho sociology in the context of revolutionary war: As the Arabs had become mentally disabled by dint of subjection to the despotic violence of the French, they were now engaging in collective mass therapy by employing retaliatory violence to overthrow the colonial regime. The impact of this book included, among other things, the practice of *Fanonization* within the youth movement of the 1960s, which denoted the self-purgation of fears of intimidation by engaging in provocations of members of victimizing social categories.

The difficulty with the Freudian model, as with all variants of the theory of the unconscious derived from it, lay in its positing of a static ahistorical model of the psyche; by contrast, the Marxist model posited a psyche perpetually evolving in history and susceptible to sudden leaps in the complexity and sophistication of consciousness whereby the individual qua participant in a social-conflict collectivity might rapidly be qualitatively transformed.

Heroically futile efforts were made to fuse the Freudian model (and derivatives thereof) with the Marxist. Wilhelm Reich, in the early 1930s, suggested that the "reality principle" was—like the Marxian concept of subsistence—

historically relative; this idea was, however, not developed. There remained the question of the contradiction between an *unconscious* fixed in childhood and *consciousness* existing in dialectical relation to practice. (It is to be conceded that there was a dialectical kernel in Freud never appreciated by the Freudians et al., for whom the unconscious tended to be a species of passive receptacle by day with the capability of going bump in the night.)

The various subjectivist ideologies of the 1960s were more prone to the Freudian than to the Marxian side, that is, if anyone could be induced to read a book without fear of left-McLuhanoid charges of literacy in the postliterate epoch. There was accordingly in each dissident subculture posited an idealized, eternal *true authentic real self*, which the establishment, as variously perceived by Blacks, "freak" radicals, women, and so on, hid, stole, and concealed from "us." To find out who "us" were as opposed to "them" it was necessary to disinter this self and rummage around in it.

By the late 1960s the perfection of the self or the removal of impurities therefrom was the sole objective common to all tendencies within the movement subculture, however much they may have favored cultural radicalism, incipient neo-Leninism, feminism (not quite fully differentiated), overt political conflict without theory, or sheer self-absorption as their top priority. There was no political tract not autobiographical and no argument not ad hominem (or ad feminam); purity of motive had to be established before the merits of one's argument could be taken up. Ideally, the movement participant was "together," this connoting the alleged true self consolidated in a posture of revolt. This posture was sustained by many until 1970–71 when they "mellowed out."

New Humans

The most intense social movements and in particular those that eventuate through social transformations, which by convention are known as Great Revolutions,[1] invariably are associated with the confident assertion that in the light of history the revolution will ultimately be judged on the basis of a wholly new type of human being, collectively created in the context of antistructure, which it is bringing into existence: the Puritan saint, the French citizen of republican virtue, the new socialist man of the Russian Revolution, and more recent Chinese and Cuban claims to promote the creation of a more advanced socialist or communist humanity. In all such instances it has been maintained that the more highly evolved human type advances inextricably and simultaneously the welfare of the collectivity and the individual. This more highly evolved being is the collective idealized expression of disalienation and the "therapylike" intrapsychic effects of social-movement participation. Few are capable of exemplifying it or otherwise living up to it, for they have been molded, crippled, or contaminated by the psychic warpage induced by the old order, now understood from the radical-relativist and environmental-determinist perspective, as a Great Child Crippler. But surely one's children, enrolled in the Young Pioneers or reared on all things natural and organic or sent to Black Consciousness Academy, will attain heights that one cannot oneself contemplate or that perhaps resemble those spelled out by Trotsky: Genius on the order of that of Goethe or Shakespeare would be commonplace, "with further peaks

envisioned beyond that." He took it for granted that the Russians would abandon
vestiges of tsarist barbarism such as drinking or cursing.

The revolutionary ideal of the new human being, like disalienation and social-
movement "therapy," ultimately fades out, for most of the former participants,
in that the collective development of the human subject in the context of
antistructure transcends the limits of what may be sustained upon the reimposition of "structure." Whether the upheaval has eventuated in social transformation, a change of political regime, mild concessions, or even nothing at
all, the reimposition of structure is ultimately dictated by the need to ensure
the continuity of the material reproduction of society to first of all guarantee
the level of biological reproduction. Otherwise there would be mass privation
by hunger, cold, disease, and so forth. This in turn dictates the production
and continuity of the levels of political and cultural reproduction, whereby the
animals are herded back into their cages—freshly painted ones, perhaps, but
cages nevertheless—where they are coerced into "getting things done" while
care is taken that these things make a modicum of sense to them while they
are getting them done. On the side of the participants there is the sheer
impossibility of living for prolonged periods in a state of nervous exhaustion
possibly accompanied by extreme material privation and the perpetual threat
of death in civil war. There comes a time to take it easy, relax, enjoy the fruits
of the revolution or otherwise make one's peace, "cop out," "sell out," or
"mellow out." The routine carrying on of everyday life has returned. Also, let
us recall that Turner (1966) posited an innate or immanent human need for
antistructure by way of complementing the structuralists' positing of a need for
structure, that is, that the animal has a need for herd formations of determinate
patterns or organization.

When structure is reimposed or reconsolidated, the human subject accordingly shrinks back into the limits dictated by the fact that, given the developments on the level of material reproduction that determine the relative
magnitudes of appropriated, redistributed, and collectively consumed surplus,
the development of certain human capacities is possible only in the context of
exploitation (the cultivated refinement of those who do the civilization as opposed to the labor), cultural alienation (e.g., that art is that which is hung in
museums and galleries, which are environments that only the wealthy feel
comfortable in, and it is certainly not to be confused with what is painted on
the exteriors of subway cars; or that music is what the wealthy pay to listen to
and is not to be confused with what members of racial minorities play at
deafening volume in the subway on enormous portable radios and in violation
of the law), and domination (statecraft, generalship, and the managerial arts).
In our lighter moments we have used the expression "the Law of the Destruction
of Surplus Consciousness" to denote the post movement consequences upon
both individual lives and the cultural ambience of the reconsolidation of structure.

In Gornick (1977), there is an oral history taken from an individual pseu-
donymized as "Ben Seligman." The latter is now retired from employment by
reason of advanced age, though still an enthusiastic Communist. As a youth
he had been reluctantly thrust into the trade of a garment cutter. He was a
classic Jewish *schlemiel* type, and for his weakness was singled out for extra
exploitation by his employer, who denied him normal wage increases. "Selig-

man" joined the Communist party in 1935 and by his own account was transformed into a veritable tiger of a class-conscious organizer and militant. Even
during the less intense labor movement of 1946–48 he was capable of heights
of exaltation: "We were thousands! We could have had the whole country!"
But at the time of Gornick's interview he is once more the *schlemiel*, shuffling
off dejectedly and haplessly to the picket line. Thus, also in the wake of the
youth movement of the 1960s, many former participants ultimately found themselves in occupations and careers not unlike those that would have been their
lot anyway. ("Some are mathematicians.") We are reminded of one individual
who, when we met him in 1970, was an archetypal "freak"-radical of the period.
In the early 1970s he studied radical history at the City College of New York
while immersing himself in New York left circles. He took an interest in the
"oral history" method, which in turn led him to radical anthropology and South
America. Five years after that—early August 1979—we met him in Central
Park. He was entering his second year of law school, which meant that he was
following in his father's footsteps. "Ten years ago, could you have imagined
that this would happen?" "No," he answered sheepishly. But there were others
whose lives were and remain permanently changed and who have either been
sustained by inner conviction and fortitude despite endless psychic pain and
soul searching or have been involuntarily fixed in their changed condition by
reason of having "dropped out" so far that they can no longer drop back in.
("Some are carpenters' wives.")

Soviet society, having abandoned the ideal of the new socialist man along
with the ideal of a noncoercive state operated by the mass participation of the
"broad masses" directly in the work of the Soviet organs, has reproduced a
state apparatus that in its crude, authoritarian centralism is much in the tradition
of tsarism, as well as a stifling cultural atmosphere reminiscent of the Old
Regime; this allows, of course, for the modernization of appearances, e.g., in
that Soviet policemen do not carry whips. The regime and the surplus-absorbing
strata who comprise its principal beneficiaries presuppose for their existence
a passive and alcoholic working class whose indulgence in the latter vestige
of barbarism would exceed even the worst fears of so harsh a critic of 1930s
Soviet society as Trotsky were he alive to see it. The Soviets regard efforts of
Cubans to create a new human being emancipated from the need for "material
incentives" (this is by now pretty much in abeyance) with a mixture of amuse-
ment at such adolescent romanticism and a touch of nostalgia: Richard Barnet,
in *The Giants*, recounts the story of a Soviet diplomat who, informed that the
Cubans were voluntarily organizing unpaid clean-up brigades, was said to have
sadly remarked, "It was the same here years ago." The same sort of doings on
the part of the Chinese have if anything aroused fear and loathing in the Soviets.

The withering of the new human ideal in a social movement is always most
bitter among those who had been intellectuals once preoccupied with articulating this very ideal. The cultural movement following the Revolution of 1905
among the youth of the intelligentsia known as Saninism (cf. Bertram Wolfe,
1964), whose principal features involved preoccupations—often simultaneous—with eroticism and suicide, for which reason we have characterized it in
terms of postmovement adaptation No. 2, "Dissipation," was rather precisely
reproduced following the spectacular suicide in 1925 of the poet Sergei Esenin
(best known in the United States as the movie lover of Isadora Duncan in

Isadora) whose amorous and alcoholic proclivities were as well-known to the Soviet public as his poetry. There ensued the cultural movement among the younger intelligentsia called the Eseninshchina, which involved a wave of suicides and a preoccupation with the erotic remarkably evocative of Saninism.[2] The culmination of the Eseninshchina was a succession of scandals involving members and even executives of the Communist Youth League (Komsomol), who were found to have been flagrantly involved in spectacular "sexual debauchery," usually drunken orgies. At their 1926 convention, the Komsomol were scolded by one of the luminaries of Soviet literary criticism:

> Polonsky, Editor of *Novy Mir*, to Komsomol Congress, 1926: There is little respect for man because there is little respect for oneself. There is no will-power, no desire to create a good strong type of new man; . . . even the Komsomol does not breed the kind of man who could serve as a model. In our time, when it is said that the quality of shoes, galoshes and other manufactured goods must be improved, *we must first of all improve the quality of socialist man.* [Carr, 1976:179]

Conclusion

As dissidents engage in conflict with their dominators, the experience of the conflict alters their conscious awareness of the nature of the social order and the social meanings within it. This we have referred to as the reinterpretation of social reality. As social reality is reinterpreted, new implications for personal identity are realized as members of dissident collectivities *self-consciously act* in their collective interests. The mere fact that one acts rather than passively accepts one's life situation is bound to have purgative effects on the individual's identity. As identity cannot be separated from social structure (Berger and Luckman, 1966, called it "objectivation") when society evidences the appearance of the forcible assertion of antistructure, the identities of those involved in the struggle are necessarily changed as they are now members of self-acting collectivities. It is in this sense that the limits of human consciousness are the products of history.

Within dissident collectivities, the reinterpretation of social reality and the process of disalienation form a totalization, in that it becomes impossible for one to occur without the presence of the other. They fuse into a dialectical synthesis, with each positing the other as its presupposition. That is, the reinterpretation of social reality cannot occur without having implications for the position an individual occupies within a set of social relations; especially when they are presently under attack by oneself and others, including other dissident collectivities. Moreover, it would be impossible for one to learn new understandings of onself without it having consequences for the understanding of the social relations in which one was engaged—especially if those relations were undergoing transformation.

As we have pointed out, social movement collectivities necessarily undergo processes of collegialization. They also tend to manifest a "cascadation" process, whereby dissidence penetrates downward in the social order. The consequences of these processes are twofold: upward mobility for the more talented of the lower orders and the healing of psychic maladies, such as the lack of self-esteem, which were the consequence of membership in dominated social categories. As social movement members participate in unalienated learning, engage in self-governance, and struggle against their subjugation, they participate in mass therapy, helping each other overcome the crippling effects of their socialization to positions of subordination within the social order. This very process liberates new human potentialities, which, in the following period of social quiescence, are alienated from their possessors and incorporated into new forms of alienation at a higher level of contradiction. Within social movement periods, however, capacities are disalienated faster than they are realienated.

As new human capacities are liberated, images of "new humans" are proffered within dissident collectivities. These images are the idealization of the aspirations of the members of dissident collectivities: more intelligent, egalitarian, humanized, aware, and sensitive than the enemy and even themselves. As the movement fades into the past and the possibility of the achievement of these new capacities in their unalienated form declines, social structure is reasserted. Dissidents are then faced with the prospect of abandoning the idealized image and accepting something less, nothing at all, or punishment for former sins. This necessitates the (often forceful) alienation of those capacities cultivated within the social movement that had been incorporated into the self. Such realienation is a painful process, often requiring authoritarian organizations to impose a harsher and more rigorous control over a former dissident's life than necessary in conventional society. Those for whom the pain is overwhelming, consciousness obliteration becomes an alternative through suicide, use of drugs of consciousness contraction (e.g., heroin, alcohol), or engaging in mindless hedonism.

Notes

1. There is of course an element of racist myopia in the characterization of Great Revolutions: That Oliver Cromwell defeated Charles I is familiar to schoolchildren in Nigeria and India, whereas the feat of his contemporary Li Zecheng in overthrowing the Ming in 1644 is not. The White Lotus rebellion, contemporaneous with the French Revolution, for similar reasons did not "make history" except locally. The Taiping Rebellion, contemporaneous with the U.S. Civil War, was unknown except to specialists in the United States (despite it having been the bloodiest revolutionary struggle of the nineteenth century, if not of all times) until China became a focus of fear and secondarily of admiration in this country.

We should also remind the reader at this point that social movements—even spectacular and cataclysmic upheavals such as the Taiping Rebellion—may leave little trace on the social order without eventuating in social transformation except provisionally prior to their suppression. Contrarily, vast and sweeping social transformations may be carried through, say, by the combined action of the exploiting class and the political regime without the presence of or even in opposition to a social movement, e.g., the eighteenth-century English enclosures and 1930s Soviet industrialization and collectivization.

2. The Soviet Union may be said to have entered a postmovement period following about 1923. The political aspects of this, including the stiffening of authoritarian control and discipline within the party and the Soviets; the economic, including the conciliation of the peasantry and the enforcement of stricter discipline in the factories; and the

diplomatic, including a more conciliatory foreign policy and the enforcement of strict discipline within the foreign Communist parties and their subordination in like manner to the Communist International, which together constituted "Bolshevization," are described at great length in Carr (1971).

Chapter 7

Social Movements Versus Political Violence and Mobilization

Now that the theory of the natural history of social movements has been fully elaborated, we can turn our attention to issues raised previously, but which could only be developed further after gaining familiarity with the perspective presented in the previous three chapters. There are two issues to be taken up in this chapter in relation to social movements: First, what are the relative theoretical benefits of the social-movement perpective to the use of the concept of "political violence"? Second is the problem of "mobilization" in reference to social movements and revolutions. Our efforts will be directed at demonstrating how the social-movement perspective rids the field of confusions that are inherent in such conceptualizations. In addition, as we concern ourselves with the problem of mobilization, we will take up issues related to revolutions and the maintenance of the state.

Before proceeding to the subject matter at hand, we would like to point out that the confusions that have existed in the fields of collective behavior, social movements, and political sociology are related to the overlapping definitions of seemingly similar phenomena. Conceptualization of social-movement phenomena has been most problematic because of the overly inclusive definitions proffered from within the field. Such terminology as "collective action," "political violence," and "resource mobilization" has been erected in its stead as a result.

Political Violence

We must insist most emphatically on the point that "social movements," as defined herein, should not be confused with the currently popular term "political violence" (see, e.g., Gurr, 1970; Laquer, 1977). "Social movements" and "political violence" comprehend overlapping domains. In the first place, though an indispensable defining characteristic of a social movement is social conflict involving the use of force by dissidents, such force is, as noted elsewhere, not necessarily violent, especially in the early stages of social-movement development. A brief consideration of two of the most tremendous popular upheavals of recent years should suffice to drive the point home. The 1968 "Events of May" in France began with occupations of university buildings in Paris in imitation of the U.S. model (the immediate precedent having been the occupation of five buildings at Columbia University, New York City, in April) by "students," i.e., candidate members of the bourgeoisie. The Gaullist regime retaliated by closing the University of Paris (including the Nanterre campus, where the trouble began, and subsequently the Sorbonne, the main campus, whose students had sided with those of Nanterre) and arresting some students. This led to street clashes of a strictly symbolic character—involving barricades, a Parisian tradition since 1588, and weaponry limited to paving stones and truncheons—between students and the Republican Security Companies (CRS, the Gaullist riot police). The political importance of the street clashes in fact derived from their character as media events. Coverage of the rioting, in particular that of May 11–12, had an impact upon affluent and politically connected French "public opinion"—obviously greatest on parents of participants, especially those beaten or arrested—not unlike that of the Chicago "police riot" of August 1968 upon well-heeled liberals in the United States. On May 12, the regime, as a consequence of its own *retaliatory* violence, announced seemingly prudent concessions to student demands, including the release of those arrested. The immediate reaction of the French working class, however, was outrage and *competitive insubordination:* Here were the pampered and spoiled children of capitalists and career bureaucrats getting away with goings-on that, had they been perpetrated by mere workers, would surely have been punished with the sternest repression; this was not to be tolerated. As the sociologist Gilbert Mury (1969) put it, the student movement was "the detonator" and the workers' movement was "the bomb." But the latter was a most peculiar bomb in that it went off without any direct instigation from the detonator or any awareness on the part of the latter that the bomb existed. Specifically, the "bomb" went off on May 13 with the occupation of a state-owned aircraft factory in remote Brittany by workers who had no contact with the action in Paris or any other center of student radicalism. By late May, 10 million workers were on strike and over 3,000 factories were occupied by their employees, surpassing all previous records for general strikes (e.g., Belgium, 1912; England, 1926; France, 1936) in terms of the percentage of factory workers participating, percentage of factories occupied, and extent of economic disruption. In accordance with the Law of Emergent Contradiction, protests and disruptions began to appear among farmers, civil servants, junior executives, entertainers, police (some of whom vowed to refrain from attacking workers, though students were still fair game), and fishermen (who flew the red flag on their boats in Marseilles harbor). Yet in all this social upheaval there was only one death attributable to action by dissidents (a police official in Grenoble accidentally killed by a wagon load of debris rolled down a street by students) and remarkably little destruction of state or private property outside Paris (where cars were overturned to blockade streets and other handy objects cannibalized for barricades; an attempt to burn the Stock Exchange in late May failed).

The other instance, the events leading up to the Iranian Revolution, is even more instructive. Sustained conflict began in November 1977 with demonstrations by the secular opposition in Tehran and by the religious opposition in

Qum. These were of course illegal but in no sense violent. The regime responded with summary massacres of participants; the unofficial figures for the death toll in the Tehran massacre are given in the hundreds and range up to 1,000. (The official figure, twelve, is ludicrously low.) The rhythm of demonstrations was thereby set: Each massacre, by tradition, called for a forty-day mourning period to be observed by processions in the streets in honor of the slain. Whether or not these were sanctioned by the regime, further massacres inevitably occurred. Traditional Shi'ite Islamic days of mourning, which crowd the calendar, also require processions through the streets, and these were forbidden by the regime only at the risk of charges of the gravest impiety. Martyrdom was courted by unarmed demonstrators. During the events leading up to the insurrection of February 9–11, 1979, the correspondent of the *Economist* (February 3, 1979) oberved a youth dip his hands into the blood of a victim shot dead in the street and hurl himself screaming at the troops. The total number of unarmed victims slaughtered in this fashion or in the shah's prisons by SAVAK—the secret service, ranked by former CIA executive John R. Stockwell as, along with the South Korean KCIA, the "deadliest" of its kind in the world; (cf. *In Search of Enemies)*—has been variously estimated from 10,000 to 30,000, with the latter figure officially adopted by the Khomeini-Bazargan regime. Although it is true that a wave of arson, looting, and assassination attended the collapse of the old order from December 1978 to February 1979, this never aproached the level of violence committed by the state apparatus under the orders of the shah and his immediate successor, Bakhtiar. The worst atrocity attributed to dissidents, the Isfahan theater fire of August 1978, in which 477 were killed, was subsequently attributed by the Khomeini-Bazargan regime—according to captured files—to a SAVAK major alleged to have set the fire as a provocation intended to discredit the clergy. (To be fair, we must point out that the alleged perpetrator was shot after a secret trial.) In any case, as the avowed revolutionary organizations had either been domesticated by the shah's regime (e.g., Tudeh, the Iranian Communist party, whose organizational talents were put to use by the shah in the management of the oil industry in a fashion reminiscent of Batista's shrewd dealings with the Cuban Communists) or rendered innocuous by SAVAK (cf. Halliday, 1978). The February 1979 insurrection would scarcely have been possible without the mutiny of part of the armed forces and the passivity of the rest (excepting only the Imperial Guard) in a fashion closely paralleling the events of March 8-13, 1917, in Russia.

In the second place, the usage of the expression "political violence," notably by Gurr, is susceptible to vulgarization to the extent that, according to the latter,

> The concept subsumes revolution, ordinarily defined as fundamental sociopolitical change accomplished through violence. It also includes guerilla wars, coups d'etat, rebellions, and riots. . . . The properties and processes that distinguish a riot from a revolution are substantively and theoretically interesting, and are examined at length in this study, but at a general level of analysis they seem to be differences of degree, not kind. (Gurr, 1970:4–5)

One error in the preceding may be quickly disposed of: Riots, like strikes, may represent episodic dissidence; that is, routine and highly specific forms of social conflict that should they occur in the overall context of a period of social quiescence, are not susceptible to further development as to either the intensity of conflict or the grievances in dispute. George Rude, in *The Crowd in History* (a book cited by Gurr, 1970:6n), pointed out that in eighteenth-century Europe urban riots were quite predictable when the price of grain rose above a certain level regarded locally as traditional; in such eventualities the state would normally take steps to lower the price by decree, subsidy, drawing upon reserves, or importing additional supplies.

There is a species of riot—we might call it the "celebratory riot"—that does not involve a social-conflict intent at all, but rather marks the onset of the New Year, the end of a major war, or the eve or victorious conclusion of football or hockey games in certain cities. (The dangerous condition of the streets of either Austin, Texas, or Norman, Oklahoma, on the night before the annual Sooners-Longhorns game is well known.) These events are commonly replete with drunken brawls and rapes; arson and looting are not unknown but are treated indulgently by the guardians of property. (Nevertheless, the fact that the predictable fisticuffs between partisans of the Greens and the Blues at the chariot races in the Hippodrome at Constantinople did not materialize such that fans of both coalesced into the entirely unpredicted Nika insurrection, A.D. 532, must find its explanation in our "natural history" approach to social movements.) Yet the celebratory riot has in common with episodic dissidence of all kinds its predictability, absence of developmental possibilities, and the comparative lack of significance with which it is treated by both participants and custodians of order. Therefore, though there may be some truth in an assertion to the effect that a social movement that eventuates in revolution differs in degree, not kind, from one that does not, it is yet more truthful to assert that a riot that occurs in the context of a period of social quiescence differs in kind, but not in degree, from one that occurs in a period of ongoing social movement development. A riot that occurs in the context of social quiescence differs in degree, but not in kind, from the routine shootings and stabbings at Mardi Gras time.

Let us proceed to consider coups d'etat. As noted earlier, the professional military in any state-type polity—whether Zulu impi, Roman legions, or the officers and "lifers" of the United States Army—constitute a distinct status group physically and culturally segregated from the civilian population. This status group is itself subdivided into numerous hierarchical gradations of formal status, which themselves mask contradictions of interest and outlook among various groupings such as functional formations (i.e., service arms), the High Command and its privileged staff, ambitious career officers, junior officers, noncoms or "lifers," and conscripts.[1]

Consequently, one may identify a military coup with a social movement only under two circumstances: The first comprises those instances in which the whole military acts qua status group to impose its rule upon society as a whole, especially if in so doing it forces the hand of a reluctant High Command. Coups of this sort presuppose a soldiery ethnically or ideologically distinct from the mass of the population and even from the exploiting class itself; they are, accordingly, typical of states and empires antedating the emergence of the "national army" in modern times (e.g., the Roman Empire, where the legionnaires adopted a distinctive religion, Mithraism, and on several occasions coerced genuinely reluctant commanders to make bids for power; similarly in the Byzantine Empire, Armenian and Isaurian troops twice thrust to power generals who adhered to the iconoclast heresy to the outrage of the ethnically Greek exploiting class; also in the Abbasid and Fatimid caliphates where ethnic Turkish soldiers ruled through shadowy "legitimate" monarchs). The second, previously discussed, comprises instances wherein simmering social conflict in society as a whole is effectively stifled by a despotic regime, yet is reproduced in the guise of sharpened contradictions among interest groupings within the military.

Generally speaking, military coups either have nothing to do with social movements at all or are expressions of counterdissidence carried out by the High Command or ambitious career officers disturbed by the inability of the preceding regime in maintaining "order." Coups of the former type represent the normal type of change of government wherever peripheral capitalism prevails; no more social significance should be attached to coups in such countries than to elections in those of the capitalist core: Orders are given, the troops obey, and Lieutenant General Tweedledum is ousted by Major General Tweedledee who, having promoted himself, institutes policies of minor substantive difference from those of his predecessor; the outs are nevertheless now in, whereas the former ins are now out of the country plotting their return. For example, in 1975, a dispute arose in Ecuador over petroleum policy; the country thereupon held a coup rather than an election.[2]

The paradigmatic case of the military coup is probably Bolivia, which has averaged at least one violent change of government per year during its history as an independent state. Nearly all of these changes were coups of little if any social-conflict significance or were—like the two coups in 1978—of counterdissident intent. The one noteworthy exception was the regime of Victor Paz Estenssoro, president and leader of a radical-populist party, the Popular Revolutionary Movement (MRP), which came to power following uprisings by peasants, tin miners, and part of the army.

Our contention that the coup d'etat is merely the normal form of change of government in the peripheral capitalist countries is fortified by the trend away from absolute monarchies (North Yemen, Birundi, Thailand, Egypt, Iraq, Afganistan, Libya, and probably Morocco) and civilian autocracies installed under other than social-revolutionary conditions (Indonesia, Zaire, Uganda, Benin, Brazzaville Congo, Nigeria, Ghana, Sudan, Central African Republic/Empire, Chad, Syria, Algeria, Comoros, Mauretania, Pakistan, Bangladesh) and toward straightforward military rule.[3] There is a telltale pervasive tendency for military expenditure to rise faster than per capita income throughout the peripheral capitalist world, where few countries can afford to fight any enemy except their own civilian populations without foreign subsidy and even internal security is sustained by lavish military aid in many cases. (The 1978–79 war between Tanzania and Uganda cost the former over $250 million—approximately the box office gross from *Star Wars* or less than a quarter of what is spent in the U.S. on pet food annually—leaving Tanzania broke and Uganda picked clean by troops of both sides. (cf. *Time*, June 25, 1979; cost figure attributed to President Nyerere of Tanzania).

Let us turn now to guerrilla warfare and terrorism. The difference between the two in contemporary usage is frequently dependent on the perspective of the speaker, as in the former Zimbabwe-Rhodesia, where the forces of the Patriotic Front—an uneasy coalition of the Zimbabwe African National Liberation Army, led by Robert Mugabe, a Marxist-Leninist based in Mozambique, a country of similar political coloration; and the Zimbabwe Internal People's Liberation Army, led by Joshua Nkomo, whose politics are less distinct and whose base was in pro-Western Zambia—were called "terrorists" ("terrs" for short) by the Salisbury regime and "guerrillas" by everyone else. The Reagan administration has been accusing the Russians of sponsoring "terrorism" around the globe, especially in El Salvador, where an ill-equipped left-oriented guerrilla force is resisting the junta. The Russian involvement in El Salvador consists primarily of a visit by a leader of one of the guerrilla armies to Moscow on a mission to acquire weapons. The only hard evidence of Russian-sponsored terrorism in El Salvador was a free trip to Vietnam for the weapons procurer.

This confusion of nomenclature is nothing new, and has sound empirical foundation: Guerrilla rebels who are abetted and succored by the mass of the population, from which they also recruit, unquestionably represent ongoing social movements; this has been true for millennia. A "war of national liberation" was led by the Maccabees (or Hashmoneans) against the Seleucid Empire from 166 B.C., when a spontaneous revolt broke out under Matathias, priest of the village of Modin, and his five sons, until 131 B.C. when Simon—the only survivor of the five sons—secured the recognition of his sovereignty (actually as a protectorate of the Roman republic). Guerrilla war, likewise, has been a traditional recourse of exploited masses against homegrown tyrannous regimes for many centuries, especially in the Far East: The first all-China peasant war began about the time of the death of the First Emperor (Shih Huang Ti, who had completed the unification of the country and founded the Chin dynasty in 221 B.C.), 210 B.C. Liu Bang (or Liu Ji), a rich peasant turned petty official, fearing execution because the slave laborers in his charge whom he was conducting to the Great Wall for construction work had escaped, himself fled and raised a rebel army. He then proclaimed himself king of Han; having overthrown the Chin in 207 B.C., he triumphed in a civil war against Xiang Yu, a representative of the old feudal nobility (whose reign the First Emperor had sought to encompass through the establishment of a rigorous bureaucratic administration throughout the country), he founded the Han dynasty (202 B.C.). Other spectacular peasant wars included those that led to the rise of the Ming dynasty (1368) and its fall (1644), as well as the Taiping (Heavenly Kingdom of Great Peace) rebellion (1850–64), suppressed with the aid of Anglo-French intervention. Vietnamese, too, waged peasant wars against Chinese occupiers and indigenous rulers prior to the advent of the Western colonialists. In medieval Europe a problem arises in the identification of guerrilla qua guerrillas, in that the latter are defined in contradistinction to "soldiers" (the word guerrilla derives from the Spanish for "little war")—merceneries or conscripts in the service of a territorial state—and consequently loses a certain applicability in feudal polities where the state is mostly notional; there is a sense in which "feudalism" is merely guerrilla war formalized and legalized. The line was, however, drawn between the petty wars of nobles and knights, which were respectable, and those of peasants and "outlaws," which were not.[4] With the resurgence of territorial states, large-scale peasant wars became a feature of political life— however temporarily—in the fourteenth and fifteenth centuries. Guerrilla wars, in something approaching the modern sense of the term, however, became "traditional" expressions of political strife in modern times (that is, after circa 1550–1600) primarily in Spain, eastern Europe, and Latin America. As in China, regimes threatened by such insurgencies called them bandits and brigands much as their contemporary counterparts call them terrorists.

Eric Hobsbawm, in *Primitive Rebels*, points out the incapacity of the states of southern and eastern Europe even in the nineteenth and early twentieth centuries to suppress brigandage and banditry in remote and inaccessible regions or even in rural areas generally. Banditry, as an obvious recourse for the poverty-stricken and desperate, was hence endemic and there arose in all such places the social type that Hobsbawm calls the "social bandit," who took from the rich and gave to the poor not necessarily from altruism but always from necessity: The rich had what there was to be stolen and the poor could hide, protect, lie to the gendarmerie, and occasionally join up. (This is hardly to say that bandits did not steal from the poor or that the latter did not betray the bandits.)

In places as far apart as China (where guerrilla rebels were depicted living a banditlike existence in the classic novel *Romance of the Three Kingdoms*, set in the third century A.D. but written much later) and Mexico, bandits were drawn into guerrilla armies during major social upheavals; their enemies correspondingly disparaged them as mere "bandits" until quite recent times: In the 1930s the Guomintang army waged four major campaigns against the Communist forces of the Jianxi Soviet under Mao Zedong; these involved hundreds of thousands of regular troops, artillery, field fortifications, and dive-bombers, yet were euphemistically called "bandit-suppression campaigns." The Mexican revolutionary General Francisco ("Pancho") Villa, was beaten in 1914–15 by the U.S.-supported forces of General Obregon. Reverting to guerrilla tactics, he sought to use a Chicano-populated area north of the border in New Mexico as a refuge and staging area, but his forces were pursued into Mexico and destroyed by the U.S. Army under General "Black Jack" (a sobriquet denoting the segregated Black troops under his command) Pershing; the latter is still celebrated in U.S. high school history texts as victor over the "bandit" Villa.

Having established that guerrilla warfare and terrorism (or social banditry) are frequent expressions of social movements, we must now declare that this association is *not necessary and in most cases does not exist*. Guerrillas or terrorists today, for example, have several possible relationships to social movements: (1) those who intend to instigate collective dissidence through exemplary action; (2) those who represent "encapsulated" (see "Postmovement Adaptation Illusions," Chapter 5) vestiges of social movements; (3) those who carry on "armed struggle," which at least a substantial minority of the population actively supports or identifies itself with; (4) those in the pay of foreign states for the purpose of subverting or "destabilizing" the countries in which they operate; (5) those who operate on foreign soil for the purpose of seeking publicity against regimes in their homelands where they may have no support or are even unheard of; and (6) those who operate against genuinely unpopular regimes and claim to act on behalf of the mass of the population although the latter actively favors none of the visible contestants for power. These categories do not have precise boundaries: The IRA, for instance, has endured for decades, i.e., through long periods of social quiescence, and shifting from encapsulation to waging a supported struggle—or even from instigators through encapsulation to armed struggle with support in the populace—during social-movement periods; the latter leave traces on the organization in the form of splits along generational lines as between the "officials" and the "provisionals." The same may be said of the Russian Narodniki (populists, from *narodnaya volya*, meaning "will of the people"). These had genuine popular support during their terrorist campaign of the 1870s among the urban intelligentsia (though none among the peasant masses upon whom they rested their hopes). In 1878, Vera Zazulich shot and wounded the governor-general of Saint Petersburg; when tried she was acquitted by the jury and rescued by a friendly crowd before the police could rearrest her. The organization barely succeeded in assassinating Tsar Alexander II (1881) before the definitive police crackdown. The feeble effort of 1886, in which Alexander Ulyanov (Lenin's elder brother) was hanged, elicited no popular response. The exploits of the Fighting Organization of the Socialist Revolutionary party (SR), doctrinally the heir of the 1870s Narodniki, both preceded and survived the social movement of 1904–1907, which is known to history of the Revolution of 1905.[5]

To conclude: "Political violence" and "social movements" are cross-cutting concepts. Most forms of political violence listed by Gurr can—as we believe we have demonstrated—occur either in the context of social movements or outside them. We have, by the way, refrained hitherto from citing Gurr's definition of political violence, since in this Gurr unwittingly supplies the clincher, as this definition is so vague that one cannot legitimately exclude from its wording even the most routine criticism of a constitutionally elected government by a "loyal opposition":

> In this study political violence refers to all collective attacks within a political community against the political regime, its actors—including competing political groups as well as incumbents—or its policies. The concept represents a set of events, a common property of which is the actual or threatened use of violence, but the explanation is not limited to that property. [1973:3-4]

Does this definition cover, say, situations at election time wherein "liberals" criticize "conservatives" for (1) excessive use of violence against a common enemy; (2) failure to use violence against a common enemy; (3) sanctioning the use of violence by a third group against a fourth group; (4) failure to prevent a third group from using violence against a fourth group; (5) scheming and plotting to use violence without regard for due process of law (e.g., Watergate); (6) pursuing a misguided policy that eventuated in the use of violence unanticipated when the policy was formulated, etc.? One can hardly imagine an election campaign, even in territorial subdivisions (states or provinces, counties, cities), without issues of this sort.

Gurr has called his book *Why Men Rebel*; this does indicate some concern for "social movements" as the object of analysis. Yet the unit of analysis is a sequence of events leading to an act or acts of "political violence," as we have seen, an evidently inapplicable concept. Why? Perhaps because acts of political violence are quantifiable, at least in principle, whereas whole realms of the study of social movements, for example, "the reinterpretation of social reality," are not (e.g., you can't ask people to tell you what they don't know that they know). Quantifiability (at least in principle), even if it explains little or nothing, still affords the authentic look of real simulated science; it is serious. Small wonder Gurr's work on this book was supported by at least three federal agencies and at least three major universities; and that it received the official sanction of organized social science: the Woodrow Wilson Foundation Award for 1970 from the political science profession and a rave review in the *New York Times* by Lewis Coser, president for 1974–75 of the American Sociological Association.

Mobilization

It was not against centralized power that we fought, but in whose hands it was.
—Member of Parliament, 1653

In social contexts and historical epochs that predispose social movements to formal-organizational cohesion, the military metaphor mobilization fails to distinguish between a mobilization effected by a mass or vanguard dissident (or counterdissident) organization engaged in the contest for power or by a revolutionary dictatorship defending a social order. In the latter case social relations have been newly transformed by revolutionary upheaval against counterdissidence within and interventionist powers without, which are expressions of social movements; and a mobilization effected by a totalitarian apparatus, which is not. That such confusion should exist is hardly surprising in that the objective of the totalitarian apparatus is the simulation of the appearances and ambience of a social movement and the perpetuation of the same indefinitely. The elucidation of this distinction, particularly that between the revolutionary dictatorship and the totalitarian apparatus, requires a digression.

As stated or implied in various places in Chapter 3, "The Reproduction of Social Privilege," the polity (which may be of the state or the feudal type; for purposes of brevity we shall henceforth exclude the latter and simply refer to the "state") in class society guarantees (1) the political reproduction of society by (forcibly) ensuring its own reproduction and that of despotic and patriarchal authority relations in society as a whole. For this purpose the use and possession of the means of violence (but not the effective means of violence) are sanctioned within the household (the *patria potestas* and its variations) and without (by slave overseers, night watchmen, "respectable" citizens permitted to own guns for fear of plunder by the lower orders or as hobbyists, aristocrats as badges of status, and so forth; or on a semiauthorized basis by mafiosi and their Japanese counterparts, the yakuza; the Ku Klux Klan in the United States or the pre-1971 Union of the Russian People, commonly known as "Black Hundreds"; and latterly in capitalist core countries by union goons to enforce discipline upon wildcatters, rank-and-file dissidents, and other troublemakers who threaten mutually advantageous union-management relations). (2) The state also guarantees exploitative relations on the level of material reproduction. It ensures that the normal level of cultural reproduction itself does not threaten the reproduction of the hegemonic ideology whether in a specific doctrinal form (the burning of heretics "relaxed to the secular arm"; or latterly the persecution or "reeducation" of deviationists, Trotskyites, Zinovievist wreckers, Bukharinists, Titoists, revisionists, social chauvinists, hegemonists, or "Zionists," also called "rootless cosmopolitans") or as commonsensically understood in society at large. In the latter version, the action of the state—whether effected by prior restraint, suppression, or awareness of the likelihood of these measures, i.e., the "chilling effect"—is commonly called "censorship." The absence of censorship is indicative of the utter innocuousness of overt assaults upon the hegemonic ideology and the absence of subversive implications as stimulants to collective action. The deliberate liquidation by the bourgeoisie of the hegemonic ideology as found on the level of cultural reproduction for sound business reasons (although its reproduction continues in fragmentary form due to the effects of structure in generating "the normative power of facticity") and the repositing of the censorship function wholly in such extrastate devices as the market mechanism or the academic "tenure" system are also indicative of the inability of subversive implications to stimulate collective action. All systems of censorship break down when they are most "needed," that is, under conditions of such intense dissidence that the capacity of the state to deploy the means of ideological supervision has utterly broken down or when efforts at censorship lead to consequences precisely opposite to those intended. A notorious recent instance of the latter was the assassination in early 1978 of the publisher of the only anti-Somoza newspaper in Nicaragua, Pedro Joauqin Chamorro; this crime set off the chain of events that led to the overthrow of Somoza in July 1979 by rebels far more radical than the bourgeois clique represented by Chamorro. In earlier periods, it is well known that, prior to the English and French revolutions, for example, official censorship was either ludicrously ineffectual or was more trouble than it was worth, for example, when, in 1637, the ears of three heretical Puritan writers were publicly cut off, this instigating far more outrage and opposition to the regime than it instilled fear in the opposition.

It is a commonplace of political sociology, perhaps dating back to Niccolo Machiavelli and certinly to Alexis de Tocqueville—it is certainly restated by Gurr (1970) and Oberschall (1973)—that revolutions, in particular those proceeding to the transformation of social relations, are associated with the overthrow of political regimes understood—rightly or wrongly—as incompetent, socially and politically isolated, lacking the means of violence adequate to the suppression of intense collective dissidence, or irresolute in the means of violence actually at their disposal. Substantially the same effect, as in Iran, may be induced by appeals to the alienated supernatural for succor against a regime ostensibly armed to the teeth, manifestly prepared to slaughter unarmed civilians by the tens of thousands, and self-confident by reasons of the long-standing passive compliance of the mass of the population. Where the transformation of social relations eventuates from the overthow of such a regime this presupposes the destruction of the whole state apparatus, which in recent centuries has occurred in only two ways: that of the *classic revolution*, sometimes called "the revolutionary process"; and that of the *protracted war*. The first type includes Bohemia during the Hussite War (1419–33), the English or Puritan Revolution (1640–49), the French Revolution (1789–94), and the Iranian Revolution (1979–81). The second type most prominently includes the revolutions in this century in Yugoslavia, Albania, China, Vietnam, Cambodia,

Cuba, Algeria, and Mozambique. Mexico (1910–14) and Nicaragua (1978–79) combined elements of both types idiosyncratically.

In the classic type, the principal political events take place in the capital city, which may be hypertrophied with respect to lesser towns and the countryside (London in 1640) or the nerve center of an administrative apparatus long accustomed to despotic sway over the countryside as well as the locus of cultural and intellectual activity (Paris, Saint Petersburg/Petrograd), or both. The initial overthrow of the regime, or its reduction to political impotence due to popular insurrection or the threat of it, unleashes a wave of collegialization everywhere, usually with the participation or even the numerical dominance of classes or strata previously debarred by law or custom from holding any official post. Events in the countryside may give impetus to this: In 1789, the fall of the Bastille on July 14 set off (or in places was contemporaneous with) a mass panic with admixtures of peasant revolt; the peasants of one village, hearing rumors of "brigands" in the service of the aristocracy, charged off pell-mell so that their approach would be taken in the next village as that of the brigands; in "retribution" the peasants would here and there burn chateaux or otherwise destroy manorial rolls listing feudal dues they owed to their lords (cf. Lefebvre, 1973). This effectively demolished the state administration in the countryside and induced or even compelled the bourgeoisie in each town to supplant the royal officials with improvised administrations and armed forces to teach the peasants respect for private property. In Russia in 1917, a crescendo of rural riots and full-scale peasant uprisings (following the precedent of 1905–1907, as was true of the movement in the cities) likewise reduced to impotence the internal security forces at the disposal of the provisional government.

The initial period of collegialization is often characterized by celebratory euphoria masking potential disunity not yet actualized in keeping with the Law of Emergent Contradiction; and the falsity of the sense of security corresponding to the faith that liberty is at hand, which has not yet been dispelled by the awareness of the absence of organized coercive force capable of defining a revolution whose precise content has not yet been settled. Effective power is in the hands of bodies improvised on the spot: committees of correspondence, patriotic societies, political clubs, county committees (England), communes (France), soviets (councils in Russia), komitehs (Islamic revolutionary committees in Iran). Most important of these are always the bodies that control the streets of the capital itself: Committee of Public Safety (London); Paris Commune; Petrograd Soviet, superseded by the Central Executive Committee of the All-Russian Congress of Society; Islamic Revolutionary Council (Tehran; moved to Holy City of Qum, retaining overall hegemony over komitehs). Provisional revolutionary authorities, such as those of Parliament in England; the Constituent Assembly, Legislative Assembly, and the Girondins in France; and the provisional governments of Russia and Iran, must govern with the consent of these bodies or must take them into account in public declarations of policy while pursuing other policies covertly. (The latter, when exposed, are invariably characterized as "betrayal of the revolution" and "high treason.")

This situation necessarily prevails because collegialization has pervaded the armed forces: In 1639, the army raised by Charles I to fight the rebellious Scots simply broke up. The French army in 1789 was of such dubious loyalty following the attempted coup against the Constituent Assembly that it was patently useless against the rebellious Paris populace; the mere rumor of the approach of foreign mercenaries to the city incited the Parisians on July 12 to plunder military stockpiles, loot gun shops, and—two days later—storm the Bastille. Following these events, soldiers mutinied in various places, refusing to obey the aristocrats—who monopolized the officer corps excepting the artillery arm—and assassinating them. The new National Guard, wherein officers were elected (as they were in new volunteer units sent into battle in 1792), was under the control of the commune in each municipality, most important that of Paris. In Russia the Petrograd Insurrection (March 8–13) succeeded thanks to the fraternization of mutinous troops with the masses in the streets. Mutiny became institutionalized almost immediately when the Petrograd Soviet of Workers' and Soldiers' Deputies issued Order Number 1, which abolished the death penalty in the army and provided for committees of soldiers in each unit to ratify officers' commands, World War I not withstanding. In Iran the crumbling relations between conscripts and officers prior to the flight of the shah (January 19, 1979), which had been punctuated by assassinations, small-scale mutinies, summary executions, and barracks massacres, continued to deteriorate during the following three weeks. On Febraury 9 the Homofars, noncommissioned air force technicians, mutinied and, for their own protection against the fanatically monarchist Javidan Guards, threw open the weapons stockpile at their base to all takers, among whom guerrillas of the Mujaheddin (Warriors of the Holy War) and Khalq-e-Fedayin (People's Suicide Commandos) were especially eager. The rebels repeated the scene at other military bases around Tehran until small arms were distributed in such superfluity that a weapon was unwittingly issued to a supporter of the incumbent Prime Minister Bakhtiar, no questions asked (*Economist*, February, 1979). With the defeat of the Javidan Guards and the completion of the conquest of the capital, the Islamic Revolutionary Council ordered the return of the distributed weapons at the mosques; but compliance was necessarily voluntary and incomplete. Following these events, which were consummated by the execution of most of the High Command, soldiers' committees proliferated throughout the army; this was precisely paralleled by the collegialization of the remainder of the state apparatus, which, even prior to the February insurrection, had contrived to prevent Bakhtiar's ministers from entering the government buildings; now there were scenes of low-level civil servants demanding higher salaries and asserting veto power over the decisions of their superiors.

In the next phase of the "classical" pattern of revolution, collegialization proceeds in conformity with the dictates of emergent contradiction. The state not only cannot guarantee the conditions of exploitation and domination in society at large; it cannot guarantee its own reproduction, which is at the mercy of bodies whose juridical status is very much in flux. Outlying regions inhabited by suppressed ethnic groups may assert claims to autonomy or secede (Ireland and Scotland in the English Revolution; Brittany in the French Revolution; Finland, the Baltic States, Georgia, and—more equivocally—the Ukraine in the Russian Revolution); local bodies behave in a semisovereign fashion, ceasing to collect taxes or to forward the receipts to the center (as in France and Russia, where the currency depreciated; the Russian currency was not even worth the paper it was printed on so that larger denominations were printed on much smaller bills). Social inferiors (English Levellers; French sansculottes;

Russian workers and peasants) assert claims against their "betters," and ri-valrous armed forces spring up, choosing sides as their inclinations and the momentary balance of power appears to dictate. The Iranian Revolution illus-trated all of these developments to perfection.

By way of background let us explain that Iran under the shah had been a most peculiar parody of capitalism of the periphery, itself further parodied in Nicaragua. The shah in person controlled the economy almost to the extent to which Stalin personally controlled the Soviet economy under the first two five-year plans. This control was exerted through: (1) state ownership of what in the USSR in the 1920s was called the "commanding heights" of the economy, including the oil industry, the basic steel industry, part of the aluminum industry, the (planned) copper industry, industrial-development banking, and agricultural credit; (2) the outright ownership by the royal family of 293 business enterprises in every imaginable sector of the economy; (3) the assets (U.S. $1.1 billion) of the Pahlavi Foundation, including an office building in Rockefeller Center, the ostensible purpose of this foundation having been among other things the provision of eleemosynary aid to hitherto-undiscovered and indigent relations of the Pahlavi dynasty; (4) some fifty-odd private capitalists owning the remainder of large industry, department stores, etc., not in the hands of foreigners and all necessarily on close terms with the shah and his fanatical partisans. (Most of these are in exile. One was shot for Zionism and another for sexual procuring on behalf of high-ranking generals whose proclivities in this area were allegedly exotic.) The shah was a species of multinational cor-poration dealing with others of his kind; thus it transpired that he purchased—in his guise of the Iranian state—25 percent of Krupp Steel.

The Iranian bourgeoisie was a caricature: Mutilated in its economic or en-trepreneurial function, it was consequently reproduced only as politico-military specialists; that is, as state bureaucrats and executives in state-run, state-controlled, or foreign-owned enterprises. Their opportunities for going into business and accumulating capital as private owners or investors depended wholly on a career of service to the state and the shah. The latter was a gigantic tree in whose shadow no capitalist grew. Three groups of would-be capitalists resented this: (1) small industrialists, e.g., Prime Minister Mehdi Bazargan, the owner of a small factory engaged in the manufacture of prefabricated air-conditioning equipment; (2) lawyers, engineers, executives, and others pos-sessing the privilege of Western education who foresaw greater opportunities, whether in business or in electoral politics, upon the shah's removal and constituted the base of the initial "secular" opposition, especially the National Front; and (3) the "traditional" bourgeoisie and petite bourgeoisie—sometimes called "bazaar merchants"—who, without possibilities for expansion under the shah, were destined to liquidation or relegated to the niche of tourist trap and who, consequently, bankrolled the "religious" opposition personified by Aya-tollah Khomeini. (This is not intended to imply any generous nature on their part: The working conditions in an Iranian carpet workshop are strictly four-teenth-century, with wages to match.) These groups were sufficiently strong and numerous to demand a semblance of real capitalism, but far too weak to sustain it. Consequently, the question of capitalism or socialism was never very serious. The expropriation of the royal family (January and February 1979), other large industrial capitalists (completed by early July except for foreign business), "private" banking (mostly foreign-owned subsidiaries, including an agency of the Soviet state and a state-owned French bank) on June 8, and insurance companies on June 10 saw to that. *Cultural* issues, including the autonomy of national minorities, the status and rights of women, the power of the clergy, the prohibition of hashish in the land of the hashishin,[6] the execution or whipping of prostitutes and homosexuals, the banning of any and all music from (entirely state-owned) radio and television, etc., aroused the most passion. Meanwhile, the following—as reported in a periodical distributed by the Iranian Students Association in Southern California—has been transpiring:

> Workers and other employees of the "Lavan" Oil Company,[7] have asked for the nationalization of the company which is owned partially by the four American corporations; Sun Oil, Union Oil, Murphey [sic] Oil, and Atlantic Richfield. . . .
>
> On March 28, 20,000 people marched in the Northern city of Bandar Turkoman in support of the just and democratic demands of the Turkoman people. Marchers condemned the killings of Turkoman people in the previous days. One of the slogans was: "Yesterday in Kidistan, [sic] Today in Turkoman Sahra, where will it happen next?"[8] They demanded the immediate release of all those who had been arrested in Turkoman Sahra, and also the freedom of political acitivities for the Turkoman people.
>
> Workers of "Jean Mode" factory in Amoul[9] established their syndicate after they went back to work to get their postponed salaries. The representative of the employer at the beginning was not willing to confirm the workers' organization, but finally with the strike of the workers recognized the syndicate and agreed to pay the postponed salaries of the employees. But he didn't honor his promise on the specified date. The elected council of the workers compulsorily decided to sell the factory's products, and collected $10,000 which was distributed among the workers.
>
> Peasants of many villages around Iran, have sent letters to the government and expressed their support for the revolution. They have also categorized their demands into three articles which are the following: 1) Cancellation of all the peasants' financial debts to the Agricultural Bank. 2) Providing loans to the peasants with no interest. 3) Providing agricultural machines for peasants' use. [*Iran News & Review*, vol. 1, no. 1, June 1979.][10]

The same source also lists the eight-point "Demands of The Kurdish People," undated, attributed to "representatives of the revolutionary councils from the cities of Kurdistan Province of Iran, in a gathering in the city Mashabad" and submitted to the Bazargan government. These include:

> 2. The Kurdish people, like other peoples of Iran, demand the elimination of "national oppression" and ask for the right of self-determination in a "federation" from within the country of Iran, and deny the charge of being seperatist. [sic] . . .
>
> 5. All the garrisons in Kurdistan must be operated under the supervision of revolutionary councils. Therefore, a joint military committee, from patriotic officers and representatives of revolutionary councils, must be formed.

6. The criminal officers who ordered shooting and martyred thousands of people must be sent to the revolutionary courts. In order to transform Shah's reactionary army into a people's army, all its anti-revolutionary elements must be filtered. . . .

That is, in other words, that the Iranian state and army may undertake nothing or appoint nobody in Kurdistan without the prior agreement and subsequent supervision and control of a Kurdish political entity whose powers are to be defined by the Kurds.[11]

In keeping with the conservatism customary in revolutionary nomenclature, former Prime Minister Shahpur Bakhtiar, overthrown in February, was called the "Iranian Kerensky" by his enemies. At the time we said, "Nonsense. Bazargan is Kerensky. Bakhtiar is Rodzianko (the leader of the state duma, the tsarist parliament, who arranged the abdication of Nicholas II and forthwith disappeared from the political scene along with the duma) or Prince Lvov (first prime minister of the provisional government formed in mid-March; overthrown the next month in the "April Days"). This was borne out: Like Kerensky, who was constantly embroiled with the Soviet for the purpose of acquiring more than titular power, Bazargan and his ministers—originally appointed for their reassuring bourgeois respectability, strove to become more than mere marionettes. Imam Khomeini—the title "imam" must be bestowed by popular acclaim, as it is blasphemous heresy to claim it for oneslf; there had previously been only twelve canonical imams, of whom the last, the "invisible imam," is said to have disappeared into thin air in the tenth century—and the Islamic Revolutionary Council played cat-and-mouse with the government, the latter cast as the mouse: When, for example, Bazargan offered to resign unless the summary executions by ad hoc Islamic courts were halted, the resignation was refused by the imam, who also agreed to Bazargan's demand; but executions resumed the following day (March 1979). Subsequently, conflict developed over the government's desire to subordinate the Islamic militia or Pasdarans, an undisciplined rabble constituting the armed support of the komitehs, to the regular army in the interests of public order. This was suspect in that the officer corps—however innocent of murder or torture under the shah—were *eo ipso* vestiges of the monarchy. In the politics of revolutionary social transformation it is not what one did but who one is or was that constitutes the crime. On July 2, Bazargan caved in and offered an apology: " 'This country needs the Pasdarans more than any other time. When the Imam gave me the mission of leading the Government, I did not appreciate this need. I thought the old regime was gone and the new regime had replaced it. But later we saw that this was not the case.' "(*New York Times*, July 3, 1979).

Spectacular indiscipline ensued within the regular armed forces: The Homofars, their heroic role in the February insurrection notwithstanding, were suspect to the dominant religious faction by reason of their secular-technical bent, and not least because this was imparted to them by U.S. instructors. Stripped of their political importance, e.g., as Bazargan's bodyguards, and otherwise harassed, they staged a sit-in at their base; several dozen were arrested by order of General Rahimi, commander of the military police (*New York Times*, July 11, 1979). This raised the broader issue of the need for technically trained personnel, which seemed to the Bazargan government to dictate not only the release of the Homofars and acceptance of their demands but additionally the recall of some of the U.S. instructors; without these measures the air force was so much very expensive junk. ⟨⟩

The Marxist-Leninist Left—the Khalq-e-Fedayin and its supporters, inclusive of the Iranian Students Association of Southern California—called for the outright dissolution of the regular army and its presumable replacement by a force of its own persuasion. In an editorial entitled "Why shah's Army Must Be Dissolved" the Iranian students declared:

> The establishement [sic] of a new revolutionary army along with the dissolugion [sic] of the Shah's anti-people army, are among the issues which are most vital. The resolution of these two issues is necessary to safeguard the victories of the revolutin, [sic] and to facilitate the struggle of the people against imperialism and reaction.
>
> We believe that the revolution can't reach its final goal, unless it destroys the nerve center of the enemy which is the anti-people army, and replaces it with a new revolutionary army made-up [sic] of the people themselves and the revolutionary personnel of the old army who have shown their loyalty by joining the people. We believe that the Shah's army, in all aspects, had been formed and extended to serve the interests and desires of imperialism.

This divided the secular Left not only from the Islamic Revolutionary Council, inevitably hostile to Marxist atheism, but also from the Bazargan government, which, faced with secessionist revolts and possible war with Iraq (which finally materialized in 1980), secretly hankered for a modified form of the alliance with the United States to revive the firepower of the military. Otherwise, given the curious politics of the situation, Bazargan regarded the Marxist-Leninists as de facto allies against the IRC in that the Fedayin were at least secular. Consequently, it was not until Bazargan delivered his self-abasing speech of July 2 (*New York Times*, July 3, 1979) that he was finally compelled to denounce the Marxist peril.

Like Kerensky, too, Bazargan was steadily compelled to replace the aging pillars of bourgeois respectability in his government with figures reflecting the power in the streets: Dr. Karim Sanjabi, leader of the National Front, resigned as foreign minister in April; in May the post was filled by Dr. Ibrahim Yazdi, thirty years younger, rhetorically more militant, and a close associate of the imam. Justice Minister Assadollah Mobasheri resigned in June; his duties had become patently impossible given the predominance of extrastate courts enforcing the Higher Law. In late July, Bazargan finally offered to appoint to his government a number of high-ranking clergy from the Islamic Revolutionary Council; but the precise identity of these personages was not known to the public nor was there any evidence that they wished it to become known.

All this was only the beginning: The seething unrest among the masses of workers and peasants was not reflected in the Islamic Revolutionary Council nor were the autonomist demands of Kurds, Arabs, Turks, etc. One recalls that much the same was true of the Soviet until shortly before Kerensky's overthrow; the convening of a new Congress of Soviets with a Bolshevik majority in fact dictated the timing of the coup of November 7. Similarly, the Girondin regime in France did not reflect the growing disaffection of the sansculottes before the Jacobins came to power in the insurrection of May 31–June 2, 1793.

The latter two events marked the installation of revolutionary dictatorships in power in the respective countries. The coercive power bestowed by control of the means of violence at the disposal of these regimes was initially negligible; but in the face of counterdissident insurrection to the point of civil war supplemented by the intervention of reactionary foreign regimes, they were charged with the defense of the revolutionary order by whatever means, as delegated by the resolute or even fanatical support of strategically located minorities of the population. With this support they organized recentralized despotic states; created huge well-disciplined armies that defeated their enemies; and massacred counterdissidents whether overt or merely suspected. (This was the "reign of terror" in France, 1793–94, and the "red terror" during the Russian civil war, 1918–21; in fairness it must be recalled that in each instance there was a "white terror" on the other side at least as bloody.) Throughout 1981, partisans of Khomeini engaged in bloody street fighting with the People's Fedayin. The head of the Islamic Revolutionary Party was lopped off by assassins who apparently infiltrated the Islamic Guards, their security force, and were able to plant bombs in meeting places of the party leadership. In response to the threat, the regime summarily executed over 1,600 suspected members of the leftist opposition. The violence was maintained at a high level, but did not compare to that which led to the overthrow of the Shah's regime. The French revolutionary dictatorship was overthrown with the passing of the military emergency in mid-1794. The Bolshevik regime, on the other hand, managed to hang on, though not without difficulty; the difference can be attributed to the circumstance that the sansculottes were a status group riven by mutually contradictory economic interests whereas the Russian proletariat constituted a class; and to the development of formal-organizational technique for political purposes throughout the intervening period. The Bolshevik regime was thus enabled to make the transition whereby it became the first totalitarian state. Even so, the end of the Russian Revolution as a social movement may be dated rather confidently in 1923 and the full panoply of totalitarianism established by 1926 (cf. Carr, 1971).

Where social transformation is the outcome of protracted war, the transition to totalitarian mobilization is far more difficult to detect. The Cuban, Yugoslav, and Albanian wars were relatively brief and, in the Cuban case at least, it is clear that the guerrillas triumphed over Batista long before the social movement had reached its peak intensity. Hence the Cuban regime quite visibly went through the phase of revolutionary dictatorship during 1960–62 (the arming of the population; the formation of committees for the defense of the revolution analogous to the revolutionary committees under the Jacobins; etc.) prior to the transition to the totalitarian state.

On the other hand, the Mozambican Revolution (1961–75), the Chinese Revolution (1925–49), and the Vietnamese Revolution (1940 or 1945–1975) involved wars of such length that it is out of the question to consider that the same social movement persisted throughout. It is more reasonable to infer that totalitarian mobilization was effected by counterstates within zones wholly or partially or even intermittently under their military control, whereby the mass of the population was affiliated to numerous and cross-cutting mass organizations (e.g., the party, military and paramilitary units, village cells, peasant organizations, women's organizations, workers' organizations, youth organizations, schools, medical services, financial apparatus, the other officialdom of the counterstate, etc.), the complexity of all this being unimaginable to U.S. observers at their first sight of squalid peasant villages (cf. Douglas Pike, 1966, for organizational charts, auxiliary bodies, and assorted entities loosely affiliated with or under the clandestine control of the party and in opposition to the regime). Protracted war, like the classic model, gives rise to what Trotsky called *dvoyevlastiye*, or "dual sovereignty," whereby two would-be states, representing irreconcilable social interests and disposing of rival means of violence contest control of the same territory by means partly political and partly—and ultimately—military. The protracted war model, though, does not necessitate the persistence of the social movement until the final destruction of the state by the counterstate, as the latter may through totalitarian mobilization achieve a social transformation immanent within the social movement whose prior existence is the precondition of the initial emergence of the counterstate as a revolutionary dictatorship.

Summary

Our pupose in this chapter has been to demonstrate the shortcomings of the conceptions of "political violence" and "mobilization," while offering the social-movement perspective as an alternative that adds clarity to the field. "Political violence" and "social movements" comprehend overlapping terrain. However, the problem with the terms "political violence" and "mobilization" is that they are defined so broadly as to include everything from routine political behavior to social revolutions. Second, they make no distinctions between qualitatively different phenomena. For example, "celebratory" riots that are not dissident actions are grouped with social-conflict riots. In the case of "mobilization," no distinction is made between mobilization effected by dissident vanguards or by a revolutionary dictatorship defending a social order. Terrorism, social banditry and guerrilla warfare may be defined, not by the nature of the activity, but in terms of perspective. That is, what the Left considers guerrilla warfare is likely to be called terrorism by the Right. No distinction is made between episodic dissidence and that which is susceptible to further intensification. Third, "political violence" makes no distinction between violence and force that is non-violent. The social-movement perspective treats collective action occurring within a social movement context as qualitatively different from that which does not. In so doing, political actions can be analyzed in terms of their social meanings—whether they are dissident, counterdissident, or routine (as in the case of coups d'etat in the capitalist periphery). By virtue of the fact that we seek to understand the meaning of political action, we can gain a more comprehensive—and historical—analysis of the phenomena.

"Mobilization," with its overtones of militaristic maneuvering, presupposes formal-organizational cohesion and downplays the process of collegialization within social-movement collectivities, which, as we have pointed out above, in the cases of classical revolutions, can even pervade the military. Such was certainly the case in both the Russian and Iranian revolutions. By overlooking the collegialization process, resource mobilization theory distorts the reality of social movement phenomena, especially the process whereby the dissidence of one collectivity triggers the dissidence of other collectivities in conformity to the Law of Emergent Contradiction. Even in the case where revolution is the consequence of protracted war, the revolution itself may cover several social-movement periods, thus making it difficult to detect the transition from social movement to a formalized revolutionary dictatorship.

Notes

1. The contradiction between the latter two groupings was perhaps nowhere sharper than in the eighteenth-century African kingdom of Dahomey: The standing army cadre, that is, the "lifers," consisted wholly of women, the famous "Amazons," about 5,000 in number. These were all volunteers. Men were by contrast conscripted for the annual campaigns; their distaste for service may be deduced from the fact that a village chief's life was forfeited when the number of recruits specified in his local draft quota was not met at muster (cf. Polanyi, 1968).

2. The analogy may be pushed further: Coups of the so-called "Nasserite" type (a term in vogue among political analysts in the early 1970s), whereby avowedly radical-nationalist officers seize power, might be fancied as the parallel in the peripheral-capitalist world of the election of social-democratic governments in capitalist core countries. In either case the extent of the transformation of social relations is not comparable to the rhetorical militancy of the regime's (or government's) declared objectives (or electoral manifesto). "Nasserite" regimes in most cases have come to power in the absence of intense dissidence among the civilian masses, and have usually dealt harshly with those groups, civilian leaders, and organizations actually intent on revolutionary social transformation. Pursuing our analogy, this might seem comparable to the repression of socialist revolutionaries by German Social Democratic party governments from 1918 to the present. (The 1958 Iraqi coup by General Abdul Karim Kassem presents an exception. This touched off a massive outbreak of revolutionary mob violence in Baghdad in the course of which King Faisal was torn to pieces in his palace and Prime Minister Nuri as-Sa'id was hanged from a lamppost. General Kassem legalized the Communist party and gave it a subsidiary role in his regime; but this apparently constituted grounds for his overthrow in the 1962 coup.) Moreover, "Nasserite" regimes have in most instances been replaced (Egypt, the prototype) or overthrown (Peru) by more conservative ones, or else have survived by moving to the right (Sudan). Colonel Qaddafi of Libya relies on magical authority at least as much as on his army; but the same personality that animates the regime is also stifled by the circumstance of being confined to a country—however oil-rich—whose population is about 4 million; consequently, the regime may have begun to autodestruct thanks to Qaddafi's foreign adventures, in which he has made numerous enemies and incurred disasters (most dramatically during the Libyan intervention on behalf of ex-Field Marshal Amin in the Tanzanian-Ugandan war, March–April 1979, when the entire Libyan force was killed or captured); presumably he will be overthrown by more "level-headed" if not "moderate" (U.S. media code for "conservative" or "pro-Western") officers.

3. The issue of whether President Sadat of Egypt was a military or a civilian autocrat should be confined to the plane of image manipulation. He liked to pose in a business suit abroad and in uniform at home.

Syria and Iraq underwent successive military coups after 1956 and 1958, respectively. They are presently governed by rival wings of the Ba'ath (Arab Renaissance) party which affects a civilian appearance in each country. Although both states are allies against Israel and clients of the USSR, not to mention their espousal of the same official ideology, they have until recently been bitter rivals. (In June 1979, they announced the formation of a joint military command. [New York Times, June 20, 1979] This may have had more to do with the anticipation of war with Iran than with military planning against Israel: During the preceding months Iraq demanded that Iran evacuate three islands in the Perian Gulf; detained a religious leader—who had been a close friend of Ayatollah Khomeini while the latter was in exile in Baghdad—on charges of fomenting religious subversion; and warmly encouraged Arab secessionists in Iran's oil-rich Khuzistan Province.) There are two possible explanations for this enmity. The *religious* interpretation points to the circumstance that the Iraqi Ba'athists are a Sunni minority governing a country with a Shi'ite majority, whereas their Syrian counterparts constitute an Alawite (Shi'ite) minority governing a Sunni majority. The military explanation points to the enormous military establishments maintained by both countries, which dominate the state apparatus in each (e.g., the Syrian minister of the interior is a brigadier-general), and to their geopolitical rivalries (specifically, the right of the Syrians to use the headwaters of the Euphrates for irrigation, and Syrian charges for the passage of Iraqi oil through a pipeline to the Mediterranean). These analyses should not be taken as mutually exclusive, in that the officer corps in each country is recruited from the dominant religious minority. The "Islamic revival," personified in 1979 by Ayatollah Khomeini, predictably aggravated Shi'ite dissatisfactions in Iraq; but simultaneously—and to the U.S. observer somewhat paradoxically—encouraged Sunni dissidence and terrorism in Syria: Sunnis have been blamed, for example, for the assassination of the country's attorney general on April 11, 1979 and for a massacre of military cadets—thirty-two dead, fifty-four wounded—on June 16, 1979 (*New York Times*, June 23, 1979). This may explain part of the Syrian motive in the decision to huddle closer to the Iraqis, presumably under the common denominator of "Arab socialism."

4. The legendary exploits of "Robin Hood" are a composite of the deeds of several individuals, often déclassé knights, who operated circa 1200. One of these gave King John so much trouble that he had to be bought off with an official post (cf. Painter, 1949).

5. Type (1)—instigators—is mainly to be found in the countries of the capitalist periphery, where its contemporary practitioners are commonly Marxist-Leninist in political thought. In Latin America, guerrilla war has been a traditional participatory sport of the *jeunesse doré*, going back at least to the time of Simon Bolivar (who finally succeeded in his third try, 1818); it is even older as the recourse of African slaves (Republic of Palmares, Brazil, seventeenth century) and downtrodden Indian serfs (rising of Tupac Amaru, Peru, eighteenth century, whence "Tupamaros"), though these latter groups were always squashed by a united front of all factions of white "civilization." Even Fidel Castro did not break with the tradition whereby privileged urban contenders for power took to the hills: Contrary to subsequent myth, he did not mobilize the peasants, but awaited reinforcements and arms from young radicals in the cities—whose friends, especially the Revolutionary Directorate in Havana, played a key role in eroding the morale of Batista's army (cf. Hugh Thomas, 1971)—and disarmed public opinion in the United States by holding press conferences for successive yanqui media representatives. The mass of the Cuban population may properly be said to have become participants in the movement only with the outbreak of strikes in 1958. Thus Castro, who was clearly in type (1) at the time of the Moncada attack (July 26, 1953), had become type (2) before his conquest of power and still more strongly so after his victory when he appealed to the mass of the population against the pro-U.S. strata.

Epigones of Castro in Latin America have almost uniformly fallen into type (1). The strategy of creating guerrilla forces in the rural areas failed, possibly because of the tedium encountered by young educated rebels in rousing skeptical peasants (much like the experience of the Russian Narodniki in the 1870s), and possibly because of the greater lure of more publicity-laden activities such as urban terrorism and press conferences (cf. Laquer, 1977:178ff.,217ff.).

Type (2)—encapsulated—is today most commonly found in the capitalist core countries as a vestige of 1960s student or youth radicalism: Weather Underground (U.S., defunct); Red Brigades (Italy); Red Army Faction (West Germany); Japanese Red Army; Quebec Liberation Front (Canada, defunct); Black Liberation Army (U.S., perhaps defunct; and possibly also the Symbionese Liberation Army (California, defunct). The strategy of such groups has as its common denominator the unmasking of the parliamentary regime in each country as a mere facade of police despotism (this having to some extent "succeeded" in West Germany, but only to the enhancement of the prestige and power of the police). Their substantive importance lies elsewhere, specifically in their incomprehensibility to liberals and the legal-parliamentary Left; in this respect perhaps the SLA was most "successful" because of its manifest "senselessness" to the rest of society as a whole.

Type (3)—those paid by foreign states—included such historical specimens as the Serbian "Black Hand," an outfit funded by some officials of the Serbian secret service prior to World War I; their objective was the creation of a Greater Serbia at the expense of the Hapsburg Empire, and their most notable success was the assassination of Archduke Franz Ferdinand at Sarajevo in 1914. In the same class was the Internal Macedonian Revolutionary Organization (IMRO), which between world wars was on the payroll of the Bulgarian state for the purpose of detaching the Macedonian region of Yugoslavia for its annexation by Bulgaria. More recently, the CIA funded the war of the Khmer Serei ("Free Khmers," i.e., rightists) against Prince Sihanouk of Cambodia (deposed March 1970); that of the FNLA (National Front for the Liberation of Angola) and UNITA (Popular Movement for the Liberation of Angola); that of the Kurdish Democratic party in Iraq, only to leave it to the slaughter when the latter country struck a deal with Iran, which subsequently unraveled during the Iraq-Iran War); and the terrorism of the Chilean Right from 1970–73.

Type (4)—operating on foreign soil—comprises the South Moluccan terrorists of the Netherlands, few of whom having ever seen their "homeland"; and the tiny and mutually-hostile bands of Serbs and Croats whose activities in the United States (one airplane hijacked by Serbs, one by Croats; one New York City policeman killed by a Croat bomb; threatening letters, etc.) and Europe mystify the public and sometimes amuse it. (Sources cited by the *New York Times*, June 22, 1979, give the figure of Serb "activists" in the U.S. as six, though Croats are said to be "more numerous.") Though we are not certain of this, the FALN terrorists who set bombs and rob banks in the cause of the independence of Puerto Rico may well have more popular support on the mainland (where the terrorist acts take place, where the terrorists are not easy to capture, and where—like Willie Morales—they readily escape) than on the island.

It is possible these days to start a "guerrilla movement" with only a set of initials and a dime for a phone call: With the latter one takes credit for a fire or explosion set by someone else or wholly accidental. This possibility is not merely theoretical: When in April 1979, a bomb wrecked part of the Rome headquarters of the Italian Communist party (CPI), both leftist and rightist terrorists called to claim credit. The claims of either group to represent any sort of social movement must be taken advisedly, especially those of the ultra Right, since these in their guise of a legal political party call themselves the Italian Social Movement (MSI).

6. These were the original Assassins, founded as a Shi'ite mystical brotherhood circa 1070 by Hasan-i-Sabah at the fortress of Alamut in Tabaristan (south of the Caspian Sea) for the purpose of eliminating heretical and infidel rulers. Hashishination continues in Iran, among the most deadly have been:

a. *Forghan*. The name is a Persian word for either the *Koran* or "that which discriminates between good and evil." It designates a terrorist organization inspired by Dr. Ali Shaariatei, murdered by SAVAK in 1975, who was, it is hardly necessary to add, a sociologist. He advocated extreme social egalitarianism legitimated by a literal reading of the *Koran*. This egalitarianism—a species of communism with God—extended to advocacy of the suppression of the Schi'ite clerical hierarchs and the end of their moral hegemony over the faithful. Since the February insurrection *Forghan* shot several close associates of the Ayatollah Khomeini, including a general and two or three important clerical figures in the Islamic Revolutionary Council.

b. *Black Wednesday*. These are terrorists supplied by Iraq, which covets the Iranian province of Khuzistan; the latter is the site of the Iranian oilfields in their entirety and its Arabic-speaking population is rife with autonomism and separatism. Black Wednesday would rather blow up pipelines than people, but does not shrink from killing persons in the vicinity of flammable substances.

c. *Khomeini Crusaders*. Elite gunslingers who fanatically support the Ayatollah/Imam Khomeini and the rule of the Islamic Revolutionary Council. These are deployed to protect the members and high-ranking adherents of the council, especially against *Forghan*.

7. Lavan is a small island in the Persian Gulf.

8. This refers to the killings of people in those provinces.

9. Amoul is a city on the coast of the Caspian Sea.

10. As an indication that this is no mere propagandist eyewash, here is the story from the capitalist side: "Some of the big farms were occupied by peasants during the revolution. In many, the owners have vanished. Those who remain wonder whether the regime's attempts to buy off discontent will push it into nationalisation of land. . . ." (*Economist*, July 28, 1979). Having described the heroic efforts of a textile manufacturer to break even, the same source notes:

> In other plants, operations are hamstrung by committees led by enthusiasts for workers' control; by the discontented (e.g., locally trained engineers at last able to lord it over their foreign-trained rivals); or by workers furious at their betrayal by employers now safely abroad with the company's funds.
> One Iranian banker, newly appointed by the revolutionary government, said it was difficult to lend because he could not find anyone capable of taking responsibility in many firms. Managers have nominal legal responsibility for the actions of the company, but find their actions thwarted by committees who mistrust them, or are determined not to pay out to firms and foreigners they dislike.

11. "We've got independence, but we are willing to compromise and settle for autonomy within post-revolutionary Iran," said Amir Qazi, one of the leaders of the Kurdistan Democratic Party.

The armed Pesh Mergo guerrillas are the only authority in many towns and villages throughout Iranian Kurdistan. Qazi's claim of "independence" apparently leads the government to doubt the Kurds are willing to settle for autonomy instead of secession. . . .

Kurds have a historic reputation as tough mountain warriors, and Qazi estimated that as many as 500,000 are armed. Four million members of the ethnic minority are believed to live in the region.

"They love guns and are ready to fight for their rights," Qazi said. [*New York Daily News*, July 30, 1979]

But these are not the same Kurds whose demands are published by the Iranian Student Association of Southern California. Those Kurds, in their Demand Number 8, denounce these Kurds as CIA agents and warn the Bazargan government to have no dealings with them. So contradiction begets contradiction. . .

Chapter 8

Thematic Recapitulation

The Definition of a Social Movement

We argue for a definition of social movements wherein the *decisive* criterion is the resort by members of dissident social categories to *nonroutinized* countercoercive *physical force*. The latter criterion demarcates social movements from cultural, artistic, and religious movements; from "reform" movements abiding strictly within the confines of routine politics; from the nutritiously edible "social conflict" of the Simmel/Coser (1962) variety or routinized dissidence, e.g., strikes at the expiration of contracts, which "function" to reinvigorate the bureaucracies on either side; and from recourses to force situated from beginning to end within established elites. Our criteria are noninstrumental and nonteleological. We reject the position that they occur as rationally calculated efforts to attain goals envisioned at the outset. As we have seen, "goals" are provisional artifacts of the level of intensity of conflict behavior.

An admitted drawback of our definition, at first sight, at least, is the fact that social movements can, and in "real" history, *have* emerged from the phenomena listed above, from which we have distinguished them. We must, therefore, apply a modicum of hindsight in delineating the course of a social movement (subsuming the issue of whether it existed at all). We offer no comfort to those who, with premeditated rational calculation, would snuff out or divert a social movement before it occurs (the hidden agenda of a Chalmers Johnson or a Ted Gurr) and we offer none to those avowed subversives who would, with premeditated rational calculation attempt to "build a movement" and thus mix their metaphors before they hatch. Woe betide subversives who are simultaneously sociologists, for in the former capacity they must give a prospective social movement the benefit of the ontological doubt on the basis of scattered early returns, whereas in the latter capacity they must refuse to concede until the returns are nearly complete and perhaps they must even demand a recount.

Our definition offered in Chapter 1, "The Guises of Social Movements," is the most restrictive in the field—and for good reason. At the writing of this

130

work, sociologists still do not have a clear understanding as to the distinction between "protests" and social movements. A glance at the conceptual confusions deriving from the 1960s gives evidence as to the nature of the problem: Was there an "antiwar" movement? A student movement? A civil rights movement? A hippie movement? From our perspective, none of the above were, of themselves, social movements, but, rather, aspects or phases of other social movements. Antiwar protests, student disruptions, hippie and civil rights protests were all parts of a middle-class youth movement. Civil rights protests, however, were more centrally located in the Black movement, which, in 1963, intensified into Black nationalism and moved north. Though the antiwar protests recruited from a larger constituency than the youth movement, certain manifestations began on college campuses, and only later did antiwar protests spread to other sectors of the population. According to our definition, there were at least four and perhaps as many as six social movements between 1960 and 1973 appearing in strict conformity with the Law of Emergent Contradiction: the Black movement, reciprocally influencing and coterminous with the middle-class youth movement, the women's movement, and the gay rights movement, the latter two of much shorter duration than the former, which lasted the whole decade from 1960–70. In addition, these movements, especially the Black, spurred collective dissidence by Hispanics and Native Americans. We speculate that the women's movement began in 1967 and had been effectively coopted by 1972. The Gay Rights Movement was even shorter, beginning in 1969 and ending in 1973. Dating them is difficult because of the the small amount of overt physical conflict manifested in each.

Social categories are accepted a priori at the outset of social movements. Social-movement participants, comprising minorities within them, act in their name ("we the students," "we the workers"). ("What is the Third Estate? It is nothing, yet it is everything."—Mirabeau)

A social category is *not* a behavioral entity. It designates the specific location within the system of social classification from which social-movement participants are drawn. It may even be a *residual* category, i.e., defined negatively by reference to those categories accorded special privileges and prerogatives, e.g., "Third Estate."

In the course of intensification of social conflict and the unfolding of emergent contradiction, social categories are renamed and redefined. For example, during the French Revolution, "Third Estate" became "the people," which then legislated a distinction between active and passive citizens. Subsequently, this distinction was erased (e.g., 1792) and replaced by the category of "patriots" within which the sansculottes, a newly delineated category, furnished the political muscle for a faction of bourgeois politicians to organize a revolutionary dictatorship. Note that, throughout, the lines demarcating categories remained subjective and tangential to "class consciousness." The sansculottes were more aware of their common interest as consumers than of their "relation to the means of production"; they were hence easily aroused against "hoarders," "speculators," and "middlemen," but had no sense of "class interest" antagonistic to that of the bourgeoisie. Duby (1981) makes the point that a system of social classification, once established in subjective awareness is extremely conservative despite its having been nonempirical from its inception and progressively more counterempirical with the passage of time. The case of the "three orders" dates from 1025–1030 and persisted until 1789, becoming progressively irrelevant to empirically observable social behavior from about the year 1100 onward. The Indian caste system, a hierarchy of ritual purity, has had at all times only the most notional relation to the distribution of wealth and power in India.

In defining social movements as confined to *major* social categories, whose collective action *interferes* with the cultural and/or political reproduction of society, we have given sociologists conceptual tools by which they can judge whether or not collective action is part of an ongoing social movement. That is, when a social category forces its way into the system of historical action (to borrow from Touraine, 1977) to the point of disrupting the normal functioning of cultural or political institutions, one can conclude that a social movement has begun. However, a definition is not sufficient. As we have indicated elsewhere, institutions can be disrupted episodically. The difference between a social movement and episodic dissidence is that it builds upon itself in a process of intensification, wherein the hegemonic ideology is rendered problematical by dissidents. This "reinterpretation of reality" provides the subjective basis for further—and more drastic—action. As social reality is reinterpreted in the struggle, movement participants attempt to reclaim those aspects of human subjectivity that have been alienated from themselves as part of their socialization to positions of social subordination. So long as these three aspects of a social movement are a mutually reinforcing totality—intensification of conflict, reinterpretation of social reality, and redefinition of the self and its capacities—a social movement is ongoing. Their fragmentation signals the point of incipient decline of the movement. When movement participants retreat from confrontation or when they begin to believe that revolutionaries can (or must) be made prior to or independent of the revolution, the point of incipient decline has been reached. Such phenomena must be viewed as a whole, since there are often temporary defeats and retreats within the process of intensification of a social movement, as well as phases of overt conflict alternating with cultural (or subjective) intensification.

Our definition of social movements differentiates them from periods of quiescence and, therefore, establishes boundaries around social movement periods. The advantages of conceptualizing social movements as recurrent (as opposed to continuous) phenomena are manifold: It prevents lapses into idealism and reification (i.e., the study of trends and ideas), allows for the examination of social movements without necessitating the use of conceptions abstracted from periods of social peace, and it helps to understand the distinction between movement and postmovement phenomena. The latter is important, since the concept is relatively new in social-movement theory. Bureaucratic organizations and other flotsam and jetsam from social-movement periods call themselves "movements" beyond the social-movement period and have rather easily deluded sociologists into believing that they in fact are social-movements. Take for example, the fall-out from the youth movement of the 1960s: religious organizations (Hari Krisnas, Jesus freaks, Nichiren Shoshu, Divine Light Mission, etc.), organizations that practiced dissidence only at the cultural level (e.g., the new American movement, the human potential movement), and Marxist sectarians all claimed themselves to be "movements" or "building movements," especially since their recruiting grounds were among former social-movement participants, many of whom joined thinking they were carrying on the revolution by alternative means. However, none of these organizations engaged in overt conflict, unless with each other, often over minute distinctions in doctrine, and they had quite different functions than groups within the movement. The sociology of "new religions" has been fairly unanimous in its characterizations of "new" religious organizations as conduits back to conventional life from social-movement participation (see, for example, the review by Robbins, Anthony, and Richardson, 1978).

The one exception to the above characterization has been the isolated underground terrorist organizations. In the wake of the 1960s, a number of such organizations existed, including the best known: the Weather Underground, the Black Liberation Army, and the Symbionese Liberation Army. All engaged in violent acts of terrorism. However, none had a mass following. None of their acts precipitated increased action on the part of the masses in whose name they were acting. In the case of the latter, its acts were as incomprehensible to the then-existing Left as it was to the rest of the population. To conclude, in our conceptualization, society moves from periods of quiescence to movement, with a transitional phase following the movement, whereby former movement participants are forced to accommodate themselves to the recrudescence of dominant structures. Dissidence during the postmovement period is fragmented, ritualized, and isolated.

Reproduction

Social movements are extremely complex phenomena, and, if the literature is any key, are more difficult to apprehend and understand than ongoing social structure. Asking what "causes" social movements is a bit like asking the causes of social structure. That is, causality is overly narrow in conceptualizing the origins of complex social phenomena. Instead of looking for "causality," which presupposes variable analysis, we must look to the reproduction of social relations in order to understand the recurrent outbreaks of social movements. Such an effort requires historical rather than teleological explanations.

More specifically, since social movements are attacks upon the prevailing set of social relationships extant at the time of the movement, we focus on the reproduction of social privilege. This provides correctives to such theories as relative deprivation, which attempt to assess the psychological "mood" of the masses in order to predict "political violence," or the alienated "dialectic" between trends and movements as advanced by Roberts and Kloss (1974). For us, the important phenomena that underlie the cyclic recurrences of social movements are contained in the processes of the reproduction of social relations in class-based society. Exploiting classes are able to exploit because they have effective control over the means of violence and the means of ideological reproduction (the latter of which has become increasingly important during the twentieth century). The former may be characterized as "power," and the latter can be described as "legitimacy." Thus, the social relations of privilege become the bases of our explanation of the recurrence of social movements, instead of the tried and not so true, industrialization, urbanization, relative deprivation, and anomie.

As noted in Chapter 1, "The Guises of Social Movements," social movements are engaged in by all sorts of social categories, spanning practically every possible social distinction. It is because of this that economistic and psychologistic theories are inadequate. A more "totalistic" analysis of social relations is necessitated at the material, political, and cultural levels, since social categories are primarily differentiated by their mental life; they are differentially affected by alterations at the material and political levels; and society is continually manifesting new divisions. Since social collectivities (having been social categories in periods of social peace) are the main actors in social movements, it only makes sense that we analyze social reproduction as a foundation for understanding their historical development materially, politically, and culturally.

We have now arrived at the question "When is a class of itself for itself?" Although this question tends to make scholars' eyes glaze, suffice it to say that the identity of groups engaged in social-movement behavior begins with the *appearances* of the social order. That is, social categories assume political and cultural identities prior to identification at the material level of social reproduction. "Consciousness of kind" appears as a consequence of both the reproductive process and the forcible assertion of antistructure. Within the reproduction process during periods of quiescence, a common mental life evolves out of similar material and political relations. The forcible assertion of antistructure allows for the rapid development of the subjective: (1) The social category becomes a social collectivity in that members begin acting in behalf of the collectivity; (2) the members of the social category experience new relations within their collectivity and between themselves and other collectivities; (3) their social action alters their understanding of the nature of the social order; and (4) they collectively experience altered states of consciousness.

Though a social category may share a common mental life, it is reproduced in alienated form such that members are being socialized along parallel lines without a clear understanding that other members are subject to the same social forces and experience alienation in similar ways (cf. Kenniston, 1959). In bourgeois society, this is reproduced in the form of the isolated individual. Thus, consciousness of kind is repressed or obliterated until events occur that raise common experiences within a significant sector of the social category to the level of consciousness (e.g., the consciousness-raising groups of the women's movement). Therefore, in order to understand the recurrence of social movements, one must be able to grasp the mechanisms and forms of development within a given historical period, major social categories and their shifting relationships, contradictions and fractionations, and internal laws of motion operating within a given social formation. Without analysis of the relations of exploitation, domination, and hegemony, this is impossible.

The Natural History Approach to Social Movements

James Rule and Charles Tilly (1972) have strongly criticized the conceptualization of natural histories of revolutions and cite evidence from the overthrow of the Bourbon monarchy in France and the elevation of Louis Philippe of Orleans to the throne, known to history as the Revolution of 1830. Rule and Tilly's main targets are Crane Brinton (1965) and his revisionists. Brinton develops what he calls a "fever-chart" theory of revolution that posits several distinct stages: escalating discontent, the fall of the old regime, the honeymoon period, the rule of the moderates, the accession of the radicals, the reign of terror, and the period of reaction; that is, the phases of the "classical" revolution. (The term "fever chart" has become a pejorative among contemporary theorists.) In addition, sociologists have set forth a variety of "natural histories" of social movements, such as Blumer's (1948) phases of collective behavior and institutionalization, Touraine's (1977) utopia, confrontation, and institutionalization, and so forth. The evidence that Rule and Tilly advance is in the form of tabular data indicating that the incidence of violent uprisings was highest in 1830, when the king was deposed and again in 1832, when the regime used violence to consolidate itself against the populace. (The Revolution of 1848 had a similar progression in France, with collective violence at its height in 1848 and 1850, the former resulting in the exile of Louis Philippe of Orleans and the latter the consequence of the Bonapartist coup d'etat.) Rule and Tilly use this evidence to demonstrate that natural histories are not of much use, since in the case of 1830 and others like it, the emergence of violence was neither gradual, nor escalating, but rather cyclic.

Rule and Tilly demonstrate only that the intensity of social conflict is no guide to political outcomes: In 1830, the political issue, i.e., distribution of the political pie between titled and untitled rich was settled rather quickly by the removal of Charles X (1824–1830) despite and largely because of the imperative, faced by all sectors of the propertied classes, to stifle the claims of the propertyless class for whom July 1830 was merely the opening round.

The problem with such natural histories is that if they are specific in their designation of phases, they are doomed to have more exceptions than cases that adhere to the rule. Contrarily, if they are too generalized, they become useless and subject to gross distortion as in the case of Blumer. The problem has been that theories of social movements and revolutions that have employed the natural history approach have used *descriptive* categories. Each social movement has its own natural history depending on the historical conjuncture. For example, the middle-class youth movement of the 1960s increased steadily in intensity throughout the decade, alternating between phases of overt politics and cultural intensification until its most radical phase in 1968–69. The women's movement, which was spawned full blown from the youth movement in 1967, had its most radical phases at the beginning, until it was coopted and deradicalized in the early 1970s. Likewise, in the Iranian Revolution, there was no honeymoon period to speak of since the civilian populace was able to rapidly arm itself following the overthrow of the shah. The natural history of social movements must be determined on the basis of *analytical* categories. That is, the internal laws of the development of social movements must be determined and the natural history must be constructed in light of the interaction of those laws.

We have posited that social-movement natural histories are the consequence of two major factors: historical conjuncture and the internal laws of motion of the movement. Historical conjuncture includes the forms and means of domination and exploitation, the level of development of social relations, the reproduction of social categories, the development of apparatuses by which social order is maintained, the nature and level of contradictions within the social formation, the historical development of relations between social categories and the level of development of the historical subject. By internal laws of motion we mean that all social movements develop in conformity to the laws detailed in Chapter 4 ("The Intensification of Conflict"): the Law of Mounting Stakes, the Law of Emergent Contradiction, and the Law of Shifting Terrain. These laws are not merely asserted a priori, but are the consequence of detailed analysis of social movements through recorded history. They are the logical consequences of the forcible assertion of antistructure by dissident collectivities that occur whether or not the regime under or overreacts to collective dissidence. Dissidence, by definition, is not a social movement unless it builds upon itself and collective action becomes a spur to further collective action. It is an empirical fact that dissidence by one collectivity will stimulate action by other collectivities, both within a particular state and between states. (One only needs to look as far as Eastern and Central Europe during the Polish labor crisis of 1980–81, as industrial worker strikes in the shipyards of the north spread to miners, farmers, and students nationwide in a process of rapid collegialization. Regimes in Hungary, Czechoslovakia, and Rumania passed legislation in attempts to head off similar confrontations in their own countries.) A necessary condition for a social movement to build upon itself is the collective reinterpretation of reality, which means that boundaries between "issues" as defined and isolated within the hegemonic ideology are breached and become increasingly understood as manifestations of conflict between two major social categories. (Again, the Polish worker movement of 1980–81 is instructive. Within the movement emerged the notion that the Communist party was responsible for the operation of the "state," whereas Solidarity was responsible for "society," a term consciously rendered problematic, since "society" subsumes "state." As protectors of society, Solidarity took on issues of state; that is, all relations of political domination.)

It is generally regarded as pretentious to refer to any social (or historical) phenomenon as a "law," although a few have been pointed out from time to time, such as Michel's "iron law of oligarchy," or Parsons's law of social differentiation. In science, a phenomenon is termed a law by virtue of the fact that it has been observed to operate without exception on repeated occasions. Once the phenomenon has been characterized as "lawful," such lawfulness becomes a defining characteristic of the phenomenon (e.g., "differentiation" becomes a defining characteristic of modernization). Subsequent discoveries may present a variety of exceptions to the law, which then can be used to proscribe the conditions under which the law works. If we return to the internal laws of motion of a social movement, we find (1) they become visible as a consequence of the development of a definition that separates phenomena that conform to these laws from that which does not; (2) through the process of reification, they are raised from observations of consistently recurring phenomena under a given set of circumstances to laws of historical development. By raising them from universally repeated observable phenomena within the process of the forceful assertion of antistructure to laws of historical development, we have elevated them to defining characteristics of social movements.

Laws are tools of science that allow the researcher to make distinctions between phenomena. The application of laws allows the scientist to make order out of the universe of phenomena he or she is studying. Although, as Kuhn (1970) has shown, laws can interfere with the understanding of disjunctive phenomena, i.e., that which violates the laws or assumptions of the observer is systematically screened out; they paradoxically also allow for the possibility of their own supersession in that they establish an order that, when violated, leads to the undermining of the paradigm of which they are part. Though some may believe that the theory of social movements is too primitive to assert the existence of laws, we would point out that there are 2,500 years of historical record from which to draw. In addition, the question we should, as social scientists, ask ourselves is whether or not they provide clarity over earlier conceptions. Obviously, we think they do.

Sociocharacterological Revolutions

We have indicated that within social movements the locus of motivation among movement participants changes; that such alterations in the human subject lead to movement conceptions of "new humans" who are perceived to be an advancement over earlier *sapiens*, including the most recent forms out of which the movement participants have evolved. Following social movements, including revolutions, the human subject must be forced back into boundaries necessitated by the reimposition of social structure, which is, in itself necessary for the material reproduction of society. For the most part, then, the psychic consequences of a social movement become denatured in the forms of psychic healing and upward mobility of former members of dissident collectivities. We have referred jokingly to this process as the law of destruction of surplus consciousness, in which movement sensibilities are effaced by the necessity to return to the production of the material necessities of existence.

Under certain conditions, such as when social movements combine with a rapid increase in the material surplus, movement sensibilities are incorporated into the social structure and are institutionalized as a characteristic of an emergent social category. We have alluded to just such a phenomenon in the English Revolution of 1640–49, in which a rational-calculating, profit-maximizing merchant class emerged victorious over a status-conscious, military-maximizing aristocracy. Additionally, those sectors of the gentry and upwardly mobile yeomanry that sided with bourgeois elements against the crown were forced by historical necessity to engage in rack renting, intensive cultivation, refraining from conspicuous consumption, and watching the ledger, all characteristics of rational calculation and profit maximization. Thus, out of the English Revolution, we see the rise of a new social type as dominant in English society— the rational calculator. From this time forward, England has portrayed itself as a nation of shopkeepers. Out of the revolution, then, emerged a qualitative change in English character that was institutionalized in the occupational structure. This we have referred to as a sociocharacterological revolution.

Of course, the emergence of the rational calculator was not limited to England, but was manifested throughout the north of Europe as capitalism evolved out of feudal social relations and mercantile capitalists gave way to industrialists. While Max Weber (1950) may have attributed this to Protestantism, such characterological changes affected capitalists who did not become Protestants, such as the Fuggers and Amsterdam bankers. Nevertheless, the rise of Protestantism in the areas of capitalist development in the sixteenth through the nineteenth centuries indicates the extent of the characterological change necessitated by bourgeois society. As E. P. Thompson (1966) has demonstrated, the industrial laboring classes of England used Methodism as an instrument of self-discipline for the purpose of altering rural-based peasant orientations into a working-class consciousness necessary for functioning in subordinate positions in industrial society.

Thus, we see the dialectics of character. First, the altered characterology emerges as a necessary element of newly rising accumulators in the seventeenth and eighteenth centuries. By the latter part of the eighteenth century, such characterology was being imposed on an industrial working class as part of their being forged into a reliable labor force. The working class resisted such imposition when they were insurgent. When worker movements were supressed and structure was reimposed, they flocked to such Protestant religions as Methodism to help increase their value as individual workers in the labor market.

Within the social movements of the 1960s, all of which developed a "subjectivist" reinterpretation of reality and were organized around dissident subcultures, each dissident collectivity intensified its subjective awareness of the imposition of the forms of domination that pervaded bourgeois society: ageism, racism, sexism, and homophobia. More important, each social movement at its most radical phase rendered the whole of bourgeois social relations questionable, including the sacrifice of the human subject to the discipline of the reality principle. That is, the necessity of performing labor under the conditions of the capital/labor nexus was called into question to the point where opinion surveys routinely assessed the perception of the public as to whether or not business had a right to make a profit.

Within dissident collectivities, there was a perceptive characterological change that resulted in a relative deemphasis of the reality principle vis-à-vis the pleasure principle. There were strong indications that the characterology of the rational calculator had been eroding throughout the twentieth century as the fundamental problems of capitalism altered from inadequate forces of production to inadequate modes of consumption. Capital attempted to solve this problem by creating consumption formations and "producing" culture in the form of consumer hedonism (see, e.g., Mills, 1951; Riesman, et al., 1956; Ewen, 1976; Bell, 1976); however, it was not until the 1960s that the characterology of the rational calculator came under attack by a self-confident minority. The social history of the 1970s attested to the alteration in the American character structure. Scarcity-based bourgeois institutions, such as education, the nuclear family, patriarchy, and work were on the defensive. The forms of bourgeois discipline have all suffered a decline in legitimation since the 1960s. The state, business, organized religion, and the media all lost "trust" among the populace throughout the 1970s. The "work ethic" has been a major issue in presidential campaigns since 1968; three recessions have been induced since then to assure labor-force discipline. Their consequences have been to both conservatize and alienate workers, who, if current assessments are correct, seem to be compelled to conform out of sheer necessity. "Management" has been able to increase its power over "labor" since the mid-1970s and demand such "give backs" as a declining standard of living; increased control over the labor process, hiring and firing procedures, and strikes; and fewer benefits. This has increased the facticity of bourgeois social relations.

The new characterology is reproduced primarily within capitalist consumption formations; that is, the surplus-absorbing strata. However, it is not limited to those strata. It has also infiltrated sectors of lower strata, especially the younger elements of the industrial laboring class. One is reminded of such examples of age stratification in the working class as younger members of unions have been at odds with and more radical than union officialdom. This cleavage was demonstrated most dramatically in the Lordstown wildcat strike of 1972 and the unruliness of young workers in the union-sponsored "March for Jobs" against the Ford administration.

The new characterology emphasizes the following: (1) increased sensitization to the imposition of authority, (2) desire to experience states of consciousness outside the boundaries of bourgeois rationality, (3) the questioning of the necessity of having life controlled by the market mechanism, (4) liberation of the sexual impulse from bourgeois prudery, and (5) the increased importance of "love" as a necessary component of life. Each sensibility can be expressed in an oppositional or alienated form. For example, number 1 can be manifested in open conflict or as mass apathy. Number 2 can be experienced as an artifact of opposition (see, e.g., the next section, "The Greatest 'High' There Is") or as altered states of consciousness induced by drug use, sexual contact, psychotherapy, religious rites, violence, or in combination, with conflictual elements vetted. The third element can be demonstrated by making attempts to extricate oneself from the market as did landed hippies in the late 1960s and early 1970s under the guise of self-sufficiency and ecology, or in its alienated form of profligate spending, gambling, and dissolusion as engaged in by Elvis Presley before his death. Sexual liberation in the 1960s took the form of an attack on bourgeois sexual taboos and body alienation. However, in the 1970s, sexuality was reincorporated into the social structure in the forms of an intensified and extended sexual-competitive struggle. As for "love," in the 1960s, it became a code word for a new form of social order that included erotic love with the love of humanity and admonitions to love neighbors and even enemies. Within dissident collectivities, members were called "brothers" and "sisters." Following the 1960s, there was a visible increase in romantic love, with a concomitant increase in fear, hatred, and yearning for times when interpersonal competition was not so intense and people could feel as members of a cohesive collectivity. This has been the underlying motivation for the nostalgia that has been characteristic of the post-1960s period.

At the writing of this work, the five aspects of the altered locus of motivation are experienced in their alienated forms. However, they remain as important traits in the American character, especially the middle-class surplus-absorbing strata. They did not recede as ephemera of the 1960s and therefore must be viewed as manifestations of a sociocharacterological revolution.

The Greatest "High" There Is

In Chapter 3, "The Reproduction of Social Privilege," we contended that the continuity of culture, that is, its *reproduction*, presupposes the periodic interference with its reproduction. The adaptive and innovative character of the human subject dictates the interference with cultural reproduction for intrinsic reasons even without the extrinsic provocations that precipitate those responses Anthony F. C. Wallace (1966) calls "revitalization movements": Few archeologists, for example, would assert these days that a change of pottery style here or burial customs there—as one digs into the accumulated garbage of millennia—necessarily implies demographic change, conquest, or even "cultural diffusion." The empirical observation of interference with cultural reproduction undertaken by Victor Turner (1969) among the Ndembu was, however, inevitably limited to ephemeral events, themselves periodically reproduced: the *isoma* and *wu'bwang'u* fertility rituals. These in turn assert *within* the "liminal" state[1] the resolution of the contradiction between matrilinearity and virilocality on the spiritual plane. This, as noted above, has the effect of limiting Turner's attention, in his extension of his concepts of "antistructure," "liminality," and "communitas" in class societies, to such festivals as Holi and Mardi Gras, which despite the blatant "status reversals" are equally ephemeral as well as socially conservative in their effects (in that, e.g., the untouchables of India and the Blacks of New Orleans are permitted "safety valves"); to religious movements without conflict dimensions, specifically those of Saint Francis of Assisi (Italy, early thirteenth century; subsequently throughout western Europe) and Sri Chaitanya (Bengal, late fifteenth century; revered by U.S. Hare Krishnas as their founder while rejecting the sexual practices instituted by him); and subcultures such as the Hells Angels, who despite their perpetration of acts deemed revolting by the "citizens"—the conventional people of California—are not in revolt (though they did dabble with both dissidence and counterdissidence during the 1960s).

"The battle of the sexes" described by Turner as the culmination and conclusion of *wu'bwang'u* gives a clue to a slightly different perspective: The central contradiction of Ndembu society is at bottom that of gender, that is, patriarchy. This central contradiction is common to all preclass societies. It may be mitigated or aggravated by changes in social structure like those discussed by Levi-Strauss as found among the "faddish" Australian aboriginals; but it is invariably reproduced. This contradiction, obviously, is located on the level of *biological* reproduction; we posit that explanation as follows: It is evident that in some ultimate sense and with the benefit of epochs of hindsight that, as Erving Goffman puts it in *Gender Advertisements*, "gender is not really all that important." But, though "anatomy" is certainly not "destiny," it is likely that—especially under conditions of low levels of material technique—possession of female bodies as opposed to male ones is conducive to *slight* differences in the construction of "reality." That is all that is required, since two "realities" cannot coexist *permanently* in the same culture (as opposed to "alternative realities" deriving from "nonordinary states of consciousness," such as those peculiar to mystical transcendence, sex, and violence, which may be situationally encapsulated or delegated to specialists). "Reality," to be convincing as such—and that, in a sense, is its "job"—must consequently be *either* male or female: In the beginning the former was decided upon.

Class society posits patriarchy as its presupposition. However, the material basis for the transcendence of class society has been built in a number of countries. Class society is of course defined by the production of products by some people in part for consumption and possession by entirely different people who do not produce but instead provide "service," including repression, military command, administration, organized religion, indoctrination, marketing, and surveillance of the population, all of which entail the *consumption* of products. (Note: To repeat, only the production of products is production and only that labor power objectified in products is productive. This is not to imply a moral condemnation of those not directly engaged in production but rather of structural conditions that *require* some do the work while others do the civilization, especially wherein this is no longer necessary.) The rising levels of technique, especially in so-called "industrial society," proliferate standardized products— "commodities"—whose relation to cultural reproduction is taken for granted, as they are produced collectively and increasingly consumed collectively (freeways, office buildings, data processing equipment); they constitute the "ground"[2] against which products more patently associated with the reproduction of mental life represent the "figure." While specific human capacities are developed pari passu with the introduction of new products, a point is reached where the emergence of the human subject in history comes, generally speaking, into contradiction with the acquisition and accumulation of products-in-general, especially the standardized kind; the human being simply has more important things to do. Yet the environmental envelope comprised of products constitutes a *de facto* ideology promoting the acquisition and accumulation of products-in-general and implicit in "reality" itself, with the corresponding legitimation of the exploiting class in capitalism—"the system delivers the goods," though increasingly to itself as collectivized consumption—and derivitively in socialism. This human predicament is perceived, however dimly and confusedly, by reason of the "sociocharacterological revolution" (defined earlier) of the present epoch.

Capitalism (and by extension socialism, where it is rich enough) compensates for the consequences of the sociocharacterological revolution by "scarcity-simulation"; that is, the restraint upon the level of household consumption and the relative shift to collectivized consumption, in particular that of the state as consumer of last resort (which unlike the household may go indefinitely into debt and unlike the "private sector" need not fear Japanese price competition). At this point, too, the maintenance of the industrial working class at an artificially large magnitude for the purpose of enforcing social discipline ("functioning") upon the surplus-absorbing strata above it stands revealed. But the new society has been gestated in the womb of the old, since the objective for which the human subject unfolding itself in history is striving posits as its *precondition* the carrying on of collective production for collective *use*, this to objectify as little human labor as possible and to be deemed appropriately insignificant. (Elsewhere we suggested that industrial production be relegated to "those with a romantic urge to return to the primitive.") Human beings would then get on with whatever it is they have to do. It is here and now that the central contradiction shifts—though patriarchy and exploitation persist—to *the level of cultural reproduction:* that is, the struggle for the control of "*reality*" *itself.*

The location of the central contradiction on the level of *material* reproduction precludes the easygoing suspension of the "status hierarchy" as with the Ndembu; and in fact the holding of "status reversal" festivals in class societies presupposes their geographical isolation (e.g., Mardi Gras in New Orleans, the Carnival in Rio, Holi in encapsulated Indian villages), a docile and disarmed population (as is true wherever Mardi Gras is held and even more so in India, ruled for centuries by Muslim princes and English Protestant administrators), or the watchfulness of a lurking constabulary (the lack of which during the 1979 New Orleans police strike caused the cancellation of Mardi Gras). It will be obvious that, whatever underlying antagonism between the genders may be comically ventilated by the Ndembu during *wu'bwang'u*, male and female must still combine to reproduce society biologically; the same is not true of classes, especially prior to the advent of capitalist industrialization; a mass of dependent peasants could observe empirically that they produced the wealth of the exploiter whose exactions may have palpably interfered with the biological reproduction of the peasant community in the form of malnutrition, war, overpopulation promoted by enserfment, and consequent vulnerability to disease. Until quite recent times, specifically until the point when the decomposition of the bourgeois hegemonic ideology in the capitalist core countries turned out to be very good business (see Chapter 3, "The Reproduction of Social Privilege"), the tendency of exploiting classes and political regimes has consistently been toward the interference with society's own spontaneous tendency to interfere with its own cultural reproduction. They tended to restrict "communitas" to pallid imitations: the mysteries, rites, and public celebrations of organized religion; and local village festivities of the exploited mass. The latter were often observed bemusedly by the local representatives of the exploiting class or even conducted by them as officiants, as for example at the slave wedding on an antebellum southern plantation: These occasions would reinforce their sense of superiority and paternalistic noblesse oblige vis-à-vis their charges, who were obviously simple pious children or savage drunken brutes or both.

The *real* "communitas" is, as the argot of fifteen years ago would have it, "really something else," and emerges most clearly in the context of major social upheavals when the dissidents have forced at least a local interference with the political as well as the cultural reproduction of society. Readers with long memories will recall the refrain of white youth at "be-ins," music festivals, or the first heady flush of campus building occupations: "Why can't it always be like this?" They will recall, too, the street festivities in flaming, riot-sacked cities like Newark and Detroit prior to the arrival of the troops; or perhaps a pop song hit, "Dancing in the Streets," best known among whites in the version released in 1966 by the Mamas and the Papas, but originally Black soul music: Whites understood the title literally, but to Blacks it had the additional connotation of Watts-like riots and insurrections. "Communitas" might be posited as a "nonordinary state of consciousness," that is, more colloquially, a "high," perhaps comparable to states of mystical or sexual transcendence with which it is frequently reported in combination: the former in religious movements and in social movements exhibiting religious solidarity (e.g., the Taoist-derived revolutionary sects of China, from the Red Eyebrows and Yellow Turbans down to the Boxers, or Loyal Order of the Harmonious Fist); the latter especially in the 1960s, whence the French student slogan of May 1968, "The more I make revolution the more I make love. The more I make love the more I make revolution." Unlike the other states, though, "communitas" is accessible to the individual *only* as part of a social collectivity.

Social movements are, in terms of the collectivity that emerges during the social-movement period, in a sense comparable to so-called peak experiences in the life of the individual. For movement participants the imprint of "communitas" upon their lives may be even stronger than that of major wars upon the soldiers who fought them, since dissidents are not conscripted (except perhaps by dint of peer-conformist pressures in the most intense phases of movements). This is the "it-changed-my-life" syndrome, after a common feminist refrain in the 1970s (and used as a book title by feminist Betty Friedan). But by contrast to the "peak experiences" of individuals, the "communitas" felt by members of a dissident collectivity during a social-movement period survives as idiosyncratic memories of the constituent individuals once each has undergone a "postmovement adaptation" to the return of social quiescence and may be subsequently able to communicate with each other about what the movement had been "all about" no better than an individual of merely average linguistic skills may be capable of informing a stranger as to the precise nature of a "peak experience" such as mystical transcendence. Social movements exhibiting formal-organizational solidarity and secular-rationalist doctrinal ideology may mask this development, or perhaps even defer it; but movements exhibiting subcultural solidarity and subjectivist ideology displayed the process quite dramatically.

"Communitas" and the "peak experience" each provide a standpoint for the critique of everyday life, but quite differently: The latter posits "individuality," takes it for granted, and points the way only to the individual enhancement of it *qua* individual. The former progressively dissolves "individuality" into the *human subject evolving in history*, whose level of development is an artifact of the density and complexity of human interdependence; that is, of social relations (cf. Marx, Introduction to *Grundrisse*, 1973). Human interdependence itself develops pari passu with human capacity to transform "nature," that is, the material and in this capacity *the level of development of the human subject is paramount, the most important objective "material" condition*, capable of further developing itself once it has become *conscious* of its existing level of development. The relation between the "human subject" and "individuality" is thus dialectical: The heightened, more developed powers of the human subject is the presupposition of greater individuation, whereas the latter implies—among other things—an enhanced capacity to discover its own preconditions and thereby contributes to the former.

Let us in conclusion restate the three processes found in social movements yet again: (1) the intensification of social conflict, that is, the forcible assertion of antistructure; (2) the reinterpretation of social reality that is, the collective development of the thought forms of antistructure; and (3) the redefinition of the "self," "human nature," and human capacities, that is, disalienation and the collective refashioning of the human individual in the context of antistructure (this process having been colloquially connoted by the expression "getting it together").

The second and third of these processes must fuse into a totalization (given, of course, sufficient intensity and duration of the movement as a whole) expressive of the historical condition of the emergence of the human subject *and* the form of ideological critique—e.g., religious, secular-rationalist, subjectivist—characteristic of the particular epoch.

Notes

1. Latin *limen*, threshhold; whence Turner's "liminality" (noun) and "liminal" (adjective) denoting a state of the social collectivity wherein the routine behavior and status hierarchy prevailing in everyday life are suspended and "communitas" is experienced.

2. Until they are suddenly unavailable:

> But growing anger and frustration all too often erupted in name calling, fistfights, occasional stabbings and shootings. While a gas-station owner in Freemansburg, Pa., rushed to help his bleeding wife, who had been accidentally struck by a car waiting in line, other motorists filled up their tanks and drove off without paying. In Levittown, Pa., in an outbreak originally caused by truckers demonstrating against high diesel fuel prices, some 2,000 motorists and thrill-seekers clashed with the police in three days of rioting. Police arrested nearly 200. Local officials declared a state of emergency and enforced a curfew that prohibited more than five people's getting together on the streets after 9 P.M. Pennsylvania Governor Richard Thornburgh helped restore order by bringing another 500,000 gal. of gas into the area and imposing a statewide odd-even purchase system. Said Bristol Township Police Chief Richard Templeton: "We're sitting on a powder keg." [*Time*, July 9, 1979]

At the bottom of the same page is a photograph captioned, "Angry rioters burn automobiles as violence erupts over continuing gas shortage in Levittown, Pa." In the picture, a shirtless young man whose hair falls below his shoulders is shown in what appears to be the act of consummating the fiery destruction of the twisted wreck of a car listing to starboard against what might be a gasoline station-entrance signboard painted over with a grafitto in fifteen-inch letters, which reads "!MORE GAS NOW!"

This is a localized instance of people refusing to "function" and interfering with the functioning of others.

Chapter 9

Conclusion

In attempting to interpret the 1970s, we quite understandably saw the period in terms of a "recuperation," or a recoil from the political dissidence of the 1960s whereby some of the cultural dissidence was incorporated, shorn of oppositional content, into a drive to expand the domestic market, in particular by replacement of the market-limiting "nuclear family" by a more frivolously consuming household or family type.

The substantive issue of the 1970s was how to stimulate personal consumption in a period of declining—absolutely or psychologically—purchasing power or, from a somewhat different angle, how do you get people to enjoy themselves harder and harder on less and less money? The solution adopted by both the state and big business was the generalization of "repressive desublimation" in the direction of a societal norm. "Repressive desublimation," epitomized by "the *Playboy* philosophy," had initally manifested in the 1950s as socially and subculturally encapsulated among young men who, it was understood, were within a few years to cofound their own isolated nuclear families and commence the "serious" business of life. The notion of the isolated nuclear family pursuing an idealized consumption career, the "family home," the "family car," and so forth, formerly known as "the American Dream" had been dinned into the heads of the population for years; the American Dream would have constituted a formidable obstacle to the generalization of repressive desublimation had cultural history proceeded unbroken after the 1950s since it posited as a presupposition the isolated nuclear family. It in turn posited as its own presupposition, as did the rest of bourgeois cultural and institutional forms, the rationally accumulating individual to whom the endless accumulation of exchange values for its own sake appears to "make sense" even if said individual is for reasons of class relations or personality deviation precluded from engaging in it. In bourgeois culture it is by definition impossible to develop a "sense of worth" if one lacks a "net worth" since one is unmistakably a "worthless good-for-nothing bum."

Given the availability by the 1970s of millions of under-35 well-educated, hip, quasi-hip, radicalized, consciousness-raised, personally growing, or merely vulgarly hedonistic surplus absorbers, it was clearly going to prove impossible to fit them neatly back into the framework of the American Dream and the isolated nuclear family. On the other hand, it was definitely possible to convince them, given a hint of recession, a whiff of tear gas, and the inevitable tendency of social movements to expire after a few months or years of intensifying social conflict, of the advisability of continuing or resuming "functioning," however reluctantly in the interests of what has come to be called "survival." In 1970s argot, this meant either "maintaining a level of social privilege commensurate with one's educational qualifications" (e.g., "What do you mean, why get tenure? The name of the game is survival," said an ex-colleague who did not get it) or "obtaining additional educational qualifications commensurate with one's expectations of future social privilege" (e.g., "Why am I in law school? Survival, that's why," a law student told us).

Thus, throughout the 1970s, in addition to the generalization of repressive desublimation, the scarcity-simulation function of the state has become increasingly important as an apparatus of social discipline. These two mechanisms are in many ways antithetical and mutually contradictory: (1) Repressive desublimation is based on the assumption that the system "delivers the goods," whereas the scarcity-simulation function posits that there is not enough to go around. This particular contradiction contains explosive possibilities. As long as such "scarcity" is structured into social relations in the form of intensification of competition in the sexual, hipness, and self-development spheres, it will continue to be experienced as individualized malaise. It is, however, entirely possible that large sectors of the population may come to the collective conclusion that the struggle is not worth it, given the ever-intensifying competition and the decreasing rewards for participation. (2) Repressive desublimation presupposes a payoff for political submission, whereas the scarcity simulation function exacerbates the fiscal crisis of the state making it less able to make the payments. (3) Repressive desublimation operates by harnessing the pleasure principle to commodity consumption, whereas the scarcity-simulation function operates through the reality principle, enforcing the necessity of "functioning" in the "real world." The former presupposes the repression of political freedom, and the latter presupposes the repression of emotional freedom. Thus, functioning in the 1970s and 1980s requires a dual repression that demands even greater self-vigilance than was demanded in high-Victorian bourgeois society of the late nineteenth century. One aspect of the cultural revolution of the 1960s was an attack on the "performance principle." In the period following, we have found that the performance principle has rebounded back in a more pervasive and vigorous form than it existed prior to the 1960s.

As the cultural revolution of the 1960s, now divested of its dimension of social conflict, was chopped up into its constituent parts—sex, hipness, human potential, feminism, mysticism, nature and the organic produce thereof, drugs, music—and turned into competitive struggles or packaged as new-product fads or both, the younger and more fashionably inclined surplus absorbers were confronted with more and more dimensions of human life in which they could be identified as *publicly* inferior, e.g., if you did not trade in your obviously unsatisfying mate, you were a failure in the human potential competitive struggle because of your indifference to "personal growth." Meanwhile, the traditional occupational-competitive struggle raged more fiercely than ever because the objective necessity—"survival"—had increased while expectation did not diminish. Meanwhile, the objective rationality of "functioning" had not been enhanced, but the subjective necessity for it had, so a tremendous psychic toll was exacted: Though college students were not rioting, in the 1970s they were committing suicide in record numbers; in addition, within youth culture, the punk subculture developed in the mid-1970s, which glorified suicide, violence, failure, and drugs of consciousness obliteration (e.g., heroin, PCP or "angel dust," and Quaaludes), and disco, in which the consciousness was obliterated through mindless dancing to a never-ending beat. By 1977, 8 million Americans were said to suffer from a mysterious disease called "depression" of whom 1.5 million were so incapacitated that they could not function. In 1975, 100 million prescriptions were written for tranquilizers, of which 56 million were for Valium, consumed by an estimated 18 million addicts. When it was determined the following year that some of the addicts had become so strung out that they could no longer "function," the drug was classified as a controlled substance, forcing the addicts to see doctors more often for renewals, generating a new industry of "stress clinics" which are thinly disguised covers for downer dealers with MD's who charge $75, on the average, per prescription. There is a thriving business in self-help books, and instant therapies are consumed by millions desperate to "function more effectively" or feel less inferior about something; if their message could be boiled down to a least common denominator, it would be: There is no such thing as right or wrong, virtue and guilt; only winning and losing. Everything that happens is your fault. You have no obligation to any other person unless you are paid hard cash; your sole obligation is to be whatever it is necessary to be in order to win. Likewise, don't count on anybody else's help, because if you need them that means they've outgrown you and don't need you; but if you concentrate on outgrowing them then you'll get to the point where you don't need them and can get rid of them at your leisure.

With the growth of predatory anarchy in the personal sphere, faith in love and happiness reaches the point of mania. Sexuality had always assumed the form of market relations in bourgeois society, with romantic love serving as the fig leaf covering the dirty secret of rational calculation. But the market had, up though the 1950s, been twofold, with each positing the other's existence as its own presupposition: There was, first of all, an extramarital sex market, which posited marriage, in which women were scarce; if women were not "cheap" then they were expensive. There was simultaneously a marriage market, in which men were deemed scarce, which posited extramarital sex; the height of Victorian prudery was the veritable golden age of prostitution. In the post-1960s period the two are combined into one, which you are debarred from leaving by the possibility of getting traded in, which in turn requires you to periodically ascertain your market value. But in that case, the bourgeois isolated-nuclear-family form has been qualitatively liquidated, i.e., the *modular* family, vulgarly known as the "relationship."

The nuclear-family form posits the permanence of the couple in principle. There may be adulteries and separations, of course; but as late as the 1950s, divorce, desertion, and "living in sin" definitely constituted deviance, and conferred upon the women involved "bad reputations" even if—as was usually the case—the men took the initiative. Even the men, if they belonged to the surplus-absorbing strata, could be looked at askance by their employers and deemed unsound, immature, or unstable. So it is implausible to us that any social institution that has undergone such a high level of "structural deviance" (divorce, desertion, and cohabitation), not to mention "role deviance" (which, after all, is what feminism is about), can still be said to exist. The vulgar language is appropriate: The "relationship," whether or not legally formalized, is not anything in particular.

In construing the 1960s as a rebellion against "functioning," i.e., the mechanism whereby social discipline is implanted and reproduced in "everyday life" routine, we posited a *sociological law of motion* according to which a limit of capitalism had been reached whereby a ceiling on household consumption was necessitated by the erosion of the fundamental bourgeois ideological construct of "scarcity"; the state would henceforth act as a "scarcity simulator," rendering the construct plausible by highlighting the privileges of a minority against a backdrop of a stagnating or deteriorating material standard of living for the majority (a trend that appears to have been sustained), low productivity growth (as to which we are less sure), and high *apparent* unemployment (which, even apparently, may not be true).

To recapitulate and clarify: A historic watershed had been reached or approached such that employment, first and foremost that entailing the performance of unproductive labor, was no longer necessitated for primarily economic reasons, i.e., as the "incidental costs," *faux frais*, of capitalist production, but as a device whereby the employed were inured to having someone else prescribe where and when their bodies were going to be placed under bureaucratic supervision. This is the essence of "functioning": It entails departure from the domicile at a (preferably) inconveniently early hour of the morning; and the partition of the day into "getting ready for work," "working hours," and "after work." It represents the minimum criterion for both moral virtue and mental health; and those who do not do it, and lacking valid "student deferments" from the "labor force," are partitioned into relatively small privileged groups (academics, practitioners of the creative and performing arts, the hereditary rich, and the virtuously retired who have served their time for forty-five years), and large stigmatized social categories (the insane, criminals, "bums," women who must admit to being "just a housewife").[1] In pecuniary terms alone, the normative prescription of universal labor force participation was irrational. According to Lester Thurow (1984:45): "Analysis demonstrated that it was often cheaper to give many low-skill individuals a lifetime income than it was to raise their earnings capacities by the same amount." We would add that it's even cheaper to do the same for a high-skill individual the necessity for whose job is of a subjective character and whose activities entail the consumption of lavish office space, sophisticated equipment, and a supporting staff.

In 1980, we believed that the observed low productivity growth in U.S. industry, i.e., retaining larger numbers of productive laborers than was warranted by existing productive technique and preserving their jobs by means of subsidies, import quotas, "trigger pricing," state purchases, and so forth, against more efficient foreign, especially Japanese, firms was dictated by the soberly disciplining effect their very presence had upon the nonproductive workers, whose sense of privileged exemption from the worst degradation of the "capitalist labor process" was thereby enhanced. The totality of these charges upon society, we thought at the time, represented the underlying, essentially noneconomic, cause of the seemingly indefensible inflation of the 1970s.

In 1980, André Gorz (1980) in France and Rudolf Bahro (1977) in East Germany were putting "free time" at the head of the agenda of the liberation struggle against capitalism and "actually existing socialism," respectively.

If something wicked this way came, it would be the condensation of relations of cultural alienation in guise of forms previously developed to subserve the administration of the extraction of surplus value such that opposition would be liquidated without resistance, without the realization on the part of anyone that it was occurring; without it being conceivable what an opposition that opposed would be against.

In 1980 we lacked the words to describe it, no portable high-level language code, just an isolated cross-section here and there, no two of which we could link into an executable module; that is, the future is here, debugged, and it works!

We call it the Garbage State.

The Garbage State flourishes by secreting a poisonous miasma of pure information into the sphere of cultural reproduction. Its purity inheres in the fact that it is not about anything in particular; just endless lists of things that can be printed out, displayed, formatted, stored on-line or on tape, just any old (or new or projected) thing that someone else finds necessary or desirable or advisable or a good thing just in case (you never can tell) to have accessible.

The life energy of most people misleadingly called "productive" is consumed in keeping track of things and keeping track of the things that have been kept track of or keeping track of the people coding literals in the *working-storage section* of the *data division* so that more things can be kept track of. The Garbage State is made possible by, and spawns the proliferation of, what is glorified as high-technology industry.

Hi-tech works like this: In August 1981, the *New York Times* included in a Sunday edition an advertising supplement paid for by the office-equipment industry. It featured an essay by the best-selling writer Alvin Toffler. This was quite informative, though perhaps not for reasons intended by Toffler and his paymasters. Fifty-two percent of employed citizens were at that time "working," or whatever it was they did, in offices. Every day (it was not clear from the context whether weekends and holidays were included) these functioning appendages of collectivized consumption output 600 million pages of computer print-out, 245 million pages of photocopies, and 76 million pages of business letters (that is, real letters, exclusive of junk mail, form letters, computerized mailings, "mailgrams," what have you); all of which represented an average of forty-five pages of documents generated per employee daily. The authors would like to take this opportunity to declare, in the words of the slogan of the National Recovery Administration (1933–1934), "We do our part!"

As we have noted above, given the impossibility of adequately quantifying the "productivity" of those paid to consume, plus the steady cheapening of the costs of consuming information-processing machines relative to the cost of the labor of those paid to implement the consumption of the machines, it was inevitable that managers would be inundated by an exponentially growing deluge of information. Toffler's essay actually cited executives' complaints of deepening obfuscation the better "informed" they were. The office equipment industry's remedy, in the proffering whereof they were perfectly sincere apart from the element of "relative use value creation" to be found in any advertisement, was redolent of iatrogenic disease: Faster, more sophisticated machines capable of generating yet vaster masses of information at the hands of still more ignorant and untrained employees at even lower unit cost.

As so often happens in social life, what was substantively rational on the "micro" level, much like the lone farmer increasing acreage under the plow in hopes of selling more crop for incremented income, had begun to turn into substantive irrationality on the "macro" or aggregate level: The more information that was output faster, the more complex, difficult, and expensive it was becoming to keep track of its flow, evaluate its importance relative to the mass of other information with which it competed for attention, ensure that it was stored in orderly fashion ("database management") and up to date, and troubleshoot the bugs, flaws, bottlenecks, and malfunctions, any of which could precipitate chaos without backup equipment, backup files, and backup personnel. Less than two years earlier, the North American Air Defense Command had been sent on a World War III alert due to a programming error. It was entirely reasonable for any given office to deal with the inundation of information by acquiring newer, faster, more sophisticated equipment that could process vastly more information coming in and send information out in the same proportion. The latter then became someone else's problem.

That was in 1981, a long time ago. The apparently successful intensification of social discipline in the "Let's catch up with Japan!" ambience of the early 1980s has at last permitted a drastic shrinkage of the "classical"—or, in the more contemptuous usage, "smokestack-industry"—working class, whose continued high visibility is dispensable: In these pitiless times it has become possible to enforce aversion to a "bad attitude" upon the "information processors," not by the mere threat of manual labor, but by the outright terror of a shelter for the homeless—if lucky: sleeping in doorways otherwise.

The Reagan administration, elected in 1980 principally because the pitiful policyless political drifter, Carter, deserved to lose, generated an amazing amount of out and out blind faith in the empty slogan "supply-side economics." We are not professional economists, but naively bewildered readers of the political press who cannot make any sensible distinction between encouraging an increase in supply and the stimulation of aggregate demand by an increase in purchasing power somewhere: the so-called Keynesians would have done it by means of deficit spending accompanied by a redistribution of income to encourage household consumption. Part of the subsidizing of the latter would have taken the form of "social programs," too small in the aggregate to subserve anything but a legitimation function, aimed at raising the consumption levels of households in dire need of basic necessities.

The Keynesian school is now in disrepute and has been the explicit target of the "supply siders." But the fiscal policies of the latter have certainly entailed deficit spending, and that unprecedentedly. The purchasing power "pumped" into the economy was, however, now sloshed onto the upper- and upper-middle income strata, i.e., those who already had acquired plenty of practical experience in squandering money and the only people in a position to save part of their incomes in that they could not possibly spend it all.

The monetary policies of the early 1980s complemented and supplemented fiscal policies: High interest rates subsidized such savings as the domestic rich chose to make, while draining capital out of Europe: $83 billion in 1983 alone. As, partly by consequence of this, Europe languished in the depression from which the United States was emerging just in time for the 1984 elections (sheer coincidence), the hi-tech sector of U.S. industry was crushing its feeble counterparts: In late July 1984, the ITT subsidiary in England was scheming to acquire that country's largest computer manufacturer, while IBM did a deal with British Telecom that "revives fears among its rivals that an IBM standard may come to dominate data communications as effectively as it already does mainframe computers" (*Economist*, August 4-10, 1984). In New York, as if in rebuttal, *Time* (August 13, 1984) ran a feature story blaming the Europeans' troubles on obsolete national rivalries while, a couple of pages later, announcing U.S. plans to abolish the withholding tax on interest payments to foreigners.

Part of the proceeds of the Reagan tax cuts was indeed squandered on luxury goods and frivolous speculation. Some was saved, thus potentially available for investment as the Reagan administration hoped. Other tax subsidies were handed over directly to corporations. Some "investment" did take place, but in terms of the categories of bourgeois economics it is most difficult to differentiate "productive" investment, i.e., on facilities and machinery for increasing the output of goods, from expenditure on office buildings, office equipment, computers, interoffice and intraoffice communications equipment, and other tinker toys wherewith management keeps better track of things while cosmetizing itself with a more advanced, hi-tech appearance. All of the latter is unproductive.

We got our most recent figures from a glance at a *Newsweek* column by Robert J. Samuelson:

> The 1981 business tax cuts . . . bloated corporate treasuries and made new investment highly profitable. In 1983 corporations collectively covered their investment needs from internal cash flow—that is, retained profits and depreciation allowances. . . . The Federal Reserve estimates that the effective corporate tax rate dropped from 56 percent to 32 percent from 1980 to 1983. [August 13, 1984]

Where is the demand coming from, though? Barring centralized control of investment decisions, as practiced by the Japanese Ministry of International Trade and Industry, wherein it is guided by the opportunities for creation and penetration of markets perceived by the mammoth export trading companies, it is quite fantastic to expect corporations to invest, rather than raise dividends, bloat salaries, squander money on advertising to marginally increase market shares, export capital, indulge in international currency speculation, or, most spectacularly, consummate gigantic mergers.

The answer was given in the following paragraph: the office.

> The boom is concentrated in computers and electronics gear as prices drop while computing power increases. Last year the proportion of business' equipment spending on computers and office equipment (14.2 per cent) was nearly double the 1978 level. Communications and electrical generating equipment, instruments and office copiers also rose; together these items now constitute about two-fifths of all equipment investment.

(Equipment accounts for about two-thirds of business investment; the rest is buildings.)

So, between 26 and 27 percent of all business investment is on nonproductive office—read "information processing and information generating"—equipment, which as we hinted above, has a way of ensuring the expansion of its own market by the very nature of its output. To this must certainly be added a portion of the 33 percent spent on buildings, as it is obviously necessary to put the equipment somewhere. Of the remainder, the portion of investment actually spent on machinery and factories for manufacture of products, a not inconsiderable fraction may be presumed to be destined for the expansion of, and research and development for, the "hardware" output of the information processing industries themselves. This is not to mention "software," of course: That is a can of worms on the level of theory, which we approach with the greatest trepidation.

An applications program written, usually in COBOL, by 500 denizens of cubicles for keeping track of inventory or personnel efficiency ratings is common clerical work. Entertainment software, e.g., home electronic games, is part of the sphere of cultural reproduction with potential for soon becoming one of the fine arts. An operating system and related system software—loaders, linkers, assemblers, compilers, file-management services, peripherals interface programs—is at least as important to the machine as any of its parts, of which by the way, none move except the peripherals (tape and disk drives, printer card reader if any).[2] Deciding whether writing system software constitutes "productive labor" may well be comparable to a rabbinical decision as to whether opening a refrigerator door on the sabbath constitutes building a fire, hence performing labor as prohibited in the Torah, if the light goes on.

To the collectivized consumption in the office must be added the collectivized consumption in the military. The predominant industry in which the energies of Americans who are paid to get through the day are expended is, materially, using stuff up; on the political level, keeping themselves under surveillance and fostering the readiness and refinement of the means of violence, and on the cultural level, generating the fog of information pollution whereby their monitored behavior is qualitatively transformed where it is not actually thereby constituted.

Considered exclusively in terms of the level of material social reproduction, the office is parasitic. It consumes products and human labor while producing nothing within its confines. The office-in-particular keeps track of things and people, as it has always done. The office-in-particular, as the facilitator and radiator of domination and exhibitor of the magical metalanguage associated with domination remains as it was since the beginning of recorded history, which was of course first written down in an office. But it was a computer scientist, not a sociologist, who pointed out that, in order to maintain the reproduction of domination at the *same level* of intensity in the period following World War II, the development of the digital computer was dictated (Wisenbaum, 1969). Otherwise, the bureaucracies of the major capitalist states would have "collapsed" under the weight of information to be processed.

We find the aggregate impact of the *office-in-general* even more interesting for purposes of abstract speculation: Over half of those recorded by the payroll-program-output-in-general as being paid money to do something are keeping track of things. That is, they are monitoring behavior.

The office-in-general is, via its ever-growing capacity to monitor an ever-expanding range of behavior, engaged willy-nilly in the reproduction of stupidity and inferiority on an extended scale: All behavior monitored, from the extent of your debt to your scores on assorted "instruments," is susceptible to the construction of being reflective of your degree of inferiority in terms of ever-proliferating invidious distinctions, i.e., who is inferior to whom on something or other and, this being bourgeois society, by *exactly* how much. A determinate relation is posited between inferiority and stupidity (nothing new here excepting only quantitative precision; recall Mencius, "Some labor with their minds and rule others..."), though it is that exception, in its mass, the very magnitude of the quantity of quantities, which imparts the quality of "reality" to the results): The inferior must be stupid; some kind of "cognitive deficit" can always be yanked from the files, printed out, or displayed on the screen.

Curiously, these inferiorities, as measured, may have little of a causative nature to do with aggregate inequalities. Economists take the word of psychologists and sociologists that "skills," "work ethic," "intelligence," and such-like are important, but according to Lester Thurow, "standard economic variables (skills, IQ, hours of work, etc.) could explain only 20 to 30 percent of the variance in individual earnings" (1984:44). Earlier, Bowles and Gintis (1976), had found that, in explaining variance in intergenerational mobility, operationalized as the probability of movement from parents' income decile to children's income decile, found that IQ contributed nothing at all.

It is curious that the social sciences have never seriously explored the alternative interpretation, by which inferiorities and stupidities, rather than representing intrinsic personal attributes determining human fate, should rather be construed as mediators of the hereditary transmission of social rank, hence concomitants of purely stylistic aspects of behavior. This corresponds to the picture that emerges when one groups the scores of children or adolescents on any standardized test: The larger the parents'-income interval used, the closer do the observed correlations with children's test scores approach unity.

Beyond the measurement of relative inferiorities, which has come to be the entire practice of the academic social sciences and their applied versions, i.e., the "management sciences," there is a realm of not-yet-quantifiable behavior susceptible to monitoring; slip-ups therein, usually of a stylistic character, can have consequences most painfully quantitative, especially in the upper-middle strata; and equally so for the professional-academic and the corporate-managerial sectors: a deficiency in your "way of relating" here or a violation of intricate "dress for success" rules there; and in either case any violation of the demanding ritual norms of bodily purity, as legitimated and medicalized in terms of "health." The advertising industry, whose business it is to propagate insecurities, reminds you of the terrible consequences: "I've had poor scotch and I've had rich scotch. Believe me, *rich is better!*"

The detection and communication of advantageous behavioral styles, deemed simultaneously fashionable and intrinsically good, for and to the relevant specialized audiences, and standardized therein, is accomplished with amazing rapidity by journalists, scholars, artists, writers, and other wielders of formidable capacities for shorthand depiction and conceptualization of the doings of fast-rising young upper middles. Some of these, in select circles, may even pass for radical social critics. We mention no names.

There transpires a generalized "speed-up" of life: Sex roles persist, but have become more difficult and complicated on either side. Men are required to become passably adept at the domestic and emotional skills formerly relegated to women, and increasingly essential for the maintenance of appropriate appearances during foreseeable episodes of singleness in the epoch of the modular family; and they must "achieve" at least as ferociously as before to outcompete and outrank the women they intend to be good enough for. Women are held to standards of pulchritude and fashionable display at least as exacting as before, to which have been added criteria of physical fitness previously enjoined—and less stringently—on men, while psychosexual passivity is taboo among the better sort as clinical norms of good sex are propagated in explicit detail by experts and their popularizers; and meanwhile women must be at least passably good as "achievers" to maintain an upper-middle standard of living both before and, again foreseeably, *after* marriage (especially with custody of children) to be good enough for men who somewhat outrank them.[3]

In the mid-1970s, it occurred to us that monitored behavior—whether kept track of by bureaucratic superiors and minions of agencies with which one has dealings; phone company and credit card computers whose presumed purpose is compiling your monthly charges only moderately inaccurately, media operatives, survey takers, market researchers; pollsters, and last and least social and behavioral scientists—is somehow qualitatively different from "naive behavior."

Monitored behavior, or potentially monitorable behavior, occurs as if it might be documented by someone else, or even oneself as surrogate, for other, and necessarily higher, purposes, precisely because of its realistic-seeming ostensibility as ordinary quotidian activity. Monitorable behavior finds its reflection in the impulse to self-document—whose remote origins are found in diary keeping and writing letters at least in part for their ultimate collection and editing by future scholars for publication and eventual textual analysis by specialist scholars yet unborn—whether by audio or video cassette devices, home movie cameras, 35mm cameras for slides, or, today, by personal computer: A behavioral scientist of the authors' knowledge keeps an Apple IIe at each of his business locations—and of course at home—whereon he maintains a log of what he does, accurate to the half hour or less, while somehow he manages to do it all ("5:00–5:30, update references including references to instrumentation; 5:30–6:00, Eat"). If Daniel Boorstin could term a news conference or a press release a "pseudoevent," the totality of monitored or monitorable or self-documentable behavior is "information pollution." This is not pseudo anything—as the imitation fur coat commerical would have it. It's real whatever-it-is.

Whether or not one agrees with Barbara Ehrenreich's reconstruction of the cultural history of the 1950's "Silent Generation" in her *In the Hearts of Men*, it is reasonable to believe that there was a single "middle-class" behavioral style stigmatized by the epithet "conformity," and, further, that this was itself a legitimate heir of nineteenth-century high bourgeois culture whose passing was so eloquently—if vapidly—mourned by Daniel Bell in *The Cultural Contradictions of Capitalism*. It was, by contemporary standards, both less demanding to conform to, the sixties having not yet occurred or been imagined, drugs having not yet been invented, "good sex" having been hitherto a mere rumor; and sufficiently coherent as to have been rejectable (as well as, of course, acceptable), at least conceptually—all sorts of behavioral compromises short of the beat generation having been tried—as a totality. Even at the most abstract theoretical levels (cf. Foss, *Freak Culture*), its seamless unity was posited if not hallucinated: Parsons's *The Social System* presenting the benign version; Marcuse's *One-Dimensional Man* the malign.

In the 1980s, there are several contending jigsawed fragments of culture, all in part confusedly interpenetrated and unto each there corresponds its variant of "appropriate behavior," each difficult to perfect, expensive to sustain, demanding of time and energy, and rigorous in its standards. Behavioral lapses, often, as noted, stylistic and superficial, may precipitate the disasters that once accrued to ideological lapses in the Joe McCarthy era: Academics do not get tenured, law-firm associates do not make partner, executives are "dishired" with exquisite delicacy.

What is appropriate behavior?

About "appropriate behavior" very little is known, scientifically speaking. A great deal was learned about interactional rituals in everyday life in the 1960s and 1970s by sociologists. This body of knowledge may or may not have some bearing on a definition of appropriate behavior: Mention of sociology is inappropriate behavior in the presence of behavioral scientists.

Of inappropriate behavior a great deal is known, as it is measured on rating scales and symptom checklists. Usages such as "role-inappropriate behavior" and departures from "age-appropriate behavioral norms" suggest that, first, inappropriate behavior must be highly contextual, second, appropriate behavior is definable merely by not being noticed; and third, inappropriate behavior invariably gets the perpetrator into trouble.

Already, by 1960, secular-rationalist doctrinal or theoretical interpretations and reinterpretations of social reality had become "deconstituted," even for purposes of lame political reformism, to such a degree that a leading candidate for the ruling political idea of the time was called "the End of Ideology," after the title of a book of essays by Daniel Bell. To the extent that "ideology" was generically identified with intellectually coherent formulations in the realm of political economy, the point was well taken. The ensuing social-movement period, witnessing as it did an innovative exuberance of subjectivist ideologies followed by the dawning awareness that the latter are no less vulnerable to standardization, trivialization, and recuperation than the ideological forms they replaced, did not at its close yield to a recrudescence of "isms" of the traditional sort, with the minor exception of a flurry of neo-Leninism among former movement participants and a more influential school called "Neoconservativism." In a period generally characterized by every form of conservatism from the knee-jerk reactionary to the mock evangelical to the steely-eyed murderous, the "neo" may have alluded to prominent practitioners applying argumentative styles acquired in the Jewish socialist intellectual subculture of New York City to the irrititation of their former friends by opposing that which, in the given situation, it had been uniquely conventional to favor and vice versa. Note the telling implications of Norman Podhoretz's book title: *Breaking Ranks*.

Withal, it is acknowledged that the post-1960s period must surely rank as one of the great eras in the intellctual history of the United States and its culturally kindred satellite states, though we insist that this impinged not at all upon the image huckstering and sophisticatedly contrived "political process." Perhaps this had something to do with the sheer mass of the cultural practitioners or the volume of their output, ever increasing under the lash of the familiar quest for wealth and fame and the increasingly more typical need for tenure. In our highly mannered civilization we have developed what heretofore might have been a contradiction in terms: a vigorous, vital, dynamic decadence, subsumed within which, in a small corner to be sure, are hitherto unimaginable cultural contradictions of socialism.

We have focused here upon the "upper-middle" strata in a desperate and rather tortuous effort to account for an obvious political fact: There is today no political opposition; and not only is this of no great concern outside an exiguous subculture of career politicos; it is hardly noticed.

In the political sphere all sectors of the upper-middle strata are collectively known as "public opinion." This is the upper 5 to 10 percent of the population that comprises the popular support of the regime as a whole. Within it, the nominal opposition chose as its candidate an entity who could not even be characterized as a gray blur, rather, he seemed a mere patch of smog: His major career advancement had been due to his capacity for making Jimmy ("Who?") Carter appear exciting by comparison. A nothing who stood for nothing, he was thought mismatched against a president who was naught but a fabrication seeking to become a facade.

Before Mondale's nomination, curiously, he faced what could only have been a serious challenge to one as insubstantial as himself. This was from a certain Senator Hart(pence), exuding mock glamor, who won a string of primaries by announcing "new ideas." This was too good to be true, and indeed it was fraudulent. There was nobody capable of generating any "ideas" whatsoever; the habit and practice of political thought had been lost.

Daniel Bell (1960) had already announced that political "ideas" were obsolete. The Germanic depths of this notion were plumbed by Marcuse (1964). The recrudescence of social-movement political dissidence in the 1960s did, in fact, bypass what had been *conventionally* understood as "ideas," "ideologies," "policies," "issues," and "positions" altogether. For this reason the 1960s movements passed the socialist tradition, which was uncomprehending utterly as liberal and reactionary adherents of the conventional interpretation of social reality, in that all of these continued to posit the primacy of the material level of social reproduction in social development.

In the 1980s, we have attained a new level of distortion in social reality. The conventional interpretation continues to posit the primacy of the level of material reproduction, ever harping as it does so on "productivity," technique, employment, and "the bottom line." The liberal variant, in the elections held in 1984, typically emphasized *material* social justice as opposed to the *material* rewards of predation, and was rejected by the voters as mustily obsolete, albeit neither winners nor losers even attempted to analyze wherein this was so.

The predominance of the level of cultural reproduction combined with new technique—so-called high-tech—yields a new social formation wherein the most privileged large stratum of the population, and occupationally the most prestigious, comprises those paid to concoct plausible excuses for other members of their own stratum, not to mention vastly more numerous subordinate strata, to waste their time generating, printing out, copying, text editing and formatting, publishing, inputting, outputting, mailing out, or throwing out strings of characters and digits. This is the *informationalizing of mental life*. An elaborate prestige hierarchy, from "knowledge" at the top to mere "data" at the bottom, corresponds to the range from professionals to minimum wage-earning data entry clerks.

At the core of Marx's (1973) analysis of capitalism is the notion of *using-up*—or consumption—of the *time* of human life. In the 1850s and 1860s, this was *productive consumption*. A solid majority of those "gainfully employed" in the most advanced version of bourgeois society are enduring the consumption of their time in the reproduction of symbols (or their symbolic representation as eight-bit characters in EBCDIC or ASCII) of which only a diminishing portion ever attains material existence.

Never before has so much of human lifetime been so unproductively consumed by capitalism, literally for nothing, with this nothing embodied in a commodity—information—which ever cheapens itself while air and water become more expensive! As earlier noted, the delusion as to this commodity's importance reproduces social discipline whose underlying logic thus becomes social discipline for its own sake. This is compounded, in turn, by the facticity of the dataness—the aggregate of all data bases—whose content, with quantitatively speaking, minor exceptions, is the monitoring of human behavior at greater or lesser degrees of abstraction.

As hinted, social theory—our own not excepted—must be subsumed within the process of the informationalizing of mental life. To ask social theorists to transcend this new stage even to the point of acknowledging its advent is to ask them to become unserious, unprofessional, unconcerned with external grant support, unaware that "previous studies have found that . . . " whereas "the present study . . . " suggests "the need for further study." This is not merely the problem of "abstracted empiricism" first noted by Mills (1959), but the ultimate dilemma of sociology: the point at which the investigator construes that he, she, or perhaps it, has stepped outside the object of investigation is a matter of subjective judgment that posits as its presupposition the prior existence of the critical faculty for making such a judgment. The constraints upon this critical faculty reflect the impossibility of construing that those with whom one wishes to communicate are in the aggregate wrong and that one is oneself wrong to the extent that dialogue is maintained. That is, all the individuals the investigator *knows* are "doing good work," and one does and should ask for reprints, but the *whole* is hallucinated. All individuals *qua* individual can generate high quality knowledge-product, but the product *in the aggregate* has the effect of legitimating the structure of information production and the monitoring of behavior.

What has been presented here is not a theory in the scientific sense. We can neither predict qualitative changes in the bases of social-movement cohesion, nor in the emergence of wholly new ideological formulations. Social movements have shifted bases in relation to the industrial era. Preindustrial social movements were formed on religious-ethnic bases using religious interpretations of reality; social movements during the industrial era (1820–1950) used secular-rational interpretations of reality and formal organizations constituted their bases of cohesion. In postindustrial societies, social movements have taken the form of dissident subcultures and the interpretations of reality have been sub-jectivistic-experiential. Yet it is problematic to posit that the next social move-ment—we promise there will be a next one—will cohere around dissident subcultures, since as we have already noted, dissident subcultures posited as their presupposition a unitary bourgeois culture.

What we have done is present a reconceptualization of an accepted body of fact. This reconceptualization has, we hope, provided a framework to clarify the nature and processes of a social movement and to delimit them as episodic and recurring processes in social development. Although this reconceptuali-zation does not have predictive power, it does provide a point outside conven-tional social theory from which currently popular theories can be shown to be egregiously inadequate for the understanding and interpretation of social move-ments and social revolutions.

There is an inevitability to the recurrence of social movements in class society. Eruptions that have occurred would have occurred anyway, because issues raised within social movements are artifacts of the historical conjuncture in which they emerge. Issues do not create social movements, but vice-versa.

Since the founding of the United States, social movements have roughly followed a cycle of recurrence every thirty to thirty-five years. Peak years were: 1828, in which laborers in major cities struck and fought for union represen-tation and the first stirrings of feminism were heard; 1860, in which one of the bloodiest social movements ever occurred in the West, combining abolitionism, labor insurgency, and regional conflict; 1894, with labor troubles and the Populist revolt; 1912, again labor was rebellions and feminists were on the move; 1921–22, working-class and racial insurgency; 1937, working-class re-volt, with Blacks as a category subsumed within it; and 1968–69, insurgency of middle-class youth, Blacks, women, homosexuals, Amerindians and His-panics, this time with the working class being counter-insurgent.

In 1959, we had no notion that there would ever be another Left, little idea that we ourselves would be in it, and certainly no inkling of what sort of Left it would turn out to be. The 1960s were capable of giving rise to those who knew somehow that they were a "New Left," though not why this was so nor why there had, of necessity, to be an "Old Left." In the future, we cannot count on participants in whatever social movement may emerge of having any sense of what a "Left" is or was, or that they are it. Of the next Left, we are sure only that it will laugh at us and that we will be too old to know it for what it will *post facto* be known to have been.

The social movement to come will somehow confront, and itself invariably bear the mark of, the recuperations of the 1970s, the emergent Garbage State, and the informationalization of mental life. We wish we could identify the rebels of tomorrow and tell you how they will do it. We do not have the slightest idea.

Notes

1. A loose formula translates exemption from functioning into privileged high income within the same occupation: We informed the graduate program director in clinical

psychology at a large State University of New York campus of the base salary rate of a clinical psychologist with the title of Research Scientist V, but required to show up at the office at 8:30 A.M., who might be employed at a research institute, an arm of the Office of Mental Hygiene, housed on the same campus; the figure excluded seniority "step" increases and raises for favorable efficiency ratings. The professor exclaimed, "Why, that's twice what they're paying me!"

2. "As measured by the number of moving parts, the System/370 operating system is undoubtedly mankind's most complex creation. The computer hardware is less complex, but complex nonetheless" (Gary DeWard Brown, *System/370 Job Control Language*. New York: Wiley, 1977. pp. 1-2). "Moving parts" is to be read figuratively.

3. There is no sign that the hypergamy-hypogyny rule (cf. Jessie Bernard, *The Future of Marriage*, pp. 25-26, for a pithy formulation thereof and certain logical corollaries therefrom) is in desuetude; witness the chronic complaint of career women that "there are so few good men around," i.e., that they have priced themselves out of the market; notwithstanding, of course, the conspicuous flouting of the rule by a few celebrities. It is arguable that the rule is sexist, but we didn't make it. The rule is to such an extent embedded in social relations as to represent a sufficient explanation for the so-called Cinderella Complex in that the logical consequence of "success" is a drastic restriction of mate selection. The structure of bourgeois social relations that constitutes the "career" as both mental structure and configuration of behavioral dictates is equally accountable for other psychic disasters discerned by mental health professionals; notably, the "identity crisis," i.e., the trepidation at "career" inception; and the "midlife crisis," i.e., that point at which definitive consignment to one side or the other of the "success-failure" dichotomy is made by conventional definition. Fortunately, the vast majority of the population is spared all this anguish in that, by conventional construction, they never had "futures" ahead of them to begin with, being left with the comparatively manageable problem of living with being inferior by reason of some combination of "lack of ability," moral depravity assessed post facto ("not motivated," etc.), and deliberate intentions of which they were never aware yet "really wanted to."

References

Amin, Samir. *Accumulation on a World Scale*. New York: Monthly Review, 1974.

Aronowitz, Stanley. *False Promises*. New York: McGraw-Hill, 1971.

Bahro, Rudolph. *The Alternative in Eastern Europe*. London: New Left Books, 1978.

Baran, Paul and Paul Sweezy. *Monopoly Capital*. New York: Monthly Review, 1966.

Barnard, Jessie. *The Future of Marriage*. New York: World, 1972.

Barnet, Richard. *The Giants*. New York: Simon and Schuster, 1977.

Baskir, Lawrence and William Straus. *Chance and Circumstance: The Draft, the War, and the Vietnam Generation*. New York: Knopf, 1978.

Bell, Daniel. *The End of Ideology: On the Exhaustion of Political Ideas in the Fifties*. New York: The Free Press, 1960.

———. *The Coming of Post-Industrial Society*. New York: Basic, 1973.

———. *The Cultural Contradictions of Capitalism*. New York: Basic, 1976.

Berger, Peter and Thomas Luckmann. *The Social Construction of Reality*. New York: Doubleday, 1967.

Bettelheim, Charles. *Class Struggles in the USSR: 1917–1923*. New York: Monthly Review, 1978.

Billington, Ray. *The Protestant Crusade: 1800–1860*. New York: Quadrangle, 1964.

Block, Fred. "Contradictions of Capitalism as a World System." *Insurgent Sociologist* 5 (1975).

Blum, Jerome. *Lord and Peasant in Russia*. Princeton, NJ: Princeton University Press, 1961.

Blumer, Herbert. "Social Movements." In A. M. Lee, ed., *New Outline of Principles of Sociology*. New York: Barnes & Noble, 1948.

Bowles, Samuel and Herbert Gintis. *Schooling in Capitalist America*. New York: Basic, 1976.

Braudel, Ferdinand. *Capitalism and Material Life: 1400–1800*. New York: Harper, 1973.

Braverman, Harry. *Labor and Monopoly Capital*. New York: Monthly Review, 1974.

Brinton, Crane. *Anatomy of a Revolution*. New York: Vintage, 1965.

Carr, E. H. *Foundations of a Planned Economy*. Harmondsworth, England: Penguin, 1971.

———. *Socialism in One Country*. 3 vols. Harmondsworth, England: Penguin, 1976.

Cheyney, Edward. *The Dawn of a New Era 1250–1453*. New York: Harper, 1936.

Cohen, Norman. *The Pursuit of the Millennium*. New York: Oxford, 1961.

Coser, Lewis. *The Functions of Social Conflict*. New York: The Free Press, 1956.

Davies, James. "Toward a Theory of Revolution." *American Sociological Review* 27 (1962): 5-19.

Dill, William. "Environment as an Influence on Managerial Autonomy." *Administrative Science Quarterly* 2 (1958): 409-443.

Dobson, W.A.C.H. *Mencius*. Toronto: University of Toronto, 1963.

Dollard, John. *Caste and Class in a Southern Town*. Garden City, NY: Doubleday, 1957.

Douglas, Mary. *Purity and Danger*. London: Routledge and Kegan Paul, 1966.

Duby, Georges. *The Three Orders: Feudal Society Imagined*. Trans. by Arthur Goldhammer. Chicago: University of Chicago, 1978.

Ehrenreich, Barbara. *The Hearts of Men*. New York: Doubleday, 1983.

Ewen, Stewart. *The Captains of Consciousness*. New York: Harper, 1976.

Fanon, Frantz. *Black Skins, White Masks*. New York: Grove, 1967.

———. *Studies in a Dying Colonialism*. New York: Grove, 1967.

———. *The Wretched of the Earth*. New York: Grove, 1968.

Farber, Jerry. *The Student as Nigger*. New York: Pocket, 1969.

Foss, Daniel. *Freak Culture*. New York: Dutton, 1972.

Foss, Daniel and Ralph Larkin. "From 'The Gates of Eden' to 'Day of the Locust': An Analysis of the Middle Class Youth Movement of the 1960s and its Heirs in the 1970s—the Postmovement Groups." *Theory and Society* 3 (1976): 45-64.

———. "Roar of the Lemming: Youth, Post-movement Groups and the Life Construction Crisis." In H. Johnson, ed., *Religious Change and Continuity*, San Francisco: Jossey-Bass, a special issue of *Sociological Inquiry* 49 (1979): 264-85.

———. "Lexicon of Folk-Etymology of the 1960s." In S. Sayres, et al. (eds.). *The 60s Without Apology*. Minneapolis, MN: University of Minnesota, a special double volume of *Social Text* 3 (3) and 4 (1), 1984.

Gamson, William. *The Strategy of Social Protest*. Homewood, IL: Dorsey, 1975.

Goffman, Erving. *Asylums*. Chicago: Aldine, 1961.

———. *Gender Advertisements*. New York: Harper, 1976.

Goodwyn, Lawrence. *The Populist Moment*. New York: Oxford, 1978.

Gornick, Vivian. *The Romance of American Communism*. New York: Basic, 1977.

Gorz, Andre. *Farewell to the Working Class*. Boston: South End, 1980.

Gramsci, Antonio. *Letters from Prison*. New York: Harper, 1973.

————. *Selected Writings*. New York: International, 1977.

Grier, William and Price Cobbs. *Black Rage*. New York: Basic, 1968.

Gurr, Ted. *Why Men Rebel*. Princeton: Princeton University, 1970.

Habermas, Jurgen. *Legitimation Crisis*. Boston: Beacon, 1975.

Halliday, Fred. *Iran: Dictatorship and Development*. Harmondsworth, England: Penguin, 1978.

Higham, John. *Strangers in the Land*. New Brunswick, NJ: Rutgers, 1955.

Hill, Christopher. *Puritainism and Revolution*. London: Secker & Warburg, 1958.

————. *The Century of Revolution: 1603–1714*. New York: Norton, 1961.

————. *The World Turned Upside Down*. Harmondsworth, England: Penguin, 1973.

Hobsbawm, Eric. *Primitive Rebels*. New York: Praeger, 1963.

Hofstadter, Richard. *The Age of Reform*. New York: Harper, 1955.

Huizinga, Johan. *The Waning of the Middle Ages*. London: E. Arnold, 1924.

Josephus, Flavius. *History of the Jewish War*. Harmondsworth, England: Penguin, 1970.

Kardiner, Abram and Lionel Ovesey. *The Mark of Oppression*. Cleveland: World, 1951.

Kenniston, Kenneth. *The Uncommitted*. New York: Dell, 1959.

Kolko, Gabriel. *The Triumph of Conservatism*. New York: The Free Press, 1963.

Kuhn, Thomas. *The Structure of Scientific Revolution*. Chicago: The University of Chicago Press, 1970.

Laquer, Walter. *Terrorism: A Study of National and International Political Violence*. Boston: Little, Brown, 1977.

LeBon, Gustav. *The Crowd*. New York: Viking, 1966.

Lefebvre, Georges. *The Great Fear*. London: New Left Books, 1973.

Levi-Strauss, Claude. *The Savage Mind*. Chicago: University of Chicago, 1966.

Livy, Titus. *A History of Rome*. Trans. by Moses Haddad and Joe Poe. New York: Modern Library, 1962.

Lyon, H. R. *The Norman Conquest*. New York: Harper, 1967.

McCarthy, John and Meyer Zald. "Resource Mobilization and Social Movements: A Partial Theory," *American Journal of Sociology* 82 (1977): 1212-41.

McNeil, William. *Plagues and Peoples*. New York: Doubleday, 1976.

McPhail, Clark. "Civil Disorder Participation: A Critical Examination of Recent Research," *American Sociological Review* 36 (1971): 1058-72.

Mannoni, O. *Prospero and Caliban*. New York: Praeger, 1964.

Marcuse, Herbert. *One Dimensional Man*. Boston: Beacon, 1964.

Marx, Karl. "Economic and Philosophical Manuscripts of 1844." In T. Bottomore, ed. *Karl Marx: Early Writings*. New York: McGraw-Hill, 1963.

————. *Capital*, 3 vols. New York: International, 1967.

————. *Grundrisse*. New York: Vintage, 1973.

Milliband, Ralph. *The State in Capitalist Society*. New York: Basic, 1969.

Mills, C. W. *White Collar*. New York: Oxford, 1951.

————. *The Sociological Imagination*. New York: Oxford, 1959.

Mury, Gilbert. *La Societe de Repression*. Paris: Editions universitaires, 1969.

Oakley, Ann. *Housewife*. Harmondsworth, England: Penguin, 1976.

Oberschall, Anthony. *Social Conflict and Social Movements*. Englewood Cliffs, NJ: Prentice-Hall, 1973.

O'Connor, James. *The Fiscal Crisis of the State*. New York: St. Martins, 1973.

———. *The Corporations and the State*. New York: Harper, 1974.

Olson, Mancur Jr. *The Logic of Collective Action*. Cambridge, MA: Harvard, 1971.

Painter, Sidney. *The Reign of King John*. Baltimore: Johns-Hopkins, 1949.

Parsons, Talcott. *The Social System*. New York: The Free Press, 1951.

Pike, Douglas. *Viet-Cong*. Cambridge, MA: MIT, 1966.

Polanyi, Karl. *The Great Transformation*. Boston: Beacon, 1961.

———. *Primitive, Ancient, and Modern Economies*. Garden City, NY: Doubleday, 1968.

Poulantzes, Nicos. *Classes in Contemporary Capitalism*. London: New Left Books, 1975.

Reich, Wilhelm. *Sex-Pol*. New York: Vintage, 1971.

Riesman, David, Nathan Glazer and Ruel Denny. *The Lonely Crowd*. New York: Doubleday, 1956.

Roberts, Ron and Robert Kloss. *From the Balcony to the Barricade*. St. Louis: Mosby, 1974.

Rowbotham, Sheila. *Women, Resistance, and Revolution*. New York: Vintage, 1972.

———. *Woman's Consciousness, Man's World*. Harmondsworth, England: Penguin, 1973.

Rude, George. *The Crowd in History: A Study of Popular Disturbances in France and England, 1730–1848*. New York: Wiley, 1964.

Rule, James and Charles Tilly. "1830 and the Unnatural History of Revolution." *Journal of Social Issues* 28 (1972): 49-76.

Sachs, Wulf. *Black Anger*. New York: Greenwood, 1947.

Satin, Mark. *New Age Politics: The Alternative to Marxism and Liberalism*. Vancouver, BC: Whitecap, 1978.

Sinclair, Andrew. *Era of Excess: A Social History of Prohibitionism*. New York: Harper, 1964.

Smelser, Neil. *Theory of Collective Behavior*. New York: The Free Press, 1963.

Snow, C.P. *Two Cultures*. New York: Cambridge, 1959.

Stockwell, John. *In Search of Enemies: A CIA Story*. New York: Norton, 1978.

Stone, Laurence. *The Crisis of the Aristocracy*. New York: Oxford, 1965.

———. *The Causes of the English Revolution: 1529–1642*. New York: Harper, 1972.

Tawney, R. N. *The Agrarian Problem in the Sixteenth Century*. Santa Fe, NM: Gannon, 1970.

Thomas, Hugh. *Cuba; or the Pursuit of Freedom*. London: Eyre, 1971.

TenHouten, Warren. *Cognitive Styles and the Social Order*. Springfield, VA: National Technical Information Service, 1971.

Thompson, E. P. *The Making of the English Working Class*. New York: Viking, 1966.

Thurow, Lester. *Dangerous Currents*. New York: Vintage, 1984.

Tilly, Charles. *The Vendee*. Cambridge, MA: Harvard, 1964.

———. *From Mobilization to Revolution*. Reading, MA: Addison-Wesley, 1978.

Tilly, Charles and Edward Shorter. *Strikes in France: 1830–1968*. New York: Cambridge, 1974.

Tilly, Charles, Louise Tilly and Richard Tilly. *The Rebellious Century: 1830–1930*. Cambridge, MA: Harvard, 1975.

Touraine, Alain. *The Self-production of Society*. Chicago: University of Chicago, 1977.

Trevelyan, G. M. *England Under the Stuarts*. New York: Barnes and Noble, 1965.

Trotsky, Leon. *History of the Russian Revolution*. New York: Sphere, 1957.

Turner, Victor. *The Ritual Process*. Chicago: Aldine, 1969.

Useem, Michael. *Protest Movements in America*. Indianapolis, IN: Bobbs-Merrill, 1975.

Veblen, Thorsten. *The Theory of the Leisure Class*. New York: Macmillan, 1899.

Wallace, Anthony F.C. *Religion: An Anthropological View*. New York: Random House, 1966.

Weber, Max. *The Protestant Ethic and the Spirit of Capitalism*. New York: Scribners, 1950.

Wedgewood, C.V. *The Kings Peace: 1637–1641*. London: Collins, 1955.

Weinstein, James. *The Corporate Ideal in the Liberal State*. Boston: Beacon, 1968.

Weizenbaum, Joseph. *Computers and Human Reason: From Judgment to Calculation*. San Francisco, CA: W. H. Freeman, 1976.

Wiel, Andrew. *The Natural Mind*. Boston: Houghton-Mifflin, 1973.

Willis, Paul. *Learning to Labour*. London: Saxon House, 1977.

Wolfe, Bertram. *Three Who Made a Revolution*. New York: Dial, 1964.

Wright, Eric Olin. *Class, Crisis and the State*. New York: Schocken, 1978.

Yglesias, Jose. *In the Fist of the Revolution*. Harmonsdsworth, England: Penguin, 1970.

Zagorin, Perez. *The Court and the Country*. London: Routledge & Kegan Paul, 1969.

Index

WE STOOD ALONE ·

DOROTHY ADAMS

LONGMANS, GREEN AND CO.

NEW YORK · TORONTO

1944

Jan and Dorothy Kostanecki dressed for a costume ball at the
British Embassy

ANDREW

*These were your parents —
this was your country*

WE STOOD ALONE

CHAPTER *1*

"*HERBATA! Mleko! Herbata!*" — "Tea !
Milk ! Tea !" . . .

Waking, I looked out on a half-lighted station platform
where baskets of geraniums swung in the early morning wind.
A boy was holding a tray with glasses up to a man in the next
compartment. A man was running down the platform.
Then, smoothly, the train pulled out of the station.

There was no more sleep for me, though the day had hardly
broken. Since leaving Berlin, I had been wedged upright
between seven others in a first-class compartment designed
to seat four. All during the night there had been movement
in and out of the corridor.

Now as I peered through the window, the train seemed to
crawl across a great plain. In the faint morning light bent
figures with milk cans tied on their backs, and capes drawn
over their heads, scuttled across the fields. Was this the way
milk reached the cities ? The grey sky and greyer landscape,
dark figures and the mournful cries brought tears to my eyes.
Foolish to feel sentimental about a people you did not and
could not know. Yet over and over went the words in
rhythm to the wheels on the rails : "The Poles are bowed
down by woes . . . the Polish woes."

However, this melancholy dispersed when the sun came out
and we arrived in Warsaw. The station was gaily decorated
for the arrival of the League of Nations Association's delegates, with whom I was traveling. A red carpet had been
laid down for us. We were shown into the first-class waiting
room, a little red plush Victorian drawing room with sofas
and chairs and palm trees, where someone was making a wel-

1

coming speech in French. But this first-class waiting room was like an oasis. In the stampede just outside, enormous bags like steamer trunks, huge bales of blankets and hampers were pushed and tumbled. Here were more bearded and befrocked Jews than I had ever seen in my life, and peasant women, their arms filled with baskets and babies, trailing lines of children.

The elegant little station building might have made a suitable background for the leisurely Victorian ladies in their ruffles and satins when it was built in 1880. Now, like the train on which we had come from Berlin, it was utterly inadequate to the throng of desperately poor returning refugees. A whole population was straining through this little doorway to return and rebuild Poland. More than three-quarter million Jews had come from Russia alone.

There had been no reserved places on the train for the hundred or more delegates to the League of Nations Conference, of which I was a member. In the first-class carriages, as in the third, we exchanged seats with those who stood all night in the corridor. This was in 1925. Only five years before, the Bolsheviks had been camped in the very suburbs of Warsaw. Hardly had the Germans been thrown out of Poland by the Polish Legions than the Russian Communists had invaded her from the east. The weary Legions re-crossed Poland on foot, over roads mostly destroyed during the first World War. The ammunition sent by the Allies was held up by the Germans in Danzig, and by the Czechs who seized Cieszyn ; still the Legions had defeated the Bolsheviks at bayonet point. Though the Russians had fled out of old Poland, foreign pressure had forced the Poles to make a treaty favorable to Russia, which ran the new frontier through the center of the eastern provinces of old Poland.

However, all Poles were anxious for peace, for the opportunity to rebuild their destroyed country. Proud of their regained country, the Polish League of Nations Society was one of the earliest to invite other League of Nations Associations to an international conference. My first job on leaving college was to attend this conference for the League of Nations

2

Committee. Since my parents would not let me go so far alone, I was accompanied by a childhood friend from Boston. She was my own age and spoke no better French nor German than I. Together we arrived in Warsaw, and were sent off by the reception committee in an old Model T Ford to the Bristol Hotel, where one of the finest rooms had been reserved for us.

It looked more like a drawing room than a bedroom, with windows to the floor, consoles and gold framed mirrors, crimson damask curtains, and Gothic brass bedsteads (discreetly hidden) which stood in an alcove. We were soon to take a violent dislike to all this elegance however. When we awakened from a short nap we found our arms peppered with ugly red lumps. Drawing our clothes about us, we called the concierge. But all the perspiring protestations of the chambermaid and denials of the management could not persuade us that fleas were to be found only in the south, and that we must have been bitten on the train. I now imagine that we were suffering from hives, but at the time, with my typically American imagination, I was sure that the place was infested with bugs. The crimson welts were a week in disappearing, and during that hot week of conferences and gala balls we had to wear long sleeves or long white leather gloves !

Between Conference meetings we tried to buy something which seemed to us characteristic of Poland. Our treasure hunts were always unsuccessful. We found poor little food shops, or candle kerosene shops, or perfumery shops where the few bottles of French perfumes and soaps were obviously window decoration. But on every street were various junk shops. I was told one could find marvelous treasures in them, but I shuddered at the moth-eaten fur coats and the dirty Oriental rugs heaped in the windows, and never crossed their sills. Women like those I had seen from the train window came barefoot through the streets, carrying a live hen, a few eggs, or milk on their back. No one wore hats. Those who were shod, wore heavy boots and coarse stockings. Most of the women were wrapped in steamer rugs from head to foot.

We were taken to see the Royal palaces in which Napoleon

had stayed, now arranged as museums. Other Eighteenth Century palaces were used for offices, law courts and ministries. I looked in vain for the signs of tremendous and unequal wealth of which I had so often heard. Everyone seemed equally poor, the only difference being that there were the educated poor and the uneducated poor. The many houses that were opened to us seemed all equally shabby. None had been painted or refurbished since 1914. Wherever we went, even the highest nobility served only tea with dried little cakes. Yet everywhere it was evident that we were received with a great effort at being hospitable.

When we left for Cracow, roses were brought us to the station. Little did I guess that those forlorn flowers, which I threw out of the window as soon as the train started, cost more than five dollars — in a country which had no luxuries.

The trip down to Cracow was very comfortable. Special sleepers had been reserved for us, and the whole train moved smoothly over the vast plain. The little hotel where we stayed was clean and simple. In Cracow we felt we had come back into Europe. Obviously here were privately owned houses, here were villas set in gardens. Oleanders in tubs stood by open doorways which gave a glimpse of well-watered courtyards, cool and inviting. In many an open window birds were singing. None of the houses had bullet holes. The streets, though paved in rough cobblestone, had not recently been torn up for barricades. Well-dressed people sauntered on the streets. Maids in uniform and children in peasant costume were actually strolling in the parks. No one was scurrying and scuttling and it was plain that war had not come so close to Cracow as to harried Warsaw.

As there were no conferences, the whole time was devoted to sight-seeing and receptions. On the first afternoon we were taken to a large private palace. It seemed very dank and gloomy that sunny July day. On the tennis courts musicians were playing, and a few people were dancing. As my friend and I were the only youthful delegates, we had many invitations from partners varying in age and obesity. But a few hops and skips on the hard cement court made the

4

precarious chairs and teetering little tables under the trees seem very attractive. Two young Poles introduced themselves and found us a secluded spot. They asked why we had come, admired our courage at dancing with the delegates, and laughed at our earnestness. They asked for our home addresses with violent protestations that they would never forget us. They would surely see us again, even if they had to cross the ocean to do so ! When we returned to the hotel we read over the names : Zbygniew Grabski, Warsaw ; Jan Kostanecki, Cracow.

Each had the finely knit six foot physique, noble features and bubbling gaiety of the romantic Pole. We were both delighted with the commotion our dashing cavaliers created about us on the lengthy sight-seeing tours, the pompous lectures at the picture galleries, and heavy dinners given by the city dignitaries. Jan Kostanecki was always by my side. He would ferret out some obscure painting in a far end of a gallery and make it stand out in place and history comparing it to similar pictured scenes in other European galleries as if he had had the catalogue in hand. Painters of whose existence I had not dreamed were to him the indispensable links in the development of different styles. He never spoke in general terms of Roman, Gothic or Baroque architecture. He classified the various buildings, subdividing them into sects and schools from various cities. He was also passionately fond of music, and at the concert of Polish Seventeenth Century Chamber Music he showed a musician's knowledge of the pre-Bach relationship between England and the continent. He would pick out the various motifs in the themes and place their antecedents. When our party had to leave by an earlier train for Prague, I felt sad not to have said good-bye to him. With all his erudition, he had made me feel at home in Cracow.

As guests of the Czech Foreign Office, we spent three days in Prague where we were taken to meet both Beneš and Masaryk and shown about the city. I had made many friends among the English delegates, including Mr. Wilson Harris, now editor of *The Spectator*, Mr. Philip Noel Baker and Lady Asquith. On the long train ride to Geneva, they urged me to come to England and write about the Polish-German-Silesian boundary. That I knew nothing in the world about it, nor even exactly where it was, did not in their eyes seem the major obstacle that it did to me, nor indeed the fact that I was employed by the League of Nations Non-Partisan Association in Baltimore. "You should do it," they urged, "you can easily take a year's leave of absence." So it was arranged. Mr. Hugh Dalton, then Economic Advisor to the Foreign Office and now Minister of Economic Warfare, would see to it that I met Mr. Bourdillon.

Mr. Bourdillon was the British member of the international commission made up of a French and an Italian general together with their respective staffs, for the Silesian Plebiscite. The new Polish frontier had not been established by the ethnological maps of Imperial Germany showing the Polish pre-war population, but at the insistence of the Germans at Versailles, the boundary had been settled by Plebiscite. Even after the Plebiscite had shown a Polish majority, the German claims had been given scrupulous consideration and only one-third of the province was allotted to Poland. In all the victorious Allied countries, much had been written in Germany's favor. Lloyd George, for instance, found it preposterous that the rich Silesian coal fields should be given to Poland. "Poland is too poor a country to develop such resources," he had said, "whereas Germany is too great a nation to be crippled for lack of raw products."

"The Poles would be better off buying good German products with their farm produce," I was told by men in authority.

All writers seemed to agree that the Germans would surely sell coal to Poland who could never be trusted to mine it for herself.

All modern German statistical data tried to prove that Silesian coal was of a special quality indispensable to the development of their metallurgical industry. It required no knowledge of statistics to realize that if coal were needed at home, the Germans could not export it. Yet statistics from 1900 to 1914 showed this very coal was used as the basis of

6

pre-war barter with Russia for foodstuffs essential for feeding Germany. By a strange coincidence, I found the same figure used in different books to prove these two opposing contentions. Only then did I realize I was totally unprepared to undertake such a serious study. I therefore decided to spend the winter of 1926 at the London School of Economics and take a post-graduate course in Statistics and International Law. Mr. Philip Noel Baker was to be my tutor.

Besides classes at the London School of Economics, I worked at the Royal Institute of International Relations where I had access to the unpublished documents of the British Commission to Upper Silesia. I was allowed to take no notes. Every little while I would run out into St. James Square to jot down what I had just read. As I had spent the summer in Geneva, studying the League of Nations reports, I had already a bewildering collection of contradictory figures.

An International Boundary Commission had divided the Silesian province giving Germany 75% of the territory although in the Plebiscite the Germans had barely 54% majority in the towns and had conceded all farm lands to the Poles. The Commission based its decision on the fact that during the 19th Century, German capital had developed this area, bringing engineers, tradespeople, and capitalists, into this wholly Polish province. The new Polish-German boundary left one German on the Polish side of the frontier for two Poles on the German, the Commission believing that it was a greater hardship for Germans to live in Poland than for Poles to live in Germany.

Many of my acquaintances and, among them members of the British press, were of the opinion that the whole province should have been given to Germany. They would tell me "It's undignified to imagine a German working for a Pole," or "What chances have the Poles of mining their own coal without German experts, or German capital or German machinery?"

"After all, the Poles are really barbarians!"

Hearing so much adverse criticism of the Poles, I began to

7

think so myself. I forgot about the law, stringently enforced after the time of Bismarck, prohibiting Poles from investing their money in anything except farming and agriculture, which had kept Polish capital out of Silesia. I had seen milk brought to town on the backs of women, I had seen the shabbiness of Warsaw.

Foreign students at the London School of Economics had a club where reference books were kept and where they met after lectures. There were Indian and Chinese, Polish and Dutch, German and French students, and quite a few Americans. As soon as the German students learned what I was doing, they invited me for lunch, to talk over my work. They had no doubt the Province should be returned to Germany. It was a "spiritual insult" for a great nation to be humbled before a little one. They took hours of my time explaining the racial inferiority of the Poles and they ended with the saying : "You'll have to restore the German Colonies. You can't keep a great nation in chains."

The Poles had no ready-made slogans nor arguments, but they were willing to help me look through the great books of statistics published by the Germans from 1910 to 1917. They discarded the propaganda pamphlets the Germans had given me and searched for the figures the Germans had quoted. Strangely I found more coal was mined under the new Polish management than had been mined under the old German concerns.

"Why don't you Poles do something to make counter-propaganda ?" I asked. "Why do you let the Germans take the initiative ? Why don't you publish these facts and tell the world ?"

"Money spent on propaganda is wasted," was the reply. "In the long run, truth will tell, and in the meantime there is too much else to be done."

"What a ridiculous idea !" I said ; "Germany by capturing world opinion will control the world."

"Do you believe," they asked, "that once Germany invaded Poland, however strongly Americans might feel on the moral issues, that they would attempt to stop the Germans ?"

8

I knew that these Polish students were right, yet I still felt it a pity that somehow the American public should be unaware of the fact that while the Germans were building up their case against the smaller nations, the smaller nations were too poor to spend the money necessary to present their case.

During the fall term the foreign students drove down to Kent for a long week-end. In the bus one of the Poles sat down beside me. I went back over our conversation of the preceding days about the return of Upper Silesia to Germany.

"The real issue is," I said, "can the Poles run a modern industrial democratic country ?" He did not reply and I went over the evidence I had collected. Finally he burst out with :

"What you say ultimately boils down to your belief in German racial superiority. You would sacrifice Polish people and all the natural resources of Silesia to satisfy German megalomania."

"In the best interest of the greatest number of people, the Poles should choose a middle ground."

"There is no middle ground!" he protested angrily. "Either you side with Germany or following the Fourteen Points you let the Poles re-unite."

We both sat silently until he said : "Don't you remember me ? I met you in Cracow. My name is John Kostanecki."

Since leaving Poland I had deliberately forgotten him. I was determined to write a just and unbiased thesis in the "broader interests of Science." I had put away as sentimental and emotional that instantaneous sympathy I had felt for Poland. In order to be fair, I had erased all feelings of friendship with Poles. When we met six months later, the memory of John had become so faint I could not have told his name. I had made it a business to eat with the German students and ask their help in my work. Yet John had a magnetic quality that compelled me to watch every move that he made. His presence in our commons was so distracting, I had been unable to concentrate on my studies. Though his clothes were used and threadbare, they were

9

always neatly pressed and brushed. His shoes were always cleaned, his shirt was spotless and his immaculate grooming was in the greatest contrast to the other tousled students. Now, even in the cold jolting bus I felt the net of enchantment slipping over me like a heavy, suffocating drug.

In a flash of self-recognition, I realized I had identified John with Poland and my obstinate refusal to understand the Polish point of view was a reflection of my fear of understanding John. This silenced me, and I was frightened. I vowed to myself I would never be alone with him again, and during the rest of the trip I managed to chat only with the others.

Yet that night after dinner, while we were all about the fire, John drew his chair beside me. In some mysterious way, we felt we were friends. First we discussed books, then paintings, then architecture — all the world of abstractions that lay dazzling before us. We became utterly absorbed in our discovery of each other, which drew us on as one races through the chapter headings of a new and fascinating book one is about to read. The joy of finding each other was so intoxicating that we had forgotten the time. We had not noticed that the others had, one by one, drifted away and were probably long since asleep. We were busily discussing the earlier form of the little Celtic church nearby, and the changes that hid its original structure. John was saying : "You see, the narthex was incorporated into the façade, it has a primitive rotunda. If you will stay after church I will show you. The Saxon font is one of the finest in England."

"Stay after church ! Heavens !" I looked at my watch. It was 2:00 A.M. I left at once, fearing how he would interpret my staying so late, frightened at talking half the night to the very person I was determined to avoid. I reproached myself for weakly becoming infatuated. What an impossible situation to fall in love with a Pole ! Like a rabbit caught in a trap ! But all my efforts of will could not keep snatches of the evening's conversation from spinning around in my head. There was little sleep for me.

"This will never do," I thought, "tomorrow I won't stay after church."

At breakfast, armored with stern resolve, I did not look up as the other students, one by one, came into the dining room, for fear that if it were John, he would at once understand my struggle. Yet as each person came in my heart stood still, waiting for the now familiar throaty voice. Months afterwards, he told me he was late because he had gone to ask his great friend Tony about my family. John knew even then he would marry me.

During the day we took a long walk. The day had the chill damp of the late autumn. John had his sketching box, and while he drew, I lay on his Burberry which he spread on a flat stone for me and watched the never ending clouds moving across the faint blue sky. At last John put up his water colors. His hands were cold. He recited the little song :

> *"My hands are cold and nobody loves me,*
> *Sit on your hands for God loves you."*

Then he plunged into a long ramble about when he was a child in Cracow his mother had made him go to Dancing School in a white sailor suit and how he disliked it.

I listened entranced. Those were the very years when with tears of protest I too had gone to Dancing School in a stiff linen sailor suit at the Hotel Somerset. I could hear my mother saying : "A sailor suit looks neater on a plump girl like you." Yet how I longed to hide under a frilly dress with bows and sashes, to wear ringlets like the other little girls in my class at Miss Windsor's School. They might have helped efface my earliest memory. I was sitting on the floor under the library table. My parents were reading aloud the life of Madame Brzeszkowska, and how she suffered chained to a wheelbarrow in Siberia.

Her story awakened a deep feeling of pity which during all of my childhood burned deeper into my heart. I would flood my pillow at night over the trials of some poor immigrant family I had known in my father's settlement house, or the account of a Jewish pogrom in Russia, or the news of the poor Serbians dying in their mountain fastness, or the plight of strikers in the desolate mill towns around Boston. As I

11

grew older the happiest moments I can remember were those insignificant services I was asked to perform for the poor mothers who came to Osterville where my father directed a summer settlement house.

My father had given up a promising literary career to direct Lincoln House in Boston. My parents' attention was wholly centered upon the daily problems of this settlement house ; raising money to buy coal or food for some destitute family, and all the regular work of a big community house. Unlike my classmates I went to few parties or dances and mostly wore made-over clothes. Even my reading was different. On our shelves, side by side with current sociological writers, the most recent novels were those of Hardy or Meredith. When in secret I borrowed the *Forsyte Saga,* my father warned me that I was following the footsteps of "The Scarlet Woman." We read only the Classics. At nine I was given *Pendennis,* and the lightest girlhood fiction was Louisa May Alcott.

It grew dark as we returned along the Kentish lane. The others were already waiting for us in the car. During the drive up to London, we continued comparing our childhoods. We had suffered the same childish miseries and enthusiasms. Neither of us felt a part of the well-established social scheme in which we had been brought up, John in peaceful, sheltered Cracow, and I in Boston, each dressed in linen sailor suits, each detesting the dancing schools and children's birthday parties which we were forced to attend, each having the feeling, if only vaguely, that Fate had other plans for us.

"You can't go on living in Kensington. It 's the most deadly part of London," John told me. "When we get back to London, I will find you something in Chelsea where I live."

I heard myself reply : "I 'm leaving for the Continent shortly. It would be foolish to move before I leave." When I had said it, I felt better. To leave would be an excellent way of breaking the spell. "Above all," I said to myself, "I must not let myself fall in love with a Pole." Aloud I said, wishing to clinch the matter beyond argument : "I must learn German if I am to finish my work properly."

12

Back in my room, while undressing for the night, I heard over and over again the conversation we had had and the throaty voice of John. Once more there was no sleep for me. Impatiently, I turned on the light and read.

When I came down to breakfast, a note was by my plate :

"Dear Dorothy :
I will wait for you for lunch, No. 11 Soho ; unless I find a message at school you cannot come. I hope Mr. Cranford is not engaged and will join us."

Mr. Cranford was my uncle. He had come to London to chaperon me while my parents, who could not face the London climate, spent the winter at Nice. He had seen John several times at the school when he had come to fetch me in the evening.

"No good can come of this, Dotty," he warned. "I believe you are being carried plumb off your feet by this Pole's magnificent physique."

"Has he a magnificent physique ?"

"Don't quibble," he said, "I won't be party to this romance."

I told him I had decided to leave London and go to Germany to study the language, and besides, I had a dinner engagement that evening with a Dutch architect.

During the morning, I was unable to get to work. I found myself on the bus an hour too soon. My head swam and the houses went by in a blur. I got out at Regent Street to kill time looking at shop windows. But I found myself looking up in the expectation that John, too, might be coming this way. "I can't go to pieces like this," I said to myself, "where would it lead to ?" At the mere thought of becoming a Pole, I grew so distraught I did not see him approaching.

His voice made me start. "What luck finding you here !"

But instead of greeting him I used the most matter-of-fact tone I could muster. "I was looking for a new pocketbook," I explained. "I shall need one for my journey." The silk pocketbooks in the window were quite unsuitable for tickets

13

or passport. Yet perversely I insisted on entering the shop and keeping him waiting.

During lunch I told him of my plan of going to the University of Heidelberg where I had friends. Since I was to cross Belgium, John persuaded me to spend a week on the way and see the Rubens.

"How can you stand all those mountains of pink fat ?" I asked.

"Rubens is a new era," he explained, "a wholly new conception in painting. Wait until you have seen the *Descent from the Cross*. I wish I could show it to you."

After lunch we went to Cook's to leave my passport and make reservation for the train. John knew all the boats to Ostend and decided which one to take. In two days I would be leaving. We walked down the Mall to the National Gallery. There were things in the Flemish Room he wanted to show me. We passed by the Frans Hals and spent the afternoon before the Rembrandts and Rubens. He had also wanted to show me the Chardins, but suddenly it was so late, I had to run to get back and dress to go out to dinner with the Dutch architect.

The last day in London was spent with my uncle. Toward evening a messenger arrived with a bundle of books, a worn Baedeker, catalogues of Museums, and several brochures on special painters. With it was a little note which said, "I will be at the train to say good-bye."

In an effort not to be at the station too soon, I nearly missed the train. It so happened that several of my League of Nations friends were on the platform seeing off Lady Asquith, who was leaving by the same train. They were astonished to see me there.

"I thought you had just come back," they said.

"What, off to Berlin again ?" I was too confused to answer.

Lady Asquith pulled my arm. "Do come in my compartment, child, it will be so pleasant not to travel alone."

The train pulled out. We had not said good-bye. John ran by the carriage. "I will write you Poste Restante to Brussels and Heidelberg," he called.

14

Lady Asquith was very kind. She asked me many questions about my studies, but I was too distracted to answer. She tried gently to find out whom I had met in London. "Lady Astor receives on Sunday. Let me know when you return. We must see that you meet the right people."

In Brussels it rained steadily. During the first week I was so depressed I hardly went out. I spent the time working over my notes in the hotel. One day, a telegram came. "Why don't you answer my letters sent Poste Restante?" The telegram sent simply to "Brussels" reached me with hardly any delay due to the system of registration of all visitors with the Police. At the post office, a whole bundle of letters was waiting Poste Restante. I sat down in the nearest bistro and tearing them all open, laid them in sequence on the table. There was hardly any room for the *cassis à l'eau*. John had written every day.

MONDAY: "This has been a marvelous day. A long motor trip to Dartmouth and along the beach to Clapton Sands and back through hilly Devon with the people just dull enough to make me realize the whole thing wasn't a dream. I talked to you as much as possible without being obviously rude to the others, and even much more. You liked particularly a marvelous church in Dartmouth, mixture of Norman and early English with Tudor screens of sculptured, painted gilt oak. Some of the views from the top of the hills were so much like around Cracow that I got quite homesick, a thing I rarely do."

TUESDAY: "I had the first really pleasant morning today lying on the rocks and gazing in the sea. Of course, it wasn't complete. You know why. Out here is really something wonderfully calming in 'les sentiments de la nature.' I have been lots at the seaside, but parts of the beach here are absolutely the most wonderful thing I have ever seen. I am waiting for your letters with more and more impatience. Tonight I even dreamed of someone getting seasick. Isn't that a nice Freudian dream?"

WEDNESDAY: "I seem to spend days in ups and downs of hope at the arrival of each post. I quite see that I have no right to ask anything of you, but how a letter from you from Brussels would cheer me up."

15

THURSDAY : "I have never felt as much cut off from the world as I do now. Tomorrow I am going to Exeter in the morning, then London, where I hope to find some mail at Oakley Street. (Do you imagine how my heart beats at the thought) and then I am taking the train via Harwich to Brussels. I hope you will get this in Brussels or else that it will be forwarded to you if you go anywhere in the meantime. I haven't made up my mind yet as to whether meeting you there is a dream or not."

Walking back to the hotel, I wondered what I should do.

This was Friday. John would be arriving that very evening. I wondered how soon he would find me. I went up to my room and re-read his letters again. My room seemed suddenly unspeakably shabby. I found myself shivering with the cold. As I sat on the bed pulling the unyielding red comfortable about me, channels of air blew down my back. I suddenly realized John was the wide open door through which the sun was pouring, the broad sea on which the waves were dancing, the timeless vision of unlimited space. The future without him would be as drab as this little room. I told myself over and over that John couldn't possibly find me that evening ; that I should undress and go to sleep as the best way of composing myself. Every time someone walked down the hall, however, I stopped breathing until he had passed my door. Though my head was burning, I was shivering with cold when the night porter wrapped on my door.

"*Un monsieur est en bas, mademoiselle déscendera ?*" With a bound, hardly glancing at my hair, I had grabbed my coat and was running down the old yellowish marble staircase. John was standing at the bottom, covered in his voluminous Burberry.

"When did you arrive ?" I asked inanely.

"A half hour ago. I'm in the hotel across the street," was his smiling reply.

"Then you knew I was here ?" My head was still spinning.

Outside it was drizzling and dark. The ornate pseudogothic buildings looked mysterious, softly beautiful in the misty lamplight.

16

"I have come over to bring you back. You can never leave me again," he said, gently propelling me along the narrow sidewalk as he stepped over the puddles at the curb.

"But I couldn't become a Pole," I protested. "I am too acutely American. I was brought up to be a Unitarian. I fear and distrust your Catholicism ; it would suffocate me."

Under the Cathedral, the sidewalk was wide. We paced back and forth ; our feet were wet. No one was on the street. I heard myself speak as though it were not my voice.

"No, I could never live in Poland," I was saying. "I would be deeply unhappy in a country in which I would have an underlying contempt for everything and everyone. I know the feeling would grow on me."

John did not reply, but as I spoke, all the poison flowed out of me and I no longer felt so superior. I felt my heart would break. I had tried to run away, I had tried to go back before the day of the drive to Kent. Still I knew my life was as surely bound up with Poland's as on the day when I had first looked out on that station platform in the early morning and felt pity and sadness for that country so grey and flat, so bitterly oppressed.

"I know," I begged, "you will forgive me for all the mean and unkind things I said, because it 's true, we can never be parted. There is no decision to be made. It was settled that day we met. And all this running away from myself is childish. I will go back to London."

However, John asked me not to return to London for a few days so that he could show me the museums of Brussels, Antwerp, and Bruges. Though it was as clear to me as it had been to John that we were both caught in the wheel of destiny, on our walks between the galleries, I still struggled to find a way out — torn between my love for him and my fear of becoming Polish, or having Polish children, and finally of dying in a foreign land and being buried under Polish soil.

"I 'll have to visit your family first," I said, thinking I had found an excuse to put off the final decision. "They may dislike me. I may take a loathing to them. Having tried being in Poland without you, I can then see whether this is

17

an infatuation or whether I could really decide to become a Pole."

It was settled that I would go back to London for a month and then as soon as it could be arranged, leave for Cracow to visit John's family.

In March once more I crossed the Channel; changing trains in Berlin, I took the midnight sleeper for Cracow.

CHAPTER *2*

I ARRIVED in Cracow at eleven in the morning. It was an early spring day. In the fields water still stood on the ground and the trees were bare. The shabby workmen's houses were splashed in mud — but so were the better houses along the unpaved streets. I immediately recognized Michael, my brother-in-law to be. As he was quite unsuspecting of all this, I had difficulty in telegraphing John of my safe arrival, before leaving the station. Michael insisted we take a taxi. But I longed to ride in an open carriage under the great bearskin rug which was strapped up against the seats. To him, the *dorozka* was a relic of the past, and not even in the greatest emergency have I ever seen him consent to get into one.

"It's certainly pleasanter to walk," Michael said. "In a *dorozka* you don't gain time over walking."

Riding, I found out, had nothing to do with comfort. It was exclusively a question of getting there faster. Certainly the *dorozka* would have been infinitely more comfortable than the stiff-springed Austrian taxi, whose seat of hard stuffed horsehair gave neither purchase, nor comfort as we bounced along the crowded street. We swerved between market carts, each with its one horse attached to a long pole which swung perilously out at the side. With every hurtling jerk, I expected to be speared through, as on a skewer. I thought to myself, "I will never take a taxi from choice!"

Michael cringed when I said, "Oh, how quaint!" pointing out the women in gay flowered shawls, sitting in the straw on those galloping carts. Those peasant carts made him very sad, as did the log cabin model tenements we were passing.

Michael explained to me, "They were built two years ago

19

in that ridiculous style to house refugees from Russia. Other building material would actually have been cheaper, but the arts and crafts movement uses outward forms of an authentic style in an unauthentic manner."

Nevertheless, I found the houses very attractive. They were built for two families, and set irregularly in the lots to give larger gardens about them. I saw nothing wrong in making log houses in the suburbs of a city. But within ten years they became obsolete and were replaced by modern apartments. They are the only houses I know of which did become obsolete, in a country too poor to tear down anything because of faulty construction or a poor plan.

"That's our house," Michael said, as we turned a corner. It was a Colonial house with a large two-storied portico of columns, and a high plastered wall hiding the garden within. As we drove up, the door flew open, dogs and servants came running out, while on the steps the Professor and his wife waited in smiling expectation. My hands were kissed, my bag grasped by an old woman who, to my horror, picked up the heaviest one and ran upstairs with it.

"Was your journey comfortable? Did you recognize Michael at once? Lunch will be served presently. Surely you will want to rest in your room."

I was taken up a broad staircase before I had time to say more than "bon jour." Every inch of the stairway walls was hung with engravings, and in the large hall above stood four great carved chests on which were Delft vases.

I remembered John's explanation that sets of Delft vases were always in fives, to complete the line of such chests. These Danzig chests held the clothes and linens in every Polish house ; if not the old ones, then heavily carved copies. The brass chandelier hanging from the ceiling was also Dutch in feeling.

"This is John's room."

I was to use John's room ! I confusedly muttered something about its being so cozy.

"You have an hour to lie down and rest," John's mother spoke softly, as she closed the door. The highly carved bed

20

had been turned down.   The sheets were of the finest handkerchief linen, inlaid with old lace and beautifully mono-
grammed.   They buttoned on to a golden yellow quilt, which
was also soft and of the finest satin.   Two gigantic beruffled
pillows left me little room in which to stretch out, but as I
wriggled down into all this cool freshness, I felt a great peace
flooding through me.

John's room!   It was so different from what I expected.
John seemed adventurous.   This room was so protective.
Old Persian shawls hung on the walls and covered a large
deep ottoman piled with pillows of ancient cashmere.   All
the bright colors in the room had sombered to a soft mono-
tone.   At the windows were apple-green moire curtains
which veiled the light.   On the wall were John's sketches
and sketches by Polish painters.   Over the bed was a photograph of the Holy Family by Luini.

As I lay there studying every detail, there on the bookshelf
were the familiar brown bindings of Louisa May Alcott's *Little Women*, the red *Alice in Wonderland*, and the blue *Wind
in the Willows*, beside the *Peter Rabbit* series that had always
stood in my own room in Boston.   I imagined the deepest
reaches of John's mind were brightened with the same childhood pictures.   The reassuring sight of these books had put
me into a comfortable doze when, out in the street, I heard a
strange throaty cry.   I ran to see what it was.   Only a woman
on one of those heavy carts we had passed in such numbers
coming from the station.

We were on a street of new houses.   Behind us and at one
side were similar streets lined with stubby little trees and big
white houses, most of which had red tile roofs and were too
big for the plots on which they stood.   From the second
story I could see over the walls into the other gardens.   Overgrown with shrubbery, they had winding paths and benches.
Here and there a summer house was jammed into a corner,
in a futile attempt to condense a whole acre's planting on a
city plot.   The workmen's model houses with woodbine over
the porches and grass close about them seemed to fit the
ground much better than their fine neighbors.

21

While I was gazing out of the window, the door opened and the old woman who had brought up my bag came in. From her smiles and gestures, it was obvious that lunch was ready and that she wanted to unpack my things. I hurriedly dressed and went downstairs.

The Professor and his wife were standing under an immense palm in a room so full of furniture that it was impossible not to bump into something. The sun streaming through two French windows caught on the gold bronze of the Empire furniture, the gold threads in the wall hangings, and glistened on the crystal chandelier. The whole room shimmered before my eyes. Perhaps I was still unsteady from the two sleepless nights of the trip, for my head reeled. As through a mist, I heard them apologizing for receiving me alone. They wanted to ask me questions about their son. For dinner, they had invited some college friends of John's. For lunch tomorrow, some professors of the university, who could perhaps give me some help in my studies. One of John's oldest friends had invited me for dinner tomorrow evening.

Luncheon was served in another dazzling room where the windows seemed disproportionately large. The furniture, rugs, and carpets had all been bought in 1900 at the time of their marriage. The furniture, made in Paris by Gallet, had chairs, the backs of which represented the petals of a lily! The rug had the same pattern. The silk curtains, designed by William Morris, had come from England. The walls were dotted with Copenhagen flower plates. Complete in its period, the room held my breathless attention. My faulty French was certainly no proof against such an overpowering distraction.

"You are tired," John's mother gently suggested. "One can never speak a foreign language when one is tired."

I was amazed that she and Michael spoke such good English, more perfect even than John, who lived in England.

"Neither of us has ever been in England," she told me.

"That seems incredible! How was it possible?" I asked.

"I learned my English from a Swiss governess. She taught

me English and German. My mother was French, my sisters and I still talk it together."

The Professor apologized that he spoke no English. He had been brought up in the German-occupied Poland under Bismarck, and had studied in Berlin University, where he lectured before he became Professor in Cracow.

"How is John's English?" he asked in French. "He and Michael went to an English school in Switzerland, but John had to do his primary work in Cracow, in German, of course. My wife took the children abroad when Michael was seven, so that he would escape starting to school under the Germans. She intended to remain only a couple of years. But then the war came, and they were able to return only after the Russian collapse." He told me sadly, "Now he will never lose that dreadful guttural 'r.'"

I thought, "If we marry, we will not be separated like that."

My voice quivered when I had to speak of John. I hoped they would think I did not know him well enough to tell them anything they did not already know.

"*Vous ne suiviez pas les mêmes cours ?*" the Professor asked with a sweet smile.

"No, I am studying only International Law and Political Science." Ah, was it possible they suspected something?

"John has had a sore throat for the last month," I said, meaning to imply I knew no recent details of his work. This put them in a panic.

What doctor had he seen? Did he take proper precautions? London is so damp — they hoped his room was suitable and properly heated. I had embarked on an enthusiastic picture of his new room on Oakley Street, and the pieces of Meissen China he had picked up for nothing at the Caledonian market, when I was choked by the idea, "What will they think about your knowing so much about his room?"

But they thought nothing, and went on asking questions about their son with a most natural solicitude.

Coffee was served in a large library. Books in green bookcases stood as high as my head. Above them, pictures and prints covered every inch of the wall. Carpets, furniture, curtains were all dark green, and in spite of a fire, the room made one shiver. Here again, the maximum number of high-backed chairs had been crowded in around a long table covered with a green felt cloth edged in heavy fringe, with a darker green felt applique. It was hard to imagine this dark room in a recently built house.

John's mother took out her embroidery, while father and son paced the length of the room behind each other. Every few minutes the Professor looked at his watch, although a fine French clock seemed to be keeping time on the marble shelf. When a half hour was past, he said, *"Je vais à l'Université. My son will show you about Cracow."* A well-rehearsed string of names which meant nothing to me indicated what I was to see.

It was a beautiful afternoon. The sun was hot, but a chill damp came out of the ground. On the broad street where the street car ran, a scraper was piling up the mud into little piles. Even so, the mud was often ankle deep. Since there was no taking a cab, I suggested we should walk. Now I wanted to talk about John. "Show me his school. What did he do with his free time?" I tried to make it clear I was more interested in the way they lived, than in the museums of Cracow.

Michael refused to understand. "Since you were here last summer three new rooms have been opened in the Wawel."

I didn't want to see the Wawel.

"Was the altar of Panna Maria opened when you were here before?"

"Which church is Panna Maria?" I asked.

After struggling to explain which was Panna Maria, it became clear that I had not seen the Church of Our Lady.

As we walked into town, Michael pointed out the renaissance houses, re-constructing them back through their various additions and modifications. We stepped into open doorways to see coffered ceilings or arcaded courtyards. By the time we reached Panna Maria, the sun was no longer

24

shining through the golden twelfth-century windows, and the great carved wood altar tryptich of Wit Stwosz was shut. We went on to the Wawel. It was closed.

Now I was thoroughly cold. It was only four o'clock, but the several coffee houses we passed were packed to capacity.

"What about something warm ?" I suggested.

"Excellent !"

I then discovered we would have to walk some six or eight blocks to the Café Michael always frequented. He explained that never in his life had he been in the coffee house we were passing.

"Is there anything wrong with them ?" I asked. "Isn't the coffee the same everywhere ?"

"Yes," he replied humbly.

"Then why go further ?" It was hard to understand why there were only two places Michael and his friends ever patronized.

"Does John have all these same prejudices ? I am cold and have walked enough," I said belligerently. "I don't feel like meeting anyone anyway."

"This one will do, but you won't like it as much as our regular place," he said as he pushed aside a heavy felt which hung over the door which resulted in retaining all the smoke inside.

During the coffee, I tried to ferret out the family prejudices and traditions. "You have to go to church ?"

"Naturally we go to church every Sunday."

"You have to ?"

"We want to."

I could not understand why, not through duty, nor because the right people did it, nor to meet friends there, nor because you were afraid of punishment if you did not. It was as much a part of life as the routine of eating and sleeping, working and playing. It rounded off existence. Well, my existence felt no need of that kind of rounding off.

Outside it was dark and cold. Michael called a taxi. When we arrived at home both parents were anxiously waiting in the hall.

You have not much time to be ready," they said. "Dinner is at eight."

Upstairs on my desk was a letter from John.

"Dearest :

I was so miserable when you left that I had nothing better to do than to go back to Elm Park Mansions. We sat on both sides of the fireplace and pretended that we were bearing it bravely.

Everything is strange, but the change is so great that I really can't quite realize that you are gone. It doesn't seem like the same world, but with you not in it, it seems like two entirely different worlds.

I enclose 'the letter.' I hope that it will be like taking an umbrella, that it will prove unnecessary. There is nothing more in it than what we talked about last night. It isn't very very important anyway whether I write or not ; I know you will charm them. I only hope it will give you a greater sense of assurance. My thoughts are with you always. I keep looking at the watch, wondering what you are doing at each moment. I hope this arrives before you do."

Would John's family guess without my telling them anything ? Would they both think it the right thing to do ? For, after all, marrying John would also be marrying his parents. I read over the letter once before I began dressing, and again when I was dressed.

When I came down, two guests had arrived, and were seated deep in the shadow under the palm tree in the drawing room, where an even sharper shadow underlined their gaunt features. The gentleman, Professor Heydel, was hardly 30 but his red hair had become putty colored and his freckles merely intensified his sallow complexion. The lady, I learned later, was Mary Rosner. Her black eyes were the only features one saw in the white face framed in jet black hair. She could have been 40, but I learned later she was only 23.

But I had forgotten their pale ugliness within five minutes' conversation. Their ideas, crudely expressed because of poor English, betrayed an intelligence that put me to shame. I found myself in a passionate discussion about Nineteenth

26

Century art, which I had never, except for the French impressionists, thought worth notice. Whereas they carefully discussed painters and paintings, I had indulged in a sweeping statement about the whole period. It was soon obvious that they were interested in a variety of techniques, the colors and themes of specific painters, and not their qualities in the general way for which my college days' discussions had trained me. There was no question of like or dislike — they judged museums more by the number of schools represented than by the numbers of Raphaels, Rembrandts and Van Dykes. The great and known names were put aside as accepted planets, in a search for new stars and new constellations. I found this very disconcerting of course. Soon I found myself being urged to go once more to the little museum over the market.

Professor Heydel explained : "It's true Matejko painted historical scenes which probably are dull to you, but he uses a very different technique than that of his contemporaries : English Burne-Jones, or French Delacroix, Ingres, David. His themes are conditioned by the times. No Polish history books were allowed in circulation during that period. Poland's long and magnificent history was cunningly obliterated by German and Russian historians, whose statements were accepted as fact by American and English historians. No one questioned the German version that Poland had always been partitioned, that the brief periods of its independence were marked with internal disorder and anarchy, and that when Poland became too much of a nuisance, Germany had felt itself called upon, in the interest of a peaceful Europe, to subdue."

I admitted that this was my vague impression of Poland's nebulous past.

"Matejko as a painter was painting for Poland. Every child knew that Poland under Sobieski had been one of the most powerful states in Europe, twice or thrice as big as present Poland. Poland was a united nation when, in France, the king, with the help of Jeanne d'Arc was struggling for recognition by the French people. The history of every nation is not without internal struggles even as recently as the

27

American Civil War. England had her Cromwell, her Mary, Queen of Scots. Yet no foreign power had ever dominated Poland until the expansion of Prussia in 1770. For five hundred years Poland was the great power of Central Europe. During all that time Germany could not unite as a nation. From the fall of the Holy Roman Empire until after the Napoleonic Wars, when the Austrian Metternich tried to revive it, Germany was split into a hundred little principalities."

"If Poland was so strong and Germany so weak, why did she fall?" I asked.

"Her very strength was her weakness. Her power had been unchallenged for so long, it was hard to persuade the people to vote for a sufficiently strong army. No one believed either Germany or Russia would dare start a war against Poland. Some members of the great Potocki, Branicki, and Radziwill families thought it better to let Prussia have Danzig than fight. There were plenty of northern ports. Perhaps they even imagined this would strengthen the Port of Memel. But Poland found it too expensive to ship so far north, or pay the heavy toll through Danzig. Actually the rump state existed nearly thirty-five years, growing weaker and poorer. The men fought without pay, and when ammunition gave out, they were cornered and disarmed."

"But the Liberum Veto?" I exclaimed. "I thought that was the great weakness of Poland."

"Have you never read the letters of Catharine of Russia to Prussia and Austria?" Professor Heydel asked. "You must understand the hatred of democracy which existed under those autocrats. She wrote 'It is the greatest danger to our thrones that a country governed by democratic principles should be at our very gates. How can we ever expect to fulfill our divine mission, when in Poland every man can freely speak his mind?' Poland's constitution of May 3, 1792, begins, 'Since it is axiomatic that all men are created free and equal . . .'"

"What? — Actually that —"

During our discussion, the room had filled up. Not wishing to break into our conversation, the other guests had stood

Mme. Curie and Prof. Kostanecki at the dedication
of the Curie Cancer Institute in Warsaw

John Galsworthy with
the Professor, during
a visit to Poland

Peasants
at Lowicz

Costumes on Whitsuntide Monday

at the door of the room by a little table on which were tiny glasses for *wodka* and a tray covered by myriads of *zakanski*. As soon as we stood up, the phalanx moved forward, each gentleman bowing stiffly as he shook my hand. I had the impression that the ladies were either short and fat or tall and thin. With their lack of make-up and the bulky bulginess of their very plain dresses, they reminded me of any Cambridge tea party in the Boston of my childhood. The men, as soon as they could go back to their conversations, walked up and down in little groups with their heads together. The host kept running between them, urging a little white *wodka* on this one, a little amber *wodka* on that, while the hostess seated the two eldest of the ladies on a sofa, placed a little table in front of them, and directed the maid to serve them sandwiches.

Unconsciously, I found myself in the corner under the palm, where from a safe vantage point I could watch the scene and muse about John. Try as I would, I could not fit my preconceived picture of him into this frame. The flouncing curtains, the ruffled lamp-shades, the opulently upholstered chairs, even the hairdress of my hostess all seemed like something out of the drawings of Charles Dana Gibson. This was like a memory of gaiety which had been crystallized and preserved through wars and devastations. The fin du siècle conserved at all costs — a tradition of Poland maintained against the onslaughts of style. But John was modern, wholly preoccupied with the problems of a new Poland.

"What is your idea of God?" said a voice just at my side. "You are my partner for dinner. Will you take my arm?"

"God?" I gasped. "I'm a Unitarian."

"That is why I am to take you to dinner," the gentleman continued. "I am the curator for the only Unitarian Chapel in Poland. It was built by one of the Radziwills during the Thirty Years' War."

"I thought that was a German war."

"It was. At that time many refugees fled here from religious persecutions in Germany; all the Protestant congregations here date from that time."

"But, this is a Catholic country !"

"If you mean by that," he said laughing, "that we have a conglomeration of all religious orders here, it is. We have Moslems, Jews, Greek Catholics, Russian Orthodox, Lutherans and anything else you like."

We had reached the table, at which eighteen guests, some in evening dress and others not, were seated. There were so many candles, China figures, antique bowls of flowers, that the ugliness of the Gallet furniture and walls hung with plates was lost in the dazzle before us. Little did I imagine, from the profusion of flowers, their cost. Alas, when I wished to send some to my hostess, I found they were worth their weight in gold. A few poor roses cost five dollars ; a presentable plant, fifteen.

There were no olives, celery, nuts, or jellies, but a long menu of many curious and good dishes :

Barszcz, with ravioli filled with mushrooms ; a giant pike, smothered in crayfish ; quails on toast, with a stuffing of juniper berries, served with a coldslaw of red cabbages ; and, to end the meal, a baba filled with ice cream, followed by fruit piled high on a silver platter.

After dinner as the guests filed past their hostess, they tried to kiss her hand, to thank her for the meal. But with a sweet smile she would reply to one, "It was a pleasure !" or, "You should come more often," to another, "Tell me what news you have of Marysia," or, "Is your mother in town for long ?" Was she smiling from graciousness or a feeling of shyness and unreality ? How different from the pious woman always working among the poor whom John had described.

All the doors were now thrown open, and the gloomy library was a blaze of lights. The heavy high-backed chairs were very comfortable after the heavy meal. With the curtains pulled, the fire blazing, and the cheerful light, even the dark corners appeared soft and inviting. "A room that came to life by night," I thought. Here I could see the family grow, each with his work laid out on the long table.

"You must be very weary after the long trip from London," several persons remarked.

I tried without success to keep my mind on what was being said. On every side violent conversations in Polish were rolling about me. It seemed as if at least half the guests were quarreling. Many appeared furiously angry, and with clenched hands called heaven to witness the truth of their own arguments. As if in turn, each guest sat by me for a while, politely taking leave whenever a new one appeared.

I was too bewildered by the noise of the strange language to follow what was being said to me, even if an effort was made to speak English.

When Professor Heydel, with whom I was to go in the morning to see the Matejki pictures, came and sat by me, I felt that he was an old friend. At last, here was someone with whom I had had a discussion, whom I knew .John loved.

"What are they fighting about ?" I asked.

"They are not fighting," he smilingly replied.

"Is that a conversation ?"

"The fat lady over there has just published a book of verse. They are talking about her book. Everyone admires it profoundly. The poems are very fresh and simply expressed. Don't you want to meet her ?"

As I came toward the group where the poetess was sitting, a gentleman, without stopping what he was saying, pushed nearer the person next him, letting me wedge my chair into the circle. The lady looked up with a preoccupied smile, *"Nous discutons mon livre, qui vient d'être publié,"* she said, and let loose a torrent of Polish to the man who had given me a place.

I sat patiently, but as no one paid any attention to me, and I could not understand a word of what was being said, it was ridiculous to sit there grinning, and I got up to go. The lady poetess grabbed me by the arm.

"Can you come to tea Thursday ? Just a few friends. There are so many questions I want to ask you. You will tell me what is being published in England and America. Perhaps you have some poetry with you. . . T. S. Eliot ? Or, of course, the latest Aldous Huxley ?"

31

I murmured something about traveling light.

"When you come to tea at five you will give me lots of notes. That will be lovely. Madame will direct you."

"I will bring her," promised Professor Heydel, relieving me of trying to learn her name, which I felt in advance would be hopeless — and her address.

The guests were saying good night ; I would be able to escape. The dogs, who had been tied up in the kitchen, now stood in the hall waiting for their beds to be brought in. As soon as they were put down, they sprang to their regular places, Jock the Dobermann, by the wall, and little Jip, the dachshund, pushed to a corner.

I tried to express my appreciation for the lovely evening, but an abstracted look now dominated my hostess' face. The party was over and past. Her mind was already far away. The Professor tucked in the dogs, and barricaded the stairs — "Otherwise they will try and come in your room during the night," — he asked whom I found the most interesting. He was full of the party. Turning to his wife, he said, "No use giving women good wine. Did you see how Marysia left her Burgundy until the sweet, and then sipped the Tokay first ? Janio was the only one who refused. The others paid no attention. I thought Franek knew more about wines. He let the maid fill his glass, and then left it. What a pleasure to see how Rostworowski went through two glasses of the Sauterne. That, by the way, was bought in 1864 for the marriage of his wife's father." The Sauterne in question had become so dry that I thought it was sherry. I hastily said, "I never drank anything so delicious in my life. Un-iced too !"

"Of course," he said impatiently. "Did you like the Raki sauce for the pike ? That is my invention."

My longing to go to my room, unnoticed by the Professor, for whom this was the perfect moment of the evening, was clear to his wife.

"Miss Adams has had such a long trip. She should go to bed," she spoke gently, and turning to me she asked, "Can my maid come to help you ?"

I hoped my refusal was polite, that my expressed gratitude was commensurate to their efforts on my behalf. At last my door was shut. I rushed to the desk to write John, telling him of my loneliness at being so far away from him, the stupidity of not letting him come and show me what Michael was trying to show, my sense of humility before his parents, who, in my superior way, I had pictured as tight-faced, threadbare individuals, living in a cold cheerless apartment like those I had seen in Heidelberg. I had imagined varnished linoleum on the floor of the Victorian dining room; a dark court room, entered from a long, narrow hall; on one side an umbrella stand and on the other would be a pressed wood hat-rack, where all the overcoats were hung. The drawing room, too, would be very sparsely furnished — perhaps with a round highly polished and carved black walnut table, covered with a filet, and a fern standing in a greenish yellow pot. In the corners of the room I could see pairs of stiff, uncomfortable black walnut chairs.

"My mother has worn black ever since the war," John had told me. "I hope you will influence her to buy a new dress. She only thinks of her charities. Now you will give my parents something to talk about. Father is so much in his laboratory, and mother so absorbed in her good works." What a cold and forlorn picture! His mother's dresses did have a timeless plainness. The body of a Dana Gibson dress, from which all the ruffles had been removed — but neither she nor the house was bleak. Quite the contrary, the very house itself exuded permanence and peace, as something that has withstood war and change.

Seeing the light under the door, the old woman who had unpacked my things came in. In broken French, she asked to help me. "I was John's nurse," she explained, 'I have been with the family since I was sixteen, and the Madame fourteen. I have taken care of her for forty years. Kazia and Helka have both been here nearly thirty years, Bronia only ten. Before the war we had two men servants, but Madame doesn't care for that now. We live very quietly." She had rapidly put away my things. "Mademoiselle must go to bed," she said with authority. "There will be much tomorrow. When you are awake, ring this bell and Kazia will bring your breakfast. She is a very stupid girl. If something is not right, let me know." She then found out that I drank coffee, could not eat three or even two eggs, and quickly left the room.

John had warned me, "Be careful. You can hide nothing from Andzia. She washed my diapers and emptied the night pots."

The arc light outside the window swung a beam of light across the room. To go to sleep, I had to pull the heavy moire curtains, which I feared would keep out all the air, but I fell asleep at once.

When I waked, the dogs were barking at the postman. I rang — perhaps there was a letter for me. Almost instantly the door opened. The dogs bounced about the bed. An old woman with jet black hair in braids tripped in to curtsey and to kiss my hands. She shut the window, making at the same time a long giggling speech in Polish, then she felt my arms to see if I was cold, dived into my cupboard, rushed out of the room, and soon was back with a bed jacket. Having arranged the breakfast table with squeals and giggles, she took all my clothes away, and finally reappeared with the breakfast tray, on which was the letter from John.

My deliberate indifference did not conceal anything from her. With more squeals and giggles, she made me realize that her romantic heart had seen what neither father nor mother had ; that this was no ordinary visit of the erudite American lady, bent on completing work for a thesis.

John wrote :

"Darlingest,
Life is getting more and more hectic. Your letter from Berlin came yesterday and the telegram today. I spent yesterday and today trying to persuade myself that a letter from Cracow might come last night. Of course, it didn't. Then, my hopes were concentrated on the morning mail, then on the lunch mail. Now I must write to catch the 8:40 train. Darling, thank you so much for the sweetest letter. It's just you all over.

34

"I didn't realize you were going to see Eble in Berlin, or I would have written him. By the way, how do you spell 'nauseating,' 'financial,' 'propaganda' ?

I was just thrilled to get your telegram, but now am getting more and more restless awaiting the explanation. Some details I can picture, — what a time you had sending the wire, the diplomatic difficulties centering around it. I hope you get my letters in time."

The door to my room was ajar. The dogs, whose patience was exhausted, were barking for crusts. Jip jumped up on the beautiful satin quilt. This made Jock furious, and he bared his teeth. Jip sprang at his throat, while I held the little table to keep it from being overturned.

Black-haired Kazia rushed in with a pail of water, which she hurled all over the rug. The old nurse came running with a shawl, hoping to disentangle them. By this time, Michael arrived and the Professor appeared, both in blue dressing gowns. One pulled ; the other gave frenzied commands. The dogs were dragged, dripping with blood, from the room.

A dog fight, of course, didn't trouble me. I was concerned for the frightful mess. The youngest servant, Bronia, soon had the water back in the pail, while Helka, the cook, waved her apron, and moaned that such an accident should have occurred before a guest. She curtsied, then glanced at me, having forgotten in her excitement that she had greeted me half a dozen times before.

Madame Kostanecka was the last to arrive. Showing the bystanders out of the room, she apologized for the intrusion. "They all lose their heads when the dogs get into a fight." Looking at her wrist watch she remarked that it was late, already ten. "If you are to be in town by eleven, you will have to hurry. The housekeeper, John's old nurse, has your bath running." You could hear the thumping and bumping of the water boiling in the gas geyser.

Dressed as usual in a tremendously full black alpaca skirt and apron over a striped gingham shirtwaist, Andzia came in, her heavy bare arms dripping with water, to inquire how hot I liked my bath. "Does Mademoiselle like the water 35,

35

36 or 37 ?" she asked. What precision ! Not knowing centigrade, I went to see.

In a large tiled room, the tub stood high off the ground and well out from the wall. The better to clean behind it, I supposed ! In the corner the hot water was roaring and spouting out of a handsome nickel-plated geyser. Beside the tub was a chair, hidden under an immense bath towel which stretched to the ground and covered the footstool, by which I was to climb into the tub. On a table were all kinds of brushes and wash cloths, soaps and powders. "You may not like scented soap," Andzia said, putting a new cake of Castile soap in the dish.

Not to seem ungrateful for all her effort, I stayed longer in the tub than was really necessary. It was late when at last I reached the museum ; Professor Heydel had already gone up, leaving Mary Rosner, his companion of the previous evening, to wait for me.

"I had a letter from John this morning," she said. "He wrote me I should talk to you as freely as I would to him." Looking at me more intently, she remarked, "Marrying John will be a very great responsibility."

"What did John tell you ?" I asked. "How do you know ?" I was stifled by this precipitation of my affairs.

"What else could we expect when you came here ? I am sure you have all the qualities, but John is the finest person I know. Besides, his family means a very great deal to Poland. Intellectually it is one of the most important families of Cracow." She then went on, "How do you like Madame Kostanecka ? She frightens me. I never dare talk to her. Professor Kostanecki is easy to get along with though he has a very big position here. Do you think you could live all your life with us ?"

"John could get into the Bank of England. That is the subject of his thesis, and he has seen the Director, who may take him," I told her.

"John's place is in Poland," she spoke vehemently. "He would never be permanently happy outside his country. If you keep him out of Poland you will ruin his life."

36

"You can't know how John has changed. He has become very international now," I replied.

"That's your influence on him."

Professor Heydel looked down the stairs of the museum. "Well, there you are," he laughed, waving his hat.

He told me later that he had never had a more attentive listener. It almost encouraged him to give up lecturing on economics at the University and become an official museum guide. But I heard not one word of his explanations of the great historical scenes painted on enormous canvasses, with life-size figures, depicting Sobieski receiving the vanquished Turks before Vienna, and the protesting of the first partition of Poland by the Polish Parliament. I saw them in a daze. When at 12:30 Michael appeared to take me home, Mary's remarks were still ringing in my ears.

Lunch was to be at one. The guests began arriving ten minutes before the hour, Archbishop Sapieha and some ten of the professors. No ladies had been invited. Everyone stood for the *wodka*, except the Archbishop, who sat on the sofa, took precedence going into the dining room, and sat at the head of the table. The sun, which in the morning is hidden by the mists that hang over Cracow, came pouring into the dining room. The wine, the sun, the heavy meal thawed out my heart, which had been frozen by Mary's words. But it was hard to dispel the feeling that this was a little island of comfort and safety in a wilderness of savage peasantry living like animals in mud, poverty, and disease. I thought, "I will only marry John if he promises to become an American."

The gentleman beside me tried unsuccessfully to catch my attention. "These are a special kind of Polish mushrooms," he said. "They are red, a great delicacy. The peasants find them in the woods."

They had a strange leathery consistency that remained tough under the parmesan sauce in which they were baked.

There was a moment of silence when the maid brought in a row of birds on a platter, which was passed first to the Archbishop. "Do you have pheasants in your country?" my neighbor asked me.

I told him that we did, though infrequently.

"Those red berries grow in the woods too. The pheasants eat them, so we eat them on the pheasants," he said, laughing heartily at his own joke.

Finally a large bowl of immense peaches, preserved whole, were served. These were framed by little cakes which had been laid around the serving plate. Our host explained that this was the first crop of his peaches. He had brought the slips from France in a valise, and budded the trees this year. He had picked two dozen peaches, he told us with pride and pleasure. We must have had all of them. A murmur of approval went up from all the guests, who I imagined were complimenting him in Polish for his great success in ripening peaches in such a cold country.

Coffee was, as usual, served in the dark library. The little side lamps were lighted, though the window shades had been pulled well back, and there was brilliant sunlight in the next room.

Now the moment of business had arrived. I mustered all my forces for the discussion ahead and fetched paper and pencil to write down the answers. "Was it true," I asked, "that industry in Upper Silesia would be hampered by lack of rail connection to the sea?"

"A new road was in process of building," they replied. "A new port in Gdynia would be completed within a year or so, subsidized by special rates, of course." Could such a program be accomplished in time, I wondered? "How would machine parts be replaced? Poland had no machine tool industry and Germany had closed her frontier to the export of machine parts."

"Poland was beginning to produce them. This stupid policy of Germany's had played into Poland's hands. The Germans would be the first to regret having made her neighbor independent," I was told. "Best see for yourself in Silesia." Letters to managers of such new industries were offered me and the gentlemen plunged into an animated discussion of which factories I should see. There was no use asking if the quality of Polish machine tools would be as good. They would say yes, and I could not believe this possible.

As for the question of maintenance of order ; the Germans had told me the Polish police were inadequate for the protection of a mining community. The training of police to handle strikers requires them to have a tradition behind them. Patiently I was told that the English had been invited to organize the Polish police. "We prefer the English system. The British police protect the individual. The German protects the state against the individual. Our police are still under English supervision. They are not allowed to shoot, except in self-protection. We have had no trouble, and expect no trouble." Poland based her assertions on promises for the future ; Germany on accomplishments in the past. My American training had taught me to prefer the tried and known to the untried and unknown. Yet within two years, I learned, five hundred miles of railroad was completed, which carried fourteen million tons of coal a year to Gdynia, the most modern, the best equipped, the most efficient port in that part of the world.

I was then offered letters of introduction to business men or engineers in Upper Silesia. At last, I should see the province under Polish guidance. But what I was groping for, which I could not then, and never was able to find in the Poles was that self-assurance which would make the world believe in them ; that booster club spirit which would convince me that under Polish leadership the Polish half of the Silesian province would develop the finest little mining towns in the world. Polish modesty could hardly be a match for German high pressure salesmanship — that salesmanship which trumpeted the slogan of the unjust Peace abroad, while squeezing little neighbor nations.

After everyone had gone, Father Michalski, the professor of medieval philosophy at the University, stayed on at the request of my hosts. He had spent his life identifying manuscripts in the libraries of the Vatican, of Paris, of Oxford and Cambridge ; manuscripts, the contents of which, as well as the authors, are uncatalogued and unknown. They hoped that in talking to him, I would find an answer to the most fundamental part of the problem I wished to solve — the worthiness of the Poles to rule Germans, the capacity of Poles to take the responsibility of running such a valuable productive enterprise.

What I had just heard seemed to my ears but rash promises. I was still inclined to believe that it would be better for the Poles to appease the insatiable appetite of the Germans, in order to promote international prosperity, to speed repayment of German debts and to preserve the peace.

How terribly sad that such wonderful people as these should be part of a nation whose future seemed so obscure and grey. They must be different, I tried to believe, they must be different from everyone else. Their wealth makes them international, I thought, their friends must be a little isolated group in this great forlorn sea of unfriendly beings. Yet I had to acknowledge that when I had studied at Heidelberg I had never spoken out so frankly to anyone. There I could never forget I was in Germany. I had never seen the counterpart of my Boston friends among them. Nationality, like a curtain, had always hung between us. Such discussions about art or about religion as I had had the evening before, or such questions as I had asked the professors this morning could not have been asked without causing great offense in Germany.

All those fine qualities I loved most in John were reflected in his people — his sweet and forgiving nature, his understanding grasp of the essential details of any problem and his perseverance irrespective of all obstacles. How patient everyone was with me! My impudence suddenly became unendurable to myself, and through my mind flashed all the details of my papers whose answers I would never know. The docket litigations between Poles and Germans which filled several volumes at the Supreme Court — one must be a lawyer to understand these! The five shelves of volumes on civil cases settled in a civil court — how superficially I had looked over them! The answer lay in these volumes, in the daily settlement by law of great and petty charges. There could be no going back on the Treaty of Versailles, which for better or for worse had drawn a boundary, and provided that for fifteen years two international courts, one presided over by a Swiss, the other by a Belgian, were to arbitrate all differences. For fifteen years, all Silesian Germans who wished could liquidate their affairs and go back to Germany. How presumptuous then to suggest that this reasonable settlement should be upset because of the Germans' desire for more territory. I realized suddenly that because the Poles had not adopted the German tactics of shouting loudly over what they had lost, the world would believe that the little they had received should be taken away.

My throat tightened as I perceived the level of my questions and the quality of the answers. Madame Kostanecka must have seen the change in my face. She suddenly seemed to understand the cause of my humility. "Oh, my poor little girl — my poor little girl !" she said and flung her arms about me. Father Michalski, whom I had completely forgotten, left the room with the Professor.

"What made you guess ?" I asked.

"I fear it will be very hard for you," she said as she burst into tears. Even then I realized she was a person who did not cry easily. As I put my head on her shoulder I knew nothing could ever be too hard for me as long as she was alive. In her embrace I felt the protective love which would shield us both. In the instant she had perceived why I was there, she had accepted me as her own child.

"I have always longed for a daughter. Now I have you."

"John wrote a letter for me to give you in case you didn't guess. Do you want to see it now ?"

We went out in the hall where the Professor was still standing. Madame Kostanecka said, "*Elle sera nôtre fille.*"

"Is it true ?" he asked, and holding my head in his hands, he kissed me on the forehead.

They put their arms about me as we went upstairs. I gave them the letter which they took to their own room. Once alone, I threw myself down on the sofa, and burying my face

41

in the soft cashmere pillow, wept bitterly, not only from pent up emotion, but because of the decision to become a Pole, to cut myself off from my family forever, putting the great ocean and all these miles of land between us, and from the English language, which I had loved and, in school, had tried to write. As I lay there, the years stretched ahead of me like a road across an endless plain. Around and beside me were children, all speaking Polish, and no familiar face or sign were near.

When the door opened, the Professor was bringing in a bunch of red roses. "We have telegraphed to John," he told me. "We are so glad. Mother will go back to London with you as soon as you are ready to leave, and as soon as I can do so I will follow. I must be in London in April anyway." He did not add that it was because he was to receive from King George's own hand the distinguished Order of the British Empire, not only for having been Mayor of Cracow during those war years when Austrian Poland was overrun by the Russians ; but for his internationally known work on the appendix, for having been Dean of the Medical School, for his many years as Rector of Cracow University, and for having organized the Polish Academy of Science.

What he said was : "All engagements are cancelled. The servants have been told that no visitors will be received. Plans for the future are too pressing. There is no time for idle visiting."

CHAPTER 3

*A*LL at once I had ceased to be a stranger. Even the house seemed more welcoming. Bedroom doors were left open, and father and son walked from room to room in easy familiarity. Madame Kostanecka had put on a Japanese kimono, a Whistlerian touch she always wore en famille. You could hear her bell ringing, and when she spoke to the servants, it was no longer in hushed tones.

Without knocking, she opened my door. "Is your head still aching, dear? Come lie down in my room. I have ordered tea sent up for you to take with a migraine powder. Here is a letter from John, which came in the afternoon mail."

Poor John, waiting in London! He wrote, "My, how I wish I could be in Cracow. I sit in Battersea Park, basking in the sun. It makes me wild to think that Michael is doing for you what by all human and divine right I should be doing! I hope you get on with all my friends." And he ended with the words, "You are living, while I am merely putting in time."

How could I tell him how different Cracow was to what I had expected? So much warmer and brighter.

Having quickly read the letter, I went into Madame Kostanecka's bedroom. It was upholstered and curtained in the same gay chintz that made the background for all John's baby pictures; red poppies, blue cornflowers and white daisies in prim rows against a white background.

"What a lovely light room!" I exclaimed. "Is it really the same chintz background in the photographs of John as a baby? How did it keep that fresh color?"

43

"Yes, it was sent out from England when I was married," she replied. Turning the dogs off the sofa, she made a great pile of soft, fluffy pillows. "Now lie down and take the powder. Perhaps it will help you," she spoke gently.

Father and son were pacing up and down the length of the room and into the adjacent little boudoir. Watching them from the next room I thought how similar the three were. I could see why people often mistook John for Michael and vice versa. Both were nearly six feet tall and powerfully built whereas the father who was a half a head shorter, was slight and finely boned. Yet both boys were the image of their father, the same wide-set eyes in a broad high forehead, the same aquiline nose and well balanced chin, the same hypersensitive mouth curved in a gentle smile. All three had heads like the bust of a Roman senator yet tempered with such intelligence that one could not conceive anyone of the three losing their self control.

Madame Kostanecka sat down at her desk, which was stacked with papers and letters. Like the rest of the room, every inch of space on her desk was overflowing. On the walls, between paintings, were photographs of the family, taken at various times. Under the glass table tops, snapshots covered the entire surface. Bookshelves were crammed with double rows of books. Besides the siphon and glasses on one table, there was a lace-drum, to which a half-made piece of lace was pinned, a heap of knitting, a piece of embroidery, the latest newspapers, and many odds and ends scattered among books and letters. Yet the room was not untidy. It gave the impression of being lived in by a fully occupied individual. Madame Kostanecka, who was in her fifties and fast going grey, was as capable of keeping a great many objects in order as she was able to carry on a multitude of charitable activities at the same time.

"We were making plans when you came in," the Professor said.

"It is so kind of you to come to England to meet my parents."

"No use discussing what's all settled," he quickly replied.

44

"We were just saying that it would be enough if we each took two portmanteaus. Can one count on warm weather at this season ?"

"London ? — In spring . . ."

"I will take a train for Warsaw an hour later than you leave for Silesia," said Madame Kostanecka, "to be certain my passport is ready as soon as your work is finished."

"All this trouble of taking an extra trip to Warsaw !"

"I am glad to see my sisters," she insisted. "The mail might be slow if I wrote for the passport."

"In Warsaw you will seem so far away." I shivered.

Her dark eyes glowed as she replied, "The day I receive your telegram, I will take the evening train to Berlin, where we will meet and continue on to London together."

The Professor pulled a telegram from his pocket. "I sent off a wire to my cousin Lignewski, the one to whom John wrote asking if you could stay with them while you are in Silesia. Here is the reply," he said, reading it. "At the Katowice Station you are to watch for his chauffeur. He has some business meetings. He sends his apologies he cannot be there to meet you."

"How I wish one of you could go with me !" I sighed, already enmeshed in the gentle protective grip of the family.

"The sooner you get your work done, the sooner we can all be together again," John's mother sensibly remarked.

Once all the arrangements had been made there was nothing more to keep me in Cracow ; the next day I was put aboard the local train for Katowice by Michael and the Professor.

"They will see you on to the right train," Madame Kostanecka had said, "and we will be meeting so soon that this is just au revoir."

I hugged these comforting words as I gazed out of the slowly moving train. During the week of spring sunshine, little lines of faint green wheat cast a light over the muddy ground and the bare brown orchards. Now, water stood only in the center of the fields. The many streams had receded to their banks. On the fences of brush about the farm cottages, lengths of linen woven during the long winter were

45

bleaching. Children were jumping up and down at the road crossings, the wind blowing their hair. The train ran along the base of sleepy little hills, which were black with evergreen woods. A wide valley stretched to the horizon, where chalk cliffs, jagged like ruined castles, were honey-colored in the afternoon sun. On the unpaved road that ran beside the tracks, occasional peasant carts were slowly moving under heavy loads of coal or wood, the driver walking at the horse's side, a long knotted whip in his hand. At every siding were freight cars, stacked with great quantities of lumber, coal and iron. The increasing numbers of freight cars and chimneys along the horizon showed that we were approaching an industrial area. The train stopped more and more frequently. Less and less farmed land was to be seen between the little towns, and hillocks of slag and coal dust, and open pits increased.

As we neared each station, I peered anxiously for the name. Zebrzydowice . . . Trzebinia . . . Zabkowice . . . at last Katowice! Here everyone got out of the train. The big covered station reminded me of the old South Station in Boston with trains made up on many platforms. I must have been conspicuous in the crowd. A chauffeur touched his cap, saying, "Lignewski?" and led me to a car where a girl of my own age was sitting.

She greeted me in perfect English. "I am Helen Lignewska. My father apologizes for not meeting your train, but he has an important conference."

We drove across Katowice, a handsome town with fine banks and stately administrative buildings and out a long muddy road. Their house stood in a large garden beside the Pit head of Michalkowice. This was the coal mine where Lignewski worked as Director. It was one of the few mines the Poles had been able to buy from the Germans.

"The house is not very home-like, I am afraid. We have been here only two years," Helen sighed. "We had to leave everything in Russia, of course, when the Bolsheviks took over the mines where father was employed. We were lucky to come out alive. How many of my Polish friends were

46

caught there !" She told me of being in Odessa while the Bolsheviks shelled the town, of their escape on a Black Sea freighter to Constantinople, and their difficulties in reaching Poland.

It was an enormous Victorian mansion large enough for a hotel, built by the former German mine owners. Of irregular shape with wing turrets and carvings, every window was of a different size and height. Palm trees, wicker furniture and linoleum laid down in the hall, exaggerated the cheerlessness of the high ceilings.

Helen apologized as we entered the living room : "You see, we simply can't seem to make it cozy ! Give me some good advice. See, I have samples of curtains. Tell me which you think best." We passed on into a baronial hall designed in the best brewery tradition, with Gothic ceilings and mullioned casements. Over the mantel were elks' heads and rows of buck horns. Yellow stained-glass windows threw a checker-board pattern over everything. The heavy sofas and chairs scattered about did not improve the hopeless prospect of arranging the room agreeably. On a table was a pile of Waring and Gillon catalogues from London, which had been torn to pieces in an effort to find the right furnishings. The manservant brought up tea in heavy shapeless cups. Helen said with a grimace : "We bought also this, from the Germans, when we took over the mines."

While we drank our tea, she asked me whom I wanted to see. We looked over the letters of introduction that had been given me in London and Cracow. Taking the telephone, she soon had made all the appointments, putting down each hour and day on a large sheet of paper. It would take about a week's time. I was to see the German Consul and the Polish Provincial Governor, the judges of the two courts, the President of the Chamber of Commerce, Mr. Korfanty, leader of the Silesian Rebellion, the Bishop of Silesia, the representative of Harriman, Mr. Brooks, and the managers of the principal mines and foundries on both the Polish and the German sides of the province. The car, Helen repeated, would be at my disposal at any time.

47

When I came down for dinner Mr. Lignewski had returned. He made no effort to hide his absorption in his own work and his lack of interest in my study. The conversation lapsed after a few casual questions about his cousin, Professor Kostanecki whom he rarely saw, and of the progress John was making in London. To him the boundaries of Poland had been settled, for better or for worse, and there existed only the pressing problem of running and managing a tremendous coal mine, working in three shifts of over a thousand miners each. He would be delighted to take me down whenever I wished. Had I ever been down a mine? No? Then I could hardly appreciate the improvements he had made. The whole mine was now electrically run, and lights, elevators, trains, drills were all a great improvement on any pits in England. Under his reorganization, production had stepped up twenty-five percent above the German production.

Pleading a headache as soon as coffee was served, I went to my room. It was stiff and white, without a single comfortable chair. The springs in the white wood bed sagged in the middle. The waxed linoleum on the floor and faint sweet odor of disinfectant was like a hospital. I quickly undressed and, having no mail, re-read the last letter from John which he had sent to Cracow:

"Sweetheart,
Your letter from Saturday came last night, and your letter from Friday just now. So that's how things happened! I love you more and more for all the things you are going through for me. Your letter made me blush and burn for shame that you should have to tell the family, though I really saw no other way. It was impossible for me to write them, not being able to foresee at what exact moment the letter would arrive. Fortunately, everything is over. Darling, this is a miserable state of affairs, being away from you at just this moment. Not that I find any reasonable reason why this moment should seem so particularly different from any other, but I am even getting jealous of Jock that he can go for a walk with you whenever he wants to, while I have only your photograph and letters to relieve my utter loneliness. In the dark I can

hear you breathe, and can talk to you for hours, but it is rather hard to do nothing all day long but lie in bed with my head under the pillows.

How quickly will you finish your work in Upper Silesia ? I have received the fourth letter from my mother. She is really delighted with you, — a great discourse on those qualities which will make you 'une femme fidele.' I do wonder all the time how you are getting on with them.

Last evening I was at dinner with Lady Napier, a cousin of the Napiers of the League of Nations. We talked about Mr. Marburg. It's a very nice house. Two most delightful dogs fight on the drawing room carpet all evening to entertain the guests. The world is full of you. We played roulette. I lost 1 shilling, and your face was flashing all the time over the green cloth. I've had a charming letter from Mary R. You won her approval. Also, a letter from the housekeeper. Of course, they all love you."

In a new room amid changed surroundings, I wakened frequently during the night. Even in my sleep I heard the strange noises of the nearby coal mine. Snatches of the information I should need tumbled through my mind. There was so much to do before I was free to go back to John. His honor too was staked on how I should accomplish this task.

My first visit in the morning was to the German Consul, Herr Von Greenow. He called for me with his car at nine sharp, and we drove the length of the Silesian frontier. He wanted to show me the utter preposterousness of drawing a frontier, where here the entrance to a mine was on one side, while the seams ran all on the opposite side ; or there it ran through the middle of a town, causing it to be divided by a stream, half in Germany, half in Poland. He showed me many places where workmen from one side crossed to the other side to work. Some twenty-five thousand persons passed the frontier daily ! "No logic — just pure maliciousness !" he would repeat at each point. He ignored the obvious conclusion that the frontier itself did not cause real hardships among the workers.

The morning was spent seeing how badly the frontier had been drawn. The afternoon would provide examples of the "bestial nature of the Poles." During luncheon I was prepared for what I should see.

"The Poles are no better than Jews," the Consul told me. "Poland is full of Jews because the Poles have no feeling of racial superiority over them. They have always let the Jews settle among them freely. They all live alike, in cellars like animals. I will show you some in the towns this afternoon."

"But I have seen Cracow. I know how Poles live."

"Not the rank and file. Those Poles you visited are the exception," Von Greenow told me in all seriousness. "Poles never bathe, they are lousy with typhus."

After we had inspected a couple of towns, not yet rebuilt since the war, with most of the houses still partially in ruins, I was shown one of the new Public Schools built during the last few years, where the German children were being educated at Polish expense. "That only proves that the Poles feel our superiority. They send their own children to school in pigsties."

"It couldn't be because they were trying to do the right thing by the German minority?" I asked. "I thought by the terms of the treaty two Poles were left in Germany for every German left in Poland. What are the Germans doing for the Polish children?"

"They don't want to go to Polish schools now that they have the opportunity of learning according to German methods!" I was told.

The Consul had arranged for us to have tea with one of the German ladies in Katowice, and in the evening I was to go to a working men's club. We were late returning from our drive, and were the last to arrive at the tea. All the ladies were knitting for the miners' children. At Christmas baskets would be given out to all the families who declared themselves German. Several ladies invited me to their houses, but I was not sure whether I would have time. They all wanted to show me how much they were doing for Germany. It never occurred to them that I might consider them disloyal to their new country, or that their good works were seditious.

In the evening I heard singing and speeches in German in a large hall decorated with German flags and maps showing Poland and Alsace Lorraine as part of Germany. This was in 1926 yet lines of thumb tacks, like those in the maps at home in my childhood during the World War, showed the present boundaries.

"When the boys are eighteen," I was told, "they are smuggled over the frontier, so they don't have to serve in the Polish Army."

"Why smuggled ?" I asked, "when they cross it every day openly. Surely they can become Germans if they wish."

"But if they did, we would lose the province," they said.

"But it is Polish." I was very confused.

"Not forever. Besides it's most important that they should learn Polish." At the time I could not understand this.

Probably my astonishment was misinterpreted as admiration. They begged me to see more — the work of the school teachers, the text books. They would show me all the stupid naïveté of the Poles.

I could hardly sleep all night. I wrote John a long letter, telling him what I had seen and heard. I told Helen in the morning that she should organize the Polish women to counteract the German work. I could hardly wait for my interview with Dr. Grazynski, the Governor of the province.

The provincial building had been recently completed. It made no effort to impose with large stately rooms or magnificent fittings. The Governor's office was a small paneled room with peasant *kilim* rugs on the walls and floor. The Governor, Mr. Grazynski, received me promptly at the hour set. Without waiting for him to speak, I told him what I had seen the previous day. "Why do you let the Germans foment bad feeling among the miners ?" I asked.

He smiled generously. "They would do so anyway. It's better that they should do it openly."

Like so many other Poles, his interest in my studies was purely polite. I found it impossible to explain the impression current abroad that Germany had been wronged by the Treaty of Versailles, and that her frontiers should be rectified.

51

"But it's we who were wronged, if you put it that way. The Silesian Plebiscite showed by a majority that the whole province was Polish, yet we only received a third of it. We are not demanding a change in the frontier. We are trying to return as quickly as possible to a normal working basis."

"But why don't you shout louder than the Germans, so that the world would know?"

Dr. Grazynski stood up and held out his hand. "We have other more pressing needs for our money than propaganda. Do you really believe you can influence justice? Eventually the world will see that we are right. In the meantime, schools and roads are everywhere necessary."

Poor Grazynski! Poor Poles! They never learned to estimate properly the long arm of German propaganda. Nor were they respected for making the best of a bad bargain.

That afternoon I was to see Mr. Brooks, the American representative of Harriman. Mr. Brooks is one of those American business men who, by their respect for the achievements of others have done so much towards making Americans loved in every country.

I asked him why he had settled on the Polish side of the frontier.

"It is much easier to work with the Poles," was his comment. "The Germans are used to being regimented. You can't run a business that way. I was able to organize this plant with fewer men than the Germans had employed, and yet I increase my production. The Germans would never have been allowed that."

"And train facilities? The Germans claim business will be choked for lack of rolling stock and yard equipment."

"We think the Poles are going to build what they need. The Poles are good engineers," he said. "I prefer the Polish workmen. They are full of initiative and do more than follow orders blindly."

It was the first time I had heard anyone who was not a Pole speak kindly of them. The Poles were gallant; they died bravely; but they were an impractical people, and lived in poverty and ignorance. Now here was a hard-headed

52

American business man choosing to live among them. He had actually sold his property in Germany, and had deliberately bought in Poland.

I approached the Polish business men with a new-born respect. I listened attentively while Mr. Korfanty, leader of the Polish uprising, explained his successful military coup, which resulted in the Allies granting a plebiscite. My last appointment was with Mr. Kackenbeck, the Belgian judge of the Supreme Silesian Court. I told him why I was writing on the Silesian Frontier.

"Go back to America," he said. "The Polish-German frontier has been established by law. Further legal problems surrounding it are being handled by the Courts."

"You really think I can't do anything about it ?"

"You will be sorry if you try," and as if to prick my self-confidence, he went on, "if you believe in settlement by law, you will attempt a learned treatise which no one will read. Or, if you believe in the possibility of change by force of propaganda, you could write a popular and amusing bit of journalism but not a University thesis. Whichever you do will benefit the Germans. Opening the question, even to support the present frontier, gives Germany free publicity."

"Why Germany ?"

"Germany wants the frontier changed. Arguing the pros and cons implies the possibility of turning a part or even the entire province over to them."

My self-confidence was now completely gone. "You think there is no ground for discussion ?"

"Not," he emphatically replied, "when the principle of Law and the right of self-determination is involved. You are wasting your time looking for it."

"Tell me," he added, "who put you up to writing this ?"

"Some friends in England." And I told him the whole story.

"That's the difficulty of laymen meddling in legal affairs, even with the best will in the world. Do stay for dinner, if you like Haydn. My colleagues from the Court will be here this evening ; we play quartets every Thursday. Last week,

Brahms; next week, Mozart. During the year, we read through quite a bit. It's the great compensation for living in Beuthen."

On the way home that evening, I asked the chauffeur to drive me to the telegraph office. There were two telegrams to be sent; one to John in London, the other to Madame Kostanecka in Warsaw. Both said "LEAVING BY THE FIVE O'CLOCK TRAIN TOMORROW ARRIVING LONDON SATURDAY."

I met Madame Kostanecka on the train just as we had arranged. The minute we reached London, I told John that I was giving up my work.

"After all you have done?"

"How can I write it?" I told him of my conversation with Mr. Kackenbeck, and explained my fear of turning out propaganda.

"You can base your thesis on statistics. I will help you with them."

"But how could I be sure I had all the figures?"

For answer, he showed me the introduction he had written, limiting the scope and object of my work.

"The English don't want a book showing they drew a good frontier," I insisted. "They apparently want to mobilize world opinion behind a peaceful return to Germany of everything she lost in the World War."

John hugged me. "What a Pole you have become! You don't believe in appeasement!"

CHAPTER 4

WE WERE married in June 1927 a few days after John received his Ph.D. in Economics from the University of London. He was only 25 when he passed his examinations for a Ph.D. and he had completed the work in record time even though during a summer vacation he had served on the Kemmerer commission. Before coming to London he had graduated in Law from the University of Cracow. However, he still had to finish his military training in Cracow. He was to report to the army at the end of the summer. Nevertheless we decided to be married and go to the United States for a brief honeymoon so that John could meet the rest of my family. I begged him to look into opportunities for an international banker hoping he would like the United States enough to remain here forever. He seemed at that time utterly absorbed in the problems of the international money market. I was confident his term of military service would be short because he had served in the Polish-Bolshevik War, and that we could leave Poland after a few months.

My father was astonished when I told him of my plan. "John has all the qualities that especially fit him for diplomacy," he protested, "I should think Poland would have need of his services."

"John has promised to try living in the United States."

"All the same," he warned, "I think he would be happier in a diplomatic career."

"Diplomacy isn't a serious career !" I replied very smugly. "We will be back — you will see !" I did not for an instant contemplate remaining long in Poland nor had I the slightest intention of becoming a Pole.

I said farewell light-heartedly, and sailed down the Bay, certain that we would be back within six or eight months. But later, as we passed the white cliffs of Dover, a cold chill went through me. Landing in Germany suddenly assumed portentous dimensions, as if I had stepped around the corner of the world. For the first time the waves of the sea were no longer a gentle link with home.

The train for Poland left Berlin after midnight and arrived at Cracow the next morning. The whole family was at the station to meet us. They had to my dismay reserved three of those stiff-seated Austro Daimler cars. "I can't ride in one of those autos," I pleaded, unable to hide my misery. "They always make me nervous and car-sick."

"She is tired from the trip, poor darling," said my mother-in-law offering to take me in a *dorozka*.

In the lazy autumn sun, the market carts jolted peacefully over the cobbled streets. Nursemaids in peasant skirts and ribbon streamers on their caps pushed their perambulators through the park along which we drove. The flower boxes on balconies and baskets hung around the lamp posts were sprawling in abundant autumn shabbiness, but in the Park the stiffly planted flowers were still banked in neat and formal designs around the fountains.

"With a few days' rest, you will feel better," my mother-in-law assured me, "and if not, we will call in Dr. Rosner. He brought John and Michael into the world." She put her arm about me and kissed my cheek.

As we turned the now familiar corner, the maids, who must have been peeking through the curtains, ran out on the sidewalk to greet us, with tears of emotion in their eyes, each repeating a well-rehearsed speech of welcome. John's and my hands were kissed again and again, and we were swept triumphantly into the house, and up the stairs.

In John's room bowls of roses were on every table. First one, then the other repeated, "This is your room, now you must rest," and, smiling with the joy of having John to themselves, they closed the door. John had left me, speaking a language I did not understand. To have come so far to be

56

alone in this room! How quickly the welcome was over! How really alone I was, because of his speaking Polish! "Everything will have to be explained to me patiently, as to a deaf person," I said to myself. "It's only in Poland that I would have no part in things. I won't stay here! I won't spend my life sharing nothing, counting for nothing. We must go back to America — we must," I said over and over to myself. "I can't stay here — England — America — John has promised it." I jumped out of bed and ran to the door. "John," I called wildly.

He came at once. I tried to tell him how lonely I felt, the loneliness of being without a country, but I burst into tears. He was frightened. "Of course we will go back. Father thinks because I did eleven months in the Bolshevik War, that I won't have to serve long now. If I had done twelve months then I wouldn't have to do anything and could get into the Reserve Officers' Corps now."

I couldn't listen to what he was saying, nor could I find the words to explain why his speaking Polish should have been such a shock. "You've heard me speak Polish before."

"Then you were just talking to your friends. This is part of me," I said. "If we are one, then you can't speak Polish if I can't speak Polish. What you say is part of me. You are speaking for us."

My mother-in-law opened the door. "I've asked them to bring up John's and your luncheon. I think you will feel like being alone."

After three days, one could no longer say, "She is tired after her long trip." I was still feeling ill.

Dr. Rosner was called. Like his daughter Mary, whom I had met before, he spoke excellent English. He subscribed to the American medical journals. As professor at the University, he was head of a large clinic, and had enormous experience. The whole family assembled to hear his diagnosis. He thought there could be no doubt, though it was too soon to be certain, but if his supposition was correct, I should not travel for the next three months. He was very old-fashioned, he admitted, but he couldn't with a clear con-

57

science have me leave Cracow sooner. "There is too much danger of miscarriage," he had said. "With a first child you can never know. During the first and the last three months I couldn't advise your crossing the ocean."

Everything depended upon John's leaving the Army as soon as possible, so that when the three months were ended we could leave for the United States. "Why don't you use pull?" I implored. "You don't have to serve, do you?"

"Just because we *could* use pull, Father doesn't want me to," was his firm reply.

John went up for medical examination. The examiner, an old pupil of my father-in-law's was surprised to see him. "I understand you are just married. Why don't you put off your service for a year or so?" he asked. This was one of the ways of avoiding military service until some present work was finished. If you knew the right person, you could get the term put off year by year until outside the military age. But it would mean appearing every year in the district, or else evading the law. Neither of us wanted that. It seemed more sensible to finish now.

John entered the barracks as an ordinary soldier. On the first day, the recruits pledged allegiance to Poland. The atheists swore separately, not having to put their hands on the Bible, as did the Jews and Catholics.

The barracks were in Lobzow, at the end of the street-car line that ran near our house. Here and there along the road was a store built into an apartment house, but most of the buildings were one-family dwellings set back at different angles. Many of the owners kept bees and a goat tied to an apple tree and pigeons in a dovecote of rough boards and wire. In every yard were chickens. The clucking of hens, the whir of the sewing machines was only occasionally broken by the noise of the trolleys. This street would have seemed shabby however neatly each garden had been kept for the road was unpaved, the sidewalk of broken slates.

Every afternoon, taking the dogs, I would walk the mile to the Barracks and back. A cold wind blew the leaves from the trees but the sun shone brightly and the sky was blue.

"The beautiful Polish Autumn," everyone told me. From far off I could hear the soldiers coming — the whole column singing marching songs to keep in step. About once a week John had a few hours leave, then we would hurry back in the street car. From the moment we entered it, the whole house was in a commotion. While Bronia drew the bath, Kazia made the tea — and old Andzia brushed and cleaned as best she could the bulky khaki uniform. Usually, however, I would slip the box of sandwiches and cookies I had brought into John's hand as he passed in line to the barracks. Then there was about a half hour before supper when he was free to stroll in the broad alleys under the sycamore trees. But if the men were late from drill, I would return home with only the memory of John's sad and gentle smile as he waved his hand in passing.

One day, on one of those long marches, he fainted. The men were singing, as usual. John no longer heard the real words. He had the illusion instead of hearing women's voices, crying over and over, *They are learning to murder. They are learning to kill. They are learning to murder. They are learning to kill.*" He regained consciousness after he had been put on the cart of a passing peasant. Lying on the straw, he was driven to the hospital. From there, the doctor, a pupil of my father-in-law's, telephoned.

"Why couldn't he say right off what's the matter," Professor Kostanecki fumed while putting on his coat. "Has a taxi been sent for? That doctor apologizes as if he could have prevented it!" Kissing me tenderly on the forehead, my father-in-law promised to get permission for me to go with him to see John in the morning. "There is not reason to be upset. John has only fainted," he kept repeating.

I found John the next day lying in bed in a huge ward. They had shaved off all his hair. Around him, most of the beds were vacant. Young soldiers were sauntering about the long corridors in their bathrobes. The doctor seemed to be very agitated, speaking first to me, then to the Professor, then again to me, though of course I understood not one word of what was said. We made a very brief call, just long enough

59

for me to learn the doctors had taken his blood count, made a metabolism test, a cardiograph, and still other tests. With all this there was a chance that John might be discharged from the Army.

"If, indeed, John has a heart weakness, they should discharge him," said Professor Kostanecki, once we were in the taxi on the way home. "But all this is complicated, by the doctors wanting to do me a favor. Now I do not wish to be obligated to Dr. P. His nephew will appear for examinations; then Dr. P. will ask me to see that he passes. I would give a lot for this not to have happened."

John was kept in the hospital for nearly a week, at the end of which time he was discharged from the Army. Category D was stamped in his military booklet, with the explanation, "Cardiac weakness." I was very worried, and in spite of the family's reassurances, I wanted him to be examined by the family doctor. The verdict put my mind at rest. John had no serious heart illness.

For months John had longed to show me Warsaw. At last we were free to go there. There was nothing to keep us in Cracow any longer. In the second week of November the autumn sky had gone grey with the coming of winter and the ground was frozen hard. The afternoon train was white with frost as it thundered into the little station of Cracow. Threads of ice were festooned about the springs and wheels. In the carriages, heavy smoky pieces of felt were hooked up to the windows. Thick ice gradually crept up the glass until after an hour or so it had covered the whole pane. John's mother had given me her traveling pillow and cashmere traveling rug for my knees. "With all the getting in and out of trains, there is always a draft," she told me. As the train slowly pulled out of Cracow, John made me stand in the window to have a final look at the Wawel, the Acropolis of Cracow, whose medieval towers seemed to rise out of a sea of mist and smoke which hung low over the city. Even after the city was hid from view by fields of little grassy mounds, the Wawel spires seemed mysteriously to hang from heaven like an ethereal crown.

Soon we were running along the line of beautiful little wooded hills. Only the hemlocks in the wintry evening seemed alive beside the great dead plain, that stretched to the faint horizon of jagged chalk cliffs, now eerie white below the dark grey sky. On a little rising above a village of log cabins was a little one-story house, with an immense tile roof covered with lichen. Four unimposing columns supported a simple pediment above the front door.

"That is my dream house," John whispered. "When we are old, we will buy it and end our days there. There is a garden and an old boxwood hedge which leads to the forest. From time immemorial, this has been the gateway to Poland. From the time of the Romans, people have walked over this ground."

John never lived to buy the house, and the Germans chose this spot for the opening of their campaign of 1939.

The lights were turned on in the carriage. Suddenly the outside world was blotted out by the frost, which now coated the whole window with gigantic, starry crystals. The dining car steward came through the car, giving out place numbers for dinner.

"Can we have à la carte while dinner is being served?" John asked.

"Naturally," the waiter replied amiably, as though this were the general custom. Yet just across the frontier, in Germany, the waiter would have bellowed, "Naturally not!"

The train seemed to crawl with infinite slowness along its track. As there was only one line of rail, it had to wait at the sidings for the train coming in the opposite direction to pass. In those days it took eight hours to go from Cracow to Warsaw, a journey of about 225 miles. Once the second track was completed, the trip could be made in six. Later, when a more direct route was opened up by way of Radom, you could make the trip in three hours, in a modernistic plush and chromium Diesel engine car.

As it was, we arrived at midnight, tired and cramped, for the cars had been so crowded that we had not been able to walk about. The Warsaw station at midnight was just as full

61

of peasant families as when I had first seen it in 1925. Every bench was crowded, and even the floor was occupied, except for a narrow passage, through which we stepped in single file to the door. Children were sleeping on piles of bedding, while their parents sat silent, holding their heads in both hands. "They are probably taking up new holdings under the Land Reform Bill," John explained in answer to my question about them.

Outdoors, snow falling heavily muted every sound, and only at the crossings, *dorozki* drivers' sharp cries of warning broke the silence. We drove to the hotel where John and his family always stayed, and had to wait in the line of taxis before the door. There was only one room the manager could give us, at $12 for the night. "The carnival began early," he apologized. That it was in full swing was plain to be seen, and judging by the sounds of music, more than one dance was in progress. Mothers and daughters in evening dress were hurrying through the hall, making last-moment adjustments. Men buttoning their white kid gloves were dashing through the crowd, the most serious expressions on their faces.

"No use running about looking for a room at this hour!" John said emphatically. "And at least here we will be comfortable."

Our room was not as flamboyant as the one I had had on my first trip to Warsaw. But with all its blue silk damask portieres and coverings, its little carved and gilt chairs and tables with marble tops, the effect was far from cozy. On the beds were those hard and unyielding pad-like quilts, to which stiffly starched sheets were buttoned. It was proper to wrap yourself up in them, but when I tried, I only created a funnel which drew the draughts about me! By tucking the traveling rug crossways, I finally managed to keep covered, but I marveled at John's ability to prevent his counterpane from sliding sideways or crossways to the floor.

During the long sleepless hours, I submitted weakly to bitter generalizations, trying to find in this hotel room a reflection of Poland. I knew my parents-in-law always traveled with their own sheets and blankets. I had frequently heard my father-in-law speak of "the barbaric eastern custom" of using woolen bed pads. Yet I imagined that this room had been designed to please a pretentious aristocracy. "This is their idea of Paris without any of its comforts," I reflected. From time to time I would look at John, sleeping with miraculous tranquility, utterly unaware of my discomfort and that I could not sleep.

Yet I was awakened in the morning by the sound of John's voice. He was talking on the telephone, and speaking Polish as if the sound of his own language were a pure delight to him. He made call after call, taking notes on a little pad after each conversation. When he saw I was awake, he remarked happily, "Everybody is in town. It looks as if we would be out for every meal. My deaf aunt from Rome — the one with all the daughters — is on this corridor, and so is my cousin Wladzio from Posen, with his wife. I'll run in to see them before breakfast. Uncle Anthony suggests meeting him before going there for lunch, at the wedding of Zdzisz Grabski an old friend of mine you met the first time you were in Cracow. I told the aunts we would see them tomorrow."

"Tomorrow? Will there be time? I thought we were invited somewhere for lunch."

Without further explanation, John went on, "Tomorrow evening there is a musicale at the Raczynski's. Tuesday the Czetwertynski's are having a ball. Wednesday the Palais Blue Ball will be opened for the first time since the war. Thursday the Borowski's are giving a party. Friday the President is having a reception at the Lazienki for the new American financial adviser to the Polish Government, Mr. Charles Dewey. I hear they have the rooms next to ours."

"Are people pleased at having an American financial adviser?"

"Of course, silly! Ring for breakfast when you are ready. I'll just be a minute."

I chose the button decorated with a picture of a waiter, and when he appeared, asked for *petit déjeuner* — "breakfast" — "*Frühstück.*" He in turn asked me questions in Polish, and since neither of us had come to any understanding, flourishing his napkin, he bowed and left. An hour later, fully dressed and decidedly hungry, I was wondering whether to leave John a note and go downstairs for breakfast, when John and the waiter reappeared simultaneously, the latter carrying a well-laden tray.

"I found the waiter in the hall. How clever of you to have ordered eggs!" John said, devouring the minute rolls with honey, and gulping down several tiny cups of coffee with whipped cream. "If only it had been double portions! Don't forget to order them, tomorrow." Without waiting for me to tell him that I hadn't ordered the eggs, he began translating the newspaper headlines. "Daszynski had made a speech in Parliament attacking Slawek. Slawek, you know, is a friend of Jas, my cousin, who has just been elected to the Sejm. You are sure to meet him at the party Jas is giving next week. Don't get him confused with Daszynski, whom you'll see at the Dvernicki's."

"Then tell me more about them."

John went on, "They both started as members of the Socialist Party. Now Slawek is leader of the non-partisan group supporting Pilsudski. Once you see him, you will never forget him. He has a terrible scar on his face, made by a bomb which exploded in his face when he was working in the Polish underground movement about 1910. Later Pilsudski trained him as a member of the Bojowka, disciplined guerilla fighters, capable of offering really effective resistance to Russia and Germany. During the war, he became an officer in the Polish Army.

"Daszynski is Marshal of the Diet, and leader of the Socialist Party. From the tone of his speeches, you would never think the Socialists had urged Pilsudski to come back into active politics in the Coup of 1926. When the Diet refused to have Slawek as Marshal of the Seym, Pilsudski resigned as Prime Minister. Now, as Marshal, Pilsudski is Inspector of the Army."

"Have you forgotten about the wedding?" I interrupted.

64

"We won't be late if you hurry." John led the way down seemingly endless corridors. The Hotel Europe had been built in the era of Napoleonic magnificence, and covered all four sides of a large square. But there was only one stairway, and our room was two long blocks away from it.

"Can we take a sleigh ?" I begged, as we ran along. "It would be such fun." You could hear the bells dancing merrily. They sounded romantic and foreign.

"Would it be fun in the city ?" John's voice sounded doubtful but he yielded.

The taxicab drivers who stood beside their cars clearly showed that if we preferred a sleigh to an automobile, we were unworthy of their further attention. They made loudly disparaging remarks as we were buttoned up to the chin under a pungent smelling fur rug, and laughed scornfully as, with a crack of the whip, our driver flung the sleigh into the New World Street. The horse was urged into the perilously narrow passage between never-ending lines of trolleys and rattling model-T taxis. On either side of the street was a jumble of houses. Some were weighted down under immense tile roofs, like the village shops. Others were finely decorated, with graceful sheaves of wheat in the cornices, and well-designed moldings. Some had Empire columns, some Louis XVI façades, and breaking the even line, all the Nineteenth-century buildings shot up above their neighbors, leaving unfinished sides gaping and uncovered. You could see the Nineteenth-century business philosophy of "laissez faire" had even reached to Warsaw. Here, as in America, the individual could spoil the outline of the street by building in utter disregard of the style of his neighbor's house.

By the time we reached the Place of the Three Crosses, where the Church of St. Alexander stands perilously in the center of seven radiating streets, the bells were ringing for the wedding ceremony. On the broad steps and high columned porch several hundred people were already waiting. John told the sleigh driver to let us off at the beginning of the Aleje Ujazdowskie the most beautiful street in Warsaw which runs from the Place of the Three Crosses to the Belvedere.

65

It is lined on either side with a clipped hedge of old beech trees, now fifty feet in height, and a very broad sidewalk flanked by grass-borders. Here many sleighs were parading, as was the custom every morning from twelve to one. Horse-drawn vehicles had congregated from all sections of the city. In the old days, equipage had vied with equipage, to display the finest breeds of horses and the most elegant coach and livery. John's mother's earliest memories had been of sitting on the coach seat beside her mother, whose faultless beauty was saluted by the beaux of Warsaw.

Though the grey mist penetrated the heavy bearskin cover, and I shivered in my fur coat, hundreds of open *dorozki* and sleighs were coursing up and down the streets. In some were courtesans, in others old ladies with their dames de compagnie. Many of the vehicles were shabby old hacks that must have come from the meanest parts of the city, and many carried Jewesses in their old red periwigs. It was now late, and everyone had gone into the church. With difficulty we squeezed inside. Already a thousand persons were pushing towards the altar. There were no ushers, no pews, and although many were well-dressed, there were also peasant women under heavy shawls.

"Are all these people here for the wedding?" I whispered.

"A church is free. Anyone may come in."

"Even to a private wedding?"

"How could you keep people out of a church?" John asked in astonishment. "Besides there is an exceptionally large crowd here because Zdzisz' father was Minister of Finance under Paderewski." After looking about, John whispered, "Most of the Conservative Party are here!"

Everyone had put on a mask of solemnity. No one smiled even when nodding to an acquaintance. Uncle Anthony, when we met him, hardly gave a sign of recognition, immediately resuming his prayers. Since I had not come to pray, my eyes roamed about the scene. The church was unheated, the marble floors wet from the ice and snow which had been tramped in. Though it was so cold you could see your breath, the bride wore no cloak over her white satin dress.

66

She had no attendants, and someone in the crowd near her picked up her long veil when she moved. Everyone else in the church was in black, the women in tubular coats of Persian lamb, the men in black cloth coats with fur collars, and with fur caps in their hands. At the solemn moment of the Mass, those who could, knelt on the bases of the pillars to be out of the wet. The others bowed down dexterously to avoid the slush.

When the ceremony was over, a few went forward to press the bride's hand, but we, like all those standing near us, turned to the door, as if it were enough to come and pray for the happiness of the young couple.

It was only on the steps of the church that Uncle Anthony greeted us. "Welcome ! Welcome to our family !" and taking my arm, he said briskly, "One can't talk in this cold. Let us cross the square to the *Cukiernia*." He coughed significantly as he pulled his muffler up over his mouth and pushed his fur cap down over his ears. He led us into a modest little tea room, saying apologetically, "At least they sell good cakes here ; and it 's quiet at this hour." We passed through the narrow shop to a side room, where even the morning light could not dispel the gloom of maroon and gilt wallpaper. However the room was well filled. The habitués behaved as if they felt very much at home, hanging their coats against the wall, and choosing the newspapers from the rack, which they studied with concentration, not even glancing up at the girl who took the orders.

John and Uncle Anthony at once discussed the people they had seen at the wedding.

"Raczkiewicz was next to me. He is going back to Poznań."

"What about Radwan ?"

"He 's back in the Agricultural Bank." Uncle Anthony bent across the table as if he were imparting information of the most clandestine nature.

"Osiecki came in with Kiernik. You don't know him ?

"Who was standing with Stanislaw Grabski ?" The ash of Uncle Anthony's half-burned cigarette fell on his jacket.

"Klarner, of course ! Was Janicki there ?"

These names meant no more to me than the strange words printed in the newspapers.

"Yes, he came up to consult with Klarner. They have plans for a new agricultural station in Lubelskie province."

"Old Zychlinski is coming in tomorrow or the next day." It seemed as if they must have mentioned everyone there.

Tea, served in glasses, is very hot. I tried to hold the glass with my glove. Uncle Anthony, who had put a quarter of a glass of sugar into his tea, stirred it absent-mindedly until it became cool. Though both men spoke English, it might as well have been Polish, for they talked of nothing else than who was at the wedding and what they were now doing. From time to time, Uncle Anthony would give me an encouraging smile. "How do you like Warsaw ?" he would ask. Or, "You have a comfortable room ?" But without waiting for the answer, he would mention to John someone else he had seen.

Uncle Anthony and my father-in-law were as similar in stature and features as John and Michael. Yet the way Uncle Anthony drank his tea or held his cigaret showed the absent-minded professor, while Father was meticulous to a fault. Uncle Anthony was gregarious and loved his pupils and colleagues ; Father, though a real political force, preferred solitude and quiet. The two brothers loved each other dearly and by writing daily shared every joy and anxiety.

While Uncle Anthony finished his tea and stood up to pay, John glanced at the newspaper. "It 's such a pleasure to read a newspaper where you can get all the information without repetition and a lot of comments," he said.

"The papers look like tabloids," I commented.

"But they are not. They are this small size because they handle more easily. In Warsaw there are twenty-odd dailies of every possible political complexion. They generally carry on a lively debate with their readers and other editors."

We went out and hailed a taxi. Uncle Anthony, like my

father-in-law and Michael, would never take a *dorozka*.

As we drove down the New World Street, John pointed out the façade of a large newly appointed bookstore. "That is my cousin Wladzia's shop. He bought a printing press to publish his own poems ! He makes a hobby of fine editions of poetry and artistic prose with a limited sale. Wladzia lived a long time in France and graduated from the Sorbonne."

"His bookstore has the best foreign department in Warsaw," Uncle Anthony said.

As we passed the University, which is on the Copernicus Square, Uncle Anthony, at the point where the New World Street and the Cracow Suburb merge, waving his hand remarked, "Every morning at ten I walk along there to the University. At twelve-thirty I have tea at that *Cukiernia*, and at two I walk home on the opposite side of the street." I could picture him, day in and day out, year in and year out, nothing changing the essential regularity of his routine.

Uncle Anthony had lived on the eighth floor of the same apartment building ever since the house had been built in 1910. After an interminable discussion with the doorman as to whether all of us could ride at once, we went up in a slow-moving lift. Upstairs we were let in by a jolly maid in a house dress and bedroom slippers. You could hear Aunt Anita and the children running about, but the living room was empty. Uncle Anthony took me at once to his windows from which you could see into the steep streets, running down to the Vistula, and beyond, across the river, to the suburbs of Prague and to the black line of pine forest in a circle on the horizon.

"This is where I always sit," he said, "in this bay window. I love to watch that never-ending procession of street cars as they run past day and night. There is the new Poland." I could see that in his deepest soul it gave him a profound joy to look for the new cars, each month more new cars, in a perpetual stream of traffic. All their nickel and glass were kept brightly polished, and the pale blue paint gleamed like new. These street cars moved a million people to work. He had the Socialist's joy of watching a state enterprise prosper.

69

The bay window was filled with a palm, not as big as the palm in Cracow, yet big enough to fill most of the space. Under it were little stiff chairs and an enormous flat-topped mahogany desk. There was a Steinway concert grand piano. A heavily padded sofa, and three arm chairs, covered in green leather, were grouped about a round tea table. Very fine Oriental rugs were on the floor, and the curtains were Persian shawls. On the side walls, mahogany bookshelves reached to the ceiling. Besides Polish, all the Italian, French, German and English classics were there. Uncle Anthony traced the history of economics back to the thirteenth century, using Dante as his guide, and his scientific writings were to be found in foreign journals.

John pointed out the volumes while Uncle Anthony fretted, "Anita is never ready. Dear, dear — not ready to welcome you. It 's the fault of Miss Helen. I always say Miss Helen is so bad for the children. No discipline. Just the other day Miss Helen broke this little piano lamp. She wouldn't let the maid dust it, so now I can't ask you to play. Do you play Chopin ? Here is my music."

As we were looking over the music, the children burst into the room, specially dressed, and drilled for the great occasion of greeting me in English. "We are so glad you have come," they said, throwing their arms about me, without the least sign of shyness. And both speaking at once, they let flow a torrent of Polish.

"What are they saying ?"

"They want to show you their toys."

"John, why didn't you prepare me ? Why have we no toys for them ?" I pleaded. "I can't imagine six and ten year old American children making such a fuss over a stranger."

"You are not a stranger. You are their new cousin."

"Yes, we all are so happy you are here," my new aunt said very timidly, giving me a kiss on both cheeks. "The children have been waiting so impatiently all morning. Would you care to see their room ?"

"After lunch, perhaps," I said, looking at my watch. It was nearly two, and I was famished.

70

"There is plenty of time. Dinner will be at three. Mr. Wieniawski, president of the Commercial Bank, will be here," my hostess told me, as she led the way through an enfilade of rooms. In the corner of one was a loom, on which a half-finished rug was hanging. She would have passed it, had I not paused to exclaim : "What a beautiful and unusual pattern ! Where did you find it ?"

"I just make it up as I go along. The colors for the wool ? I dye it myself from vegetable dyes, of course. Gladly will I show you how to do it. It is so very simple. As soon as you are settled, I will set you up a loom."

The children were tugging at me to come and see all their toys, which had been neatly arranged for my inspection. They had the largest room in the apartment. It was newly whitewashed, and the faded chintz curtains were freshly starched and ironed. In one corner stood a statue of the Virgin, set about with ferns and palms, before which a light was always kept burning. The beds were hidden behind screens, and in the center was a large white table with chairs about it. I had only just sat down with the children when the doorbell rang, and the bank president, a gentleman like those we had seen that morning in church, was announced.

The moment of greeting was solemn, with hardly a smile. While kissing my hand, he said, as if he had rehearsed it, "You are for the first time in Warsaw ? You are comfortable in the hotel ?" and again without waiting for my reply, he turned and greeted Uncle Anthony and John. The three then moved towards the window, and instantly became oblivious of everyone else in the room.

Having drawn me to the sofa, my new aunt rang for the servant, who entered apologizing that the *kanapki* were not ready. "Miss Helen wishes to do everything herself," she said helplessly. "It's hard to train the others." She fidgeted with embarrassment, until finally she begged to be excused. From time to time John would look up and send me that "I hope you are as happy as I am" smile. The line "They also serve who only stand and wait," went over and over through my mind. I was learning my place, but it was

71

difficult to sink into it and to fill it gracefully. In Poland, I found, conversation was about specific things; no one ever spoke in generalizations, nor were the opinions of young people considered interesting. John, his uncle and the bank president were, I knew, engaged in a technical discussion. I would be expected to discuss our immediate plans, my impressions of Warsaw and Cracow. John had more than once made it quite clear to me that a person who indulged in propounding hackneyed theorizing was avoided as a terrible bore.

When Aunt Anita came back, I tried to describe how different everything was in America. She listened politely. When I had finished, she said, "Yes, indeed. Everything will be very different for you here."

I said I did not mean in essential things. "People really are the same everywhere."

"Perhaps," she said doubtfully. "Out there interests are so different. People are occupied with other kinds of problems."

When the maid brought in the sandwiches and *wodka*, the gentlemen joined us. Drawing the three arm chairs together they continued the conversation in which they were so deeply absorbed. They made no pretense of admitting us into their circle. Finally, at half past three, dinner was served. The bank president, Uncle Anthony, John and I sat on one side of the table, while on the other Aunt Anita sat, between the two children to whom she gave her full attention. It was a long meal, consisting of wild duck blood soup, followed by a roast of wild boar with wattle berries, then chicken and a salad. For dessert, there were horns of plenty, made of wafers, filled with candied fruit and cream.

During dinner, John told me that Mr. Wieniawski wanted him to go into the Commercial Bank. He would be trained as secretary of the bank.

"What about America?" I asked.

"I am sure I could arrange to be sent over there in some capacity," he told me reassuringly.

When, at five, we staggered from the table, it was already

72

dark. Far across the river, out on the horizon, was a red streak left over by the setting sun, and from the city streets below a myriad of soft lights were twinkling. I sat in the window with the children, who loved to watch the line of trolleys, with their solid bank of lights, while John, Uncle Anthony and Mr. Wieniawski stood in the shadow of the bookshelves, talking softly. When other guests arrived, everyone made a great effort to carry on a general conversation in French. They spoke of the theatre, the various actors I must see, even if I couldn't understand what was said. But one would speak an aside to another in Polish, and bit by bit, the general conversation crumbled away. Then the four men became engaged in a heated discussion, which continued without interruption until midnight, even after the evening tea and sandwiches were brought in.

My new aunt, the lady guest and I were left on the sofa by the tea table, for the men had once more drawn back to the bay window under the palm. The lady, it appeared, was French, but she had learned Polish, which she spoke fluently to my aunt. It was not difficult, she said. She had two boys who spoke French and Polish. It was comforting to think that my children would be able to speak two languages equally well. The lady had many friends in her adopted country, and seemed to be very happy in Warsaw. She loved Poland, and every year she visited her parents in France.

"C'est pas le bout du monde !"

It was difficult to keep up a conversation of questions and answers, especially since the lady seemed so much happier while talking Polish to Aunt Anita. The hands on my watch made so little progress that I thought it must have stopped. I made repeated signals to John, which he refused to see. At last I stood up.

"I'm so very tired. I really must go to bed."

"Why don't you take her to the hotel and come back?" Uncle Anthony suggested to John. "No, no !" I tugged at John's sleeve.

"Will we not see you tomorrow?" Aunt Anita said wistfully.

I said we would join them for lunch tomorrow.

Back at the hotel, as I was undressing, John dropped the bombshell. "Wieniawski is very insistent about my taking that job. It's a perfect beginning. He will arrange to send me to New York to learn the international money market."

"Did you promise to take it?"

"Not without consulting you."

"But you want to take it?" I could see his mind was made up.

"If you can decide to live in Warsaw."

So it was decided.

CHAPTER *5*

*A*S SOON as John signed his contract with the bank, we started the difficult task of finding an apartment. At that time all old apartments were occupied. Rents in the old buildings were frozen at a very low level to protect the tenants from inflation. As a result, people only moved if they were paid a high enough price, enabling them to get a smaller apartment and still pocket a considerable sum. Finding an apartment depended on social connections, first prefaced with a call, then leaving wounded susceptibilities.

In 1927 all houses were in an appalling state of disrepair. Landlords who received about twenty-five dollars a month for an apartment which before the last war had brought them two hundred and fifty were unable to make anything but the most superficial external repairs. The appearance of the interiors of apartments which had not been re-decorated in fifteen years — before the period of the war and occupation — can hardly be imagined.

Though the newer houses were cleaner, they had central heating. This was considered a disadvantage, and everyone assured us the heating system would surely break down during the coldest days of winter.

"In the last war," they said, "it was the people who depended on central heating who suffered the most. If you have a stove you can always find a scrap of wood to burn for an hour or so."

"But there won't be a war now," I would reply.

"Suppose there is a strike and coal isn't delivered. Or suppose one of the other tenants does not pay his share, and

75

deliveries are stopped. Or suppose the heating system goes to pieces in the cold weather, and you have to wait until the blacksmith makes the new parts!" This was before the factories were rebuilt, and after the Russians and Germans had stolen all the machine tools from Poland. Everyone had recent memories of privation and suffering from the bitter winter cold.

We eventually chose an apartment in a newly built house, even though it had central heating, because the ceilings were not festooned with plaster of Paris scrolls, and the windows and doors were not decorated with wooden caryatids. Four rooms gave off a central hall, and the maids' rooms, kitchen and pantry were down a separate corridor. If we felt somewhat self-conscious at having more room than most friends of our own age, they appeared to rejoice at our good fortune. Many suggested renting a room while moving or re-settling, but we never had visitors for the night, not even guests from out of town. Rooms and beds were so scarce that no one would have presumed to expect such hospitality in the city. Yet everywhere out in the country "the guest is God in the house" as the saying goes, and no one was ever turned away from the door, however poor and meager might be the hospitality available.

We moved into the new apartment while the workmen were still painting it. Once it was ours we were anxious to be settled. Every day we combed antique shops, with the result that we had a fine collection of old brass chandeliers and silver platters before we had found anything comfortable to sit on! My husband would not spend money on anything new, not even a simple chair. "It's just pure waste!" he would say, buying a capo di monte figurine, or a fine piece of brocade to hang on the wall. Judging by the few Eighteenth-Century chairs that survived, the Poles of those days must have sat very prim and upright. As we appeared doomed forever either to sit about the dining room table or on the seven-foot square ottoman, which also served as a bed, John's family offered us a whole attic full of shapeless old stuffed chairs and sofas. "Some can be upholstered in leather ap-

76

propriate to a man's den," said my father-in-law, "and others in silk damask to go in your living room."

John refused to be cajoled from his conviction that arm chairs in a room full of antiques should be treated in a temporary manner with slip covers of printed linen. But in all Warsaw I could find no self-respecting upholsterer who had ever made or even seen a slip cover. The several I called in refused to take money for creating anything so amateurish.

"No, Madame. They will slide and tear."

"The room will look like a rats' nest."

"Now if Madame would let me nail on the cloth with a heavy fringe and tassels !"

In the end I found a seamstress, and together we made all the slip covers and curtains in the house ourselves.

John hired our cook Makowska because, he said, "You could see she had an instinctive feeling for antiques." She had lived in a wing of the old Royal Palace, now being arranged as a museum, where her husband cleaned and polished the beautiful parquet floors and stored away rugs and hangings brought out for receptions. They had first come to Warsaw when the Germans bombed the village where they lived. Their little girl had been born prematurely while the houses about them were in flames. Though their livestock had been plundered, and nothing remained but their land, they still dreamed of going back to the country and re-building their home. Now, though the husband had a good salary of forty dollars a month, and two rooms in the *oficina* of the palace, the wife wanted to earn twenty dollars as a cook, to put away for re-building the farm.

She told me how she had walked the forty miles to Warsaw with her new-born baby. She had started off in their cart with a few possessions. The Germans came nearer. They began shelling the road crowded with refugees. Her husband made her jump down from the cart and run into the field. At that moment they became separated. She went on like a crazy person, following the other refugees, having nothing to eat, and holding the child to her breast to keep it warm, and wrapping the wet diapers about her loins to dry

77

them. When she came to Warsaw, she did not know where
to go. She had never been there before in her life. She
tried to remember what she had been told about the city.
Her mother had done washing for a Countess Rose. She
would go there. It took her two days to find the house, and
she was four days without food. When she came to Countess Rose, her husband was there. It was surely a miracle
of God.

If I would hire her at the very high wage of twenty dollars,
she would take nothing from the "basket." In the early
morning when the peasants drove their carts to the edge of
the city she would buy potatoes and other winter vegetables
and wood for the stove.

Makowska had learned some German during the occupation. She begged me to teach her English. Her ambition
was to be a housekeeper and hold the keys to the larder.
From the first day she came to us, no matter what was lost,
she would say, "Nothing can disappear completely from the
house." With these comforting words, the disrupting
search would be ended. A week later she would triumphantly produce the missing object. She would never let
me take a parlor maid unless she had references from the few
bourgeois or aristocratic families that measured up to her
standard of "right and proper." If the former mistress was
known for her love affairs, or had lived beyond her means,
she would say, "Such people are too lenient with their servants. Madame would never be satisfied."

Makowska took the keenest personal interest in all objects
bought for the household. When she found that I had ordered mattresses from an upholsterer, she was dismayed.
"How can you know what they will be filled with ? You
order horsehair, but they can stuff it with seaweed, for all you
know. We must buy the hair and have it done at home."

She plagued me until, dressed in our oldest clothes, we took
a *dorozka* and drove across town where the Jewish whole-
sale shops were located. These were in the Ghetto, established under Russian domination. During the years of Poland's freedom the Reformed Jews moved into the finest

streets uptown and many of our literary and artist friends moved down into this ancient picturesque district. But in 1927 the Jewish section still looked like an oriental bazaar. Brass shops in one street, tin shops in another, streets of carpenters and streets of shops with old furniture, streets of furriers and of cloth merchants. Finally we came to the street of the horsehair merchants! It was very narrow, and we were constantly shoved off the sidewalk into the midst of pushcarts hauling bathtubs, pipes, furniture, great lengths of wire, piles of paper. Straining at the shaft, one Jew pulled while others pushed. They were spattered with mud, ragged and unshaven.

On every window ledge, women were leaning, though nothing unusual was happening on the streets. People swarmed from the houses like ants. Those who overflowed the houses jammed the shops, some sitting, others standing at the counters. All were engaged in heated conversations. No one made a move to wait on us until Makowska told them what we wanted to buy. Only when we started to leave, they would grab at us.

"You leave me go, you good-for-nothing! I would not buy that dirty hair if you made me a present of it!" Makowska appeared so angry that I was frightened, until I learned her technique.

"Not take my beautiful hair! It's fit for a princess to sleep upon. You would not recognize the quality of the fine hair I have. The lady never held the like of it in her hand." The merchant held the strand above his caftan.

"I would not touch it — it's too dirty," Makowska spat out.

"Dirty! The purest white Arabian horsehair," the salesman's voice rose to a shriek as he dangled the braid above Makowska's head.

"Not good enough," she told him. "We must be going."

Someone else caught her arm and held aloft another strand for her inspection. Still she shook her head and dragged me from the shop. Having spent two or three hours going through all the shops down one side of the street, and

79

coming back up the other side, I was faint and ready to leave.

"We've seen it all," she consoled me. "Which does Madame consider the best?"

"I can't possibly remember."

"Then, if Madame will permit, I will go into that shop over there, the third on the left. Does Madame wish to come in while they weigh it?"

"If they can be quick."

"It may take an hour or so," she warned.

"Oh, no," I said, "I will give you the money. Direct the *dorozka* to our street. I want to go home."

Hours later Makowska arrived home in a *dorozka*, sitting on a bale of glossy hair, her hat awry, but otherwise as fresh as when we had set out that morning.

Until I really spoke Polish sufficiently well to go shopping alone, everything I bought for the house was just as exhausting as buying the hair for the mattresses, whether it was the curtain rods of solid brass or the cord that was to pull them, the cloth for the servants' clothes, or their sheets and towels. It took an hour's bargaining to settle the spending of a dollar. Our linens, fortunately, were bought in shops where someone spoke a little French, and I could go alone. My husband's aunts had advised one place for fine sheets, another for those of a more ordinary quality, and a third for towels and napkins. The shops were like warehouses, with stock piled to the ceiling. Everything was tied up in paper and tapes. There was a bewildering choice of qualities. No sooner would I settle on a pattern, and it would be measured than the desired amount was found lacking.

"Yes, this is very fine," they would explain to me apologetically. "It is stock made before the war for the old Russian trade. Our Polish factories today cannot even keep up with the orders for cottons that come in, everything is so depleted."

I was shown samples of Czech and French linens. Had I been buying five years later I should have had the finest Polish linens to choose from, as it was I took the Czech. Everything had to be made by hand, and was delivered piece by piece. It took two months for my whole order to be delivered.

I was never to cease marveling at the streak of perfectionism in the Polish character. So many things were kept from being done at all, that could have been just tidied over. When a high road was repaired, its very foundations were replaced ; and once a house was built it was supposed to last forever. Even the Polish peasant wanted nothing but the best in cloth and boots, and spent hours in the choice of those few items which he purchased. My husband would never buy the simplest items for the house unless they met his exacting requirements in every respect. It was three years before we had any little tables in our drawing rooms, or a small old meat platter — there was no question of buying a copy ! It was ten years before we bought a dining room rug, though during that time we constantly searched in Poland and many parts of Europe. The ideal rug had been bought by a cousin from under our very nose, and nothing else was fine enough, big enough, or somber enough in color and design.

One day I was seized with an excruciating pain and high fever. The doctor was summoned immediately and at first we hoped the pains would pass and all would soon be well. But after a few days he insisted I should be transported by ambulance to a hospital. The baby, it seemed, was pressing against my kidneys ; an operation might become necessary. The small private hospital to which I was taken had been established on several floors of an ordinary apartment house, and John chose what must have been designed as the living room. My bed was an after thought. In the large bay window stood a dining room table with six chairs around it. There was a sofa on which John slept, two easy chairs, a desk, a chaise-longue and a couch for the night nurse, a wash stand and medicine tables behind screens. All patients were allowed their own bedding and as I was rolled down the corridor, I had glimpses of the magenta or yellow satin quilts with those lace trimmed voile covers so frequently displayed in linen shop windows.

After a few days when it became apparent I was gravely

81

ill, John engaged the adjacent room so that his mother who had hurriedly arrived from Cracow, could also remain in the hospital day and night. During the day John read aloud the *American Tragedy* and at night he sat by my bedside stroking my forehead. When he dropped from weariness his mother was there to whisper caressing endearments. Both of them helped with the nursing. As the situation grew worse, my father-in-law who at first had come only for the week-ends, left his University students in the hands of an assistant and remained in Warsaw. He searched the shops for different kinds of biscuits and fruits to tempt my appetite. When he found that pineapples at the equivalent of six dollars apiece were what pleased me most, he combed all the stores in town. He bought ice creams from all the various caterers hoping one would be better than the other. "Americans do like ices, do they not ?" he would anxiously inquire.

Every day Uncle Anthony and his children came to inquire how I was doing. They stood behind the screens for fear of intruding. Wojtek drew pictures to paste on the wall over my bed and Zosia sewed lace ruffles to a pillow for the new little baby.

Because of my father-in-law's position as Dean of the Cracow Faculty of Medicine, the greatest specialists from all over Poland offered their services. The line of physicians about my bed grew longer with each consultation. They gave little hope for my recovery and urged that my parents, be sent for. Every day for six weeks the fever rose to 105. When all the known methods for checking it failed, the gynecologist declared nothing was left but to take the child. It was then the eighth month and they feared a general infection would set in.

When the operation was over, I could feel the hot tears flowing. They wet the pillow and made me cough. I wept from weakness and exhaustion, despair and frustration. I was even unable to read. When finally I could crawl about my room and reach the window, spring was nearly over. Lilacs in the dooryard below managed to lift their fragrance above the ether-filled hospital air. Men passing in the street had thrown their coats wide open, and women in blouse and skirt carried their shawls on their arms. At last we could leave in an open *dorozka*.

Without pressing the point, on the way home John asked, "Would you like to take Polish lessons ? It would be well if you kept yourself very busy."

One of the teachers in the primary school, which Uncle Anthony's son, Wojtek attended, said she would teach me. Her name, translated, means Miss "Book." She spoke no English and she taught in the public school every day until two. But she felt it her mission to give me a thorough foundation in Polish. Her father had been a teacher during the years of Russian occupation when teaching Polish History carried the death penalty. Like hundreds of other Polish teachers, he had been shot at the citadel. Her tiny frame weighed less than a hundred pounds but her zeal for teaching gave her the strength she needed to follow his heroic career. She was well-read in theory and method of teaching and spurned the old-fashioned way of learning words — "The pencil is red — the canary is yellow." Instead she plunged immediately into the household accounts that had accumulated during the last six months. From working over them I learned the names of objects in the larder and soon I could order a meal.

I was so proud of my new achievements that I tried to give orders in Polish even before guests. I lost an excellent maid by trying to ask for the dessert knives — instead I said, "'Put your foot on the table here." She ran to the kitchen in tears. Makowska could not console her, even when she explained, "When Madame asks for the bedbugs, meaning to ask for thumb tacks, *I* do not take offense."

We used the Polish school text books, and I learned to read from the primer. Within a few months I had reached the third grade. As soon as I was able to understand a little conversation, Miss "Book" invited me to tea. She lived in a tiny flat, consisting of a living room, kitchenette and bath. The walls, the floor and a large ottoman were covered with *kilims*, which are woven like American Indian rugs. The

83

ottoman has the appearance of a big upholstered box. At night it is used as a bed and, with the bedding put away, by day it serves as a sofa. Four highly polished mahogany chairs stood around a brightly polished mahogany table in front of the window. On the walls were photographs of Switzerland and Italy and an etching of a Polish mountaineer. Decorative pieces of Polish pottery stood on top of a bookshelf containing a few Polish classics. Hers was the room of the Polish city-dweller of small means and modest taste, neat and clean, where "even a fly couldn't sit," as the saying goes.

When Miss "Book" first came to me, she was one of twelve teachers at the public primary school near our house. During the ten years I knew her, she advanced to the rank of principal. There were between seven and eight hundred children in this school. There were thirty in a class, the grades were subdivided into sections according to reading ability ; those who could learn to read by whole sentences, those who could only learn a word at a time, and those who could learn to read only by syllables.

This teaching technique and the regulation which did not permit children starting school before they were seven years old, are I am told, advanced theories in pedagogy put into practice by only a few schools in the United States. Poles believed that, before attending school, all children should have seven years of play in the open air. Even the poorest women were out with their infants in the bitterest weather, and there seemed to be more perambulators on the streets and in the parks than here in America. The pre-school children were taken care of in big playgrounds, where they were divided into age groups for supervised outdoor play. If a child's birthday fell a month after the fall term began, he had to wait until the following year to commence school. It was felt that the healthy child could learn more quickly and concentrate better on his work in later years, than if he had started school before the age of seven.

During my lessons, Miss "Book" explained this theory to me and she also told me about the public school routine. Immediately on arriving there was inspection of hands, nails and teeth. For the very poor, who couldn't afford tooth-brushes, the Parents-Teachers Association had its funds which were discreetly administered. Every morning each child brought his six cents for the lunch of milk, vegetable stew and fruit. The stew was cooked and prepared by the mothers in turn throughout the winter. Those too poor to pay even the six cents were given it free. The children themselves devised the plan that when they marched in line to give the teacher the money, even the ones who could not pay stood in line, so that no one could know who paid and who did not. The poorest women volunteered most eagerly to help with the cooking and the serving.

The Parents-Teachers Club at her school met on Fridays. The teachers prepared little talks about child hygiene and the latest theories of education. They met in the roughly plastered and whitewashed basement dining room, which was furnished with the simplest wooden benches and tables. Here they also made clothes for the needy of the school, from the materials bought with the proceeds of the entertainments and assembly days, or from old clothes donated for the purpose. They were as grateful for small gifts as if one had offered them a fortune.

Corporal punishment, freely practised in other parts of the continent, was not allowed in Poland. Once when she was preparing a Friday talk on punishment, Miss "Book" showed me with horror a booklet of regulations in German for German state schools, which sanctioned not only beating, but locking children in dark rooms.

Once a month delegates from all the Warsaw primary schools and the principals met to discuss not only their special problems, but also the latest educational theories from abroad. Articles from American journals were translated and read to the teachers. Every few years, the teachers were compelled to attend summer school.

With so many extra-curricular duties, the teachers were naturally very much overworked. They had to accept harrowing salary cuts. Moreover, the Government economized on the number of substitute teachers, for teachers could not be trained as fast as new school houses were built. In every community the one outstanding building was the new school. Poland at one time was the only country in Europe with a larger budget for education than for military service.

Because of having compulsory sickness insurance, when the teachers were ill they could have six weeks' treatments in semi-private hospitals rooms. This provision was fortunate for teachers like Miss "Book" who lived alone. She told me how she had nearly died of appendicitis — luckily, when she had not turned up for school, one of the teachers had gone over to see what was the matter. The teacher was able to call an ambulance and get her to the hospital just in time. Had they needed first to find a doctor, it would have been too late. As it was, once Miss "Book" had recovered from a ruptured appendix, she went to a convalescent home built especially for teachers. It was in the forest outside Warsaw, and administered by the State Sick Insurance. The room which was allotted to her had folding glass doors, which in good weather were thrown open to a loggia. Chintz curtains and wicker chairs distinguished it from the rooms in other hospitals. After six weeks she returned to Warsaw, but she still went twice a week to be baked by diathermy. From her description, it sounded as if half of the population of Warsaw went in for these treatments, and indeed diathermy must have been very popular in the new Polish medicine. My maid who developed housemaid's knee was prescribed a daily baking. Every afternoon I was obliged to give her the time off until she was pronounced cured. Nor had I the right of dismissing her unless I gave her board wages for the whole period.

Any servant needing a tooth filling, or eyeglasses, or any of the pleasures afforded by the medical profession, could spend hours out of the house receiving free treatment at the clinics. All of them received free sick insurance, old age and unemployment insurance, which cost me six or seven dollars a month per servant, according to their wages. To evade the insurance was a Court offense. The servant received indemnity and the right to the services of a State attorney free of charge, if such evasion was discovered. My husband's salary was also taxed for sick, old age and unemployment insurance. When tragedy befell me I was offered the choice of payment by a lump sum or a monthly dividend, though indeed I never asked for it. Everyone in the country could make use of these services.

The English Consul might have died when he had a heart attack in my garden had it not been for the city health doctor who spoke English and also read the American medical journals. Since the situation was serious, he remained until our own physician could be found. Being Sunday, it was hours before we were able to reach the great heart specialist who, when he did finally arrive, had nothing more to offer.

One morning Makowska arrived at her home to find a crowd standing around the doorway. The heartrending shrieks of her little girl rang down the corridor. Rushing into her apartment, she found her old mother tearing cloth with which to bandage the child's head. "Are you mad, Mother?" she cried. "Run to the pharmacist's and have him send the first aid man." Quickly the ambulance came and the child was taken to the hospital. She had spinal meningitis, and was delirious for weeks. She remained nearly three months in the hospital. During those anxious days I saw little of Makowska. She did our marketing every day at dawn, before the hospital allowed visitors, because, as she explained, "Mother is too old to bargain, but she will cook for you." In the evening she would return and triumphantly report on the visit her daughter had had from one of the greatest doctors in the city.

The sick of the whole country were tended by doctors sent out by the Department of Health. Out in the country few had health insurance, but disease was treated as the concern of the State. In this way malaria and typhus were stamped out, and typhoid reduced to negligible proportions. Poland was the first country in Europe to establish socialized medicine.

Every child had to be vaccinated against smallpox before it was six months old. When our child was born, the doctor warned us that if we didn't let him vaccinate Andrew the health officers would come to do it themselves. The child was born on the 25th of January; on the 25th of July the health officer arrived. Had I not been able to show the scar, proving that it had already been done, he would have been vaccinated on the spot. In order to enter any school a child had not only to be vaccinated for smallpox once again, but also for diphtheria. Typhoid inoculation was also compulsory.

Artesian wells were put down in the villages and old fashioned wells condemned as unsanitary. In those days the great circles of concrete lining the wells were a familiar sight all over the country. In many districts a little red cross by the edge of the highway gave the name of the next village where a doctor was available. It is difficult to exercise sufficient health control in a rural community, but in spite of criticism, much was done that had never been done before. Free medicine and free serums were as much a part of the State program as free education. The little hospitals in the small towns were primitive and insufficient, but clean — remarkably so, considering the general poverty of the country.

There was much complaint that the sick insurance companies were too rich and powerful, that they took too large a percent of the salaries, that in a poor country simpler buildings would have been adequate. "Why," it was asked repeatedly, "should corridors of their buildings be faced in polished granite? Hospitals and sanitariums are springing up like mushrooms. Much better to cut down the premiums than have all this unnecessary luxury."

Insurance seemed to us to take a heavy toll of our income, and to help create a bureaucratic regime, but it gave a sense of security to all. Though everyone complained of it as a financial burden, no one ever found fault with its efficiency. Even on Sundays and holidays a doctor could be at the house within ten minutes of dialing the operator. The poor man who dropped in the snow knew he would wake in the ward of a clean comfortable hospital, and because of this knowledge, poverty in the cities was a less desperate hardship. Socialized medicine is a program for the future in the United States. I saw it work efficiently in Poland.

CHAPTER *6*

WINTER in Warsaw seems endless. Being as far north as Labrador, the days are short and the nights are long. Waves of chill damp fog roll in from the north and hang over the whole land during November and December. Sometimes for six weeks the sun does not shine. The bleak cold burrows itself into your soul. You forget that the sun can shine in a blue sky. But Christmas is usually clear, and by New Year's the dry winds from Russia have gathered enough force to blow the fogs back to Germany — where they remain until spring. In January, the real winter begins in Poland. Snow falls at night and the temperature drops, but by day the sun comes out in a dazzling blue sky. It shines so brilliantly that often by the end of February there is a false hope of spring. From under the deep hot bed of evergreen branches, daffodils force up their long bleached leaves. When it begins to become warm, in March, back roll the fogs from the German lowlands and Warsaw once more is buried under a dank and heavy cloud. By April, however, spring is in the air, though the ground may be blanketed under the heaviest snow of the winter.

In those days the arrival of the first robin was the signal for spring housecleaning. Windows that all winter had been pasted together with strips of cotton wool to keep out the cold winds were thrown open. On the first fine day they were filled with great red pillows and red feather counterpanes, put out to air in the sun.

With the first signs of spring came letters from the country. "When are you coming? The few miles from the highway are passable now. On the road through the forest the sand is quite dry."

"Dabice, Charbice, Wlazy, you must see them all," John said. "The house where Father was born — Uncle John (he's the oldest brother) owns it, but it is really home for all of us. Charbice is right on the highway. You can reach it even in the worst part of winter. It is beyond Lodz, the textile center. A trolley runs within five miles of the house. Such wonderful communication !"

We packed our bags and took the train to Lódź. In those days only the diplomats and a few Cabinet Ministers or very rich merchants had automobiles. The trains were always packed to capacity. In our compartment all eight places were taken, two people, in most cases, to every single seat. The men seemed not to mind standing in the corridor, where they smoked and discussed the crops. Roaming the length of the train, they always found some acquaintance with whom to chat. In one of the third class carriages John found Prince Henry with whom he had gone to the same college in England. He was sitting between two peasants on the hard wooden bench, and eating from a package of sandwiches.

"You see," he grumbled, "Mother's economies run to third class carriages and sandwiches. Of course she is right. There is so much to rebuild in the country."

"Have you lost many acres in the Land Reform ?" John asked him.

"In our part of the country there is more land on the market than peasants to buy it." He told of the losses of others in his family who had been less lucky than they.

Changing the subject, John inquired. "What were you doing in Warsaw ?"

He told John that he was entering the Foreign Office, at forty dollars a month.

As we pulled into Lódź we counted the chimneys that were smoking. Lódź was the center of the spinning industry. Most of the woolen cloth was made there, and cheap trousers were exported even to the East Side of London. On every street were factories, surrounded by the miserable homes of

91

the workers. In a city of a half million persons, Jews numbered more than half the population. We went by taxi over the rough cobblestone pavement to the trolley that ran from Łódź out into the country.

The trolley followed down a river valley passing through villages attached to dye plants and small factories. These villages were peopled wholly by Jews. At each station, boys dressed in cassocks and *paiss* peered in through the windows at us. The six inch greased black ritual curls formed a mournful frame to their sallow faces and oozing red eyes. There was not a tree nor blade of grass about the barrack-like brown wooden houses, not a flower nor curtain in the broken-down windows, yet everywhere slatternly women in periwigs were lazying over the sills. On the streets, men were loitering with shopkeepers on their rotting doorsteps. Beside and behind the houses the hard-packed earth was barren. Gusts of wind carried the dust in clouds over the crude cobblestone streets. Not a house nor fence had been repaired or repainted.

"Why do they live that way?" I asked, pulling back from the trolley windows as though the boys could touch me. "Is there nothing that can be done?"

"It is not because they are poor," John replied. "The peasants are poorer."

"Perhaps the rent—. The landlords should do something."

"Jews own this property; all these little factories are owned by Jews."

"How can they let their property deteriorate so horribly?" I cried. "It's not good business. Besides these people live in the country. Why don't they plant gardens like the neighboring peasants?"

"These are orthodox Jewish towns, ruled by the Rabbis who administer ancient Jewish laws and teach their ritual schools. The Jews live as in a state within a state and since their kingdom is not of this world, why should they care for gardens?"

Later I learned of the deep-rooted fundamental differences

between the Reformed and the orthodox Jews from my doctor, himself a Jew. The orthodox Polish Jews lived in their mystic cabalistic past, every activity prescribed by ritual laws of the Talmud. To my doctor, their mystic exaltation over suffering was irrational and foreign. He represented more than half the Polish Jews, modern, highly educated men and women eager to be part of the new state in which they already played important political and intellectual roles.

At last the trolley plunged through a pine wood, down a little slope, and came to a stop. This was the end of the line. The wood was like a wall, closing off those terrible dirty towns from the open country.

Across the meadow on a little bluff was a Gothic church, the walls of which had been replastered over in the eighteenth century. But in spite of the baroque trimmings, its great steep roof and narrow windows betrayed its Gothic past. Nestled about the church in a haze of apple trees was a little village whose outline fitted the landscape like a soft round hummock. Though the trees were bare and the road was muddy, geraniums bloomed in the windows, and grass grew thickly before the doors. Over all the sweet scent of peat smoke mingled with the clear air of the pine forest.

In honor of this first visit, Uncle John had sent the coach and four. It had been bought for John's grandmother before the Insurrection of 1863, before his grandfather had been exiled to Siberia and the house burned down. Today, only the kitchen wing remained standing, and it was there that John's grandmother brought up her four boys and her orphaned nephew, who later became Bishop of Lowicz and Warsaw. My father-in-law had been born with Russian soldiers standing in the room. His father, in chains, had been permitted to witness the birth. He was then dragged away to deepest Russia and returned only after twenty long years of exile. The mother had brought up the boys and had farmed her land so successfully that she had been hired to run the farm of a neighbor, who was also in chains in Siberia.

The horses pulled slowly up the long hill — up out of the lush river valley with its fertile hay meadows, divided by deep drainage ditches. The evening wind blew the waving white beech fronds on either side of the road. We passed the shrine of Charbice which I had seen photographed in Cracow. The shrine and the white birch alley photographed against the sandy white road made a rich tracery against the plain Polish grain fields.

We knew we had come to Uncle John's land by the thick winter wheat which covered his fields like a bright green mat. Not a weed grew anywhere. All his fields were drained with terra cotta pipes, and as a result of this system his crops afforded double the yield of his neighbors'.

When the road turned, the horses broke into a canter. We swerved off the highway and galloped down the steep lane that led to Uncle John's house. The wooden gate was open under the lindens. To the right were the old brown barns, to the left the small village of whitewashed log cabins, their great thatched roofs thick with lichen. After the high road, the sand of the turn-around was soft. The one-story house (the wing of the old house burned in the Insurrection) was hidden by old thuja, arbor vitae, and the Japanese quince was just coming into bloom. On the end towards the river was a rustic porch covered with wistaria. A carriage step made of concrete before the front door was the only addition Uncle John had made.

Because of his great good sense and knowledge of practical economics, Uncle John had been called on to serve on the boards of directors of several industrial concerns in nearby Lodz. He had also been chosen President of the Provincial Farmers' Association because he was considered the best farmer of his province. He reinvested all farm profits above five percent back in the land. With them he had bought fertilizers, laid on tile drains and built a hydraulic electric plant to sprinkle his fields. He utilized the water of the river, which, because of nearby dye plants, was full of chemicals highly useful to the soil. He had electrified the village and his barns, to reduce the cost of insurance, but his house, which as he said, "brought no return on the investment anyway," was neither insured nor lighted by electricity.

It was five o'clock when we arrived, and the family were at tea about the dining room table. Uncle John came into the entrance hall to meet us and show us to our room behind the drawing room. There was hot water in the pitcher and in the basin on the wash stand. While I washed, John hung up our coats and unlocked the bags so the maid could unpack them. He called me to the window to see the broad drained meadows, Uncle John's pride, and the wind blowing in great gusts, flinging itself against the giant plane trees surrounding the house.

Before many minutes, Uncle John reappeared with one of his grandchildren. "That's enough prinking," he said. "They are impatient to see you." Following him into the dining room, I was introduced to my new relatives and to several of the nearer neighbors who had driven over to meet us and were seated at one end of the long table.

The dining room was large. At one end there was Aunt Stefcia's desk, the chaise longue, her Bechstein concert grand piano, and many old-fashioned comfortable arm chairs. At the other, a table for twelve or fourteen was set up, in case unexpected guests should arrive. On a white cloth, tea was laid — coffee with clotted cream, piles of brown bread and butter, pots of many kinds of preserves and honey, and a large babka cake. Once introduced, without further ceremony we had to help ourselves. There was a roar of conversation, which it was taken for granted I understood. The guests shouted at each other with free-for-all familiarity. The son-in-law, who spoke Polish with a French lisp, turned to me and asked, "We were wondering what price the farmer gets for milk in America ?"

"About four cents a quart," I told him.

"That is worse than here. We didn't get anything for our hay last year. What was the price in the United States ?"

As I was not well up on agricultural prices, this conversation soon languished.

In the hall, a bridge table always stood ready. We drank down our tea, for "they" were anxious to begin playing. John refused ; he preferred to talk with his cousin, Marysia, but he

urged me into the game. We played five-handed, and I
drew for the first four rubbers. It was nearly eight when, at
last, I was free. Outside the windows was black night, not
a light anywhere to be seen. The only sound was the shrill
throbbing of the frogs from over the meadow.

All the women were dressed in black woolens. "Do we
change?" I whispered to John.

"I doubt it." It was as he said. As soon as the last rubber
was ended, dinner was announced.

Uncle John took me in and set me by him; the others all
found their own places. The meal was served by two full-
skirted maids with white gloves. It began with fermented
bread soup. Uncle John always had it, he explained, every
day in the year. "Don't take it unless you like it. There is
always bouillon in the kitchen."

A roast boar was served next, the last of the season. A
neighbor had shot it, and they had kept it to honor our coming.

The dinner ended with a platter of meringues and whipped
cream, dotted with black preserved cherries and little drops
of red syrup.

Aunt Stefcia loved coffee. Several persons told me how
the last time she was in Italy she had bought an "Expresso"
machine, which was now brought in and put on the table.
We all watched in silence while she prepared it. Then some
began talking about crops, others about our bridge game.
Later, after Marysia put the children to bed, we would play
with two tables. Uncle John was restless; he had everything ready. "Bring the coffee cups here, it 's time to begin."

He bid on everything, even four clubs to the jack, and won.
He seemed to know by instinct where every card lay.

By midnight my head was hot, and my feet like ice. "A
cup of tea is what you need," everyone said. But John came
to the rescue. "No, she is tired. It 's bed she needs."
When we left the room, the neighbors were still playing
bridge. Having come to tea, they stayed on until after one.

Our room was dark and cold. The fire was out in the
great white tiled stove, and the lamp had been turned down.

The beds had covers of forest green felt, with the family crest appliqued in the centers in still darker green. The wash stands and wardrobes were hidden by a screen. On a round table, covered with a dark fringed felt was an old-fashioned globe lamp. In the gloomy circle of its light stood a rosewood Victorian sofa and arm chairs.

The shutters, drawn for the night, had been bolted from within with a heavy iron bar and then padlocked. On the door to the drawing room, which was lined with sheet iron, a similar bar was affixed. This had been put on during the war, when German marauders were abroad, after one had broken into the house. The night watchman had been killed, and Uncle John's nephew, who had run out of this very same room to find out the cause of the disturbance, had been shot through the leg.

In the airless room it was hard to sleep. Outside was the sound of the roaring wind, the shrill whistle of the watchman and the scratch of the dogs on the hard earth. I longed to turn on a light and read, but the candle on my bed table hardly pierced the gloom.

In the early morning we flung open the shutters and let in the spicy clear sunlight. Sunday silence and peace flooded about us. Only then did I fall asleep and I slept deeply for two hours. When we were dressed, we found a breakfast set out on the dining room table, sliced meats, goat cheese, brown and white bread baked in the village oven, and a sweet bread that was only served on Sundays. On the sideboard a kettle of water was boiling for tea. Sun flooded through the windows, reflecting the dazzling young green lawn which curled like a soft mat, clean and neat, against the house. One of the maids came to ask if we took eggs for breakfast. "The Enlightened Master breakfasted an hour ago," she told us. "But the ladies have not yet rung for their hot water. The horses are ordered for a little before ten. Church at Lutomiersk is at ten-thirty."

Having finished our breakfast, we took our hats and coats and went to wait for the horses before the house. But old Matthias, the groom, was already there with the coach. Uncle John was coming across the garden from his morning tour of inspection. "Wait for me," he called. "I will drive over to church with you." Without going into the house, he climbed into the carriage. "Stefcia had a bad night again, and may not be going. Marysia and the children will follow in the *bryczka*."

He whipped up the horses, and they galloped through the wooden gate, up the lane of lime trees, and on to the high road bordered with birches. Then down the high road they went at a brisk trot.

We retraced the road we had taken the previous day to the village, across the meadow to where the Gothic church stood, embedded in lilacs. When we arrived, Uncle John left the horses with the groom and disappeared in the crowd of peasants loitering before the door. We went in alone and sat down. Every place was taken by the peasant women who, crowded about us, had come well beforehand, while the men stood in the churchyard, hat in hand.

After the service, we visited the family vault to see where the grandparents had been laid. Uncle John showed the place he had arranged for his wife and the next generation. He waited each Sunday, he said, to let the peasants get a head start away from the church. But Marysia was so anxious about Aunt Stefcia that, undaunted by the crowd, she joined in the galloping procession. The peasants on Sunday were so exhilarated by the joy of the holiday that they galloped their horses all over the road. The men stood up, gaily waving their whips, each jockeying for the first place. Away they tore down the road, women screaming and giggling in the straw of the wagon. They raced like children, in a whirl of merriment.

After some time Uncle John looked at his watch. "If we go now, there will be time to drive over the meadow before dinner." You could see this was part of the schedule. On the way home he constantly compared his two watches without comment, counting the minutes at each mile post. Before the door of the house the children were sitting in the *bryczka* (which looks like a buck board). "Can we drive the horses in the meadows, Grandfather ?" they shouted gaily.

Uncle John held the horses while we all climbed into the *bryczka* and drove through the garden, the children jumping down to open and close all the gates. We crossed over the narrow plank bridge to the dykes along the meadows. The children knew their way about the checkerboard of ditches. As they guided the horses, Uncle John showed us his new sluice gates, and pointed out the different kinds of grasses that made up the hay. "In a good season there are five crops," he said. "The Army took it all last year. They cut it, and hauled it green to Łódź." When he told us how many tons he had to the acre, I was unable to tell him how many we grew in America.

"Those are the storks that are nesting in the village," said one of the little girls. "Look, there is one flying back." She was jumping up and down for joy. "Now it's really spring," she kept repeating.

The wind was cold. Though lightly clad, none of them seemed to notice it, neither the little girls in their red velvet dresses and sweaters, nor Marysia in her "tailor made" Angielski of dark worsted, nor Uncle John, so absorbed in the grass of his meadow. But I was glad when we reached the lea of the plane trees, by the village mill where Uncle John had put up his hydraulic electric plant. The miller was an "American." He had been born in the village, but his parents had migrated to the United States when he was a baby. When he had returned, in the late twenties, he had installed the most modern of flour mills in the old wooden building.

By the dam the river spread wide and quiet. Weeping willows protected the cropped grassy banks. On the commons children were playing ; geese hissed at the horses as we drove over the grass up to the village set back from the river — one long street of houses, some ten along a dirt roadway. Unlike the German or Jewish villages that line the four sides of a square, Polish villages, even inside Germany, always string along the roadway. Sometimes they are several miles long — houses on one side and barns

99

on the other, with long narrow strips of ribbon-like fields leading over the hills behind them. On the outskirts were newer houses of brick, with red tile roofs, the older ones low and one-storied under the gigantic old plane trees, thatched and whitewashed blue or white. Every Polish village had a steam bath house, an ice house and a bread oven. On Saturdays the fire would be lit in the oven and all the women would bring their bread to bake in it. At Charbice, the village road ran along the family garden, the kitchen garden and the outhouses.

As we passed the kitchen, Uncle John asked if we had spoken to the cook. There would hardly be time to see the grain fields before dinner. Before the kitchen door, chickens had scratched away the grass, and were roosting in the currant bushes. The kitchen, the pantry, the larder and store room formed a long low wing, connected to the dining room. In the kitchen, at an immense stove in the center, stood the cook, dressed in white. Two kitchen girls were scrubbing vegetables. Skirts tucked up under their aprons, they bent over pails on the floor. There was no running water ; a wash tub stood on a three-legged stool. The cook wiped his mouth on his sleeve before kissing our hands, saying, "Let Jesus Christ be praised, highly respected Mr. John and the new wife !"

"How are you, Tomaszek ?"

"Getting old, highly respected Mr. John. I 'm sixty-eight this autumn, and the rheumatism this winter has crippled me badly." He pulled his long mustachio. The brown hair under his tall white cap was hardly grey.

"That was a fine boar we had last evening."

"I won't be cooking much longer. I said to my wife only yesterday, 'It won't be long now before Tomaszek will be lying down in the village beside the old Master and Madame.'"

John answered, "Let Tomaszek not be so gloomy."

In the drawing room, Aunt Stefcia was waiting for dinner. She was sitting and smoking in the sunlight, a peaceful enigmatic smile on her puffy Buddha-like cheeks. "Has Tomaszek been telling you his premonitions ?" she asked. "We haven't been able to cheer him up all winter. The cold has hung on long this spring. I haven't left the house myself since I did Christmas shopping in early December."

"There was a stork in the meadow this morning."

"Yes, spring will be soon now," she replied. "If you were not too cold on the ride this morning they thought to drive over to Ruddy."

John asked, "Do the Werners still live there ?"

Aunt Stefcia pulled at her home made cigarette before replying. "The two daughters are alone now. Their brother is continually in Dabrowa. They have rented to Piotrkowski — not badly. They say for one renting he gives fertilizer sufficiently."

After dinner everyone slept, at four tea was served and we set off in the *bryczka,* following the lane up across the highway, past Uncle John's fields and woods and on to Ruddy, some four or five miles further down the river.

The houses we passed on the high road were the usual one-storied white plastered dwellings, covered with vines and wistaria. Many had the four stubby pillars at the front door and the five or six rooms about the entrance hall. Most of these farms were of four hundred or five hundred acres. Holdings of this size comprised the bulk of the cultivated land in Poland, and the "gentry" who owned them were the backbone of the country, the ones who could be depended on to outwit the invader. Usually the owner was a man of University training, eager to try out new agricultural methods. In addition to farming he would mill flour or run a distillery, raise horses for the army or operate a beet sugar refinery. Though he was the social equal of the greatest aristocrat, to American eyes he appeared to live hardly better than the peasants.

The house at Ruddy was an ugly Nineteenth-Century building that meant to be Norman. But there was a Moorish look to the windows and a Gothic tower towards the river. On the south was a Renaissance loggia of artificial marble which dwarfed the house. The rooms were somber. The ceilings were cracked and grey, the wallpaper stained and peeling.

101

It had been looted by the Germans during the last war, and the two ladies had no money with which now to put it in order.

They greeted us cheerfully, and begged us to stay for dinner and spend the evening with them. They appeared quite disconsolate when, after refusing tea, we insisted on pushing on. Before going, we must see the garden. The wind was roaring in the plane trees as we wandered through the paths, under trees so tall and thick that nothing but ferns could grow under them.

When we returned home, Aunt Stefcia was still sitting in her chair in the drawing room. The lamp was lit on the table ; the old blue velvet upholstery glowed in the lamplight. "The Director of the Agricultural Station drove over for dinner, and the village priest will be here shortly." As she smoked, nodding her head pleasantly, she told us how the village priest, a man nearing sixty, had an orphanage of boys at the village. It was a marvel how he found means to feed and clothe them from the pennies he raised at the Masses. There were seventeen or eighteen boys there at the rectory. They raised their own potatoes and cabbages. Charbice sent them sausage at Christmas and Easter ; the village women gave them bread at each baking.

The priest arrived while we were talking about him. He was a small round man with scarlet cheeks and bright childlike eyes. He did not look like the hero who had sheltered the village in the crypt during the bombardment, turned the priory into a refuge for the homeless, and himself nursed the wounded. During all the years of the German occupation he had cheered and counseled his parish. He had never known comfort and plenty, but had shared all the vicissitudes of the seasons with the impoverished folk of the region.

"Don't get up — please don't stand," he said, fearing to be an intruder. He sat on the edge of his chair and smoothed out the skirt of his cassock, which covered his coarse heavy leather boots ; he took no notice of the kitten who played with the silk fringe of his sash, but began at once to talk of the weather, the growth of wheat, and the hay fields.

"Mr. Markowski from the Agricultural Institute," Uncle John introduced a stocky middle-aged man in riding trousers and a heavy whipcord jacket.

The village priest asked, "The great agricultural expert? Are you here for the night? No? At Lutomiersk? Then you can't pass us by in the morning. A few words to my boys, I beg you."

Wodka was brought in and *kanapki*. "What fine pickled mushrooms, Madame," remarked the priest. "You do them at home? And smoked carp too! What a feast this is! And the ham — the very best in the country — from what wood do you smoke it?"

Dinner was served. During the bread soup, Uncle John poured out claret. "Is that the wine that was sunk during the invasion?"

"Tell me about it," I begged.

"After the battle of Lutomiersk the Germans were billeted in our village. The Commandant took over our house. I feared he would drink up my wine, so we sank it all behind the dam. I hoped the stream would carry off the labels. The Szetkowskis put theirs in the carp pond. A few days later, every label came to the surface, and of course the Germans had the pond drained."

"How did you save your doorknobs?" someone asked.

"I had the village smith make a set with iron before the order came out. I had heard they always took brass. These we greased and buried in the furrows of the vegetable garden. They never even suspected. When searchers came for the brass knobs, they found only iron latches."

"The way to get on with the Germans," the priest remarked, "is to foresee their plans. Don't try to cross them. Never show fear or servility."

Someone sighed, "I hope I never live to see them here again."

Another, "But if they do come, this time they will regret it."

"*Panie! Panie!* The Poles are too courageous," said the priest. "I fear they don't count the cost."

Uncle John who always disliked histrionics, changed the subject. "What do you think of the season, Mr. Agriculturist ? Was there enough snowfall this winter ?"

"In some parts the frosts came before the snow."

"My nephew writes his rye suffered severely."

Uncle John nodded in confirmation of the expert. When the ducks were served, he said, "Take the whole one, Mr. Priest. You know the adage : 'a duck is a foolish bird, too big for one, too small for two.'"

"Oh, no, Mr. Landowner. I couldn't eat it. I only take potatoes and sour milk in the evening."

"But make an exception," Uncle John urged.

"It would be a kindness if the lady permitted my taking it to my older school boys. They are growing lads, you know."

"There are surely plenty in the kitchen. I'll have two put in a basket ; take one now."

But the priest persistently refused. "Only the dessert will I gladly accept," he said, smiling.

The next morning we left the house early in order to visit the boys before they left the priory to go to the village school. The walls of the old Renaissance building were six feet thick, making the rooms hard to heat. The younger boys therefore slept together downstairs, and the older boys had a large room above. One end of the room was filled with crude cots ; the other was arranged as a study, with tables, chairs and bookcases. On every window ledge, pots of geraniums, wandering Jew and straggly ferns gave a homey atmosphere to the otherwise bare room. The white tile stoves were lighted in the afternoons. Heat was not wasted in the mornings, when the boys were away at school. In the unheated washroom were a row of wash basins, with a spigot of cold water. The priest proudly showed us the pigeonholes where each boy kept a glass, a toothbrush and towel.

The priest served hot milk and coffee for us in his bedroom. His bed, covered in a dark felt, was piled high with pillows and an eiderdown. A melodeon stood by the window, and a motley collection of plush arm chairs surrounded a black walnut table, on which was a Turkish carpet. Between holy pictures, the walls were encrusted with photographs of boys of all ages, boys he had brought up in his orphanage without a penny's subsidy from the State, with only the support of his parishioners. They left him when old enough to go to work, but all through their lives they returned to him as to a father. Such orphanages in every hamlet of Poland were considered part of the normal work of the country clergy.

During the years Poland was free, the peasants sent their sons to the University. They became doctors and lawyers and even had positions in the Foreign Office. More than thirty thousand graduated annually. They made up the new city middle class. This social revolution, accomplished without bloodshed, changed the complexion of Poland. The State provided new forms of employment in its factories, refineries, and on the roads which it was constructing. State hospitals and sanitariums called on young physicians, and young lawyers were needed for free State Legal Council. Though British and American "Leftists" on their travels rarely stopped for more than a night on their trip to Russia, foreign capitalists doing business with Poland regarded her as the incarnation of State Socialism.

CHAPTER 7

*I*N *1930* my husband was sent to Geneva to work in the Economic Section of the League of Nations. We returned in 1932 having seen the failure of the Disarmament Conference of 1931, and only too aware of the obstacles in the path of a Federation of the smaller eastern nations. Unfortunately the idealists at the League of Nations were as opposed to regional groups as were Germany and Russia. The English and French diplomats tried to bolster the democratic regimes in Germany of Stresemann and Brüning as if in an unconscious appeasement for the Treaty of Versailles.

The eastern agricultural states found it impossible to form an agrarian bloc. John's desk was rifled and his carefully prepared sheets of statistics vanished. His corrected report disappeared the very morning it was to be mimeographed for a meeting held to consider various schemes for Danubian federation. He personally felt convinced it was the work of the French Second Bureau because the French were opposed to everything tending to break into their "little Entente." By preventing the formation of the Danubian Bloc the French played into the hand of Germany who, posing as financial protector of all the small eastern nations, soon held them in economic bondage. Lithuania, for example, was one of the first states made economically dependent upon Germany as far back as the regime of Stresemann. We came back to Warsaw bewildered and saddened that none of the democracies, or so it seemed in Geneva, were pursuing a clear, logical eastern European policy.

We expected the city to seem shabby after Geneva. Instead, the Aleje Jeruzolimskie was gay with pansy beds, new sidewalk cafes had been opened, and most of the houses had freshly cleaned façades. To our amazement the taxi glided smoothly over recently laid asphalt into the Place of the Three Crosses, where many brand new houses were being built, and where most of the old ones (by city ordinance, as we later discovered) were being re-stuccoed. Two years' improvements had changed the whole slow, dingy aspect of the city to one of gaiety and motion. The smartly dressed people bore no resemblance to the barefoot, shapeless forms I had seen six years before. The pot holes in the streets, the cracked and fallen plaster on the houses, the dilapidated taxis, had vanished. Some houses were adding a story ; on others the Victorian scrolls were being removed from the pediments over the windows, or the old iron balconies were being replaced with concrete. We felt like strangers as we looked out the windows of our cab at the unexpected improvements.

Newly planted trees which lined all the streets were just coming into bud. As part of the "beautifying Warsaw" program of Mayor Starzynski, the first hundred and fifty thousand had already been planted. When we turned into our own street we saw some school children watering their gift to the city of black thorn trees, which were just bursting into bloom. We had noticed other children with spades and shovels marching across the Place of the Three Crosses.

In 1930 we had bought an apartment in the center of the city. It was in a co-operative building which had been recently opened in the old palace garden of Frascati. We had just moved in when, a week later, we had been unexpectedly ordered off to Geneva. During this two years' absence we had rented our apartment to a foreign diplomat. Before returning we had written Makowska to put it in order and now we felt all the satisfaction of coming home. When in 1930 we had joined the co-operative, the building problem had been acute. Then no one had enough money to finance a whole apartment house, even though the State granted fifteen years freedom from taxation as an inducement. All over Warsaw, co-operatives had been organized as limited stock companies. We all belonged to the Board of Directors and, without expert advice, it had taken two years to organize and build the house. Though we had had many offers to sell the apartment while we were away, the housing shortage was then still far too acute for us to consider giving up an apartment.

However, during the spring after our return, this situation was changing very swiftly. Not counting renovations of old buildings, new buildings put up during this time housed half a million people. The majority of these were workmen's co-operatives, which went up on the periphery of the city. They were built in vast units, some housing as many as ten thousand persons in a single project. On the first free Sunday after our arrival Michael took us to see the "Workers' Victory," the largest in the suburb of Zoliborz. It was as completely organized as a small town, with laundry, schools, nursery and supply shops. It even had its own bus service to the center of Warsaw.

Like many smaller projects, this great co-operative had been organized as the philanthropic housing society of volunteer architects and engineers when Michael was executive secretary. He aimed to make housing a public concern, rather than leave it to the mercy of speculative builders. Through the efforts of this society, the Prime Minister started a commission and brought Michael into his office to supervise all new plans. Zoning laws were so strict that not only architectural style of the houses, but the precise height of the buildings was kept uniform. No house could shut off the sunlight from its neighbor. Although other suburbs had houses more prettily planted, where many of the professors and Government officials of our acquaintance lived, we never tired of walking through Zoliborz. Here three hundred thousand workers had been housed.

These immense projects were financed by private and state insurance companies, savings banks and public utilities, which were required by law to invest a large percentage of their holdings in low-cost public housing at a profit of only 1½% to 2%. These were the newest steel and glass brick buildings

108

set at appropriate angles to let in sun and break up the monotony. They were surrounded with gardens and tennis courts. They had free schools, day nurseries and playgrounds, and they had been planned to house a family at ten dollars a month. It was said, "Such buildings should be so well constructed they can be amortized during fifty years without costs of major repairs."

John and I both found great pleasure in the general spaciousness and modern architecture of the new sections of Warsaw. Of a fine afternoon we strolled along one or another of the stately thoroughfares where the new hospitals and technical schools were being built — the Curie Cancer Institute, the Warsaw Polytechnic, the Agricultural Institute and the School of Aviation. Now all these fine institutions have been destroyed by the Germans and their laboratories stolen. Then they were planted with fine trees, neat lawns, clipped hedges, rose beds and hybrid lilacs. On every side street were low houses, tennis courts and gardens, built by co-operative unions of artists, professional groups, teachers and civil servants.

After 1934, because of the imminence of war, all the houses by ordinance had to be in a modernistic style with flat concrete roofs, to reduce the danger from incendiary bombs. This futuristic style of architecture and gardens attracted many of our friends, who, caught by the building fever moved to Saska Kempa, where over ten thousand houses went up after 1932. This suburb was not bombed by the Germans during their invasion of Poland in 1939, and it is that section that they have chosen as living quarters for their administrative officers.

At this time everyone was interested in building. Wherever you went people asked, "Who is your architect?"

"Is he one of the modernists?"

"Poland has such a beautiful classical style, why won't the architects follow it?"

"Where is everyone nowadays? You see no one about any more." Everyone was building; no one had time to sit about at parties.

109

Two months after our return from Geneva, we too caught the building fever. Once more it became apparent that we would soon need a nursery. Those afternoons when John finished work a little early, we hunted plots and compared various plans. The only friends that interested us were those whose houses were already completed, and those who could advise us on the choice of builders and architects.

One beautiful spring morning while I was practicing finger exercises on the piano, a gentleman called. The maid showed him into the study. He bowed stiffly as I came into the room and said, "I am Mr. Kurnatowski, from Posnań. I have heard you are thinking of building. I want to sell the land I inherited in the Frascati gardens. I will sell it at a sacrifice price of $6,000 as I need the cash immediately."

I knew, for we had previously inquired, this was half the price of other land in the garden.

"When must you have the money?" I asked. "We could hardly give it to you this afternoon."

"If you decide to take it, your husband's signature is as good as cash," he replied. "If I don't sell the land I shall take the 10 o'clock train to Posnań tonight, to see if I can sell something there."

"Come back at four for your answer," I said, showing the man to the door, and ran to the telephone to call John.

"First call up mother and see what she thinks," he advised, "and then make up your mind whether you like the plot." He promised to be home before four.

I telephoned Cracow. My mother-in-law's answer, as to all our questions, was, "You must decide. I'm in no position to judge. If you like the land, buy it, and we will help you as much as we can."

The Frascati Garden was in the very center of town. The Houses of Sejm (Parliament) stood on one side of it. The apartment building in which we lived, was built at the entrance gates. The old park had been planted in the eighteenth century about a small, one-storied "palace." Now the heirs had divided it on paper and were feverishly trying to sell their plots though neither roads nor sewers had been laid and the garden was still a thicket of ancient trees and muddy paths.

I went down into the garden. The old gnarled apple trees which surrounded our apartment building were lacy white against the vivid blue of the sky. You could see the plot proposed for sale from our windows. John had even sketched the great white birch, with its fronds sweeping the ground. Now it was feathery with new green buds. Beside it were an ancient catalpa tree and two pines. The whole plot was overgrown with a thicket of privet and lilac bushes.

I sat down on the ground under the birch tree, and looked up to the sky through its swaying branches. I felt the land was already mine. How sweet to own a little plot of earth, and when my child came to cradle him in a house strong enough to withstand the ravages of time! "The entrance," I thought, "will be between these two old pine trees, and the birch will stand by his window, so that he sees the sky for the first time through these branches." A cold March wind made the branches sway like a pendulum, but the sun was hot against the earth. A little beyond where I sat, a gardener had opened his cold frames, and pulled the straw pads across the glass roof of the greenhouse. He was sifting his compost piles and preparing his hot frames. Yet this was the very center of Warsaw. I tried to imagine this relic of a garden covered with new houses. The French Embassy, it was rumored, would build over there where the glass house stood.

I could hardly wait for John to return, and began to pace up and down. Inside again, I found it impossible to read or concentrate on the piano. I made a little sketch of the house I thought would fit the lot. In my mind's eye I pictured the outside with a timeless plainness, the inside spacious, yet compact enough to fit the changing circumstances of the present times. I called Makowska from the kitchen. "What would you think if we bought land in Frascati and built?"

"I think if Madame builds we will surely have servant quarters second to none in Europe," she said with great conviction. "My mind cannot imagine how fine it will be," and she clapped her hands with joy. "You will build us a little

111

apartment in the basement, and my husband and I will care for the house forever." Her imagination rushed on. "We will give notice this evening in the old palace."

"But Makowska," I pleaded in vain, "the land is not bought, and you should know how long it takes to build anything." She was oblivious to anything but the joyous prospect of the new quarters. Our house was hers from the day it was projected.

When at last John arrived, the decision had been taken. For me, the land was bought. It was expensive, but it was in the center of the city. It was not as though we were faced with years of walking great distances to bus lines, or waiting for the city to reach us.

When the gentleman returned, John pointed out what I had already told him, that it might be a week before we could assemble the necessary cash. But the gentleman insisted our I.O.U. was sufficient. We had only to sign a small paper. The land was ours.

We were so excited we could hardly sleep all night. We telephoned all our relatives and friends — everyone must know of our new venture. "Who is the architect?" they all asked, and each had some suggestion to make.

"My brother-in-law will build," I had said. But Michael, when asked, replied, "I will help you, but I could never build it for you. Ask Professor Niemojewski of the University. He has worked in Paris and is very artistic. His books are to be found in libraries everywhere even in the Metropolitan Museum of New York." So it was settled.

As soon as the land was registered in the Great Land Book of Warsaw under our joint names, we went to the Building Commission to find out what restrictions were placed on it, and receive permission to build. We found it was true that the French had bought the the adjacent lot for their Embassy. "The style of all adjacent houses must be French," we were told. The French had made that condition. The house could only cover one-third of the land, and no garage, greenhouse or porch could encroach on the two-thirds of garden space.

The outline of our house, then, was established by statute. It was as much fun as a puzzle putting the rooms together, to get the most sunlight and greatest number of feet of floor space. Various contractors offered to build it, but our architect preferred to do what he called "your own building." He himself hired the foreman, mason and carpenters. This proved to be no economy, for when anything went wrong, we were to blame. I had to oversee the whole work on the building. Blueprint in hand, no matter what the weather, I watched it all go up from foundation to finish. I knew every workman by name — which ones could be trusted, and which ones shirked and complained. Most of the men worked along steadily without being watched but a few needed prompting, and were always complaining, "I've a drain but no connection at two points," or, "My window upstairs is a brick further from the floor than the one down." — "The floors don't agree." — "The bricks for the ceiling have the wrong profile." — "Two of the iron beams are different lengths." — "Which one is for the balcony outside the window?" — "The sashes came all wet from the carpenter's." — "Thirty meters of piping for the hot water, and not a single elbow!" etc., every day, week in and week out.

At first I used to telephone, but later I fetched the needed parts from the dealers myself, even bringing several toilet bowls and a length of pipe with a red flag tied on the end in an open *dorozka*.

When the roof was reached, a cross with a wreath was nailed to it, and the men came for a day's extra pay and a holiday. They expected us to break bread with them, and wished to drink to our health and prosperity.

The full days had gone by so swiftly that I had scarcely noticed that summer was coming to an end. Our house was of bomb-proof construction. The roof of reinforced aero concrete was a yard thick; on top was a layer of waterproof cement. The whole surface was finally to be covered with three layers of asphalt. Before the waterproof cement was dry we had a cloudburst. Within a few hours the sewers could hold no more, and the streets were running with water.

Six inches of water stood on the roof of our house ; it poured into the rooms, running down the sides of the walls in wide streaks. The newly laid inner floors were wet. The workmen became alarmed and gloomy and muttered forebodings. "The house will have brick mold unless heat is turned on at once," they prophesied darkly.

It was a four-storied house, one floor for us, the others to be rented. There were fourteen bathrooms, four kitchens, an elaborate hot water heating system, two furnaces and centralized electric refrigerators. In every room we burned coals in open baskets to dry out the walls and ceilings sufficiently so that they could be plastered. The carpenter refused to put in the doors and windows. "They would swell up like a sponge in all the dampness." We were over a month behind with our work. The autumn rains, which came early that year, continued throughout the whole of September !

Late in October, after eight weeks of rain, the weather turned fine again. The beautiful Polish autumn came at last. Finally the house dried out sufficiently for the roof to be asphalted and the windows put in. The end was in sight, and we began to look about us after eight months of voluntary exile, to answer the mail that had piled up during the summer and the telephone calls that had come while I was out.

I had talked, thought and dreamed in Polish from the moment the house was started. I had called my father-in-law Tatus and my mother-in-law Mulka, and they had shown me all the solicitude and tenderness of my own mother and father. In the same year I gave birth to our Polish child. These two fundamental primitive activities recreated me. I had made a place for myself among Poles, who everywhere were as busy as I had been, building themselves solidly constructed homes, and unconcerned with everything beyond the present. I had learned to work with the Polish workman. We had had a hundred different men, specializing in various trades, many of whom we kept in touch with later. I knew when to depend on them and trust their judgment.

Had not our mason solved the problem of our stairway when our architect miscalculated the size of the hall? He had conceived of stairs spiraling up like a ribbon, without side support. It was the mason who carried it out, without even a drawing to go by. The mason also worked out the very complicated pitch of the flat roof, so that each drain should receive the same load of water.

The men who laid the floor had come from the Pinsk Marshes. They did beautiful woodwork, matching the grain and color. They were paid by the piece, and four or five men laid all forty rooms in three days. It seemed as if they worked around the clock, for they were anxious to be paid and leave.

The painter too worked in secret on Sundays and evenings. The sooner he finished our work, he said, the sooner he could begin another job. He was an artist, his eye was true, and even after four years his paint had neither cracked nor peeled. He could be trusted to mix with the best oils. In 1939, a month before the invasion, he repainted my iron railings, foreseeing that it might be years before they could be done over — if the house were left standing at all. He had discovered a new colored amalgam for metal which, when it hardened, formed part of the iron. There was no need of overseeing his work, done with the pride of a good artisan.

Our bathrooms were beautiful. Some of the workmen had told me where to buy odd colored tiles in small lots, hand-baked in grey, yellow, lobster red, blue or black. The men sorted them out, dividing them between each bathroom. When they had finished, each bathroom was different, but each seemed more beautiful than any of the others.

While we were building a hundred other apartments went up about us, each more modern than the last, wholly fireproof two and three room apartments, low in rent, built for the new middle classes, Government employees, civil servants, young lawyers and doctors that peopled the new democracy. Most of the front doors were of wrought bronze, the work of young sculptors. None of the houses were old-fashioned plastered brick, but were all of cut stone hauled up from Kielce. This tremendous building activity continued unabated to the very day of the outbreak of war.

CHAPTER *8*

WHEN Andrew was born I had begged my physician to arrange the birth at home. He had consented, partly because my father-in-law was Dean of Medicine and because he knew how nervously I dreaded going to a hospital. Memories of the frightful six weeks that attended the loss of my first son and the second catastrophe in Switzerland where I had lost a little daughter made me fearful of the cruel formality of hospitals. I wanted this child delivered at home so that from the moment of its birth my mother-in-law could watch over its welfare. "The house will be turned into a hospital," I promised, "and everything shall be arranged as you desire it."

"I will make an exception only for you," the doctor had said, "for it is a great inconvenience. Only you must have one of my own specially trained nurses who has worked for me now over ten years. She will come beforehand and prepare everything."

When the nurse came she made a price of $150 for the birth. She would take no other case ten days before the appointed time in order to be free at any time I needed her. I considered the price very high, but we learned it was the usual price paid a good obstetrical nurse who had graduated from the Medical College as well as the School of Nursing. My mother-in-law did not like her personality and wanted a nurse of our choosing to be responsible for the baby. After interviewing many candidates we decided to take a first cousin of our cook Makowska who had recently graduated with honors. She was to receive $100 because though she would help at the birth, she would not be responsible for it.

117

These details were settled well beforehand, for the most highly recommended nurses were always engaged six months in advance. A week before the event the nurse in charge ordered the walls and floor of my room washed with lysol, and the pictures and chintz curtains taken down. Each week she would change the drum of sterilized linen she kept in my room, so that the necessary dressings were always on hand. A special bed was prepared and kept in readiness for the final day.

When the great moment arrived, I was put in a night shirt from the hospital, and the dog and cat were locked up in the servants' room. I could hear through the walls the little bitch scratching and moaning, but the cat somehow escaped. When the nurse opened the door for the doctor, it slipped into the room. With a flying leap he was on my pillow and had snuggled down by my ear, throbbing and purring. The head nurse screamed and flung him out, but it was too late now to change everything — the anesthetist had prepared the mask. Makowska's cousin kept calm, "The cat's a clean animal, he never leaves the apartment," she said soothingly. Her words went round my head in the jumble of gas — "The cat is a clean animal, he never leaves the apartment."

"Please do not send my husband and Mulka away," I begged. In the haze I could see them in white aprons with masks on. I pushed off the gas mask, "not so much ether — I'm not afraid," I said.

I could hear the doctor tell my husband, "This is the strangest birth I have witnessed since I was a student in Cracow when Stryjenska, the artist, was having her twins. She spent the whole time sketching. She would interrupt my work with, 'Don't move your head, doctor — you spoil the composition.' And when the first child was born we told her there would be twins. 'That's splendid' she said, 'now I can finish my picture.'"

When Andrew was born I heard his first cry. John was holding my hand. "It's a boy," he said excitedly. Then I fell asleep.

118

When I waked, it was afternoon. I could see across the hall into the dining room that had been changed into a nursery. The afternoon sun flooded the windows. The nurse was saying, "The little bitch sits under the bassinet and every stir makes her so nervous she runs for help. At dinner she brought her bone and left it for the baby."

Someone else said, "The Bishop is here, may he see the lady?" The nurse smoothed back my hair. John brought in two large white lilacs in pots, "One is from Tatus, the other from Mulka," he said arranging them on either side of the big window. They are for the new garden." The house boy brought in five dozen yellow roses, "Madame hasn't a vase large enough for them."

"There," said the nurse, "at home it's always the same, the servants must come in and ask stupid questions."

Tatus was bringing in the bishop. "The Bishop waited an hour for you to wake."

"Uncle Bishop, how kind," I said, and kissed the amethyst ring on his outstretched hand.

"He looks a fine baby. I will baptize him Saturday week. I came to do it today," he spoke with his usual halting humility, "but the Rector said there is no hurry. He will return when you can be up."

My eyes closed in spite of themselves. My father-in-law, quick to perceive my weariness, pushed the Bishop out of the room, motioning me to speak no more. Nothing made him more impatient than unnecessary formalities. He closed the door, shutting out the glorious sunlight, radiant on the bassinet of my son.

I was too weak to call him back, to beg him to leave the door open. Tears of weakness and exhaustion trickled down my nose onto the pillow. I felt too tired to move my head from the wet place they made.

But soon John was back, peeping through the door to see if all was well. Many more flowers had come — he wanted to show me other baskets of white cyclamen and maiden hair too big for one to carry, the azalea bushes, some trimmed as cones and cylinders, others a yard across, bunches of pink, white and red roses. They were countless. "Love to you" — "Joyful greetings" — "For the Son" — "Our friends" — how had they found out so quickly ? Uncle shouldn't have done it. "From Stas, how beautiful." "How just like Tony." There was no longer a place to put anything. Seventy-odd bouquets and plants had been sent us. During the long afternoon, the bell rang constantly with flowers and telegrams, all the family in Warsaw came to offer congratulations. But the two nurses were decided I should see no one, no one should see the baby.

Without any preparation, John announced, "When Eva came, I gave her the cat."

"Blankus is gone !" I screamed.

"The nurse refused to stay in the house with him," was the answer. "She says that cat trails germs around everywhere. He might even jump into Andrew's bed."

From exhaustion once more tears came in my eyes.

"Try and be reasonable," John said. "When Andrew's bigger, we will get him back again." Poor Blankus — he had traveled to Geneva with us with a passport stamped at each frontier, he rode in the car like a dog — in all the changes of apartments his one anxiety had been to cling to us ; he would even hide in our suitcases while we were packing. I could not be resigned to parting with the faithful creature.

Just then Andrew woke up and gave a heart-rending shriek. "Oh, go quickly. Whatever is the matter ?" The nurse went so slowly.

"It's nothing at all — a fine healthy baby," she said indifferently.

"Call Mulka," I begged John, "the baby may die."

"Mulka's asleep now — don't be afraid when the baby cries loudly. It's only the low feeble cry that is a danger sign," he said and kissed my forehead.

"If he is awake, then surely I can see him. Do bring him here no matter what the nurse says."

A few moments later she brought the baby to me, protesting, "It will only excite the Madame. I always say the first twenty-four hours the lady must rest. Think how many years you have to admire the baby!"

On the twelfth day I was allowed to be up for the christening ceremony. The doctor gave his permission on condition that I sat in an arm chair. My legs had been bandaged to prevent phlebitis. Afterwards I had to return to bed, for I was really not allowed to walk about for six weeks. The nurse insisted that these precautions would make all the difference to future health. She said, "If a woman gets out of childbed too soon, the muscles in her face will sag along with the muscles of her belly and everything else. The lady must be patient and prepare for her getting up with proper exercises in bed and massages." She bound me from arms to thigh with a rolled bandage. I would have to remain at least four weeks in this binding — which was to be removed only night and morning when she bathed and massaged me.

My father-in-law arrived by plane from Cracow for the ceremony. Since the regular planes were established in 1930, he had never traveled otherwise. My mother-in-law likewise would say, "Now there are planes, how can one travel in slow, dirty trains?" "Planes make it possible to come to Warsaw for a day or two without weariness; we will come to visit you more often now."

Tatus' present for the baptism was a Sixteenth Century Madonna covered with a skirt of old embossed silver. It was worked in a beautiful baroque pattern of Pomegranates unlike the stiff Romanesque style of the Orthodox ikons. He gave Andrew two bottles of a hundred-year-old Tokay wine — one from which to toast his health at the baptism, the other for his twenty-first birthday. A cousin brought a bottle of a hundred years mead, and the Bishop brought a little gold locket of the Virgin.

The whole family assembled in the living room which a Deacon had previously arranged like a chapel with an altar. John held the baby while the Bishop read the many prayers he had collected for the occasion. When he poured the holy water, Andrew screamed loudly. "A sure sign he will pro-

121

claim the faith with much fervor," the Bishop exclaimed smiling kindly. Following the ceremony, tea was served to the family and intimate friends who came during the whole afternoon to offer their congratulations. The Bishop gave the first toast which Tatus had to answer. Then healths of the grandparents, the god-parents, the parents and the child were drunk from the hundred-year-old amber Tokay.

Next morning I learned that Tatus would not return to Cracow but was to remain in Warsaw for a hearing at the Ministry of Education on a bill which, if it passed, would give the State the right of nominating professors. "This bill must be opposed at all costs," he explained. "The State should indeed provide for universities, but it should not have control over them in either subject matter or the choosing of teachers." Tatus spoke seriously and was obviously worried about the outcome. When he went out, John told me, "The Minister of Education is a hothead. He threatens Tatus with expulsion from the University. Representatives of various faculties will support Father, but if the proposition becomes law, their situation too can be serious."

When Tatus returned in the afternoon, he told us nothing of his conversations. Instead he played with his grandson and asked us what plans we had made for the summer. "I won't come in to see you in the morning," Tatus told us when he kissed us good night. "I must collect my thoughts. Before an important conference I do not care to speak to anyone. Arrange for Edward to bring up my breakfast at seven so that I need not be hurried."

At three he returned to fetch his bag ; there was just time to reach the plane if John drove fast. I had to wait until John returned from the airport to learn the outcome of the hearing. "Short of getting a change of Ministers, there is no hope for us. Tatus believes his arguments made no impression."

The next morning the press was ablaze with "CRACOW PROFESSORS REVOLT — Fifty professors threaten to leave the University if their age-long privilege of selection of new members is taken over by the State."

122

Several of our more pusillanimous friends in the Ministry of Foreign Affairs came to the house to plead with us. Did we not realize the Professor risked prison by his attitude ?

A hearing was called for by the Sejm, the two houses of Parliament. During the six weeks of anxious preparation for the hearing, we hardly saw Tatus. He had daily meetings not only with the staff in Cracow but also with professors from the other universities, Vilna, Lwow, Warsaw and Posnań — trying to weld them into a unity. Among them, some of course were friends of the Minister's, others were hesitant in resigning and had to be persuaded that it was a serious matter for the government to appoint professors to a university. Some felt that the State was as good a judge as another and anyway, would probably accept the universities' candidates. The various universities were slow to pass resolutions, but public opinion expressed through the greater part of the press was strongly for the complete independence of the professors. The *Cracow Times,* closed because of its outspoken editorials against the Government, opened two weeks later in Warsaw.

But the resolution to place all Professors on the payroll of the Ministry of Education — a measure that virtually destroyed the autonomy of the universities — was voted down when it reached the Sejm. The universities had won out and the Minister of Education, who had tried by this bill to find a lucrative place for his henchmen, was repudiated by Parliament and soon dropped from his post as Cabinet Minister.

One afternoon at tea time we heard a boy calling under our windows, "Extra ! — Extra !" Listening attentively we heard him say, "Minister Pieracki murdered — Minister of Interior shot." Out in the streets groups of people collected about the boy selling papers, and as leaves blown in the wind the crowd eddied and swirled as groups broke off towards the city, not a mob running ; but separated, scuttling figures in two's, and three's, all carried by the same impulse, to reach the place of the disaster without creating a commotion.

"Strange," said John, "I was at the club where this happened just before lunch. I passed the Minister coming in as I left to return home."

The bell rang, a friend came in. "Isn't it terrible ?" she said. "He was shot in the very doorway while waiting for a taxi." Another bell, another friend — another and another.

The boy hurried away for fresh tea cups and bread and butter for the dozen or more persons who had dropped in to learn what interpretation John put on the assassination. Soon the telephone began ringing. "Do you know ?" "You have heard ?" John was unable to leave his study before the telephone bell would ring again. In the drawing room everyone was talking at once.

"The Ruthenians did it."

"No, the Ukrainians."

You could hear someone ask, "A plot ?"

And someone confirm it, "Yes, it 's part of an international plot."

"The Germans wish to overthrow Poland," it was suggested.

"No, they mean to weaken her internally," another flung out.

"Perhaps the Ukrainians wished to start a revolution so the Russians can invade us."

"Not the Russians — the Germans." The tone was authoritative.

"You are sure ?" we repeated in chorus.

"Indeed, yes. Weapons made in Germany were found on the side street where the murderer threw them as he jumped over the fence and disappeared." That was proof.

"The police searched all the buildings in the neighborhood."

"Impossible a man could disappear from under their nose." I said, offering a second cup of tea which no one accepted. Everyone was more concerned with what had become of the criminal.

"He jumped the fence ; only his revolver has been found."

"They believe the German Embassy arranged it," John reported.

John and I being received in Yugoslavia on the
Danubian mission

Professor and Mrs. Kostanecki *(Tatusz and Mulka)*

"Von Rintelen is always out for trouble !"

"If one could only get something on the Embassy."

"Or at least have Von Rintelen recalled."

"I never go there."

"Nor I."

"Nor I."

"When they asked us for dinner last winter," I confessed, "we went because the head of the western division of the Foreign Office and two Cabinet Ministers had accepted."

"We will never accept another invitation because obviously we won't ask a German under our own roof," John paced before the windows from time to time, looking out on the street.

"What will the outside world think of this latest 'outrage' ?" That was what we all wanted to know.

"Oh, the British papers will say, 'New Internal Disorders,'" someone suggested.

"The German papers will call for a re-examination of frontiers and minorities," the voice of a friend from the Foreign Office.

"Minorities — that's the worst of it. When you've seen how they were organized in Upper Silesia eight years ago, you can imagine what they are doing today !"

A lady close to British circles whispered to her neighbor, "The British Consul told me he knows for sure the Ruthenians are kept in rebellion by Germany ; their discontent is the work of German provocation agents."

"I doubt he would say such a thing. It hardly seems possible."

"Indeed he did. He goes to that part of the country every year, and visits the Ukrainians too," she stoutly maintained. "He even speaks the Ukrainian language and reads their papers."

"Pilsudski should have made Poles of them," we all agreed. "Why did he grant them so much autonomy ? Everyone knows the Germans supply them with arms."

"The Poles are the only people compelled to keep their Minority Treaty obligations under the League of Nations.

125

Imagine Germany or Italy allowing a League Commission to investigate minorities." We could hardly imagine such a condition. Yet in population Poland was second only to Italy. Because her strategic position was weaker, she was treated like a small nation.

"Little good adherence to treaty obligations will do Poland," someone said bitterly.

"If one country began breaking treaties," John admonished, "think where it would end. That would give the Germans and Hungarians the very chance they are looking for."

We were all aware of the danger. We saw no way out of it unless England and France put an end to these Minority questions. But with both countries at Geneva pursuing a policy of "hands off Central Europe" and America following an isolationist policy, Poland was forced to submit to German intrigue in the guise of carrying out Minority treaties. Text books and German teachers were provided even where there was only one child that claimed German extraction. This farce of allowing an autonomous German state to exist within Poland opened the frontier to thousands of German agents.

In despair we had discussed the whole question with Mr. Lipski, later Polish Ambassador to Berlin. Everywhere in Geneva there was a persistent refusal to face the logical consequences of Germany's underground work through her minorities, even when these Germans loudly proclaimed themselves the vanguard of Greater Germany.

"Poles are so unsuccessful with stating their positions," we agreed as we said good night, each one promising to telephone the instant we heard an authoritative report.

After the murderer of Pieracki escaped to Berlin he became the head of a Ukrainian organization that was a cover for German espionage in Poland. It was hard for anyone in Poland to understand such treachery. In the thirteenth century a pact of mutual guarantee had been signed which gave equal rights to Ukrainians, Lithuanians and Ruthenians. The idea of mutual respect and individual sovereignty was the basis of a cantonal union which held together longer than the union of Scotland and England. The oldest and greatest

Polish families came from Lithuania. Pilsudski was born near Vilna. Poles could not conceive of Minorities being used by foreign powers against them. They were mentally unprepared for German fifth column activity among their former allies. It took years to prove to them that the Germans were re-arming the Ukrainian and Ruthenian peasantry and were stirring up an animosity which never previously existed — taking advantage of social unrest. Hitler used the appeal of the worker against employer, the minority against Poland.

Only those who lived in the Eastern Provinces understood how serious was the situation. The rest of the country hoped to quiet the leaders with concessions and seats in the Diet. Our friends from the East told us of the talk current in the villages, of the effort to burn out Polish peasants in the Ukrainian province. "Many are fine people," they said, "good workers, thoroughly dependable. But the situation will grow out of hand, if hot-headed leaders are allowed to become martyrs in the hands of a routine police system."

Among our friends was a young couple whose houses and lands had been destroyed by the Bolsheviks after the last war. They had gone back to their farm and lived in their milk shed, while they had invested all their capital in machines and fertilizers rather than personal comforts. Their shed had no floor and mildew had crept halfway up the walls. As it was too damp for their children, they had to be sent to Lwow for eight years to live with their grandparents. At last in 1936 the farm paid so well — there was a turnover of $25,000 on carloads of beet seeds sold to Germany — that my friends could build a house and bring their children home. They drew up their own plans which they brought to Warsaw to show us.

Hardly was the house finished than Ukrainians with burning torches marched through the village to their very gates. The head man shouted and swore ugly epithets to drive them from the village. Joseph went out unarmed to meet them.

"Friends," said he, "have I not always paid you well ? You

have wages from me now, whereas before I built up this farm, you lived with difficulty from your land. If you burn my house and destroy my crops, who will pay you? Go back to the dishonest man who sent you hither and say, 'We are not so simple as to destroy the goose of the golden eggs.' Let him leave our countryside and give his idle talk to more foolish men."

The villagers talked among themselves. Finally one said, "What you have said is true." They began to break ranks and put out their menacing torches. "We would be foolish to burn this house," they agreed.

"Do not leave my gates before we break bread together," my friend pleaded.

Jadwiga, his wife, who was watching from the veranda, ran down the path with bread and salt. "Wait," she said, "the last year's mead is not too weak to drink our healths. Here is the bread and salt. Please come in."

The incident left them with no hard feelings. "I love the Ukrainians," she said, "they are a noble people, fine workers. If only the government would find out who are the paid trouble-makers."

Joseph came to Warsaw to tell the Minister of the Interior what he knew. "Germany is sending in agents who distribute arms and money. One of my men was approached. The government must act immediately and with great caution before it is too late. The movement started among workers in Lwow and is spreading to the countryside. They preach the land is theirs by inherent right and should be taken by force from the Polish peasants."

"Do you believe they want to secede?"

"It's more a movement to get control of everything. Warsaw is so blind to the potentiality. When I tell them, they answer, 'don't spread panic.'"

"No Pole can touch another with arms," they said.

That in the long run Poles were justified in treating the people within her borders as a great family, sharing prosperity as well as the vicissitudes of history, is borne out by the many Germans who became Poles. The Mayor of Lódź, Bajer, committed suicide rather than call himself a Reichsdeutscher when the Germans marched in in the autumn of 1939. One of the sons of the Pastor of the Lutheran Church, Professor Bursche, was a Polish pilot and killed in action. The other two died as did Bursche, in German concentration camps. The Fischers, the Wendes, the Meyers, the Wedels — all German Protestants — were so militantly Polish that not one of them has been found today who would form a pro-German Government.

CHAPTER *9*

AFTER the murder of Minister Pieracki, you could hear reverberations and echoes from the furthest provinces. During the long winter we had all been gripped with dark forebodings. Now the sweet scented air of summer, like a gentle caress, made us forget those endless winter days when the sun which never pierced the fog seemed only to emphasize our obscure and melancholy future. Here at last was the season we loved the most! There was the outdoor ballet and the theatre in the Lazenki Gardens. The alleys of beech trees were cut and fragrant. There were outdoor cafes in the parks and the promenade along the new cut stone embankment. I can never think of Warsaw in the summer without hearing again voices singing to an accordion across a meadow — and the song of nightingales in lilac-scented gardens. . .

Summer was always nearly over before we had even thought of leaving the city. I was therefore quite astonished one evening at dinner when John told me :

"Tony has asked us to meet him in Danzig."

Tony had been the best man at our wedding. "Is he really taking all eleven nieces to the seashore!" I could not picture Tony travelling with his nieces ; nor even imagine him as part of a family. He seemed to have sprung full grown into life. He never spoke of his childhood or his escape from the Bolsheviks. Though everyone knew his family had had one of the greatest Polish fortunes, he made fun of his precarious position as an émigré as if he had been born into it, with inevitable good humor. He was the art connoisseur ; he had

130

dined with Noel Coward and wore an exactly similar silk handkerchief. He had managed his love affairs so successfully no one had ever been able to tell with whom he had had them. Wherever it was smart to be seen, Tony would be there, but he also enjoyed the most Bohemian parties and could always be found at four A.M. at one of the artists' cafes.

"He is leaving the girls with some relative and then going on his pet freighter to London." London was part of his double life of which he never gave us any details.

"I wonder how much longer he will keep up his London house." This was always a source of speculation.

"I believe he wants to rent it when he leaves this time. He still has the ex-sailor manservant to care for it," John explained between mouthfuls.

"He told me he was hard up again — something about his brother making more improvements in the country, new additions to the stables and hothouses." We always felt slightly guilty sitting down for dinner unless we were certain Tony had a previous engagement. The eleven nieces, daughters of his brother, were the cause of Tony never having married.

"I must provide a dowry for them ; the poor dears have the choice either of going on the loose or taking to the veil," he would say. "My brother has piously produced them. He is far too religious to plan for their future."

"When you think of their all squeezing into that gatehouse, no wonder Tony escapes periodically to London !" They had moved into the Concierge Lodge at the time Mr. Dewey was financial adviser and continued in it while their house was used as the American Chancellory.

Tony maintained that even when he retired to the bathroom, his mother would plant her chair outside the door insisting there were things she simply had to discuss immediately with him.

Finally I asked, "Shall we go — what is the decision ?"

I could have guessed the answer. John was always ready to go anywhere at a moment's notice.

"Let's meet him but not travel with him," he suggested, "if he really seriously means to travel by river boat."

The river boats were unbearably uncomfortable. They were built to carry freight and though there were one or two staterooms, I could well believe Tony would not have the funds to use them. "He is an angel to take the trip," I said with real conviction.

"It saves his mother," John wisely remarked. "He would do anything to relieve her."

"Is it so much cheaper?"

"It must be when you count twelve tickets," John was practical. You could see John wanted to go.

"Telephone him we will meet him Wednesday morning by the quayside at Danzig."

Dressed identically in black, the eleven sisters had occupied the whole prow of the small paddle wheel river boat that had brought them from Warsaw to Danzig. The little girls were still in mourning for their mother. Their grandmother had prepared immense hampers of food, dozens of little white rolls, eggs, butter and cheeses, and a cold chicken for each of the girls. Each carried a steamer rug in which she had rolled up on the deck. Though their faces were sunburned a bright scarlet, all eleven were in high spirits. They ran down the gangway and hopped into a bus which took us to the harbor at Gdynia where we were to take the steamer that crossed over the bay to Hel. When the bus came to a halt by the quay at Gdynia, a cold sharp wind was blowing. It made us shiver in our inadequately thin summer clothes. The glaring sun which seemed to pierce our eyelids and blanch our skin gave us no warmth. The pale blue sea was streaked with white caps and marked like a honeycomb where the squalls passed over the waves. It was clear that the little steamboat to which the girls raced so innocently would be hopelessly thrown about in the choppy sea. They hopped merrily aboard, taking possession of the prow with all their rugs and baskets. They were impatient once more to be going.

"You and Uncle Tony will sit in the middle," they called, showing how they had arranged places for us.

"How much longer do we have to wait?"

"Do we really go out of sight of land?" Each shouted a different question.

I shuddered at the very thought.

Tony whispered, "Frankly, I don't look forward to the trip — let's go in search of a little fortification."

"Will the girls be alright if we leave them?" Though the oldest might have been fifteen they seemed very young to leave alone. But Tony was reassuring. "They know all about travelling after 36 hours on the river," he said.

As we walked along the broad concrete quay, I thought of the eleven little girls sitting so cozily in the prow of the ship. "Oh, Tony, what if they all get seasick together!"

"Darlings, I'm thinking of that myself. If you really love me, you will stay behind," he begged.

I had dreaded the boat trip from the instant we caught sight of the sea. Crossing the broad cobblestone street at the quay side, we felt chilled to the marrow. "Getting seasick isn't really a social pleasure," I agreed.

"Why don't we all wait over until the wind dies down?" John suggested sensibly. As with the one impulse we had ducked into the nearest bar. The two or three other persons there were sailors. Upholstered bentwood chairs and tables and plain wood panelled walls, like everything else in Danzig, were new and the smell of tobacco smoke had not yet saturated them.

"It can't blow forever; tomorrow it may drop," John continued as soon as we had sat down.

"Suppose it gets worse?" Tony replied.

"Then stay on in Gdynia," John urged. "It's very comfortable here in Gdynia."

"My dears, pay for rooms for eleven nieces in a hotel when they can all stay for nothing with Marytka? You plutocrats!"

"*Wodka?*"

"Three, please."

"And *Kanapki?*"

"*Kanapki* — "

"Don't come with me, please don't!" Tony pleaded.

133

"What could we find to talk about on the boat ?   Lay bets on which one would be seasick next ?"

"Then if you mean it, we will wait."   How wonderful not to have to go !   I tried to hide my delight but John who really loved rough weather, replied, "It seems silly not to go with you when that's why we are here in Gdynia."

Tony fortunately insisted we remain behind.   "If the wind dies down, take the next steamer ; if it holds, wait for me."

"Then we will all meet in the Hotel Riviera," I cried, anxious the matter should be settled.

Tony, evidently relieved, proposed, "Another round to meeting at the Riviera."

It was time to depart.   The tiny steamer gave its first warning toot.   We stepped outside.   The cold gusty wind sweeping across the cobbled street from the Baltic Sea felt like March.   The frantic wind and the low angle of the sun were chill reminders of the north.   But the little girls had opened their hampers and had settled down to finishing their rolls and chicken.   They were chattering and giggling, totally unaware of the ordeal before them.   With a shriek, the launch cast off.   Hardly had it left the quayside when it shipped water, and spray had drenched the eleven nieces. We last saw Tony frantically shoving them and their luggage to the lee side of the steamer.

The Hotel Riviera, where we deposited our bags, was built in the summer resort section of Gdynia.   Here the broad quay had been arranged as a park and planted with ornamental flower beds.   There was a pavilion for band concerts, a boardwalk and a broad white sandy beach which swept as far as the eye could reach along the Polish coast towards Danzig.   We followed the boardwalk to its end, along the dunes a mile or more out of town.   The dunes piled up against a high bluff thickly grown with century-old oaks.   An ancient, much used path with steps formed by the roots of trees led to the top.   We scrambled up the steep footpath that looked as if it had followed the top of the cliff since time immemorial. Here and there someone had carved a rustic seat between two trees where there was a fine view of the white beach and

broad sea.   The well kept forest had been cleared of fallen
branches and undergrowth.   The roots of the trees held large
clumps of soft moss, tiny wild flowers and such grass as grows
in the deep shade, covered the steep bank down to the sea.

Before we realized we had walked so far, we had come to
the next village.   There was a bathing establishment with
modern cement bathhouses along the shore where we found
we could rent bathing suits and towels, fresh from a steriliz-
ing drum.   The spacious bathhouses were equipped with
showers, hand basins and a broad bench on which you could
recline.   We were now warm enough from our walk to relish
a swim.   But when we had put on the bathing suits and
stepped down on the beach, the sand felt so cold and the
water was so icy that we dashed back to the cabin as fast as
possible.

While we were dressing, we realized we were famished.
John looked at his watch.   It was 3:30.   "Where shall we
have lunch ?" he said, and quoted the Polish proverb, "The
first place will be the best," and led the way across the road.
A moldy, old fashioned hotel was set back in a grove of trees.
Neither the fifty empty tables all set up on a glass enclosed
veranda nor the sight of a waiter flicking dust with his napkin
off the artificial flowers could discourage us.   We were too
tired to go further.

Luckily the waiter understood how hungry we were.
"Shall it be omelet or hors d'oeuvre while the *Panstwo* are
making up their minds on the dinner ?" he asked.

"Let it be omelet, and *starka*," (a kind of rye).

The omelets covered a whole platter and we found it impossible to eat the ragout of veal we had ordered.

Gradually we grew warm again protected from the wind
by the glassed veranda and the heavy trees.   The sea was
breaking in short high waves and the white caps came closer
together.   How glad we were we had stayed behind.   Next
summer, John repeated, I could go to Hel.   He tried to describe that long narrow cape, stretching eighty miles out into
the sea, so narrow there were places where you could see
across it from the shallow bay, into the tumultuous Baltic.

135

He pictured the old fishing villages under the neat pine trees, and the colonies of modernistic summer cottages strung along both sides of the highway and railroad line.

Tony returned to Gdynia on the following day. His usual ruddy complexion had gone an oily yellow. For all his thick sandy hair and six feet two, he looked frail. But he managed to greet us with his usual flourish, "Well, my dears, it's lucky I kept you from going on our little picnic. It was nip and tuck mostly. The girls had to be helped ashore. I am rushing back to Warsaw tonight."

"What happened to your week's holiday?"

"I have to sell something, some family jewels, or livestock — anything in a hurry."

We laughed merrily.

"Nothing humorous about it that I can see. I have to set about selling the boat tickets to London and finding the girls' fare home. They won't return except by train. Having planted them on kind Marytka I can't leave them for more than two weeks. She has other guests coming." Tony's indignation was so droll it was hard not to laugh, even though we knew how serious was his plight.

As there was nothing to keep us in Gdynia, we too left by the evening train. In Poland no one needed to take a sleeper except at the holiday season when the trains were packed. All first and second class Polish railroad carriages could be converted into sleepers. The backs of the benches tipped up and were held in place by specially made wall brackets. You could rent pillows and blankets in the station. In each compartment four persons could stretch out at no extra expense. From the time of boarding the train at Gdynia until you left the Danzig Free State, there was no use trying to sleep. The Danzig customs officers stamped about the train making such fuss and commotion it was better not to try and settle down.

We leaned back in our places while Tony broke the news of his plans for leasing an apartment in Warsaw. He had found the very place — in the basement of a professor's house, with his own entrance through the garden, near his mother's house and only around the corner from us. It would be a difficult apartment to decorate. The radiators hung high on the walls. Since you couldn't hide them or mask them he thought you could use them as part of the decorative scheme — perhaps paint them like the Venetian blinds. The large one in his bedroom could be arranged as futuristic organ pipes. We promised to take a hand in the painting and to lend him as much furniture as we could spare. At Danzig a passenger came into our compartment. When we found he was to leave the train after Torun, we gave him one of the lower berths. John and I took the two uppers hoping not to be disturbed. After we left the frontier the conductor came through the train, dimming the lights. Soon everyone was quiet for the night. We did not even hear the stranger leave the compartment at Torun and we were surprised to find a lady in his place when we waked up in Warsaw.

We left Tony at the station, expecting it would be two or even three weeks before we would see him again. We were aware it would be one of those periods when Tony had to find money.

"Don't call me up till you hear from me," he had told us. "This time I must seriously find a lot of money. You know my brother has bought an automobile. He signed my name to it. The worst of it is that he doesn't realize what he has done. Good-bye and God bless you."

How he did it was always very mysterious and as he never asked our help it was difficult to inquire into the particulars. If you telephoned to his house, however, early in the morning or late at night, his manservant always replied, "Mr. Count is at the Board of Directors." Tony's family had owned beet sugar refineries and he often complained of the number of salaries paid the officials when nothing could be squeezed out for him. He said there were times he hated to look in his pocket for fear he wouldn't be able to pay for his dinner. Yet he had always been the most sought after bachelor in Warsaw and his pockets had always bulged with invitations to Embassy functions and dinners. It was known he could make the dullest party a roaring success. However, these times of disappearing into board meetings were becoming longer and longer. He had become more restless and impatient with the "best" Warsaw society and he failed to show up anywhere except the President's receptions in the Zamek or the annual parties at the British and American Embassies. Tony had decided to be worth the salary he was determined to earn. His needs for money were endless. His brother's debts — his eleven nieces — his mother's few wants, and a host of impecunious artist friends for whom he in turn was always willing to go into debt.

In the taxi on the way home, the whole tragedy of his position burst upon us. "How I wish there were something we could really do to help Tony," John remarked affectionately. "When we are old, he will come and live with us. He will have sold everything he owns to help someone else and then we'll have to take care of him."

But we didn't have to wait long for Tony to telephone, in fact, we had hardly sat down to lunch when he called. "Did you hear Carol Szymanowski is terribly ill? (Carol Szymanowski was the greatest modern Polish composer.) "No one knows how long he will live. How much will you contribute every month? Not less than 100 zloty. Can you make it 200 (about $40)? Aunt Marylka is giving 200 zlotys, and so are the Meyers. They need at least a thousand to send him to Grasso. Thanks, darlings. I'll be around later."

As usual he came about seven, too late for tea. Even before he spoke, you felt he was bursting with news. "You haven't kept tea for me? What a day!" He always kissed both hands with an affectionate mock seriousness, saying in English: "I suppose you are so Polish now you expect it. Girls and boys, I'm going abroad."

"When?"

"How did you arrange it? Where are you going?" John and I shouted in the same breath.

"I'm being sent by the *Literary News*. I'm going to

Berlin!" He told us of his chance encounter that morning with the editor.

"Well now, be careful."

"They think I know all the 'pinks.'"

"And is Berlin full of them!"

"Do you know everyone?"

"Enough to meet plenty of people and hear lots of gossip. Most of all it's lucrative. Very! If I do well, they may send me to Paris."

"I know the articles will be good — when do they commence?"

"Not till I return. You don't think I'd send them through the mail. I'm not going to Germany as a journalist. I'm just an ordinary old fashioned traveller from the back country seeing the wicked night life of the big capital."

"You'll be gone a long time?"

"As long as I like — six weeks — or two months. Don't fret — I'll bring you a souvenir."

"There's a card from your Aunt Marylka announcing her 'at home.'"

"You'll be good lambs and go — Good-bye."

"What about the money for Carol?"

"Jaz will take care of it, or you send it to the Meyers. Don't forget."

"How did you settle for your nieces?"

"Mother once gave me a string of pearls. I sold them for a ridiculous figure — not even 10,000 zlotys. I needed five right away for Carol. I've paid for the girls' tickets; they are out of hock. I paid off my brother's automobile — I hope he understands now. With what's left I'll go abroad."

"You'll get that back."

"When I come back I'm buying my freedom. I'm moving out — definitely. It's all settled. I'm going to have a magenta room with a pink ceiling that none of my family can stand looking at."

"Good-bye, Tony."

"Such sweet sorrow!"

"Gluptas!" (Idiot!)

Tony's career as a journalist lasted up until the day he was killed in the London blitz, while delivering the Polish Overseas broadcast for the BBC.

No matter what hour you arrived at Aunt Marylka's "at homes," a great many persons were already there. In the old days she like Tony, had been renowned for her snobbishness and the pleasure she took in having an elegant salon. It was certainly proof of her love for Tony that she had gone along with him to all the recent futuristic shows and seemed to share his passion for everything new Poland could create. Though late in her sixties, she spent much of her time reading modern philosophy and she did her best to understand the reasons and causes of modernistic art. In her salon she brought together those younger members of the old Polish families who had a vague and incoherent feeling of wanting to take part in the artistic life of the country with the very young artists who needed a public.

There were always a few middle-aged matrons who still thought it smart to be seen there. They sat primly together as if afraid of being contaminated by the strange young persons chatting so loudly in the corners. "Dear Marylka is going through a phase," they whispered together, "it's her second childhood!"

"All this craze for Jozio Czapski is a pose!" the ladies put their heads together, hoping no one would overhear them.

"Anything for publicity."

"You know he's here all the time."

"There can't be anything in it."

"At her age?"

"She seems so fascinated by him."

"He is awkward and ungainly enough!"

"And seems so unconscious of women — "

"It's his talk — when he gets started he never stops. Dear Marylka does love talk."

They need not have whispered. Jozio was paying no attention to them. He was expanding his idea on art to a mixed group of people. He was the recognized leader of a school of painters called after him "Capisti." They were the first group to come under the influence of modern French painting and break with the Polish tradition which had been dominated by that very dry photographic School of Neo-Gothic painters. Czapski did not believe in any form of neo- or pseudo-art. As we came in the room we heard him defending one of the members of his group who was being loudly criticized in the press for the way in which he had painted a ceiling in the Wawel in Cracow. He was fairly shouting : "You wouldn't tear down the Gothic additions to a Romanesque Church, would you ? Well, and what about the Renaissance Choir stalls ? I suppose you would remove the Van Dykes just because baroque painting has no place in a Romanesque Church. I'm surprised you don't criticize Leonardo da Vinci for painting his 'Last Supper' in the style of the day, instead of copying the Ravenna mosaics which were contemporary to the period of the building. Can you name any ancient edifice painted in a pseudo-art ? Do we not see decorations of every period side by side ? Were the Sforza family afraid to hire Montegna while Gothic painting was still in style ? If the Polish aristocracy wish to be known to posterity, it will be through the contemporary monuments they erect. It's their honor and duty to be the patrons of modern art as during the Renaissance the nobility made that art possible."

We slid through the double doors into the dining room. The maid was passing tea and we helped ourselves from the bountiful plates of cakes and sandwiches laid out on the large table. The novelists Maryia Dombrowska and Zofia Kossak, and the poetess Illakowiczowna were chatting in a corner. They had been successful for so many years their presence no longer created a commotion. The niece of Joseph Conrad in her usual effervescent and sparkling manner was running from one to another, with an endless store of good-humored comments, "Ah there you are *kochanya* ! Do you know everyone ?" She really did. She had belonged to Pilsudski's underground organization from the beginning and she had known him well. Everyone in the government, from the Prime Minister down came to see her in her single shabby rented room. When she had an "at home" you could barely squeeze in the door and in the crush it was impossible not to rub elbows with all the most influential people. You would find yourself pinioned with the famous Bartel or Slawek, Pristor or Zaleski who always good naturedly returned to her parties. She was counted as a writer and a member of the Academy because she translated Joseph Conrad from English into Polish.

It was considered ill-mannered to remain after seven. Yet the young artists, unaware of this convention, never left as long as there was a cake on the table or tea being served. Aunt Marylka would often ask a few of her oldest acquaintances to stay through the evening and the conversation would then continue till one in the morning.

From the next room you could hear Czapski talking, "The difficulty for an artist in Warsaw is the lack of criticism, the give and take of the atelier," he was saying. "Our group will go stale unless we get back to Paris."

"Your shows have been successfully attended."

"That's important, surely!" For the first time Czapski's voice sounded impatient.

"And you have had plenty of quarrels with the press."

Like an eagle brooding over all he felt sacred, he sat high in his stiff chair, his arms embracing his unshakable belief in the sublime destiny of art. "One can't live by destructive criticism alone. Criticism must have something to offer."

"But you have sold quite well."

"That's another question. Seeing one's picture in a real room, with furniture, is a shock indeed. It is far easier to paint exhibition pieces. The point is the public treats us like a fad."

"Isn't it a fault to be dependent on Paris?" someone asked. "An artist should reflect his country of origin."

"That's to say art is not universal and should be narrowed down to the limited concepts of each country or each level of society in which the artist hoped to sell himself." Czapski nearly choked with rage at the very suggestion. He was six

142

feet tall, and had the saintly expression of a wholly selfless individual. He lived in an ill-heated attic room sharing everything with the dozen or so Polish colleagues that had studied together in Paris under Bonnard. Coming as he did from a gentry family, he was treated at first as a dilettante. It was with difficulty he established himself as a professional painter. However, he eventually gained not only recognition of his artistic ability, but also achieved considerable financial success. He was indefatigable in the way in which he attained commissions for the whole group, always making a greater effort to sell their work than his own. His title and social position attracted many persons to his exhibitions but he never accepted social engagements unless they promised to be useful for his artist friends. In posing the problem of national art in contrast to art universal to our western civilization, Czapski started an uproar. The conversation swelled into confused cross fire in which everyone shouted at the same time. Czapski was no longer able to command attention.

I had already decided to leave when Anieluszia)the niece of the writer Conrad) whispered in my ear, "Are you going tomorrow to the Marshal's ?"

"I would like to ; can you stop for me ?"

"After four then — "

Promptly after four Anieluszia arrived as she had promised. During the night it had rained hard, now it was gently drizzling. The sidewalks were brown with leaves, and more rain-soaked leaves were dropping from the trees. Though the thick mat of leaves overhead had begun to thin, the street beneath the thick branches was dank and somber.

"It makes me sad," were her first words, "autumn has come !"

How quickly the summer passed !

"It makes me apprehensive," she remarked. "This is an ill omen. The Marshal has long been overworked. This is his first afternoon in several months." She was unable to continue talking for in spite of the rain and the late afternoon, the Alleja was crowded. We threaded our way with difficulty between the women pushing perambulators, buttoned up against the rain, lovers loitering under the beech trees as if in disregard of the last few summer days. The clipped beech hedge hiding the apartment buildings bordering either side of the Alleja made a majestic frame for the whole scene. I followed Anieluszia's swift pace as best I could for many blocks. Suddenly we caught up with a familiar figure walking with a cane.

Countess Rose was nearing eighty. It was not surprising to find her alone on foot. She considered robust health as another would a virtue. When over seventy, she had flown in an open avionette, probably the first woman in Poland to do so. She had managed her own financial transactions and amassed a considerable fortune. All her life she had lived in Spartan simplicity. Following the real Polish aristocratic tradition, she never allowed herself luxuries and comforts. We both kissed her hand out of respect for her great age.

"You shouldn't do that," she said smilingly. "Are you going to the Marshal's? Then we can walk together."

"Have you come all the way on foot?" I asked, with amazement. I knew her house was at the other end of town, a good three miles from the Belvedere where Pilsudski lived.

"You should know I always go on foot," she spoke emphatically. "I never ride in town."

"When you were for dinner with us in Cracow you would not let us send for a cab even though it was a stormy night," I reminded her.

"That is the reason I am never ill. The other principle in which I believe is keeping my feet uncovered at night," she explained. "Too many covers make one soft."

Anieluszia and I both laughed from embarrassment.

"It's the Marshal's first 'at home,'" Anieluszia remarked.

"That is the reason for which I am in town. I never wish to miss such an occasion at my age." She had the gay voice and energetic step of a young woman.

"*Prosze Pani!*" we protested in unison.

"One never knows! Moreover, we must set the example

144

of self-discipline. Each generation of our aristocracy must give proof of their right to use their title. Unless they make a real contribution to society, they have no right to call themselves aristocrats. This generation must establish unity in Poland. Each young person should serve his country without prejudice. Many of us hoped to achieve Polish independence. It was Pilsudski who won it for us all. It is for history, not for us to judge his methods now. We have won our independence by our united opposition to our enemies. Today such inner unity is even more essential to raise our poor country from its ashes."

We both gave our complete assent.

She continued, "I have always said to my sons, 'Set yourself a program and follow it scrupulously.' For myself I rise at seven. During the morning I have certain hours for attending to my estate and writing letters, others for the foreign and domestic press and the reading of books by various statesmen. In the afternoon I also have a period for reading before tea-time after which one must be prepared for interruptions or social engagements." As she spoke I could picture her table stacked high like a reader's desk in an office, with books in Spanish, French and German, Italian, English and Polish. I could well believe no important book appeared in Europe without her reading it.

As we arrived before the gates of the Belvedere, she asked me, "Where is your husband?"

"He is at his office. He never knows when he can leave so I came ahead."

This seemed to satisfy her and we were all silent as we stepped into the hall. A row of doormen were taking the coats and umbrellas and helping with the rubbers of the steadily increasing crowd of officers and civilians. "I hope we are early," Countess Rose asked one of the men. "The Marshal has not as yet come in, my lady," he respectfully replied.

Waiters were passing tea as we entered the drawing room. The guests stood in groups — the military men had congregated in one room, while the writers and politicians had taken possession of another. Anieluszia immediately joined the literary group and as soon as Countess Rose seated herself on a sofa, several young men from the Foreign Office came and paid her their respects. I stood back by the door waiting for John, where I could watch the arrivals. Each dropped his calling card in a large dish before entering the drawing rooms. Some greeted the footman familiarly; all had been there before. The hallway and drawing rooms were furnished with soldierly simplicity and the waxed floors shone in the lamplight. While I was still standing by the door, the Marshal came in. Though he was as erect as ever, he seemed to have shrunk in stature and his clothes hung more loosely than the previous winter. His piercing eyes under the heavy eyebrows showed signs of the crushing strain under which he was working. He moved with simple dignity, greeting his guests with kindness. He spoke a few words with each group as he passed around the room and sat down by Countess Rose for ten minutes. With every move he made it clear he neither expected nor would have enjoyed adulation. Then before John had arrived, he went into the room where the officers were standing and soon passed out of sight. Every unassuming gesture had shown his great distinction and as I watched him, I knew some day he too would be called father of his country.

In 1926 Pilsudski had returned to Warsaw to help organize the country he had fought to establish. During the five years after the end of the Bolshevik war, the Constitution had proved itself ineffectual. The relations between President Paderewski and his ministers was ill-defined; consequently the authority dissipated, the value of currency was undermined and the army became disorganized. After Paderewski resigned, several others tried to form governments, none of which had strength equal to the situation.

Under the circumstances, Pilsudski was convinced that the country needed a strong democratic constitution and at the risk of being called a dictator, he assumed authority until the

146

new constitution was formulated by the Polish Senate and adopted by popular referendum. Having no political ambition, he preferred to be Commander-in-Chief of the Army and, under the authority of the President, Marshal Pilsudski carried the title of Chief of Staff until the day of his death.

CHAPTER *10*

*T*HE two years between our return from Geneva and our post in Vienna were the happiest in my life. Everywhere in Poland they were years of fruition. By 1935, after 15 years of autonomy, the country really seemed firmly established. The more Germany was occupied with internal revolution, the greater our sense of security. At last the world would realize that Stresemann and Brüning had only created a façade to hide the deeply bellicose nature of the German people. Perhaps an anti-German League could be formed now that Hitler and the Germans openly sponsored a violent cause. Pilsudski instructed his ministers abroad to sound out foreign opinion and he himself did not vacillate to placate Hitler. Menaced by the German effort to take over the Danzig defenses, he ordered general mobilization of Poland. The Germans, not yet ready to fight, offered their apologies and a ten-year guarantee of peace. Ten years, we believed, would be time enough to organize world opinion. Yet everywhere we were told, "Hitler won't last a year." Whether in France, Italy, Britain or the United States, everyone said, "German public opinion won't stand him."

John would reply, "Don't delude yourself. Hitler is there to stay." It was clear to him the British wanted a strong government in Germany. Even he believed that statesmen would be sensible enough to form a common front against Hitler. Germany would not attack a united Europe.

If we were over-confident and lulled by false security, it was because apparently the Germans had backed down over Danzig. Though we knew that alone Poland was no match

148

for them, we were confident the world stood solidly behind us against German armed aggression.

In Warsaw those friends who, when we first knew them, lived in miserable tumbled-down houses, had now found apartments in the many new buildings that so completely changed the aspect of the city. They were busy furnishing their new quarters from the many shops which sold the textiles and pottery, hand-woven rugs and furniture cleverly designed by the art students. Along all the old business streets, these new shops had sprung up overnight. An air of well-being spread over the whole city. It was very rare to see an old woman under her steamer rug. In 1935 the working people wore silk stockings and fancy shoes and were better dressed than many of the officials whom I first met in Warsaw in 1925. That spring dressmakers had more orders than they could fill. My tailor was too busy to promise me a new costume before the summer. The street of milliners had overflowed into a whole section, and even peasants wore hats in the city.

The old aristocratic group was no longer in control of society. Warsaw was breaking into cliques. Little by little the ministries had dropped men with title and taken on "new blood." An aristocrat was at a disadvantage — those with titles were rarely promoted. Prince L. joined the Jesuits, Stas went back to farming, Witek went into law. Finding no place in government service, many of those with the most ancient names went into business. Prince S. sold coal ; Count A. went into the steel business ; Baron P. sold automobiles. Only the very modern-minded of the gentry survived the pressure of this crisis. It was only when they had made a place in business that they were offered a small restricted post in government service. In every office were new faces. They were self-made men whose father had been a labor leader or a waiter, a carter, or a peasant. These men were distrustful of past leaders, and were the product and the proof of Poland's new democracy.

Such changes greatly enlarged the circle of our acquaintances. While in Geneva we had met the generals and military experts sent out to the Disarmament Conference, and now through them other officers of the General Staff. They asked us to their houses, to meet their plump wives from the country towns, newly come to Warsaw, who loved dancing and were excellent bridge players.

During these years my husband's work in the Foreign Office consisted in preparing the groundwork for a Baltic Union with Estonia, Latvia, and Finland and, it was hoped by many far-seeing people, with Lithuania. Everyone, even the simplest peasants could tell you that the day would come when Poland would once more join in confederation with all those states forming the triagle between the Baltic Sea, the Black Sea and the Mediterranean. These are the states which Russia considers as her west wall and Germany her natural region of expansion.

My husband worked by day and at night searching for a sound working basis that would make the Baltic countries inter-dependent.

By mutual guarantees, the new Baltic Treaty was to be based on reciprocal trade agreements. But many such obstacles stood in the way! All three countries had agricultural exports — each being rich in timber and flax. All three countries needed capital and machine-made products. In the past journalists had repeatedly asked, "Why can't Poland live with her neighbors?" Here at last was proof that we could. How secure we began to feel. This would be an answer to France and her Russian alliance; France who had never treated us as an ally but only as a tool; who expected us to promise to attack Germany if she were attacked, but refused to give us the same protection. Now we were no longer what the European press spoke of as one of the French "vassal States."

The day that Poland signed the treaty of mutual guarantee with the Baltic States, was a day of popular rejoicing. Miss "Book" had tears in her eyes when she described the excitement among the children and the other teachers. They had been allowed to go to the great square to see the Baltic emissaries put wreaths on the grave of the Unknown Soldier.

After the ceremony, schools had been closed. "No one could work on such a day as this," she said. "Poland was growing in prestige and honor. We may not live to see it but surely once more Poland would lead the Slav States from the Baltic to the Black Sea."

"But will the Germans let you ?" I asked.

"In 1410, we beat them at Grunwald, and in 1917 — we beat them again. We are twice as strong as they are — because we are united."

"The Germans are so much more powerful," I said.

"Now England and America will stop lending money to Germany," she stated naïvely. "Instead they may lend some of it to us. A Polish firm has sold a half million hams to America — can you believe it ?" She spoke with as much pride as if she were the sole benefactor.

It was impossible to explain to any Pole how much less Americans knew of them than they knew of America, if only through the cinema.

"But Wilson gave us his support," she answered, as if to prove I was wrong.

"That was solely due to the personal influence of Paderewski," I tried ineffectually to explain. . . .

In working on the Baltic Treaty, we had been forced to remain in Warsaw for two years. John felt he was growing stale and losing his perspective. When the Librarian of the new Polytechnique Library asked him to prepare a bibliography of current studies on currency, banking and economics, John seized this excuse to leave for Paris and consult the Bibliothèque Nationale. "Paris for Easter and summer vacation in England at the British Museum," John had said, "and I can find out what's been written in the last two years."

But when we returned from Paris we found on John's desk urgent messages from the Foreign Office to report at once.

"I may be late for lunch. You know the Foreign Office," was John's comment on leaving the house.

This was a clear April morning, the sun filled our living room and I opened the French windows which gave out on the courtyard.

"It's so warm the baby can be out," I said to the nurse. "Take out his pen."

I began tugging at the branches from the rose bed. The roses were sprouting blanched leaves under the heavy hemlock boughs.

"Come help me." I called Edward, our house-boy, but Makowska heard me. Taking the initiative, she soon had the beds cleared, and a great heap of boughs filled the courtyard.

"It looks so bare, *Pani* should plant primroses," she insisted. "I can get them on the Place of the Three Crosses. I saw women with baskets this morning — shall I go?"

"Tomorrow then — you will be late with the luncheon," I scolded her. But at the thought of the primroses I called the dog and ran out to the Place of the Three Crosses. On the south side women with baskets were screaming — "Lemons 10 groszy — lemons 10 groszy — lemons . . ."

"Have you seen primroses?"

"Lemons — ten groszy."

I pushed my way among the throng to the crossing. There the flower woman was putting up her stall and setting out her potted hydrangeas.

A woman with a big basket poked me in the back as she dove for the first courtyard. Turning I saw just in time that she had primroses. I ran after her but she had vanished. There was no one in the large empty courtyard. As I came out at the gate a policeman passed me. He too was looking for her. I pushed on along the square buying some blue hepaticas and little wood anemones rolled up in a corner of newspaper. But there were no primroses — only lemons, ten groszy. I came back past the doorway as the woman with the primroses was coming out.

"You have primroses? How much?"

"I have no license. I don't dare sell them."

I lifted the linen towel that covered the basket. "Follow me," I begged her, "I live nearby."

"How many does the lady want?" she asked cautiously.

"How much are they?" I asked.

"25 groszy the piece," she said crossly.

152

"Colossal price !" I said. "I will take them all at 10 groszy the piece."

"Fifteen," she replied lamely.

"They aren't worth that — I will take them all, but at 10."

"Good."

Every time I looked back she was following at some distance. As I reached the house she had quickened her pace and was abreast of me. As usual, Makowska was hanging out of the kitchen window. Not too politely she said, "So Madame went to town."

"Yes, I have some primroses."

"Bring them up," she commanded the woman.

"Didn't the lady buy them for herself ?"

Edward was walking up and down by the front door in his white linen coat. "Master has telephoned he will be late."

"What time did he say ?" I asked.

"Not before three. Madame is not to wait."

Andrew was having his lunch, blowing his spinach in great puffs about his room. His nurse was bobbing about with a napkin saying, "He is so naughty because he heard you coming." The sun came in both windows. Someone in the next garden was singing and above all there was the continuous roar of aeroplanes.

Lunch was announced. In the dining room the door to the pantry was still open. Makowska and the flower woman were counting the plants. Makowska's voice was high, "It 's a shame the Madame lets herself be cheated like this with all the primroses in Poland to be had."

I rang. "Don't announce lunch till you are ready to serve it," I said crossly.

Makowska was wreathed in smiles. "For Madame's homecoming there are veal cutlets, the first radishes, and green salad is already in — though very dear."

After lunch I lay down on the sofa in the living room while waiting for John to come home. I lay facing the light to see out of the window into the clear blue sky, so blue after the haze of Paris. How thrilling it had been to cross the Polish frontier into this country in the making — so young and vital, yet with such high standards of the past achievements — a country made and built up by a great family of people who had always been too generous with their leaders, even those who had made the most fatal mistakes. Every time we crossed the frontier we wept with joy to see the growing prosperity of our country, the weedless fields, the small cement houses, the tile roofs, which were replacing the log cabins buried under thatch ; the five million acres which by Land Reform had been given to the peasants ; the eight hundred and fifty thousand buildings which housed eight and a half million people — the little towns where sewage pipes were being laid — the swamps criss-crossed with new draining ditches. As the train sped across the great plain, we hugged each other for joy that Poland was no longer grey and poor.

Through the open door I could hear the servants laughing in the kitchen. They were the house, but they were pleased to have me in it and proud of Andrew too. They were determined to make him a very great Pole. They would bring him up to be "President of Poland" — or "Bishop of Warsaw" ! As I lay before our fireplace, I felt the warm protection of such devotion. When Edward came in to take my coffee cup, he chatted, "Prince Zdislaw is building — over there. They say Cziczewski from Silesia has bought next door. The house across the street will be finished soon."

The bell rang. It was not John, only the courier of the French Embassy leaving a card. His Excellency, the Ambassador of France and Madame Laroche — for M. Laval on 12 May, 1935. I took the card to my desk and began opening the mail which had come in our absence. An "at home" at the Greek Minister's for that very afternoon ; lunch with His Excellency, the Minister for Belgium on Thursday — I must telephone at once to explain the delay in answering ; dinner and soirée at the Swedish Legation on Monday ; a note from Savery welcoming us home — John will want to call him as soon as he returns from the Ministry ; Friday a reception for M. Laval at the Ministry of Foreign Affairs. I had just finished when I heard John at the door.

154

"Guess what it is all about."

I couldn't.

"Vienna.   They want me to report there this week."

"This week !"

"I wish we didn't have to leave Warsaw, but both Tadzio and Pawel consider I must.   The Ministry would take it badly if I didn't accept."

"What will the work be ?"

"It 's a special mission.   They want a report on the economic situation of the Danubian countries and the possibility of forming a Danubian Economic Bloc."

"These cards that have come in . . ."

"Answer them — you can go alone."

"How long are we to be separated ?"

"As long as it will take you to pack."

"Do we take the furniture ?"

"Better not.   A moving is as bad as a fire in the house."

"Then I can pack in two or three days.   Can't you wait to begin your work next Monday ?"

"I am late already.   I should have begun working to-day."

"Have you had your lunch — it 's nearly four."

"No time.   Having seen the chief of the Western Division, this means I leave the Eastern.   I signed up with the personnel office and had my new passport made out.   I had to get photographs made up in a photomat, and while waiting for one and another I saw Pawel and Tadzio.   We will wait to telephone the family this evening ; I have a few people I must see at once."

"Is your mission a secret or can I tell everyone ?"

"It 's official, but wait till I have left tomorrow."

Salary ? — baggage ? — trains !   My mind was like a pinwheel spinning out of control.   "Makowska !" I called. "Take all the linens to the sewing room where I can sort them out and have the trunks brought out and cleaned.   We are leaving for Vienna."

"Better take a week to pack calmly," John urged.   "I will come back next week-end and fetch you.   Perhaps we can

155

drive there by car. Go to the Buick Agency and see at what rate you can trade in the old car and order the international tryptich made out at the Automobile Club. You will need to get passports for the servants and Andrew, unless the Americans will let you put him on your passport."

"You know they won't."

"Well, you can try. He's only a baby. Then you could try to rent our apartment — call in Pentkowski. Now I must run."

While he was out I feverishly went over in my mind the things I must do. I tore up the letters I had just written and telephoned the Legations. "Do come alone." — Alone ! — would I have the courage to enter a salon alone ? — without John's supporting arm ? I had watched women enter drawing rooms alone, always a pace too fast or too slow. They showed their self-consciousness either by too great self-assurance or too painful timidity. It was a question of age — the young were always conspicuously graceless, and not even all the older ladies had poise.

Between telephone calls I made lists on one column of things to take and on another of things to be left. There was a separate sheet of items to be attended to in town.

That evening, on the way to the station John gave final instructions. I was to prepare the list of names and addresses where cards should be sent, marking by each name how many cards were to be left with the corner turned down and the P.P.C. in the corner. The French Embassy Ball was to be Sunday. Most of our friends would surely be there ; we would then tell them good-bye.

A week later John returned for the reception for Laval at the Becks'. There was a tremendous number of people crowded into the four or five drawing rooms. We worked our way through the first two rooms crowded with diplomats to the third room where members of the Foreign Office were talking in close groups.

"Pilsudski is very ill ; the doctor from Vienna has been summoned."

"No one knows exactly what it is."

156

"They say he is so shrunk in size."

"That means cancer."

"Perhaps he can be operated on, it need not be fatal."

Mr. Beck was standing in the center of the room where everyone could have a word with him. His mask-like face showed none of the strain of the importance of this occasion. No one looking at him could have guessed Laval had refused Poland equivocal support in any future war with Germany.

"I thought you were in Vienna," he told us.

"I am here for only three days, Mr. Minister. I am going back to Vienna with my family on Monday."

"How are you?" he spoke graciously as each person entered the room, and without listening further, passed them on to someone else.

Laval's visit was being discussed in undertones. "He has an arrangement with Russia in his pocket," someone said.

"We can't agree," John replied, "to Russian occupation of Poland if Germany should attack France."

Someone else suggested, "The Russians will attack us anyway; they want a common frontier with Czechoslovakia; better give them some of the southern Carpathians on condition they don't take more."

"Appetite comes with eating; give them some they will take more."

"It 's a question of strategy — how can the country best be defended ?"

"Bukowina could never be held."

"Our only real protection is the Pinsk (Pripet) Marshes. Napoleon learned their strategic value," with a laugh.

"The sooner Poland shakes free of France, the better. The French take, but they give nothing." There was little enthusiasm for Laval's mission.

On Saturday we sent off our trunks by express. The house looked forlorn and bare, and even flowers could not hide the chill emptiness. Though the packing had been done downstairs, there was a sense of excitement and perpetual disorder in all the rooms. Saturday passed in a frenzy of trips to the station, to the bank, and to Cook's.

Every acquaintance we met would say, "Congratulations on your appointment."

"We really regret leaving Poland just now."

"You are so lucky — all the same I wish I were leaving."

"What is the news of the Marshal ?"

"You have heard the doctor came from Vienna ?"

"Father says it is cancer ; he is shrunken beyond recognition."

"Cancer ! What a catastrophe, if anything happened to the Marshal !"

The Sunday crowds were gaily dressed in new straw hats and light spring suits, though a wintry wind howled through the half-opened leaves. We pushed our way among the loiterers strolling on the Place of the Three Crosses and the Aleja. Unlike everyone else, who was showing off his fine new clothes, we were in a hurry. We had to say "good-bye" to all our family, a duty left to the final day.

"What is said in town about the health of the Marshal ?"

"Tell us the latest news."

"It may drag on for months, but he is a sick man."

"You will enjoy Vienna, it is such a beautiful city. When I was young I knew many people there ; I must look through my address book and send you letters."

"Good-bye, dear aunt — till we meet again."

"Yes — till we meet again — perhaps not on this earth."

"Surely this is not good-bye — this is only till we meet again. We will write."

"Yes, write often."

Tony and Tadzio were coming for dinner — to go with us to the French Embassy Ball. At home order had been restored. Our clothes were laid out, neatly pressed, — on the dresser was the box of fresh flowers John never failed to remember.

"Darling, the wind has blown your hair out of place."

"Does it look hopeless ? That is the worst of a Sunday reception, you can't get to a hair-dresser."

"Perhaps Makowska can help you."

"Let 's not call Makowska," I pleaded. "Our last evening
158

in this house.   How I hate to leave home.   I feel sad with premonition."

"Are you afraid of the riots in Vienna ?   The shooting of Dollfuss left the city more peaceful than ever."   As usual, John tried to calm me.   "The German putsch was a failure."

"I feel uneasy all the time, a black premonition."   My eyes burned and for the moment the whole future seemed very obscure.

Before we had finished dressing there was a knock at the door.   "Mr. Count has arrived.   He is in the room of Andrew."

The cold morning wind had died down, the evening air was soft and still.   Arc lights, veiled by the trees, set off the streets like a stage.   As we sauntered over to the French Embassy, we joined with others also sauntering in evening dress. All the streets surrounding the Embassy were filled with smooth moving, gaily dressed crowds like the Harlequins of another epoch, like a scene from Watteau.

"Was Laval impressed by what he saw ?" each asked.

"Will France now give up her Russian dreams ?" someone else remarked hopefully.

"What a lovely evening for a party, not a cloud in the sky."

"There will be champagne until morning."

"We must be late, some people are leaving already."

"That is strange, it is only 9:30."

Then meeting one of those who was leaving the French Embassy — "Have you heard the news ?   Pilsudski has just died — only ten minutes ago."

"It is not possible.   *Boze !*   Our poor country."

"*Straszne !   Straszne !*"

"How terrible."

"What will become of Poland ?"

"Poor Poland !"

We had moved nearer and by now we were standing before the very door of the Embassy. A string of open *dorozki* that had brought guests were still loitering by the curb.

"What does the lady say ?"

"Not our Marshal !"

"I marched with him. What a leader !"

"Now our poor country will face calamity."

"Yes, the Germans will come now."

"What do you say — the Marshal does not live !"

"Does not live — Holy God !"

"What a catastrophe for Poland."

Tears ran down the cheeks of the cab driver and of the taxi chauffeur who had joined us.

"Our poor country — our poor country — Holy God."

"No one can take his place."

"No one."

Now around the French Embassy a great crowd had quietly gathered as the terrible news pierced deeper and deeper into it. As a foretaste of the doom to follow, the whole street filled with tearful people whose one and only thought was that Poland had lost her leader and her security. The frightened people roamed the streets unable to quiet the anxiety of their hearts. A moan of lament rose softly in the night from those who could find no place of rest, peace or safety.

By the next day the heartbroken people were given "something to do." They formed in line and filed past the bier on which Pilsudski was lying in state, they left wreaths on the steps of the Belvedere where he had lived. Children walked in to the city from the outlying villages. The main streets were roped off for the delegations marching on foot and the only automobiles which circulated carried frenzied officials from one government office to another. All the length and breadth of the city, every street was crammed with a seething crowd pushing its way down towards the cathedral or back to the Belvedere. The people were as numb and cold as they were sorrowful. Wild rumors of German invasion spread through the crowd, filling the hearts with panic. When the Germans neglected this golden opportunity to strike, the people believed that the Polish Army truly must be a mighty force.

By the time Pilsudski was laid in state in Cracow, the country had regained confidence in their army and their government. It had lost that utter, absolute unity which the past days of danger had given them — and began once more to complain about the funeral, and bicker over the new Minister with the complacence of security. We had gone to Cracow for the funeral. We had watched the procession of tanks and anti-aircraft guns, the motorized field radios and telephones, and had been amazed at the extent of the motorized equipment.

"The Czechoslovakian soldier is more smartly dressed," the American military attaché whispered to me, "but those motorized field radios are something very new."

"Do you really think the Polish Army is good?" I begged.

"If it weren't, Germany and Russia would have divided it long ago. Still in the long run it isn't enough — Poland is indefensible."

"You don't really mean it," I said desperately.

"I most certainly do. Poland hasn't a prayer the day Germany and Russia get together. The Army will be squeezed in a nutcracker."

"The Polish soldier is hard and enduring."

"Bravery and mechanized equipment aren't enough with production and supplies cut off. Come now, you don't really think Poland can survive?" he said. "The day the Germans and Russians move in here there is nothing the Poles can do."

"You will see," I said with bravado. His pessimism I took for defeatism. "You have something to see," I insisted. "Every man, woman and child will stand."

CHAPTER *11*

WE LEFT for Vienna in an optimistic mood because Germany had not broken her treaty and seized Poland at once.   We felt there was still time to solidify our resources within the country and strengthen our political ties, by closer alliance without.   The Polish General Staff decided to move all vital industries back from the Silesian frontier.   It chose that farming section where there was the greatest over-population.   It was in the center of the country and of the new railroad system.   It was hoped that this triangle could be defended from all sides.   Their decision was criticized by the businessmen, for heavy industry had all been organized about coal pits in the Silesian mines on the German frontier.

John was sent to Vienna to prepare the economic foundation of a Danubian League, like the alliance Poland had made with the Baltic States.   He was attached to the Polish Legation in Vienna with the special mission of making an economic survey of all the Danubian countries.   This was to be the foundation of a special trade treaty between Poland, Austria, Hungary, Czechoslovakia, Yugoslavia, Bulgaria, and Rumania, as it had with the three Baltic countries of Latvia, Estonia and Lithuania.   The Eastern European Bloc of ten, stretching from the Baltic to the Black Sea, was to be bound by such mutually beneficial economic ties that political unity would inevitably follow.   In his report to the Polish Foreign Office John based his study on fundamentals of area, population, agricultural production, of wood and metal industries, of transportation and the finances of the region.   He made a statistical study of the capacities to grow grains, corn and rice, potatoes, sugar and flax, and tobacco, wine and beer, live-stock and its products, coal, iron and steel and other metals. Czechoslovakia, he found, held a traditionally important place not only among Danubian but European countries because of its production of glass and china. It was a natural leader due to the intelligent organization of the Bata shoe industry which played an important role in Czech exports.

A large part of the Austrian exports depended on the development of its luxury trade in high class leather goods and men and women's clothes, and its tourist resorts brought in foreign exchange. He analyzed production in every country, giving tables and statistical charts to substantiate each point.

Going on into the question of transportation, he found that Czechoslovakia and Austria had sufficient railroad lines. Some lines could even be demolished because of the new express highways. Though Hungary had enough railways, her highways were insufficient. In the three southern states, however, the railroads inherited from the old Austro-Hungarian Empire were completely inadequate to the economic needs of the countries and did not correspond to the real lines of communication. In Bessarabia, for instance, lines led to Odessa, and the northern Rumanian lines converged on Budapest. In Yugoslavia, the Vienna-Budapest-Belgrade-Constantinople line ran counter to all possible logical needs of the country. The connecting of Belgrade with the wonderful natural harbor of Spalato had to be made by the new state.

But the really important line of communication, he found, for this whole region was the Danube, with its tributaries. Practically the whole oil of Rumania was transported up the river — as were potatoes from the three southern states — while Germany and Czechoslovakia filled the ships with coal on the down voyage.

The international crisis had hit the Danubian countries as everywhere else abroad. New capital rebuilt factories destroyed in the previous war as well as new factories which the post-war frontiers made possible. New capital, though

163

large in extent, was charged at a very high rate of interest. Because of the high rate of interest, costs of production were so high that products could not be bought generally, and industry was a great drain on these countries. High costs kept down the standard of life and in turn restricted the volume of internal markets. Then foreign capital ceased coming and it is a fact that the Danubian countries — new countries — could not pay their old debts without incurring new ones. Foreign capital invested in 1929, he said, "will be found to be lost."

The run of creditors on these countries first hit the agriculturists, who had to throw in their gold savings. This weakened the finances of these countries and in turn foreign creditors lost confidence in the Viennese through whom the loans were made. The run of great international capitalists on the Viennese banks started a run of the Austrian depositors. In the summer of 1937 the Austrians were forced to pass laws protecting their credit on the one hand and on the other hand to call in the League of Nations for assistance. The Hungarians, who also had many foreign loans, followed by 'freezing credits.' Thus the banks of Rumania, Yugoslavia and Bulgaria were paralyzed. In all four agricultural countries a grave fall of prices followed. All four had to adopt radical agrarian laws. In all four countries, following the agrarian reforms, savings banks then showed a slow rise — though these countries were far from coming out of the crisis before the present war.

John was still compiling statistics for his report to the Foreign Office, when on Sunday morning the Polish Legation learned from the newspapers that the German Government had given a protective guarantee to the Austrian frontiers. He dashed back to tell me that the staff was in utter consternation.

"The Minister certainly was stunned," he said. "He had boasted for a long time that Von Papen never saw anyone in the Foreign Office without sending him a memorandum."

"What does it all mean?" I asked. "It sounds harmless."

"There must be much more than appears on the surface or

we would have had a copy of the note at least twenty-four hours ahead."

"This will be a blow to our Minister's prestige with Warsaw."

"I only hope it wakes him up to the caliber of Von Papen."

"Everyone says 'Von Papen is only a tool,'" I repeated what I had so often heard.

"That doesn't make Von Papen any less dangerous. He escaped being purged by a fluke, and now he is like butter in Hitler's hands."

"He looks like such a gentleman, like a picture of Washington, and his wife and daughters seem so innocuous," I ventured. I could picture the three ladies in my mind's eye as I had seen them under such different circumstances. We were on the "first" list of the German Legation and were invited to all the German functions. Madame von Papen often asked us informally to tea and to join them on picnics. She was a faded broomstick of a woman. She and her two ageless daughters appeared to be the quintessence of the old-fashioned German aristocracy of another age. Modern dresses hung shapelessly from their shoulders. Their long white kid gloves and fans, the little ostrich feathers and the little lockets they often wore, baubles of the Eighteenth Century, were the only objects that fitted them. Even when they went on a picnic they looked as if they had stepped from the frame of an old pastel. In birdlike voices they tittered and chattered, happily agreeing to the most contradictory statements. At church they were always in the front row oblivious of everyone around them. Dressed in plain black, they knelt through the entire service. Could these pious women be the conscious accomplices of the most dangerous envoy in Hitler's galaxy? It was far pleasanter to believe that both the Von Papens and the good-natured Prince and Princess Erbach, Councilor of the Legation, then learning how to betray Greece in the capacity of Minister to that country, were simple county gentry serving their Governments. It was, however, impossible to drown out the persistent question, "Can anyone work for Hitler without having sold himself to

Hitler? No man can serve two masters. Hitler must be sure of them or they would not be here." I had to make myself believe this as I searched in vain for something to dislike in their disarmingly affable personalities.

The Polish Minister left for Warsaw in the evening to try and explain, not only what the new situation in Austria would mean to Poland, but how it was that Von Papen, his oft-vaunted close friend, had delivered the note without at the same time sending him a memorandum explaining it.

John considered the note to be an answer to the Polish effort to form a customs union with the Danubian States. He cancelled his proposed visits to Rumania and Bulgaria and decided instead to send in his report to the Polish Government as fast as possible. "Travelling about is fun, but what I did last year is enough," he said. "Now there is no time to be lost."

Although he was already depressed by the lack of time and sense of emergency, many of his friends and colleagues took the German note at its full value. After puzzling over the idea of issuing a unilateral declaration, they dismissed it as a face-saving effort on the part of Hitler, who evidently had renounced the notion of the Anschluss.

Not so the Czechoslovakian Minister, Mr. Frülinger. On the following day, Monday, he invited the members of the Little Entente and Polish Legation for luncheon. Very informally, about the luncheon table, problems connected with defense were discussed. The Czechs saw real threat of danger in the proclamation. Even then it was apparent that by making Austria neutral, Hitler had blocked the passage of Yugoslav troops to Czechoslovakia, according to the original plan of the Little Entente. If the Austrians would not allow passage of Yugoslav troops to aid in the defense of Czechoslovakia, we had to consider alternate routes. While the ladies withdrew to another room, the men hung over a map, tracing roads down through Rumania which the Yugoslavs would thus be forced to use, adding at least five more days before effective aid could arrive. Someone calculated how far German tanks could travel in five days. It was clear that help would not arrive soon enough to prevent the fall of Prague, and that the line of the Warsaw-Vienna Railway would be the place for a stand. Though everyone realized that Austria and Hungary could not be depended upon, the rest of the Little Entente seemed firm.

After the gentlemen had finished their conference, they joined us in the very room in which Beethoven had first conducted his symphonies to his patron, Loepkowitz. It was a two-storied, vaulted room with Baroque frescoes on walls and ceiling. Sprawling figures pulled aside looped curtains to show the heavenly blue sky and floating clouds. Like nearly all old palaces from Rome to Warsaw it had been rented out, and the family lived in a few rooms in a remote back wing.

John whispered, "Private capitalists haven't built a monument equal to this. They tear down as fast as they build. Why haven't they mastered a style and put their stamp on it for future generations to admire ?"

The other guests had risen and were waiting their turn to take leave of our host. When it came our time, Mr. Frülinger said to my husband, "Tell your Minister how sorry I am he could not be here. We will be seeing you very soon again, it 's always so easy to talk to you."

"It 's a privilege to be here," John replied with great conviction ; and as we went down the great round stairs, "Frülinger is one of the biggest men in Central Europe." Shortly after this luncheon he was recalled as Secretary of State of Czechoslovakia, and then sent as Minister to Moscow, where he remains today.

Out on the street the air was soft. "Shall we walk home ?"

"Let 's."

"Is war so imminent ?" I asked.

"You heard the report of the American Military Attaché just back from Berlin — unimaginable re-arming in every line. War will come within the next few years unless . . ."

"Unless ?"

"Unless we find more than just a formula for uniting the Eastern States, and get guarantees from England."

"England will never give them."

"You sound so positive. All the Czechs are more friendly of late," I said.

"They are always charming as individuals. The Government is constantly blackmailed by the French, who do everything in their power to prevent the formation of the Agrarian Bloc."

"But I should think it was to French advantage to have a strong Eastern alliance."

"If the Eastern Bloc were united they would become too strong and independent for the French. They are afraid we would slip out of their grasp."

"Are the Germans sincere about backing the Bloc?"

"It's an anti-French coalition obviously, and they hope to win the agricultural states into their orbit. That is why I don't like this statement of Hitler's yesterday."

"So many people think it means peace."

"I think it is the beginning of the Anschluss. What is the idea of guaranteeing neutrality if there aren't strings to it?"

"You are the perpetual pessimist."

"So everyone else says. But the first fruits are clear; to-day the Austrians were afraid to go into a real protective alliance with Czechoslovakia."

"Will Poland?"

"Surely, if the Czechs wish it. They prefer their alliances with Russia and France. Unfortunately they put all their faith in the big powers. You will see that they will get nothing more out of France than Poland did. Has France ever once in any treaty promised to come to the aid of the Eastern States? She has not. She expects us all to sign the Locarno Treaty, but refuses to make a treaty of mutual guarantee."

"Don't the Czechs have a secret clause?"

"Only the Russo-French treaty. In case France is attacked, Russia can occupy Czechoslovakia, like the treaty we wouldn't sign."

"Do you really believe the attack will be to the East?"

"Absolutely. No one doubts it."

"Except the French."

"Yes, the French."

"But why? The French are stronger, and why should Germany leave the stronger army at her rear?"

"For the very reason that if the French won't guarantee our frontier she obviously won't move unless she is actually attacked."

We were walking along the Ring now, and across it towards the Argentinerstrasse where we lived, in the house next door to the Legation. It was a warm spring day, and along the sidewalks every seat was taken in the enclosures of the café houses.

"Vienna still seems like an outpost of ancient Rome; the physique of the people . . ."

"Yes, and in the Aurelian philosophy of 'live and let live.'"

"That is why I don't understand Dr. Lempke being a Nazi."

"It's because he is convinced that after the Anschluss, Austria will conquer Germany."

"Well, why is Prince Liechtenstein a Nazi? What can the aristocracy get out of Hitlerism? I understand why all innkeepers are Nazi; they look for trade. But the aristocracy — ?"

"You heard Johnny say it's being abreast of the times. The aristocracy lost out in the French Revolution; they want to play winner this time."

"Austria wouldn't really join Germany of her own volition?"

"Not now. Her gold reserves are so much greater than Germany's; but if they can make a deal with the German Government they would find large popular support."

"I know. I was astonished that the neighboring shopkeepers near Aunt Marylka's in Corinthia were such outspoken Nazis. I don't see how they can patronize such people."

"Well, what about the sons and daughters of Countess Serrthoss? They went across the line to vote for Hitler a few weeks ago."

"Their mother is an American, too."

We said nothing as we walked across the Karlsplatz, feeling for the hundredth time that we belonged to another gen-

169

eration. We couldn't laugh with Carlo when he told about giving castor oil to the Italian liberals. We still clung to a definite moral code — yet how many of our diplomatic acquaintances laughed at us and believed a compromise with Fascism was inevitable in this changing world.

Suddenly John spoke. "There simply is no time to lose. I could get my report done if I were alone and didn't have to be tied down to coming home for meals and evenings, and if I didn't have to take a vacation this summer."

"How much have you still to do?"

"I don't know. But if I were alone — "

"You don't really mean you want me to go away. You have never said I interrupted your work before," I said, feeling quite desperate. "Have I ever mentioned your being late for meals?"

"No," he said very gently. "Even so, the idea that I have to turn up inevitably breaks into my time."

"You know I'll do what you want."

"Well then, take Andrew to Cracow so that I can get the report done. I may bring part of it on ahead, since I don't trust it to mail or to the pouch. The sooner you go, the quicker it will be finished."

CHAPTER *12*

*T*HE day train to Cracow left Vienna at nine in the morning, and during the long hot day it crossed the Moravian plain. On every siding were flat cars piled with war materials which kept Andrew running from one side of the train to the other.

"See the big cannon, Mummy ! See the big tank !"

All day long there was no keeping him quiet.

"Andrzej," he said in Polish, "wants to look — wants to see the big guns."

Here and there a few soldiers were on guard at way stations ; but most of the trains had no guards. There was no indication on the cars of the destination of the guns. Nor did any of the passengers turn to look. From time to time we stopped beside a train going in the opposite direction. It was often said the Czechs were wasting no money building new rolling stock that would fall into the hands of the Germans. Most of these local trains had the old-fashioned short wooden cars with exaggeratedly large open platforms like toys.

"Funny train !" he said. "Andrzej's not sleepy. Andrzej sees a funny train !"

The thick June hay was cut and drying in the peaceful summer sun. Women were slowly sweeping the rolling fields clean while men stacked the hay in neat piles.

At every station our carriage would empty out and new passengers would fill it up, women in heavy skirts and blouses, men in old-fashioned green woolen suits. The Czechs were not 'smart,' but how neat and clean, each with

171

his one little leather suitcase ! Such a contrast to the Poles who you could always recognize travelling, by the many boxes and oversized suitcases. The Poles took possession of their seats with the air of habitual travellers, with rugs and pillows, drinking cups and towels, transforming their corner into a little bit of home.

At Cieszyn, the Polish frontier, the whole landscape changed. The big empty country was cut into small narrow strips of fields. New buildings crowded even to the frontier, and people, too, were everywhere. A procession of carts was strung along the highway, and there all about the country-side people seemed to be moving, and moving swiftly.

"*Polska*, — Andrzej's Poland," Andrew said to the customs men who went through the train carriage by carriage as it dashed on to Cracow.

"What is in that box ?"

"Food for the trip. I have a diplomatic pass."

"Open it," said the customs guard. "And in that bag ?"

"The baby's clothes — the nurse's — that is mine."

"Open the child's bag."

At the sound of Polish being spoken, the dog, who had crouched under the seat all day, came out and wagged his tail.

"You understand Polish ?" said the officer pleasantly. "Where are the dog's papers ?"

I got out the dog's pass, with all his visas and exits, his ticket, his health certificate.

"Much the dog has travelled," he said, saluting as he shut the door of our compartment.

The train was travelling much faster now. Once we had passed the Czech frontier it gathered up speed on the smoothly laid tracks. At seven we would be in Cracow. Soon the old chalk cliffs appeared on the horizon. The vast plain was now drained with neat ditches, stone at the bed and clipped grass on the rims. The tall wheat blew back as the train rushed by, and birds rose up, circling high in the evening sky.

"There," I told Andrew, "are the hills that Poppy loves
172

so. That ridge runs into Cracow. Now watch carefully for the *Kopiec* Pilsudski."

"What's a *Kopiec* ?"

"A hill dug up in memory of some person like that big mound you can see over there."

"Andrzej can make it."

"Not Andrzej — hundreds and hundreds of school children, and thousands of grown people from all Poland made it by filling wheelbarrows and mounding the earth."

"All Poland ? Why, there are two *Kopieccy* !"

"The other is the *Kopiec* Kosciusko. That was made a hundred years ago. Now you can see the Wawel, — that great castle covering the hill."

"Who lives there ?"

"The Polish king once lived there, seven hundred years ago."

"Is that long ago ?"

"See how lovely ! The Wawel !" That first glimpse of the spires gripped my throat so tightly I could not go on to explain what the Wawel meant to all Poles. "Now *Dziadzius* (the grandfather) will be waiting at the station looking at his watch every minute to see when Andrew is coming."

"And Babby (the grandmother) ?"

"*Babcia* is probably waiting in the garden, with a big sand-pile for Andrew."

"Why doesn't Babby come to the station ?"

"So as not to crowd the taxi."

"Why doesn't Babby have an auto ?"

"*Babcia* gives all her money to poor people, so that the poor people can have something to eat."

"How many poor people ?"

"Seven or eight thousand poor people. Look — there is *Dziadzius* right by our carriage." He seemed to know which car we would be in and was pointing us out to two porters. As the train drew in very quickly one had jumped into the carriage and was handing the baggage out to the other who stood under the open window. I handed Andrew through the window too. All the while Tatus was smiling and blowing kisses to Andrew. "*Dzien dobry*. Bon jour. *Dzien dobry*," he kept repeating until I descended, and then said, "Michael is in Cracow; he came down for the day to see you. Let us hurry. Mother will be impatiently waiting."

My father-in-law had a pass. Taking Andrew in his arms and leaving the maid and me to run after him as best we could, he led the porter with the wheelbarrow. We were the first out of the crowded station. There was something in his bearing that impelled the crowd to part before him. By the main entrance he had two taxis, already reserved, one for us and one for the maid and bags, and away we drove through narrow streets honking incessantly, the pedestrians scattering before us.

"You are very nervous," he remarked. "A few days' rest and you will be better."

"Even if it took but five minutes longer, Tatus, driving a bit more slowly would be so much pleasanter," I begged.

"This is a good driver. I always get him when I can."

As we rounded the corner of our street you could hear the two dogs barking. The curtains in the living room were parted where Mother was watching for our approach. Before we drove up to the house, the door opened and dogs and servants had come running out.

"You must see the roses," Tatus said, "before going upstairs."

"It's so late. Andrew is way past his bed time."

"Just once won't hurt him."

Mother was hugging us, drawing us toward the doors leading to the garden. The house was cool, almost cold. It had been closed up all the day, and the curtains were still drawn. But now the hot sweet air of the garden was rushing in through open doors that led out on to the terrace. On every table both in the hall and the drawing room were bouquets of flowers, hundreds of roses and great heads of peonies.

"How sweet everything smells! Strawberries! What wonderful ones this year!"

"This basket is only of pineapple strawberries. Try some.

174

They will be refreshing after the journey. This dish is just for Andrew, the latest from the garden."

"He is only three. He shouldn't eat so many !"

"From our garden ? How could they hurt him ? Were they bought, then you could never get them clean, even if they were washed in alcohol."

Andrew had run down the terrace steps, into the garden. "May I go on the grass ?" he called.

"What a poor city child !" the grandparents moaned.

He ran across the grass to the yellow roses which bordered the outer path around the garden and knelt down to smell one. *"Jakie ladne,"* "How lovely !" he said.

The grandfather melted in ecstasy. "That's surely my child !" he said. "Neither one of my own sons understands me as well as does my grandchild !"

Taking my arm he showed me which rose plants he had put in that spring.

"How many roses are there now altogether ?"

"Over a thousand plants, but there are only two hundred and eighty different kinds," he replied, but number meant little to him. "This new rose is French. Here is a new English variety — has a fine bud, but the head droops when it is full blown."

Andrew was jumping up and down, in the abandonment of joyous excitement.

"It's so lovely now but I must take him up. He will never get to sleep."

"The evening is the finest moment of the day," Tatus protested.

But Mulka gently intervened. "Andzia has everything ready for him, his bath and a little *kasza* and milk. Come and see if it is all as you wish it. His nurse can sleep in the little hall room. Is that alright ? I know you don't want anyone to sleep with him." As we were going upstairs, we would see the preparations made as a surprise for us : a new little table and chairs and many new additions to the toy shelf, a large wooden train, molds for the sand, pail and shovel,

175

and on the shelves of the wardrobe new bibs, in cross-stitched patterns of automobiles, aeroplanes and locomotives, designs for the modern mechanical child.

"Where did you find them ?"

"I drew them as best I could, but Andzia embroidered most of them."

"New suits !"

"Yes. These Tatus designed, with a high waistline. I tried to find material that would be cool in this heat."

On Andrew's tray was half a grapefruit.

"How in the world did you find that at this late season ?" I asked.

"Tatus found them. We knew Andrew liked grapefruit."

"But now there are garden fruits," I protested uselessly. Through the open door into my room I could see Andzia unpacking my bag. She said, "Supper will be served as soon as Madame is ready. Will you change ? Mulka had me put this kimono in your room, thinking you might like to wear it."

"I 'm not so hot really."

"It is just as the lady finds it convenient."

"It 's my hair that is so dirty from the journey !"

"Shall I wash it in the morning ?" she asked. "We have an electric drier, and Mulka has found a new hairdresser who arranges hair quite presentably."

"If it is sunny I could dry it in the sun in the garden beside Andrew."

"How Madame sits in the sun astonishes all of us."

There was a soft gong downstairs. Andzia said, "That is the supper. I will hear Andrew say his prayers."

"He doesn't know any yet."

"Not the Ave Maria ! Well, I will teach him."

"Come up after supper," Andrew called, "to see if I am asleep."

"Yes, sweet. Good night."

Downstairs it was really cool. I regretted not having my jacket, and said so.

"That is impossible," Tatus protested. "The heat is ter-

176

rific. It is 76 right now, and it must have been more than 80 this afternoon."

"In America —"

"Yes, I could hardly breathe," Mulka gasped at the recollection of her arrival in New York. "I never suffered so much in all my life."

"But Vichy is so hot. Will you go there this year?" I asked.

"Later, perhaps" — Tatus sounded uncertain. "We have applied for visas and money. With money restrictions travelling becomes impossible. You can't take the little trips which make it all worth while."

"Last year we went to Puy de Dome," Mulka said. "Did you see my photographs? This year we wanted to see the Cluniac churches in Bourgogne."

After their cure, every summer for a great many years Mulka and Tatus visited different provinces of France to see the Romanesque churches, which Mulka had carefully photographed. She had been quite a photographer in her youth and had developed and enlarged all her own photographs. Sometimes she used a double-lensed camera with plates to get a three-dimensional picture, but she had quite a collection of cameras and a wonderful collection of pictures of churches and details of carvings.

"What are your plans for the summer?" they both asked together.

"We can't make plans until John finishes his report. Then he should really take a rest. John hasn't had a vacation in three years, not really since we left Geneva. But I doubt he will go away this year. He is very apprehensive about Germany."

"England wouldn't let Germany start a war."

"John says, 'England underestimates Hitler.'"

"Do you really think Hitler amounts to something? Read his speeches. He is crazy. How can you take him seriously? He has no following."

"The danger is that everyone feels as you do."

"Public opinion nowadays —" Father began.

177

"Is powerless !" I interrupted bitterly.

"Let's not talk about politics," Mulka said. "It was so hot we thought that you would prefer cold chicken and salad. There are just strawberries for dessert. Do have some more bouillon."

When we were finished, a white oilcloth was put down on the floor and the dogs' bowls brought in. The moment dessert was served, they had waked from a deep oblivion as if by signal and had begun pacing about the dining room table.

"What creatures of habit. They are more regular than men," Tatus remarked. "As soon as they have finished they will stand by the pantry waiting for the tea tray so they can get their sugar. Then they race through the garden for half an hour. Like clock work, at nine they want to go into the front yard. At ten, if we have guests, they are unhappy because they can't go to bed. From ten o'clock on they tease to have their beds brought out."

We went into the dimly lighted library where tea was served. On the table was a pile of wool skeins. "How do you like this wool ?" Mulka asked. "I want to make Andrew a new suit."

"This is no moment for knitting," Tatus protested. "Lay down the new game of solitaire Mrs. Bienacka showed you."

"By the way, how are the ladies on your Committee ?" I asked.

"Mother can tell you about them tomorrow. Now lay the solitaire," Tatus insisted.

At a quarter of ten the dogs' beds were brought into the hall, and the maid inquired if anything more was needed.

"It is late, already ten o'clock," said my parents-in-law, "everyone is tired. Good night." Abruptly we all parted for the night.

I was awakened in the morning by the familiar barking of the dogs at the postman. I rang for my breakfast and finding Andrew's room empty, jumped back into bed. Hearing my bell, Tatus opened the door. "You have one letter from

John," he told me, "and one was forwarded, but I do not recognize the handwriting."

"It's from my cousin in America.

"Read them." Tatus asked eagerly "What news do they send you ?"

"I'll translate them if you like."

When we had finished the letters, Tatus asked how I had slept, what plans I had for the day, and what dress I intended to wear.

"Is it hot ?" I asked.

"There is not a cloud in the sky. The day will be scorching." Tatus's concern for our comfort was touching.

"Then Andzia is washing my hair."

"And — ?" he looked up brightly, hoping I would propose calling on one of Mulka's friends.

"Perhaps I shall walk in town to the Lending Library," hoping to deflect his attention.

"What calls do you intend to make ?" he could not resist asking. "Mulka has a list of the ladies on whom we think you should call."

"That's for tomorrow. Today I will be lazy, just enjoying being here."

"It's better to get the calls over with. Otherwise every day they will be hanging over you. You need not telephone beforehand nor remain longer than fifteen minutes anywhere, except at Mrs. Rice and Sister Magdalene." He pleaded so sweetly, I melted.

"Alright. I'll promise to do it tomorrow."

"Always tomorrow !" he sighed.

There was a pause, then he said, "Father Michalski is coming in for luncheon tomorrow. Mulka thought you would like to see him. Of course we will have old Stryjenski — Mulka has asked Mrs. Mycielska to come too. That's the only friend he still has, poor old man."

"I am always glad to see them, really."

"Since they would be offended if we didn't have them, we will get it over with at once. Unfortunately, you know, every summer I have to have the members of the Academy. I would have put it off until after you were gone," he apologized, "but it must be on the fifteenth because of the arrival of the Lwow professors."

"But why? I think it will be extremely interesting."

"About fifty or sixty for supper," he continued. "I have been wondering whether to give them a buffet as usual or to serve them a plate as Mulka saw in America. There is always so much left over after a buffet. We have to eat it up for a week."

Mulka was coming slowly up the stairs. She was returning from Morning Communion, which she never missed, either in the greatest heat of summer or heaviest snow of winter. Then after her breakfast she would hurry to her office at the "Parish Committees." As President she oversaw the finances and decided which new applicants should be given the "dinners." All the other ladies who worked in the office were also volunteers like herself. She had organized fifteen food kitchens, most of them in the refectory of the old monasteries, but some in the parish halls. Most of the food was prepared by the Sisters of Charity and served by ladies of the parish. A hot midday meal of stew, coffee, bread and a pudding was served. Every destitute person was received until a volunteer social worker investigated his case, then, depending on the situation, the applicant was fed temporarily or permanently. Once in a while a swindler tried the round of the fifteen parishes, giving a different name each day. But Mulka used to say, "We are here to feed the poor and we cannot run the risk of turning away the truly needy. The dishonest will surely be discovered quickly enough."

Each kitchen was prepared to feed a thousand daily. To raise the funds for such an enterprise each year there was a house to house campaign, a flower day on the sidewalks of Cracow, theatre benefits and picture exhibitions, raffle sales and church bazaars. Above all, there were gifts in kind; coal offered by coal merchants, loaves of bread given by bakers and flour sent in by friends from the country. Potatoes by the truckload and other vegetables were supplied by the gentry of the Cracow neighborhood.

180

For nearly twenty years my mother-in-law had given all her strength to the work. As she wearily dragged herself up the stairs, Tatus said, "I wish Mulka would not tire herself so! It is time a younger woman took her place."

"Archbishop Sapieha has promised to look for someone for next year."

"Then promise me you will hand in your resignation now for next year." Turning to me, Tatus explained, "Dr. Oszacki does not like the condition of Mulka's heart. She has to rest now every day for several hours."

Over Mulka's tired face passed a sad look of loneliness. No one in the family had ever been heard to praise her work. Tatus had always complained that it took her thoughts from her family, and her two sons had accused her of pre-occupation. All three begged her to buy herself clothes which she always felt she really did not need, and a car which she flatly refused to have. "A car," she would say, "will cost three thousand dollars to buy. To run it and pay a chauffeur will cost me another thousand a year. With four thousand dollars we can give forty thousand people dinner at ten cents a head. I could never, never ride around in a car for thinking of that. When I am tired I take a *dorozka*; that costs me twenty cents. The street car goes right to the door of my office. Please don't bring up the subject once more." She would beg with so much earnestness that we would all feel ashamed.

"Then I don't think John and I should have a car," I would say.

"That is different. You are young. For you the car is a means of transportation. How rarely you travel in a train!"

"That is hardly giving up something for charity."

"Your time will come. Now get as much happiness as you can together. Let's not talk about it any more," and smiling very sweetly, she would try to change the subject.

Having come in from church she went to her room and lay down in the sunlight on her sofa. The two dogs, jumping up on her feet, left her but little space. During her breakfast she read the paper and listened to the news. She

181

had a little radio with earphones which she used so as not to disturb Tatus, whose room was directly across the hall. After breakfast her bath was drawn, and Andzia would brush her hair as she had done since Mulka was twelve.

By ten o'clock both parents-in-law had gone out for the morning. Downstairs above the roar of the vacuum cleaner you could hear old Kazia giggling in the garden where Andrew was playing. I felt like a spectator suspended in space, having nothing to do. My first instinct to go to the Library had been the right one — to make a plan of summer reading. Now, at last, I had time to start Duchesne's *Early History*. I hurried out of the house choosing the narrowest and most shady streets. They had been sprinkled to lay the dust and cool the air. Before many doorways, pots of oleander were airing, and caged canaries swung in open windows. The strident voices of children playing rang from the backs of the courtyards, and from the different houses came the unmelodious sounds of scales and finger exercises. A man, sitting on a loaded cart, cried out, "I am the hawker of old clothes, rags and papers!" and a woman with a large basket covered with a linen cloth was shouting, "Crayfish! I sell crayfish!" But under the newly planted trees the streets were nearly deserted, and as the hawker's cry died away, a peaceful hum of general activity settled back over the neighborhood.

The Lending Library occupied a narrow vaulted shop in a fifteenth century house. Between the windows heavy buttresses jutted out into the sidewalk. In the heavy thickness of the walls were narrow windows, and set close against the panes new books were on display. The Library listed between ten and fifteen thousand volumes. Half the books were Polish; the rest were French, German, English and Italian. Foreign books were not unusual in Cracow. Even the Lending Library on our street had a good assortment of Penguin and Tauchnitz editions in English, as well as the latest Polish books. But of the many lending libraries in Cracow this was the largest and cheapest, the books costing only a few pennies. As usual the narrow room was overcrowded. An old lady dressed in black with a heavy black veil (who looked like any other of Mulka's acquaintances) asked me when I had returned. She was rather thin and tall, dressed with nun-like simplicity — intelligent eyes in a kind face. Once again I was conscious of the extraordinary similarity of Cracow society to that of the really old families in Cambridge, Massachusetts.

My book procured, I followed the cool, narrow street out into the brilliant market square, dazzling in the noon sun. Already market stalls were being folded away on carts. Soon the clamorous bustle would be hushed, and no trace would be left of the poultry, the vegetables, the painted wooden furniture, the wicker baskets and the gaily colored children's toys. Swiftly the tables sagging under homespun linens and festooned with laces and the gaily printed skirts billowing in the wind were being piled away. This was the moment to catch a last glimpse of the twelfth century towers of the Panna Maria Church above the sea of striped umbrellas shading the flower market.

In the center of the market square the cloth hall has stood since the fourteenth century. Within the Gothic vaulted hall is a bazaar where peasants buy new velvet bodices embroidered in sequins, coral beads and gay ribbons. About the outside, under an arcade are shops for the city folk, shops of fine scarves and neckties, dress goods and woolens, button shops with a myriad varieties of colors and shapes, a handkerchief shop, and a haberdashery, neatly dusted every morning ; a goldsmith who did our small repairs, and the antique shop of Miss Konopka, who was standing in her door. She said in greeting, "How have the Mr. and Mrs. fared during the winter ? I have several fine Meissen cups I wish the lady could see."

"We will be back when my husband comes," I replied, hurrying on past my mother-in-law's corsetiere, sewing in her open window. She came to the house for measures and fittings.

"So ! The lady just arrived ?" she called gaily as I passed.

At the end of the arcade where the Virginia creeper hung

in lacy festoons was a café, set about with pots of oleander and morning-glory. In summer the tables overflowed the arcade out on the market square. But in winter it was less popular. The red velvet benches circling the walls and Gothic columns were hard and narrow, and the great white tiled stove hardly took the chill out of the heavy stone vaults. I chose a table screened from the sun with a quilt of morning-glories and ordered a raspberry syrup. Nearby, the flower women were calling the latecomers, pressing on them their last bunches. Boys were climbing the statue of Mickiewicz, the poet. Through the open doors of the Panna Maria women tugging at their bundles were pushing in and out of the church. Up in the belfry the trumpeter blew the noon bugle. The call, which goes back to the Tartar invasions of the thirteenth century, ends in the middle of the line where the bugler was struck in the throat by a Tartar arrow. On the stroke of twelve, pigeons flew up in the air and when they settled down, as if by magic the market folk had disappeared, leaving no trace that they had been there, no telltale boxes, faded flowers nor discarded vegetables. This is the signal for store-keepers to close their shops and pull down their shutters. Last shoppers hasten from the square. The *dorozka* drivers crack their whips, turning their horses to race each other off the square. The noon promenade then commences. Smartly dressed shopkeepers come out of their dark back rooms. Sales girls dressed in the latest Vogue fashions strut up and down the square vieing with each other, and young bloods bandy at the street corners.

Fearing that if Tatus had returned before me he would be pacing the hall, watch in hand, though there was still a quarter of an hour before dinner time, I took a taxi. It was well I did. The movement of Mulka's curtains showed someone was watching from the window while Tatus and the dogs were waiting in the hall by the door. "What kept you so long?"

"You were not waiting for me?"

"We were anxious when the noon hour was passed, wondering what had detained you. Mulka thought you had met Mary or Eva and would forget the time."

"I will tell you all about it," and after embracing him fondly, I ran up the stairs.

CHAPTER *13*

ON THE next day Father Michalski was to drive us out of town to a ruined convent on the upper reaches of the Vistula. He was to come at one, and for fear I would be late for lunch, Tatus suggested I make no plans for the morning, but remain at home.

To make the most of the beautiful hot June sun, I put on a bathing suit and taking Duchesne's *Early History of the Church,* retired behind the raspberry bushes at the end of the garden. Though the usual sound of singing from neighboring houses was broken by the periodic roar of aeroplanes practicing spirals, loops and dives, Andrew paddled with unconcern in an old rubber travelling tub from the "good old days." We were lulled by a hot earthy smell that rose about us in delicious soothing waves of heat. If only the morning would go on forever ! But at eleven, the old nurse came bustling down the walk, her full black alpaca ruffled about her ankles.

"Let the lady come up now. I will dress her for dinner."

"With two hours' time ?"

"Too much sun is no longer considered wise. These fads are changing."

"In a minute then."

A few minutes later, cane in hand, impeccably dressed in a black serge suit and black felt hat, Tatus stepped off the portico into the garden.

"Do come in. You will be late."

"With an hour and a half in which to dress ? A minute longer," I begged.

However, the priest professor was already in the library when I came down for dinner, and I could hear my father-in-law apologize for his delinquent family.

"My wife is always with her Committee in the mornings," he was saying as I entered the room.

"*Dzien dobry.*"

"*Dzien dobry,* Father Professor. I have taken your advice and begun reading Duchesne."

"A great work!" the priest agreed heartily. "I am, I confess, more interested in the modern problems of philosophy — Bergson and Maritain. One must read modern philosophy to understand what is happening in the world today."

"I thought you were more interested in the Middle Ages."

At fifty the Priest Rector was nearly blind. His thick glasses made his eager eyes look like bright little black buttons. He was small and neat, his soutane brushed to perfection.

"That was my work abroad," Father Michalski explained, "trying to find clues as to the author of an ancient manuscript by comparing the copies in Paris and Oxford. All chance! But my eyes didn't stand the strain. Now I am working on 'modern' theories. Would you care to see my book *God and Fascism* ?"

"Yes, please. But tell me, how can you tell who wrote the manuscripts ?"

"In the manner of making the letters. You remember the same form in another library. Abbreviations are one of the best ways."

"Are there many unidentified manuscripts ?" I asked.

"Most of the manuscripts that have come down from antiquity are unidentified and uncatalogued. We have no idea what was lost in the Spanish conflict. If war comes to Europe soon, three million priceless volumes can be lost of which not only the authors but even the contents and theses are unknown."

"I thought that just as monasteries had preserved the classic learning in the Middle Ages, they kept the libraries in order today."

187

"It takes very highly skilled and trained men to recognize the period and read the manuscripts today. One is lucky to identify a dozen volumes in one's lifetime while working on the catalogue."

I was dumbfounded. "Where are the uncatalogued manuscripts?"

"In all the great libraries — Paris — Oxford — Cambridge — Seville. The Rockefellers spend enormous sums to send ten men to work in the Vatican. What's done is only a drop in the ocean."

"You can finish your conversation at the table," Tatus broke in. "My wife begs us to go in."

"Does the young man come down for meals?" asked the Father.

"With your permission, Father Professor."

During the meal he told us the history of Tyniec, the Renaissance building we were to see that afternoon.

"It will be very hot," Mulka said. "You and Tatus go. I will stay with Andrew."

"Andrew wants to go!"

"You will get tired on such a long ride," I tried to discourage him.

"All the same, Andrew wants to go."

"I will take care of him," the priest promised. "The Sisters will give him milk. They have many children on vacation there."

"I cannot understand why the auto has not come," Tatus interposed.

"The dear colleague has the Academy car for the occasion?" the priest asked.

"I always use it for going out of town," Tatus explained. "The driver is careful and a good mechanic."

To hasten the meal Tatus refused a second helping, and he constantly looked at his watch until finally the door bell rang.

"Ah! At last! That will be the chauffeur." To the maid he said, "Tell him to wait outside. We will just finish our coffee."

188

But as soon as dinner was finished, Tatus sent us up for our wraps, promising we could have coffee when we came down. To the priest he said, "It makes the trip so late if we don't get off right away."

"And does that much matter?" Mulka gently inquired.

When at last he had us in the car Tatus relaxed. Looking at his watch for the last time, he said with his sweet smile, "The Priest Rector knows how women take long to be ready."

We drove along the outer ring, on which all the new buildings of Cracow University were being built. It was a double road, separated by a very wide park strip. The newly planted Lombardy poplars had already reached a stately height. Shrubs and permanent trees planted among them were feathery with young green leaves. As the outer road, freshly laid with asphalt, was barricaded, we were forced to rattle and bump over the old macadam one, deep with pot holes made by the heavy building trucks, and kept muddy by the city sprinkler which was laying the dust.

"How typical of the Polish mentality!" I said. "In America they would let you ride on the asphalt or at least repair the bumps."

"America is so rich," I was told for the nth time. "Cracow could not afford to pave both sides until the buildings are completed."

"Still passenger cars could use the asphalt," I persisted, already ashamed of having used the stupid expression 'typical.'

"There is so little monetary help from Warsaw," Tatus complained, wearily.

"Centralization of everything in Warsaw —" the Priest began.

"Skladkowski was a pupil of mine."

"Have you seen him since he took office?"

"I will make a special point of it the next time I am in Warsaw."

Now we were crossing the Vistula. The smooth planks of the bridge gave temporary relief from the jolting and I could look with pleasure at the play of sun on the old rosy brick turrets of the Wawel. Children were running about the beaches along the river, and horses, let out of their shafts, had waded in to drink before hauling the heavy loads of sand up to the road on top of the dykes. Across the river rooks were rising from the plane trees. Their croaking call could be heard above the rattle of wooden carts leaving the city.

As soon as we passed the quiet Cracow suburb, the road ran for several miles across the flat moor. Here and there were half deserted wooden shacks. The thick short grass looked newly mowed and every outcropping stone ledge was carpeted with tiny wildflowers and set about with hawthorn and trailing yew. We were crossing that chalk ledge which, geologists said, showed the Baltic Sea had once covered the whole of Poland, even to the Carpathian Mountains. From time to time ancient tracks ran off to unmarked destinations, and our narrow road finally petered out into two ruts. Billowy white clouds floated lazily in the wide sky, and only the noise of our car broke the perfect stillness of the empty space.

"Mr. Chauffeur knows the way?" the Priest asked anxiously.

"It is quite clear, Father Professor. Four kilometers ahead is the village where we turn off to Tyniec."

"We could have come up the other side of the Vistula and crossed on the ferry," the Priest explained nervously. "But I have been there when the ferryman was away and it took hours to find him. The Sisters always tell him when they will be returning."

"By boat is the best connection — " the chauffeur began.

"But that runs only once a day," the Priest broke in. "If you do not wish to spend the night at Tyniec, this is the better way."

"I thought Tyniec was only twenty miles from Cracow!" I exclaimed.

"Yes, on the road we are travelling, but most of the year this way is inaccessible. The moor is too boggy," Father Michalski said. "The countryside has not changed since the thirteenth century when the monks rode this path on horse-back."

The village where we were to turn was hidden in an abrupt hollow of the moor where a creek ran down to the Vistula. The village had many two-storied stone-walled houses built near the newly plastered Baroque church. The church and the houses were buried under ancient plane trees, hanging with mistletoe and dotted all over with countless nests of rooks. Most of the houses were whitewashed log cabins. The new ones had red tiled roofs required by law to protect the village from danger of fire, and the old ones still smothered under immensely deep thatch green with moss and lichen, on which the storks love to build their nest. "Where storks are nesting, a child would be born that year," as anyone could tell you. Here and there were a few cottages painted blue to indicate the owner had a marriageable daughter.

In some of the houses were shops. Above the door was displayed the Polish coat of arms, a white eagle on a red shield saying "Polish Tobacco and Salt Monopoly" —state-owned industries from ancient times. The door would be opened, you could see the wares through the bare window. In all other windows geraniums were blooming, and clean smooth grass grew close to the buildings. After the light air of the moorland, the heavy shade of the gigantic plane trees made the village seem close and humid.

We had come to a separate country, cut off by the moor. The road signs pointed to other villages ; not one sign indicated Cracow. How many of these people had ever travelled so far away as that. A wide dirt road ran from here to Tyniec shaded with willows and weird shaped stumps grown old and hollow. It was busy with carters and carriages, bicyclists and pedestrians. On either side were rich hay fields, and fields of grain, cabbages and potatoes. The ripe produce was shipped down the river to Cracow on steamers that stopped at Tyniec as the barges had done in the fourteenth century. Then all this rich land was under the jurisdiction of the Monastery.

We entered the town over a causeway. The houses had picket fences about them, with phlox growing in the front yards as in all prosperous small towns here. There were sidewalks along the roads leading to the flat grassy banks of the river that served as commons for the village and to the castle.

It rose on a pinnacle of chalk cliff where the river circled around it. Our Fiat could not pull up the bastion. We left it to climb on foot as so many others were doing — boys who rolled down the grassy slope, and women climbing with beads in their fingers. Great buttresses of brick held a high wall above us. There was a gate with portcullis, and heavy oak doors left ajar with a rope to hold them. Inside the court gate was space for a thousand soldiers. To one side of the terrace were the great defense walls, beside them the church and monastery; to the other the ruined Renaissance castle destroyed by the Swedes in 1656. On the fourth side a parapet hung over the river, providing a view of the distant Carpathian Mountains.

Father Michalski knocked at an unpainted oak door that let into part of the walled bastion. Here passages and barracks rooms built for defense, had been reconditioned by the Sisters to house hundreds of orphaned children. The openings had been glassed up to make great windows. In each room stood a porcelain stove. When we arrived the children were outside playing in an orchard of old gnarled apple trees, the trunks clean with whitewash. Several Sisters were preparing the four o'clock bread and milk, setting the enamelled mugs on rough tables covered with oilcloth. Others protected the smaller children from tumbling off the high ruins of the castle on which the older ones were climbing. Trees were growing out of the crevices in the walls and their roots tore the stone sheathing from the brick. Here and there a stone carved lintel was still in place over the immense square windows that now formed an empty arcade on two sides of the tremendous old courtyard.

"Let Jesus Christ be praised, Sister !" said Father Michalski. "I see little results from the money I collected for weeding and tarring the palace ruins."

"I will guide the Father Professor to the repaired places as soon as the honored guests have rested."

"Let the Sisters guard the child Andrew. I prefer immediately to inspect the work that was done."

"Instantly, instantly, Father Professor. The Sister Superior will show it."

Like the Priest Rector, the Sister Superior wore thick glasses. In spite of being near-sighted, she briskly led the way, climbing down the rough path that led around the outside of the palace ruins. First we walked along the wall that towered directly above the village, then above the fields which stretched far off in the golden western sun, where the little mounds of hills grew more and more numerous until they joined the mountains on the horizon. Waves of hot air shimmered before our eyes and the lush deep grass engulfed us with its overpowering scent.

The priest busily compared recent repairs with those made several years ago. "You see here how the cement crumbles off, bringing new bricks with it. Tar is more protecting," he said to the Sister Superior. Though both were nearing sixty, they climbed nimbly to the third story of corridors which were all that remained of the great bishop's place that had once housed several hundred members of his staff. From this height we lingered over the view of the Vistula sweeping around the cliff at our feet.

"What reason had the Swedes to destroy all this ?" I asked.

"During the Thirty Years' War, the Protestant Swedes wished to break up the Catholic power of Poland. Tyniec was a formidable fortress holding the Upper Vistula," the Priest answered. Waving his hand he explained the tactics of the battle.

"This view has remained unchanged through the centuries," the Sister commented to me.

"Were the forests not closer ?" I asked.

"Not judging by the records. From Roman times these have been grain fields and hay has grown on those meadows."

"Let me show the Father Professor a coin which was brought to me recently. Perhaps he can identify it."

"It will likely be one Trajan struck to the grain growers of Poland. I must show you some coins at the University."

"I could sit here forever in the company of the Father Professor, but I must make good use of his infrequent visits to beg for new roofing over the southern portion."

"Are there leaks?" he asked.

"A storm blew half the roof away," she said, speaking in a rush. "The Sisters and I took handy boards and patched it temporarily. Furthermore, may I say it, we need ten new blankets. If the Father Professor has the ear of the Archbishop, I would like a dozen. I could put two more beds into Room E. It is so hard to turn down children when I could make a little corner for them. The new beds are wonderful, Father Professor — imagine, the hospital did not need them! I know the Father Professor thinks about us continually."

"How did you come through the winter, Sister?"

"With very little sickness, God be thanked, except for those poor little twins who had all the illnesses. A quart of cod liver oil is what they need now."

"If only there were money for such luxuries!"

"Couldn't I send you some?" I asked. "It would be such a little thing to do."

"Oh, no, please, the lady is too good! She should not fatigue herself, really."

"Then I will send some."

When we returned, the children had finished their bread and milk, and the Sisters were gathering up the enamel cups in a big basket. Most of the children were pale and thin but they laughed merrily as they ran and played. They were garbed in all kinds of made-over dresses which the Sisters had arranged for them, and it was clear they felt no restraint. Tatus, who had been sitting off by himself, called to us, "Time, you know, is passing. If we are to see the inside of the church we must hasten."

"Mr. Rector will just permit the showing of our new dormitory?"

"*C'est toujours comme ça,*" Tatus said in my ear. "One
194

goes on an expedition and one is bored to death by this kind of thing."

"It was extremely interesting however, to see how these Sisters had organized everything."

While we were taken single file through corridors and made to peep into every room, Tatus kept muttering, "We really must go. Don't linger. All such orphanages are the same." Finally, in a burst of exasperation, he said, "Sister, it has been a delightful privilege to inspect your splendidly run asylum. You will excuse me, I am sure, if I now leave you." As he bowed stiffly he said in French in my ear, *"Je serai devant l'église, Depêche-toi."*

"The Rector is always so amiable," said the Sister happily. "Now the lady must come and have milk while I call Andrew."

We found Tatus fifteen minutes later, holding his cane with both hands, a cigarette hanging from between his lips, his hat pulled well down to shade his eyes. "I thought you would never come," he said. "You simply don't know how to leave."

"But she would have been offended."

"Fifteen minutes is time enough for such visits. They wear you out. Come now, let's look about the church, but not spend a lifetime over it either. If we hurry we can see it before Father Michalski gets you to go over every stick and stone of it," he said laughingly.

Just as we finished Father Michalski came hurrying across the courtyard, his robes blowing behind him like a victory.

"If you are ready, we will go down and see the ferry. Come now, you have visited the church often enough, Father Professor," he said, pleased that our duties were finished.

There was a procession of women still climbing up and down the ramp. "They bring the Sisters an egg, a pint of milk, a little bread, to help with the children," the Priest explained.

It was pleasant under the shade trees after the glare of the immense gravel court. About the foot of the castle in an alley of plane trees, townspeople were strolling. In a little orchard a woman was singing, and from an open window

195

came the sound of a Polonaise played with a flourish on a cheap upright piano.

"Brrrr" shouted a man to his plunging horses. Everyone fled from under foot. The carter reined his horse towards the river bank where the cable ferry was secured to the cliff under the castle. This ferry was a flat-bottomed scow which the ferry-man steered downstream until the force of the current carried it to the other side. The boat was small, just place for the cart. The horse had to cross the river separately. "We could return to Cracow that way," the Priest proposed. "Shall I arrange it with the chauffeur ?"

"Oh no !" I begged. "The car might go to the bottom. You need so much power to drive over these logs, the car might jump into the river."

"We could all push it on the ferry," the operator suggested helpfully.

We were standing on the crude log landing. The river was swirling in great eddies of foam, sucking down cones of water ominously. I pulled Andrew away. "This is no place for a child to play." The carter unharnessed the terrified horse and led it to graze on the grass under the trees where several of the village boys tended it. Others who happened to be standing about, helped the carter and the ferryman push off the barge which slowly drifted out into the current. The ferry swung downstream, the cable strained like a bow, and halfway across the ferry turned to the other shore. They were too far away for us to watch the unloading, and I begged to go home.

"It's only four."

"John might telephone."

The Priest suggested walking further up the river for the view of Tyniec over the meadows. "It would take too long," I pleaded, "Andrew must be home before six."

"This is the most beautiful moment of the day," he said regretfully.

The sky preparing for evening had lost its midday fleecy clouds and had settled into a still deep blue. The swallows awoke, and were flying in great circles over the meadow.

High in the sky larks were singing and the rooks rising and settling in the plane trees were carrying on a soft chitchat. But feeling uneasy and restless I insisted on returning to Cracow. As we drove up to the house, we could see Mulka had been watching for us from her window and she hurried down the stairs to meet us in the hall. "John telephoned. He had an auto accident. He had wanted to make us a surprise and arrive for the weekend."

"He is not hurt?"

"No, but the motor car is badly damaged."

"How did it happen?"

"When he heard you were not here he said he would call after seven when he could explain it to you."

The connection came at eight. John was speaking from our house in Vienna. Someone had unscrewed the wheel of our car. The car had plunged down a high ditch and the bumper had cut through the radiator.

"What a narrow escape!"

"The baggage went out of the window and the dog was hurled over the seat." John's voice sounded very apologetic. "I just hoped to make you a surprise. I was so lonely in Vienna I couldn't stand another moment not seeing you."

"I will take the morning train to Vienna. I will leave Andrew here."

"Yes, do. We simply can't be separated."

"No, no, darling."

"He is not hurt then?" Tatus said.

"God protected him. Everything in its own time," said his mother.

"I am leaving in the morning."

"That is ridiculous if he is not hurt!"

"I will leave Andrew here, but I promised to go in the morning."

"The train leaves at nine. Tickets! Money! One can't leave a country so suddenly!"

"My passport is in order. We can get the ticket at the station. It only costs about fifty zlotys" (ten dollars).

"Yes, yes. I have money enough for you. You mustn't

think of money," Tatus replied with his unfailing sense of protection.

Mulka said, "If you are really going, Andzia should get your bags down. Go tell her what you are taking."

Everything was settled so quickly and then the long waiting began, twelve hours of waiting before the train left! Over and over I kept wondering how it had happened. John had not said over the telephone who had unscrewed the wheel. How foolish of us to be parted! It must never happen again. Marriage wasn't for that. This nightmare was all totally unnecessary. Had I remained in Vienna John would not have had to set off to drive seven hundred and thirty-five kilometers — nearly five hundred miles — across Austria, Czechoslovakia and Poland alone. His very existence was so nearly ended!

In the last two years I had fought that horrid premonition that something terrible would happen to us, that vision of John lying dead in a muddy field! I had tried to keep the picture out of my eyes. Though I never thought of it by day, in the early morning it would rouse me with a chill I could shake off only by waking up completely. Then I would creep close to John, and warming myself beside him, put away the spiteful dream as an unworthy and evil fancy.

Now it had nearly come true through, I felt, my fault. I should not have left him. If he needed more freedom for work, my day should be arranged for it. This kind of separation was artificial. It might be good for other people, but not for us. I tossed about all night. In the early morning I was up and dressed and all ready to leave.

"Andrzej must be a good boy while I am away."

"Andrzej wants to go!"

"Babby wants Andrzej to stay with her. She would be very sad if we both went away. I am going to take care of Poppy while you take care of Babby."

"*Dobrze* ; Andrzej will take care of Babby," he said gaily.

CHAPTER *14*

*T*HE trip to Vienna seemed endless. I was tired after the sleepless night, sad at leaving Andrew, and apprehensive about what I would find on arriving in Vienna. Was John telling me the truth ? Perhaps he was hurt. But John, as he stood waiting at the Vienna station, looked strong and his usual tower of dependability. "You will never leave me again ?" were his first words.

"Not as long as I live." I promised with the whole ardor of my being.

" 'Absence makes the heart grow fonder' is such a shabby phrase."

"Absence makes me so deeply miserable that in self protection I have to fill my time with utterly trifling occupations not to think about you."

"We have to be together, every minute, forever."

"Till death do us part," I said, choking back an unutterable emotion.

In the taxi John remarked, "It was the Germans who unscrewed the wheel."

"Are you sure ?"

"The car was inspected as usual at the Buick place. I brought it home the evening before to make an early start next morning. It stood downstairs where they had access to it."

The Secretary of Von Papen had moved into our house only a few months before. Our first difficulty with him had been the previous Easter Sunday. That morning we were to leave at five to drive down the Danube to Belgrade. About

3:30, however, we were wakened by someone closing our bedroom door. Jumping out of bed we ran into the boudoir, where our two desks stood. The drawers were half opened and papers were scattered about. There was nothing amiss in the drawing room or in the hall. There was no one on the front stairs. Crossing the dining room we went into the servants' quarters. At that early hour our Viennese cook had already arrived and was boiling the water for our coffee.

"Was there anything unusual when you arrived?" my husband asked. "Did you meet anyone on the stairs?"

The old woman wagged her head. "Nothing, nothing, *Herr Baron*."

"How many times have I begged you not to call me with a title?"

"As you will, *Herr Gesandtschaftrat*."

"Luckily I keep all my papers locked at the Legation," John said when we returned to our room. We decided to dress first and call the two Polish servants only when we were ready to leave.

I was in the tub when John came rushing in to tell me that he had been robbed of the three hundred dollars cash he had in his wallet for our trip. His wallet was still in the drawer of his night table at the head of his bed. It seemed almost inconceivable that an outside thief could have climbed into our window. Calling the three servants, we said one of them must have taken the money, and that we would not call the police if it was returned. The Viennese cook hinted darkly that our house-boy had a liaison and might have been in need of money. On hearing this our two Polish servants were so frightened by this accusation, one could hardly recognize them. Becoming quite hysterical, they ran away, crying, to their rooms. But the cook was unperturbed.

"I have no time for idling now," was her comment as she left our bedroom. "I must prepare the breakfast, *Herr Baron Gesandtschaftrat*."

A few moments later the Polish nurse burst into the room bawling more hysterically than before. "My money is gone, gone! All my savings are gone!"

"How much was it Bola ?"

"Gone ! Gone ! Gone !" Though I shook her shoulders, she would not answer but kept repeating, "Gone ! Gone ! All my savings gone !"

In the meantime John went into Edward's room to ask him if he had lost his money. The lad was prostrate on the bed, unconscious with despair. John could not rouse him. He went to the kitchen to fetch him some coffee. The cook had left.

He telephoned the police, who ordered the main house door locked. He raced downstairs. The concierge was dozing in his box.

"Has my cook left the house ?"

"I have not opened the door since it was locked at midnight, *Herr Gesandtschaftrat.*"

"Then the cook did not come in this morning ? Keep the door locked till the police come," John ordered. "So that means she spent the night in the house !"

When the police came they found Edward too had been robbed, but even this did not pull him out of his coma of despair. Since we had all been robbed and since the cook had fled, the police concurred that she probably was guilty.

"As she has not left the building, the money is still in the house. It will be simple to recover it," the police said cheerfully and set out to search the house. When they came back they told us the cook could not have entered the cellar which was locked, and must be in the apartment of the German Secretary.

The police requested the right to enter, but the German replied, "Even if the maid were in my apartment, I will not waive my diplomatic immunity and give permission to the police to enter on mere circumstantial evidence. Search the Polish servants upstairs."

After the criminal police took over the case, it was found the cook had once been alone in the house of a Cabinet Minister who had been mysteriously murdered. Her savings account, opened in 1930, had a balance of thirty-five thousand shillings after six years, though her wages were but forty shillings a month. Still, she could not be convicted on circumstantial evidence. Although the Polish Government requested the Austrian Government to make further investigations, after two months the case was dropped.

After that, when it was known downstairs that we were entertaining guests for dinner, a mournful band would sing the *Horst Wessel* song over and over for hours on end. Sung out of tune, it would end each time on a lower note. When the bottom was reached it would start all over again on a high pitch. Conversation in our apartment was so difficult that it soon became impossible to invite anyone to our house.

And now our car was wrecked.

"Why should the Germans do this to us?"

"I am convinced they believe I am here on a military mission," John replied. "They paid our cook to look through my papers. Her stealing the money spoiled their plans. Now they resort to petty annoyances."

"Smashing the car is hardly 'petty annoyance.' You might have been killed."

"If they didn't believe I was on a secret military mission they wouldn't go to all this trouble," said John brightly.

I leaned back in his arms. It was wonderful he was alive. It was joy to be with him.

During the next two weeks while the car was being rebuilt, John worked night and day finishing his report. Except for an hour every afternoon when we would go across the street to the Theresiana Swimming Pool, he was always at the Legation. He felt certain these trade agreements would make the Danubian countries independent of Germany by opening up a free trade zone among states of more or less the same level of standards of life. All his papers were locked in the safe whenever he left his office. If the Germans got hold of his report before it was put into the form of a treaty, they would undermine the whole proposition by making attractive loans to one country, say Bulgaria, and dangling equally attractive promises to other states on condition they did not join the Agrarian Bloc. As soon as the report was finally typed, not trusting it to the pouch, we left at once for Warsaw.

Although John had been sent to Vienna by the Foreign Office, the agreements he proposed would have to be carried out by the Department of Commerce and the Ministry of Finance. Unfortunately, because the Polish Minister Mr. Gavronski at Vienna had not foreseen the latest move of Von Papen, he had become generally unpopular in Warsaw. Minister Beck, too, was accused by many persons of influence of having pro-German sympathies. The Minister of Finance Mr. Koc, perhaps for this reason, seemed little inclined to accept a proposition sent him by the Foreign Office. It was ten days before a conference hour was set, and when the conference met, no one with authority was delegated by the Ministry of Finance to attend. It seemed clear John's report was doomed by inter-departmental rivalries. He came back from the meeting discouraged and despairing.

At the Ministry of Commerce and Industry, he found a similar situation. "They had the audacity to ask what commission I got out of it," he told me. "I wish I could retire from all this and go into the University."

"Why don't you ?"

"You wouldn't like living in Cracow, and I am too young to settle back in a university. The life would be too pleasant and easy."

"You needn't let it be so. The President of the Bank of Poland was a professor. And Krzyzanowski doesn't lead a quiet comfortable life."

"Do you really mean it ?"

"I didn't want to go to Vienna in the first place."

"Put it out of your mind then until I have first seen whether there is an opening in the University."

As soon as it was clear there was nothing more to be done in Warsaw, we left for Cracow. John went at once to the head of the Economics Department, Professor Krzyzanowski, under whom he had worked for his doctorate. Krzyzanowski was a short stocky man, with a deceptively lazy southern drawl. He had negotiated more foreign loans than any other person in Poland. We had last seen him in the Hotel Plaza in New York, looking out of place and uncomfortable. He had apologized for all these unwanted luxuries, saying, "I couldn't float a loan unless I lived here." Now he greeted John with more than usual enthusiasm. "It's about time you joined us. I have been wondering how much longer you would stand the diplomatic racket!"

John explained the urgency of the work he had done in Vienna.

"Someone else, however, will draw up the treaties!" the Professor spoke with bitterness.

"The report is in the legal division now," John said.

"Now that is accomplished, what future do they offer you?"

"Commercial and Financial Secretary in Vienna."

"Routine business," the Professor said with disgust. "I will place your name on the list of candidates for Assistant Professor. You must prepare an address on the subject of your thesis for the faculty, who will ask you questions. Later they ballot on the candidates; in your case this will be a formality. We will need good young heads to carry on the University when war comes." Krzyzanowski then asked him in which field of economics he wished to lecture.

"On the effects of state monetary control laws, on general economic factors," John said.

"No one is more fitted to do it. You have had access to all the most recent exchange regulations and you know all European languages. Do you read Portuguese, as well as Spanish?" the Professor asked.

"I worked with them in Geneva. Recently I have been studying Rumanian, Bulgarian and Yugoslavian. Hungarian is the only language I absolutely can't read."

"We will all come to listen. Now prepare your lecture. I will do the rest."

Instead of going on a vacation, we settled down in Cracow, for two months, while John prepared the lecture he must give to the Faculty of the University.

We had arrived in Cracow at the very moment when Tatus

204

as President of the Academy of Science was preparing his annual reception of the sixty professors. The house was in great tumult. For a week beforehand Tatus had been pruning the garden to produce the maximum blooms for that day. Mulka had been allowed to spend only half her time at her Committee, in order to be on hand for all little changes in details. The telephone rang constantly. One professor would beg to be allowed to offer some wine. Another had raised melons under glass which were just turning ripe. Professor Nowak wished to send trout from his fish hatcheries. Amid these kind offers, others telephoned their acceptance. Until after the reception Tatus could only be approached with notepaper in hand and every consideration other than the reception was put off. Then, Monday morning, the bombshell fell : The President of Poland, Ignace Mosciecki, as Professor of Chemistry, telegraphed that he planned to come to Cracow for the opening of the Academy of Science and would be pleased to come for dinner.

The President could not be expected to stand about in a reception of professors at a buffet supper. Tatus' strict sense of propriety dismissed this notion immediately. During the hottest noon days we measured the garden with a view to serving dinner on little tables out on the lawn.

"What if it should rain at the last moment ?" said John.

"How would you ever decide who was to have the honor of sitting with the President ?" I asked.

"What kind of a meal could you possibly serve out of doors, and where could we find enough servants to serve it ?" Mulka demanded.

Tatus groaned. "There is nothing for it but to have the President on Wednesday, and the rest of the Academy on Thursday."

"That night there will be a reception by the President at the Wawel."

"If he would come Wednesday," he repeated, "it would simplify everything. We could invite just the Local Committee, the Archbishop and the Mayor of the city." Tatus held his head in despair. "How I hate these last moment rearrangements, after I have been preparing this for a month."

John offered to telephone the President.

"Operator, I wish to speak to the President of Poland."

"Do you want Warsaw ?"

"You will have to find out where the President is now staying."

During luncheon there was silence. If anyone started to speak, Tatus would motion them to be silent. "Don't ask me that now. Some other time," he would say plaintively.

When the telephone bell rang, he raced to the phone, though John was to do the speaking.

"Hello — "

"*Tak.*"

John gave the invitation. The Secretary promised to telegraph whether the President could come as conveniently a day earlier.

All afternoon we waited in a state of suspense. Nothing could be settled before the arrival of the President's telegram. The two maids, Kazia and Bronia, sat about the dining room table giggling while they polished the silver, and in the kitchen Halka baked little cakes and made pastry shells. Old Andzia ran up and down stairs with linens, counting out the six dozen napkins.

"All this rush and bustle about the house ! Andzia, why do you keep running up and down stairs ?" Tatus exclaimed.

"I 've finished. Only once more," she protested, going on about her work.

Mulka took Tatus' hand. "*Kazia Koteczku,*" she said softly, "are you not going to the club ? It 's four o'clock."

"Not this afternoon."

"There is nothing you can do by staying at home."

"I must be here when the telegram arrives."

"You might wait for hours. I can reach you at the club or at the Institute."

Taking a book, Tatus went up to his room and closed his door. At last at five o'clock the telegram arrived. "Mr. President would gladly come on Wednesday."

Tatus seized the telephone. "Now, my dear, come help

me with the telephoning. Dial the numbers while I think."

"Dear Mr. Colleague, such changes! The President is coming Wednesday. Can you alter your plans? There will be just eighteen for dinner."

"Dear Mr. Colleague — such changes! — "

Through the wall in the next room where I was feeding Andrew I could hear the tired voice.

"Dear Mr. Colleague — Wednesday — just eighteen — "

When it was learned in town that the President was coming, the book dealer Fisher sent Napoleonic Tokay; the oldest wine merchant Gross offered two priceless bottles of hundred year old Mead.

During the dinner for the President, Mulka and I ate off trays upstairs. Two ladies would have complicated the already difficult seating. Archbishop Sapieha sat opposite the President at the middle of the table, John and Tatus at the ends. No one could say who took precedence and which was the most honored position.

After dinner was over and the coffee and liqueurs were finished, we came down to help with the conversation. As we entered, the gentlemen were all seated stiffly about the long green table in the library. The President and the Archbishop sat in state at either end of the room, and Tatus was busy bringing up the different members of the Academy for a few words. Only the Mayor of Cracow was holding a rapid conversation at the long table.

"A very fine garden you have," the President said. "Please, Ma'am, let me compliment you. Your daughter-in-law is American. I speak a little English too." Mulka and I were seated and each professor in turn sat for a few moments beside us.

At ten-thirty, both the President and the Archbishop stiffly took leave, and with them, the cordon of police who had roped off our street. After they had gone a storm of conversation broke loose. Everyone spoke at once, each praising the honored guests for their wit and naturalness. Each repeated the conversation he had had.

"The President is so easy!"

207

"It is such a pleasure to talk to the President!"

"Did he tell you anything new?"

"I told him we should open a strip to the Russians across the Carpathian Mountains to Czechoslovakia."

"Once Russians enter Poland they will never leave it!"

"How else can they bring help to the Czechs?"

"The problem is to defeat Germany. We can deal with the Russians later."

"The Czechs will surely fight."

"The Czechs will not cede their territory to Germany."

"There is labor trouble in Germany — sabotage."

"Hitler has cancer of the throat. He will die in a few months."

"If war comes it will prove internal difficulties are so great that Hitler has to solve them by war."

"All that sounds like British talk. That is what they hope. They count on internal revolt. They never have understood the Germans' stubborn loyalty. Besides Hitler is popular."

"Hitler won't stop until he reaches Russia."

"The quality of Polish and Czech equipment is better than Russia's."

"What if Russia joins with Germany?"

"It would be unsafe to give Russia passage across Poland. The Russians are as imperialistic as the Germans. Once in Poland they would never leave voluntarily."

"Don't forget Russia will join with Germany."

I could only hear snatches of the conversation. One or another of the professors would ask me what America thought of Hitler. I could only repeat that I knew America would not help Poland, perhaps even Europe, until it was too late.

At eleven-thirty most of the professors pulled out their watches as if by a signal and, standing stiffly, waited in turn to bow over the outstretched hand of my mother-in-law.

The Mayor was the last to leave. Taking my father-in-law by the arm, he walked back and forth in the drawing room, talking in a low voice. They were discussing some matter before the City Council. While the Mayor repeated his argument again, Tatus maneuvered him into the front hall.

"Yes, indeed, Mr. Mayor. As I said — " you could hear him repeat. At last the front door slammed shut, and Tatus walked rapidly into the room more gay and energetic than if we had spent a quiet evening at home.

"Finished! I will be still happier when tomorrow evening is over. Now to bed! No more talking! Conserve your energies." He called the maids, and as I climbed the stairs I heard him say, "You all did very well — and Kazia too. She didn't giggle once, I noticed." Then he barricaded the stairs and went up to his room. He would sleep little for thinking of the sixty members of the Academy who were coming the next evening.

CHAPTER *15*

*J*OHN finished the work on his dissertation
just ten days before he was to deliver it to the Faculty of the
University of Cracow.   That did not leave much time to go
back to Vienna and pack up our belongings.   Yet John, who
was always ready to spend fifteen hours at the wheel, wanted
to see whether the new strategic highway to Vienna via
Munich, of which so much had been written, was completed
(and what warlike preparations were being made in the
Sudetenland).

For this reason, on the return journey to Cracow, we
crossed the Czech-German frontier several times between
Pilsen and Breslau.   The contrast between the two countries
can hardly be imagined.   On the German roads we were held
up by army lorries, trucking the harvest of potatoes, beets
and cabbages.   On the Czech side you could drive over the
usual empty highroads and cross peaceful villages for miles
on end without stopping.   Every German hamlet was choked
with heavy trucks, and untrained drivers blocked the central
market squares, delaying us for hours so that we reached the
Polish frontier a day later than we had intended.   The heavy
trucks pretended to be privately owned.   Peasant names
were painted on their sides.   It was difficult, however, to believe that these uniformly large six-wheeled vehicles were the
private property of poor farmers.   In the quiet Czech villages the German shopkeepers had put up their signs in
German.   Across the German border, no Czech nor Pole living in the German Bohemian towns would have dreamed of
such a privilege.

To add to our difficulties, a violent Autumn storm had turned the roads to quagmire and strewn them with leaves and branches. When we finally reached the Polish frontier, the customs officer was occupied in guarding a group of several hundred farm workers returning to Poland without passports. He was not able to attend to us until the Polish constable could be roused from the nearest county seat. "Every year," he said, "it was the same story. In the spring Germans go from village to village promising high wages for farm labor. They smuggled peasants out over the frontier. Once illegally in Germany, these workers have no redress from German Courts and having worked the whole season, are thrown out of the country without any pay."

"I should think that the peasants would not go back a second year."

"Naturally," he said, "the Germans must choose a different community each spring. Though our Ministry of Labor sends out warnings to every part of the country, the Germans trick several thousands of persons every year."

At 2 o'clock he was still guarding the peasants so we went into a German inn for lunch. It was raining heavily when we returned to the car. We found all four tires flat on their rims with thick iron spikes driven into them. Even our spares had been punctured. It was hard to imagine how we could have picked up on the road four identical spikes and certainly the spikes in the two spares had been driven in by hand. The German police insisted they had seen no one near the car and took no interest in the affair.

We begged the Polish frontier guard to let us go in search of the village mechanic who lived on the Polish side of town. Our clothes were thoroughly rain-soaked by the time we found his deserted shop. None of the passersby we hailed in the street knew where the mechanic had gone, but one of them volunteered to start the forges going, others offered to return with us to help block up the car and remove the wheels. While we rolled the wheels in procession across the town, strangers called out, "We haven't seen the mechanic, but we'll find him presently."

211

The rain changed into a drizzle during the afternoon, leaving the village roadway slimy with mud. While running about the car I tripped and skinned my leg on the rough cobble pavement.

"In this dirt, you could get tetanus," John said with dismay, "it's at least two miles back to the inn."

Someone from a nearby shop ran out with water in a dirty basin. John was so frightened I would touch it that he shouted, "Let it bleed. You can clean it with face cream and toilet water, and tear up one of my clean shirts to make a bandage."

As the car was still jacked up, I had to squat on the sidewalk to bandage my leg.

At the forge, every time a man passed, John called, "For a few grosze do give us a hand here," until it seemed that half the town was mending our six tires. Some pumped up the tubes to test them in water, others worked the bellows, and others held the vulcanizing irons to the tires. By four o'clock all six tubes and tires were ready, though the mechanic had only arrived in time for a final check-up. John put his hand in his pocket wishing to reward the men, and found he had only American dollars.

"How much Polish money have you?" he asked me.

"Five zlotys," I said. ($1.00)

"And I need fifty!"

The poor village mechanic had never seen an express check. As the bank was closed, he suggested, "Try the police. They may know what to do with it." But the police said, "Go to the Jew. If he will, he can change the money but you must hurry! If he has lighted his candles, he will not make the exchange."

In the street we asked, "Where does the Jew live, Abraham the Jew?" Boys ran after us to direct us to the street and ran with us to the second floor of the house where he lived.

"No, I can't do it. It's too late. Darkness has set in."

"Mr. Banker," John pleaded with him, "it is only the dark clouds. The first stormy day of winter!"

"I cannot do it. It would be against my principles. But I
212

tell you what I will do for you, Mr. Inheritor. I will lend you the money and you can bring me the check tomorrow."

"Don't you understand?" John almost cried. "I must spend the night in Warsaw."

"Warsaw is too far, too far! That is impossible, Mr. Inheritor. We will do the whole business in the morning."

"I shall put the check for ten dollars in this envelope," John said, signing it. "And I shall seal it so you cannot open it until tomorrow. Now you lend me nine dollars," he continued desperately.

The Jew stood up in his long black frock. His noble head was covered by a round cap, and his white curls hung down to his shoulders. He left us and went into the next room to wrestle with his principles. When he returned, he said, "Only for the good gentleman do I make this exception."

It was five when finally we were ready to leave the frontier, with three hundred miles to cover during the night. After the heavy rains the roads were in very bad condition. Our headlights hardly picked them out at all. We had scarcely driven ten miles when I asked, "Don't you think we are driving on our dimmers?"

"If our headlights burned out, where could we fix them?"

"Are we far from Piotykow?"

"Fifty miles."

"Isn't it more reasonable to spend the night there?"

"Then tomorrow will be wasted. I have little enough time to go over my lecture." John sounded as if he were at the end of his rope.

"And if we went now to Cracow?"

"We would arrive after midnight and frighten the family out of their wits."

I was silent. As the lights grew dimmer and dimmer it was apparent our battery was running down.

"Just you watch the edge of the road. I will go on the parking lights for a while to let the battery charge a bit."

It was so dark that even the villages through which we were passing were invisible. From time to time the moon would break through the rushing clouds, and village duck

213

ponds would mirror back the light. But in the endless forests white fog would blow across the road, carrying the dank autumn smell of forest undergrowth, blacking out all landmarks. At great intervals a bus would dash past us with blinding lights, or we would just escape crushing a carter asleep on his wagon, his rear lantern out. By two o'clock we caught up with an endless string of covered wagons carrying produce into town.

"We must be nearing Grodzisk."

"In an hour and a half we should be home," John said happily.

Hardly had he spoken when he noticed that the long caravan was turning to the left, and that the high road was heavily barricaded.

"Detour to Sochaczew," I read on a placard.

"What has happened?" John voiced our dismay.

"Heaven knows! Won't this double the distance home over narrow back roads? Why couldn't we have stayed en route for the night?" I wailed. "Can nothing ever make you change your plans!"

"Put your head down and go to sleep. I'll wake you when we are home."

"But the lights?"

"The battery will be charged by now."

"You are even more tired than I."

"Sh — sh — , Sleep — sleep."

The car jolted slowly, heavily, over the dark badly paved roads. I slumped against the seat but could not fall asleep. Every village street was torn up, and sewage pipes were lying by the road. "Oh, these terrible roads, why don't they pave them?"

"Evidently they don't want to pave till new pipes are laid."

"The moon seems to be higher. There is more light."

"That's the sun coming up."

The wagons, now darker than the road, were faintly visible. Far off we could see six lights high in the sky — Raszyn, the radio station outside Warsaw.

"That must have been Guzów," John said, as we pulled

up on the main Poznan highroad. "Now we have only twenty miles."

The car purred over the smooth pavement in soft release. Though there was a double line of heavy wagons, the great, broad Napoleonic road was visible for miles ahead. Soon we had reached the Airport and the end of the street-car line. Apartments standing desultorily in almost empty fields grew more and more numerous, closer and closer together, until they lined the city streets. We both relaxed. Nothing more could happen to us. If the car broke down now we could reach our home anyway. But like a tired horse on the home stretch, the car fairly raced through the empty streets.

"Remember how bumpy this street used to be when the street-car track criss-crossed it a dozen times ?"

"Now the tracks are set in grass and trees. This horrid old street looks actually handsome. How a well paved street looks prosperous at once !"

Along the sidewalks, beds of yellow chrysanthemums still held their color, though the young trees were bare. A warm wave of home-coming flooded over me. Warsaw ! Driving over this very street ten years before, wolves had seemed to be prowling behind broken walls and rotting doors. How was it possible the character of a street could be changed in such a short space of time ?

When we reached the center of the city, trams were bringing night workers to their homes — the never ending line of cars of the Krakowskie Przedmiescie that Uncle Anthony loved to watch. It was just five o'clock when we arrived before our house. The speedometer showed John had driven 360 miles in the twelve hours. We opened the latch and there everything was in place, as we had left it two years before. Every rug and every chair had been meticulously put back, and in our room the bed had been turned down, and I saw the fine linen sheets from Strassbourg, and all the piles of pillows of different sizes, smoothly pressed — the luxury of the warm white room ; the hot steaming bath in the yellow and grey tiled bathroom ! Neither in Vienna nor in Geneva had we had so much comfort.

"What are you doing? Why don't you come to bed?" I called. John, in his study, was sitting on the floor and filing away his new books. The rest of the night he rearranged his library of five thousand volumes. The French histories had belonged to his grandfather and the English classics were mine but the bulk of his collection were economic studies which he had collected in every language during the past ten years. The next morning without resting he flew down to Cracow to deliver his lecture.

After two years away it was hard to fit in all our friends, so that one did not have to explain how a week had gone by without seeing them. Yet during the first fortnight after our return to Warsaw, breakfast was the only meal we had to ourselves. Gone were those blissful days when we had drifted about alone together. We met at luncheon parties, arriving separately, and parted afterwards, rushing off in different directions. When John was home he sat behind a bolted door to work. Half the night he worked preparing his lectures after I had gone to sleep. Even Andrew was not allowed to disturb him long enough to say good night. He would return so late, I nearly always had to telephone that we would not arrive on time for dinner.

At our parties I often had to make the seating list out alone, or check it with the Government protocol. John would arrive after the last guests. If at the last moment someone was unable to come, I had to decide upon the substitute. This was not simple, for if "diplomats" were invited, then few of our Polish friends would care to come.

Since Government circles were inaccessible to most foreign journalists and Secretaries of Legation in Warsaw, the Opposition accused the Government of every possible crime, every internal and international intrigue. There were some Poles who honestly believed that Beck was hand in glove with the Nazis, in connivance with Germany itself. The Opposition, as everywhere else, did not see that the cure for a bad government program is not more opposition, but more constructive criticism. In the emergency they were unwilling to work with their Government, instead they stooped to

216

personal abuse and bitter feuds which widened the gulf between the Government and the Opposition and caused the Government circle to grow closer and tighter. They refused to see that the alternative to co-operation was chaos ; that Hitler was only waiting for the opportunity afforded by the inevitable disorganization attending change in government. We were only just faintly grasping these things, and we had not yet learned how to formulate them. Moreover, it was clear the intellectuals were not prepared to work together. Though we did not always agree with Mr. Beck, he represented the Government, and like the great masses of the Polish people, we believed he should be supported during his term of office. Naturally some of the Cabinet Ministers realized clearly what was going on, others, as in every other country, merely jockeyed to keep their high positions. It was against these that the Opposition launched their most successful attack.

After the October rains the sun shone brightly for the last few days of autumn before the heavy fog bank shut off the winter sky. We were having eighteen for luncheon, and an autumn menu : Baked mountain mushrooms, guinea hens with wattleberry sauce, and for dessert, Royal Riviera pears weighing over a pound apiece, grown by Tatus in his garden, stuffed with almond paste and stewed. I had had to choose the wines and change the menu. Before I had finished the bell rang and the first guests began to arrive. When John appeared, he whispered in my ear, "Victor, Makowska's nephew, is opening the front door dead drunk !"

"Tell him to go away," I whispered back. "I never did like his hanging around our house anyway. Edward can manage both doors."

"Victor has lived on our charity long enough, I 'll tell him to leave at once," John exploded. When after a few moments he returned, he was pale with anger. But lunch was served before I could find out what had happened. As we entered the dining room he looked with surprise at the re-arranged seating, and glancing at the wine, whispered to Edward, the house-boy, to change the Montrachet which I

ordered. I supposed he thought it too heavy for the Mont-
rose that was to follow. The two men to my left and right
were talking heatedly across the table, and for the instant
my thoughts wandered off to the good uncorked wine which
would mildew, and I thought, "I will have to invite the Bishop
and Uncle Anthony's family Friday. They will enjoy Montrachet with a pike." John was looking at me. "Yes, I will
pay more attention to our guests," my eyes said back to him.
"Mr. Minister has had a good vacation?" was an easy way to
begin.

The moment the guests were gone we called Makowska.

"How was the dinner? I know the lady will say the
parmesan cheese was too mild."

"It's about your nephew — about Victor. He opened the
front door, drunk."

"The lady knows my husband is away by day working on
the Zamek." I found Makowska's voice had an unexpected
peevishness.

"Makowska knows I am not criticizing her, but her nephew.
I want him to leave our house immediately."

"Leave our house! His mother — a poor widow!" Makowska wailed.

"When your husband is away Edward can open the door.
There is no question of Victor's staying here. He must go
at once."

"He has been so useful and helpful," Makowska begged.

"He has to leave this house within two hours or I will call
the police to arrest him for disorderly conduct," John said
angrily.

When Edward came in to clear away the coffee cups and
liqueur glasses, he said, "There is a fortune to be had from
the rag man for the wodka bottles in the cellar."

"I shall see he surely leaves," John promised confidently,
but half an hour later he returned and telephoned his lawyer.
"Brem says we can call the police. Victor has passed out,
and the others say he has brought girls into the house."

Makowska was not in the kitchen, where I went to ques-

218

tion her, but in a heap on her bed. It was the first time I had ever seen her weeping with uncontrollable sobs.

"Gracious Makowska, he 's only your nephew. Send him away and all will be forgiven." Makowska did not answer.

Of his own accord, Victor left during the afternoon, and we tried to forget the whole incident. On the next day we received a letter from the State Attorney saying that since Victor had worked for us as janitor of "so and so many rooms" without contract or pay, we were due to pay a fine of a year's board wages and a year's sick and unemployment insurance at six dollars a month. We sent this astonishing document to our lawyer, who promised to attend to it. About a week later, however, we received a summons to appear at Court, the day being the one on which John's weekly lecture in Cracow was scheduled.

"I can go to Court," I said confidently. "It 's surely simple to prove he came here while we were away in Vienna. We never hired the boy. He annexed himself to us ; the whole story is preposterous !"

Our lawyer, however, advised settling with Victor. "If you lost," (and we were fighting the State) "you would have all the Court fees to pay in addition."

"I would rather go to Court. I am sure we can't lose."

The date of the trial was Tuesday, November 9th, 1937. On Monday I had little time to talk it over with John before he left for Cracow. I had had a busy morning and we had had two Cabinet Ministers for luncheon. In the afternoon the Ministers stayed till four, discussing points in the Danube report.

When they were gone, John said, "It 's the last chance to plant the bulbs. It might freeze any time now."

"It 's growing dark," I protested.

"We 'll all do it together — and Andrew too. Andrew can make the holes for Poppy to plant bulbs," he said gaily.

There were two hundred narcissus bulbs and a hundred tulips, as well as scyllas, snowdrops and some daffodils to be grouped about the garden. It was drizzling faintly. The first cold icy fog had set in. John's face was streaked with mud, and his hair was dripping in the rain. "Leave the rest, let's stop," I had begged over and over again. "I will plant them tomorrow."

"You know you won't! Besides, I need the exercise."

"Please come in. It's so cold!"

"Go in and order the tea. I'll be finished shortly." His gentle voice had a low thrilling timbre.

"My back aches, and yours must too," I weakly protested.

"If you won't go in, then get a lantern and hold it for me." I held it for him for the last hour while he worked.

When we came in, my Polish teacher, Miss "Book," was sitting by the fire.

"What has happened?" she cried in consternation, taken aback by our muddy hands and dishevelled appearance.

"Nothing. Bulb planting! We will have tea presently."

"Mr. John is having tea with us!" she exclaimed. "That is an unexpected pleasure."

There was a tremendous noise in the hall, and John came in roaring like a lion, with Andrew on his back. "Andrew is going to have tea with us too."

"Mr. John, it is such an honor to have tea with you. I hope I am not intruding."

"Far from it! When I hear my wife speak Polish, I always thank you!"

"There is still much to be done with her spelling —"

"You will always help her?"

"Always, always, I promise it!" she said with emotion.

In a businesslike way, John finished two cups of tea and a plate of bread and butter, went to his study and came back with a waste basket.

"What in the world have you got there?"

"A surprise! Miss Book, please keep my wife occupied till I say 'look.'"

"Andrew wants to help."

"No, Andrew would tell Mummy. It's a surprise. You go sit on Miss Book's lap. She will tell you a lovely story."

She began, "Once upon a time —"

Andrew
at four
months

Andrew
at three
years

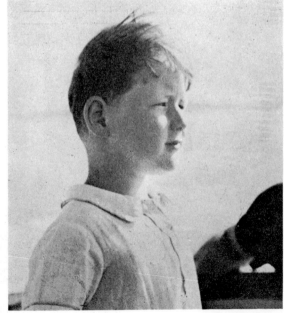

Above: Our house in Warsaw

Below: The house in Cracow

On the piano John had spread out some maps he had picked up for a penny, and was measuring them around the waste basket. He had put glue to melt in a little white enamel cup in the embers of the fireplace.

I stretched out on the sofa before the fire, thinking again how tenuous my happiness was — the frail thread of John's life so precious that everything, even this room, seemed alien by comparison. Those lovely silks hanging on the wall, which he had found for nothing in discarded dust piles, one could see how fine they were only when they were washed and pressed and mounted. These pictures whose artistic value he had by some instinct recognized! These chairs and rugs, he had found them all, but never felt he owned them. When he would bring home a piece of china, or a snuff box or a clock, he would say, "When the war comes, we will live by selling this!" Oh, Fate that showed me this peace and joy, let me taste this bliss a little longer!

John was bent intently over his work. How thin the hair on his poor bald head had gone, the half moon of hair that grew down on his neck and curled at the edges, the clean white collar, always spotless. How thin he had grown that summer! His coat hung off his shoulders.

"You must call the tailor, dear, to have him take in your jacket." Silence. "It's simply hanging off you."

Andrew was sitting spellbound on Miss "Book's" lap.

John turned suddenly around and said in Polish, "No matter what happens, my wife will always say she felt it coming."

Miss "Book" looked up and smiled absently, going on with her story.

"What do you mean, dear?" I felt pained.

"Your basket's ready. How do you like it?" he replied cryptically.

"It's lovely! The old white is just a perfect match for my room, and those baroque scrolls you painted relieve the plainness. Let me take it in and see how it looks." How quickly he had waved that cloud away.

I put the basket by my toilet table which he had designed

221

to use my mother's duchess lace. When I came back he had made a second basket in brown for his own room.

"Andrew's bed time! Thank you, Miss "Book." We will see you soon again? I shall have plenty of time tomorrow while Mr. John is in Cracow."

While we were dressing for dinner, John said, "I don't want you to leave the party at the Winslow's this evening. I'll just slip out, come home and change. You stay till the party breaks up!"

"How can you ask me to stay? Of course I will leave with you. I could help you pack."

"I won't take anything but my papers."

"Things for the train?"

"They will go in my briefcase. I will be back tomorrow as usual."

"On the train that gets in at midnight?"

"That gives me time for both lectures. If I take the three o'clock train I have to rush."

"I hate to have you go."

"I hate to do it. But don't be silly, it's only for one day."

"I shall miss you frightfully — every minute. Oh, be careful!"

"There's no more danger in going to Cracow than there is in going downtown."

"I know that," I said sadly.

"I could wait over and take the 9 A.M. plane."

"No, that's worse. You promised never to go by plane alone, remember?"

"I remember."

"You know winter is a bad time to fly. Remember what Raczynski said about flying after he married."

"Let's not go over all that. I only asked you."

"The dark cloud?"

"I never feel it when I'm with you."

Edward knocked at our door. "Evening mail," he said.

"A letter from that Lwow professor. I think I told you, there is an opening there for next year for full professor. How would you like moving to Lwow?"

222

"I'd love it."

"You don't know anyone there."

"If you liked your work I'd love it," I repeated.

At ten thirty, when John stood up to take leave of our host, I got up also.

"You stay.   You said you would," he whispered.

"I have to go too," I insisted aloud.

"I'll take you home," someone said.

"Stay on," everyone begged jovially.

I felt trapped.   Clutching at John's arm, I pleaded, "Don't make me stay, please."

"My wife is tired.   This first month in Warsaw has taxed her strength."

I leaned against him, happy and relaxed.   Alone in all the world he could understand perfectly.

We ran home gaily.

"While you are packing I will undress.   You can kiss me good night in bed, and I will try to go to sleep at once."

"Darling!"

John was running in and out of the room, putting books and papers in his bag.   By the time he snapped it closed I was in bed.

He knelt down by the bed.   "Good night," he said, and made the sign of the cross on my forehead.   "Sweet dreams."

"I love you."

"Forever."

"Forever."

I burrowed my head in his neck where I could feel the familiar knot in his throat against my eyes.

"Stop crying.   Nothing will happen.   You know I have to do this every week, and if you are going to make a tragedy over it I shall have to give it up."

"Forgive me."

"Yes.   Well — good night."

"Don't go."

"I'll miss my train.   Good-bye."   Without turning he fled out of the room, down the hall, slammed the doors.   I ran to the window to see if there was a taxi at our corner.   The falling mists had coated the sidewalk with crinkly ice. I tried to beat back the tears, the tightness in my throat.

"I'm so foolish," I thought. "When John goes out every day I think nothing of it. There is no difference. If only one were as alert to be tender when he was at home as when he was leaving it. I must try and be less impatient when he is late — and less possessive."

The bed stood in a recess formed by book shelves — on one side histories, on the other current books. I pulled out Thiery's *"Tableau de l'Histoire Romaine"* and found my place. John would be arriving at the station. I could see him running through the temporary building, his coat flying, and down to the new tunnel two flights below the street.

CHAPTER *16*

THE next morning, a half hour ahead of time, I arrived at the Court with our administrator. The Labor Courts had set up their jurisdiction in what had been the Jewish section. They had taken over an old apartment house without making over the building. Having found out in which apartment our trial would be heard, we picked our way through the crowded, muddy courtyard and climbed up a wooden back staircase. We had to push our way up among a crowd of loitering workmen. On the fourth floor the schedule for our trial was posted by a front door. We shoved our way into the inner hall. The smaller rooms were occupied by stenographers. Two main rooms had been thrown together, and here the Court was already in session. A list of the cases hung on the bulletin board.

"Our trial is next," the administrator said. "I will look for the lawyer. Does Madame intend going on the witness stand?"

"You, Mr. Administrator, should know how long Victor has lived in our house with Makowska. You know we never gave him permission to remain. But if their lawyer needs me, I will stand."

While we were looking for him, the lawyer saw us. "I advise you to settle, Madame," he told me immediately. "The State proctor is giving all the verdicts to the workers."

"Legally, how do we stand?" I inquired.

"These days when workers get free State attorneys —" he began.

225

"Do you mean to say any person you rescue in charity from the street can claim to be a hired servant ?" I exploded.

"The law says — if you accept their services — they are entitled to compensation," the lawyer patiently explained.

We were called. At the back of the Courtroom others waiting trial filled all the benches. Those whose case was being heard came up to the Judge and sat before him. Our case was read by the lawyer. The State Attorney claimed that we had taken advantage of a country lad to exploit him without payment of regular wages. He had had to work for us for nothing, only for tips as a doorman ! Our lawyer protested that Victor was the nephew of our doorman, and showed as proof the signed contract with Makowska. "Why was he allowed to stay and take tips ?" the Judge asked pertinently. "That proved you used his services. Doubtless the boy was too ignorant to know how to make a contract. The State must protect such ignorant workers, and must fine you on the basis of the equitable contract you had failed to make."

"But Mr. Judge, he was a drunkard, and refused to leave our house. He was there as a visitor."

"Drinking ? Well, he shall be fined for drinking while on duty. Your fine, then, will be eight hundred zlotys."

I was stunned. "We will appeal," I said to the lawyer. "Makowska can testify for us."

"You cannot leave Court without paying the Court fees," the lawyer reminded me.

"I haven't the money."

"I thought of that contingency. I will pay it."

"It is utterly preposterously unfair !" I was bewildered and furious.

It was two o'clock when I returned home. The telephone bell was ringing as I opened the front door.

"Hello." John's deep throaty voice. "Now, please don't worry. I am bringing Mulka back with me by tomorrow's plane. You will release me of my promise ?"

"Yes, if you ask it."

"Don't be silly ! Good-bye."

226

"John, John — the Court ruled against us."

"Oh, yes, the trial. You can tell me about it tomorrow. I must rush for my class now. Good-bye."

The telephone clicked. So that was it ! Tomorrow. To-day, all this afternoon, and tonight and tomorrow, I must wait.

"Madame will come in to luncheon ?"

"Oh, luncheon. Yes, in a moment."

I telephoned my brother-in-law. "Hello, Michael ?"

"Yes."

"John is bringing Mulka by plane tomorrow."

"I wonder if anything is wrong. Mulka was to see the doctor or something. Well — "

"Stop in on your way upstairs tonight."

"I 'll try to remember. I 'll be late, though."

The next morning, the 11th of November, the bells were ringing. The two maids came in to ask what time they could go to church.

"I will just have a light luncheon. Dinner this evening, when the elder lady and the Master will be here."

"Madame does not fear this foggy weather, for flying ?"

I tried not to think about it.

On his way out to church, Michael said, "If you will have lunch at one I will come eat with you. But I can't drive out to the field. We are taking advantage of the holiday to have a meeting of the Housing Board. I will be back at the latest by five o'clock for tea."

Andrew was playing on the floor in his room. "Babby will bring me an aeroplane."

"What makes you think so ?"

"This one is broken."

"You shouldn't have such expensive toys. They are not for such a little boy."

"Andrew is a big boy, not a little boy," he said stoutly.

I roamed restlessly about the house, rearranging the flowers, looking two or three times into the guest room to see whether fresh paper was in the drawers and towels in the bathroom. There were many letters to be written to America, but I was in no mood to write them. "An hour's finger exercises will

227

be the thing!" But soon my mind wandered and my fingers stumbled on the keys.

The living room had three French windows giving out on to our courtyard garden. John had laid the rough flagstones, gathered up from the left-over stone facing of our house. The flowering moss we had planted so carefully had died, except at the edges. Among the rose bushes which bordered the flagging, many were missing after our two years' absence. The fog was coming in closer and closer. It cut off our nearest neighbors. "Too damp for Andrew to go out." The governess complained to the house-boy. Too damp for Andrew. I shivered. By the fireplace the cat was curled up on her favorite cushion. She had made a dark spot from constantly lying there. When the dog came over to sniff at her, she jumped down and ran away. I sat down on the warm pillow.

"If I go in John's study I will telephone him not to fly. I will telephone and see if they are flying. I can at least telephone the Lot" (Polish Airlines).

They had no indication from Cracow whether the plane would be running. At lunch I would ask Michael to telephone and beg them not to fly. When at one Michael came in, he said it was nonsense to telephone. The aeroplane would not leave the ground if there were danger.

With an hour to spare I got out the car. Andrew had had his nap early so he could come with me. At two in the afternoon the fog was so thick that the street cars had on their lights. I feared to miss my crossing. Out by the old airport, used now for amateurs, there was an unusual silence. No planes were taking off. There were none of the aeroplane buses that usually raced past us. And I thought, "If something happens to the car now, no one will ever find us."

"Mummy, sing me a song," Andrew begged. "Mummy, tell me a story."

"A story of being way off in the world of make-believe as we are now?"

In an hour's time we reached the airport. We should

have done it in half an hour. We were just in time. There was the plane now — you could hear it overhead.

We ran through the building and out to the barrier on the field. A loud speaker was calling, "Plane down from Bucharest. Plane down from Bucharest. Plane down —"

"What about the Cracow plane ?"

"It's overhead. It had to leave the field clear for the foreign plane."

"It will land in ten minutes."

"Or a quarter of an hour."

On the bench in the window a friend was sitting.

"Christine !"

"Dorothy !"

"Pella's coming up. Her brother died last night. She doesn't know it yet."

"Poor thing."

"You ?"

"I'm waiting for John and my mother-in-law."

There was a tremendous roar. The plane had just cleared the hangar. We ran out again.

"They missed it !"

"Missed it ?"

We came in and sat down once more.

"What happened to Pella's brother ?"

Ten minutes later the plane came back. This time it was flying higher. From the half open door of the radio room I heard, in Polish, "Why are you so high ?" Then, "He says he can't find the beam."

A man rushed past me. "Get the Army field lights," he called.

The door shut. There was a long silence. "Where are they now ?" I asked an attendant.

"They are ordered back to Cracow."

"Back to Cracow ?"

"There is less fog there."

My heart was beating painfully. "What did the man say ?" Andrew asked.

"They are to go back to Cracow. But I will ask someone else."

Out on the flying field they were shooting rockets. You could hear them popping. It was nearly dark. Once there was a roar above us as the plane circled the field.

"Tell them to wait till dusk. The beacons will be visible after dark," someone screamed.

Andrew clenched his fist and shook it at the invisible plane. "If you kill my Poppy, Mr. Pilot, I will kill you."

"Andrew," I said, shocked, "how can you think of such a thing !"

"Please buy me something. The lady over there wants me to have an aeroplane !" Andrew begged, dragging on my arm to pull me to the newspaper counter.

The door to the wireless room opened again. More men ran out. I followed, asking, "Why don't they land ?" He paid no attention, but entering a telephone booth, I overheard one man telephone the Military Hospital for an ambulance, and the other for the Police.

I ran back to where Christine was sitting. "There has been an accident," she told me.

"Was anyone hurt ?" I asked the guard.

"Probably everyone was killed," he said bitterly.

"You are trying to frighten us. No one was ever killed on the Polish Line."

"The radio doesn't answer. It hasn't answered for the last five minutes."

Employees and attendants were running in all directions, taking their coats and hurrying to the main entrance. "Where was the accident ?" I kept asking. I asked each one, but no one answered.

"Shall we follow in your car and send Andrew back home in mine ?" Christine asked.

"Let me first call my brother-in-law." I dialled my house. Michael answered.

"There has been an accident."

"Anyone hurt ?"

"No one knows. I am sending Andrew home in the Potocki's car. Their chauffeur will bring you here."

When I reached the main door, most of the attendants had gone. Only one car was still waiting for the military doctor and the Chief of Police. "I will follow you," I said.

"That is impossible. All relatives must wait before the Military Hospital on the Langewicza."

"All the same, I am following you," I called, as the car pulled away. Now the fog was like a thick rain. It clung to the windshield and froze with the particles of mud that were flung up by the car ahead, driving fifty miles an hour along a narrow lane. I followed at a few paces, fearing to lose it. At a few yards' distance the car was already invisible. We were crossing fields by farm roads, and both cars frequently spun circles in the mud. In order to see through the windshield I had to lift it wide open. I could hear the even voice of Christine at my side, saying, "Steady there. That's all right. Steady now. Left here. Straight ahead. All right now. Steady — steady." At every right angle turn the ambulance swerved half around, and, unable to use the brakes in the heavy mud, I skidded to the side of the road. "Steady now."

"Do you think they have medicines in the ambulance?"

"They took time enough. They must have everything."

Now we came up to a main road on which soldiers were marching, soldiers, tanks and armored cars. We crept along the grassy siding. My beam headlight had burned out, and I could not see the soldiers I was brushing past. Though barely a foot from the car they did not hear me above their marching song and the rumble of the heavy guns.

"They're returning from the Armistice Day parade."

"Was there a parade?"

"This morning."

My heart was sick, my brain dead, like a stone. Nor did my imagination suggest what I should find when we reached our destination.

Five miles down the road the ranks were broken, and the

ambulance ahead plunged down a slippery bank on to a pitch black field. I followed to where it stopped, churning mud all over my car. There was nothing to be seen beyond the ring of lights made by the dozen cars that had preceded us there.

Christine got out. I shivered, pulling my coat about me. Our little dog who had been crouching in the back seat, jumped into the seat beside me. A hundred people were milling around here. John surely would appear in an instant, a little dazed. It was better to wait for him here than miss him by running about aimlessly in the muddy field.

"Are you Mrs. Kostanecka?" A peasant's voice. "I thought so by your pearls. The lady is dead there. Her pearls are just like yours. Your husband told me you were coming with your little boy. He is expecting you."

"He is not hurt, surely."

"The gentleman told me. He was wearing a grey and black checked coat."

"That was he. Thank God!"

Some of the passengers were coming to the bus, which was two cars beyond us in the field. Some were walking alone ; others the soldiers were supporting. They were visible in the light made by the cars' headlights.

"Where is my husband ? Mr. Kostanecki ?"

"He 's very bad — bad — bad."

"How do you mean ?"

"He may not be living. Oh, frightful ! Frightful ! Oh ! Oh !"

"I was a colleague of your husband. Poor woman ! He is very bad."

"Get back in your car, Madame. We must move the bus. Your car blocks the passage."

I moved the car a little to the side. After the bus had pulled out the car arrived with Michael.

"Mulka has been killed."

"Have you seen her ?"

"I was waiting here for John. We can try and find them."

"Is John all right ?"

232

"So a woman tells me. Some other passengers say he is badly — " I could not say the words.

"Where was the accident?"

"The people came from there."

Three steps, and the heavy mud had sucked off my shoes. In the black night my feet were invisible. I stooped down to pick up my shoes, and when I stood up Michael was gone. "Michael!" No answer. Our little bitch came sniffing to my feet. "Look for your master. He may have fainted on this field," I said to the dog. How indeed if he had fainted would we find John? He might die of exposure before we reached him. Even the car's searchlights could not pierce the fog but for a short distance. I fell against the soldiers guarding the spot where the plane had crashed. "Mr. Kostanecki," I begged them frantically. "I am looking for Mr. Kostanecki. Tell him the car is by the others."

About the invisible wrecked plane the soldiers stood in line. They would not let me near it. Moving in the center of the circle with a light was a doctor, bandaging figures stretched on the ground. To the left was the empty ambulance. I stood by it waiting while the first of the wounded was brought up, a man, whose bandaged head was covered with a dirty plaid coat.

"Who is that?" I asked the attendants.

"It's a Mr. Band."

"And that?"

"The lady is the gentleman's wife."

A woman was carried by on a stretcher, deathly pale, and then another.

"That will be Pella," I thought, and called her name. When the four stretchers were put in place, the ambulance drove off.

Someone shouted, "Will that cholera of a private cholera pull out!"

I heard someone turn over my motor, and the motor stall. The little bitch was whining at my feet. "Where is our master, Irena? Our master?" I tried to run back to the car. My feet were burning, caked with mud, my stockings torn off below the ankle. Michael was standing by the automobile. A man had the hood up and was tinkering with the motor.

"Look at the mess you have made with my car! Short circuited the headlights! Get out."

I switched on the motor and pushed slowly into high gear, so as not to grind deeper into the mud. Like magic the car moved to the side and the ambulance pulled away.

Christine was following. "Pella is wounded. If John should come to the hospital I will tell him where you are."

"We are staying a little longer to be sure he is not still here."

"Perhaps he reached the high road."

"He might try to hitch hike to Warsaw."

"Yes," I said, comforted. "He would try to get home as fast as possible."

"I will see what is to be done about Mulka, and be back instantly," Michael said. "Wait in the car."

Waiting in the car, I dismissed what the other passengers had said. John and I lived under a glass bell. Our life was one — John had said it. We would both be killed together. It was terrible about Mulka, but John had luck because he loved me. Nothing could happen to him. This very instant he might be along the road. He would have hailed the special bus. Already he would be in Warsaw. The necessity of finding John was so strong in me that, to the amazement of the remaining chauffeurs, I turned the car as easily as if it had been standing on pavement. The mud, the nightmare of Mulka's death, the fog which hid everything under a black pall, could not obstruct my way. When Michael returned to the car, we drove back to Warsaw as if my eyes could penetrate the dark. My headlights had gone out, but I steered a course through marching men, passing trucks and farmers' wagons. I could drive slowly. I did not feel the pressure of time, for John steadied my hand and his voice close in my ear directed my way. Unconscious of my bruised and shoeless feet, like a sleepwalker, I drove slowly into town and across the city to our house.

"John !" I called as I opened the door. John had not telephoned. The bell had not rung. "You are certain ?"

"I waited in the hall after Mr. Michael telephoned for further news."

I slipped on a pair of shoes and left for the military hospital.

A line was standing there before the desk. "Mr. Kostanecki was not brought in from the field," the attendant informed us.

"Perhaps another wing ?" Michael inquired.

"Yes . . . an unidentified corpse was in the ambulance that left for the morgue."

We tore outside.

An ambulance was standing by the door, the driver smoking nonchalantly.

"Were you at the field ?"

"Yes."

"Is there someone in there ?"

"I have orders to let no one in."

We threw open the door. Could that really be John ? The face so distorted, the whole figure so caked in mud ! He was not even covered with a blanket.

"That is my husband. Drive him to my house."

"Orders ! He will have to go to the city morgue."

"If you will not drive the ambulance to my house, I will," I said, springing to his seat.

"Orders," the driver said grumblingly, as I pushed in the stiff clutch.

"You can come with us."

"I will drive, if you tell me where to go."

"Then Michael, you sit with the driver. I will sit with John."

While John's head rolled on the hard pad, I thought wildly of letters on his desk he had not read. What had he left behind to show the world what he had been ? And there flashed through my mind's eye the Etruscan Tomb of the Volumni . . . the national monuments, and all the nameless dead whose tombs we had passed so idly. Gone without a trace ! How cruel that John should go before his book which he was preparing on the "manipulated currency" would reach its American publishers. Only one of the articles on mathematical economy for the American Economists' Society. I tried not to look at the fine features, distorted now in death, or to face the empty years ahead. Both seemed irrelevant. Why had I not protested ? Kept him to his promise not to fly ? "Because," a voice within me answered, "death is no accident."

"Amen. Thy will be done."

This, then, was my punishment for loving John too much, for basing my life on his life, for not having once paused in loving John to wonder why we lived.

"For this I am bringing John home dead. Oh God, Thy will be done."

The ambulance stood by our house. The two men carried John up the stairs. "The Master is dead." The maids stood weeping on the stairs. Only the little bitch wagged her tail and jumped about the stretcher to lick the hand that was hanging down.

"Put him in the drawing room."

"Call the Priest."

"The undertaker too."

"We must telephone to Cracow."

"Yes. Tell Tatus before he hears it on the radio."

Our door was open to the street. My grief was open now to all the world. All that was home to me would soon be carried out, away, to be buried under alien soil. Death is a public thing. John was no longer mine. Already people were entering our house — the undertaker, the Priest, some friends. I crept back to our room and to Andrew's. Andrew was sleeping. As I stood by his bed, the sight of John's orphaned child broke me completely. I wept, not from self pity. I wanted no pity ; I had had more happiness than anyone deserved. I wept for John, who could not pass on to his son the richness of his own mind, and for Andrew, who would have only me. I stood by the wall and struck my head against it in unconscious grief.

"This way lies madness. How unworthy of John! I am what he made me," I suddenly realized. "I disgrace him now when he is most helpless. From now on I must live an outward life as he would live it, with an exterior bearing that hides our secret life. This is my only chance to keep John now," I thought. "This life is over. No one will penetrate it," I told him. "Dearest, as I longed to give you liberty in life, I will be faithful to you in death. I promise not to betray through grief our secrets and our feelings. To the world nothing will be changed. Your friends will find you here when they come. No one will ever see me with tears in my eyes, for no one can comfort me but you, my beloved. This is our secret grief, as it was our secret love."

In our room some of his cousins were sitting.

"Dearest!"

"You poor, poor thing."

"Weep a little — it will help you."

"Nothing can help me," I replied.

Michael telephoned to Cracow. Andzia answered. "Call Father from the Club and tell him. Do you hear me?" Andzia had fainted at the telephone.

During the Armistice celebrations in the Grand Opera House, the Chairman of the performance paused to give the radio announcement. Friends who heard it came at once. They knelt beside his bed and prayed. What were they saying? They took John from me and seemed to help him while I stood aside.

"I cannot pray. It's all meaningless to me."

"*Swieta Mario Matko Boska —*"

I took *King Lear* and went to my room. "This," I thought, "is the level of our life. I will read at night rather than let myself slip." The full Renaissance power of Shakespeare never seemed keener than that night. Never did the plight of King Lear appear so real.

At four in the morning I saw a light shining under the guest room door.

"May I come in?"

Michael was standing in the bathroom, shaving slowly.

237

"Did I disturb you?" he asked.

"No, I couldn't sleep. I came in to talk to you."

"As soon as I am dressed I am going out there."

"I wish you could drive the car."

"I'll have to learn now. What I keep asking myself is: Why did it have to be John and not me? He had everything to live for. I have nothing. He was successful. I am not."

"You mustn't talk that way."

"John's death will be much worse for Tatus."

"*Michael!*"

Early in the morning, Andrew ran in to our room.

"Where's my Poppy?"

"He went another way."

"When will he come?"

"He won't come now. He has gone on up to the sky, above the clouds."

"That's not true. The horrid pilot killed my Poppy. He fell down and broke. The aeroplane went boom!"

How could I answer him? I tried not to cry. He put his arms around me. "I'll be Poppy for you now. Don't cry. Where is your kerkersniff?" Then, toddling into the bathroom, he sprinkled the floor with the water which he was bringing in a glass. "Mummy lie down and drink the water. I will sit here, as Poppy always did. I will have my bed brought in to sleep by you. Yes?"

Old Andzia came with Tatus from Cracow. Though crushed, her duties gave her fortitude. As Andrew wished to sleep with me, she was to use his room.

"Madame must rest," she ordered.

"Andzia, how can I ever rest again?"

"You can change nothing," she said. "The lady must learn to bear it."

"All the same, I am haunted by the thought I could have prevented it. If only I had begged John not to come by plane! Or if I had gone for my own doctor, he might have saved John's life. He was not killed outright. The peasant woman told me that he spoke to her."

238

"Let Madame not torture herself so. God appoints for everyone his day. Master John will be spared untold suffering on this earth, you will see. Mulka he has surely taken to Himself."

"John had so much still to do. His book is only just half finished."

"God would not now have taken him like this unless he was ready for Eternity."

"Eternity!" These were empty words to me.

During the long afternoon a few of our closest friends came to my room. "Dorothy dear," they said, and knelt down at my side, "be comforted. This is not an idle accident of Fate. You will see. You will live to thank God for sparing John still greater sufferings."

"Since you loved him you should rejoice that he has gone while we can still mourn and pray for him. Think if he should have died unhonored and unsung."

"Anielka," I begged his cousin, "do you really believe in God and Heaven?"

"Yes, truly."

"That nothing is pure accident?"

"Of course. I believe life is only a period of test, and that on how we pass it depends our future eternity."

"The Greeks say 'the beloved of the Gods die young.'"

"That is only part of it. On earth none of us can guess when he has finished the part he had to play."

"John had felt a dark shadow hanging over him."

"He must have known death was near."

All day long streams of people came to the house. Hundreds of people came and left their cards. The doorbell rang incessantly. The messenger boy brought telegrams — over a thousand messages from other parts of Poland, France and Italy, from England and America. Flowers — great yellow tufted chrysanthemums and wreaths of myrtle. Many came to pray, and stood beside the coffin weeping gently, leaving again without a word.

One of the cousins called a milliner to come and measure

the long black veil that reached nearly to the ground, covering me completely, and all my clothes.

Mulka's body was released on the second day after the State had completed its investigation of the causes of the deaths and had ascertained the reason for the accident. Mulka was serene in death as she had been in life. Her life had been complete. She had died a month after resigning, by doctor's orders, from the presidency of her Parish Committees. She had died swiftly, as a modern woman, in a modern way. She was spared the humiliation of a slow, lingering old age. A proud smile was on her face — a challenge to those who die supinely in their beds! But John's face was different. You could see the torture that in death he could no longer protect us both.

"Oh, God, by John's death you have brought me to my knees. I pray this is sufficient punishment to keep me humble. I am Thy handmaiden, here to serve Thy will," I thought. During those days I no longer felt crushed with impotency or a sense of guilt for not having somehow prevented the inevitable event.

At the funeral I could be calm because John wished me to be so. Our souls, I found, were more united than before. Those immense laurel funeral wreaths sent by cabinet ministers and business firms seemed but a just, fitting tribute when they were stacked about his sepulchre. I could follow the service word for word with comfort. I could feel his shadow beside me, and I could believe my "faith" had given John the peace in death which he had known in life. I held poor Tatus' hand tightly while the crowd surged past to give their last words of condolence. I remembered what a barbaric custom this had always seemed to me. But now I was glad to be able to thank this horde of friends who had waited till the end in the stormy November cold, for their evident devotion to John and Mulka.

Driving home after the ceremony, the Bishop asked, "Did the Service bring you comfort? I read a number of special prayers for you from the Anglican prayer book."

"I thank you deeply, Uncle Bishop. It all seemed so complete and excellent I felt now I really must become a Catholic."

"You would only be acting under an emotional impulse. Religion is far more important as an intellectual philosophy and way of life. In a year, after you have studied diligently, you can decide."

"The Uncle Bishop will see that I speak in seriousness."

Tatus put a restraining hand on my arm. "You know how much Mulka always prayed for it. That should not today precipitate a hasty decision you would later regret. She always said 'Dorothy must not become a Catholic from a sense of duty to the family. She has not been trained to it.' "

As we drove up to the door, Edward was standing on the sidewalk. "Will the lady come at once. There is a telephone from America."

"Hello."

"Mrs. Kostanecka? Here speaks the international telephone. Please wait. Please wait. Please now speak."

It was my family in America. I could hear my mother gasp, then my brother spoke. The family was broken-hearted. They understood my grief. Mother would take the first boat. In ten days she would be in Warsaw. Someone would come with her if the doctor did not permit my father to make the journey.

The living room in which the Bishop and Tatus were standing had been restored to its former order, and yet the room seemed entirely changed. It was as impersonal as a scrupulously neat waiting room. Books, papers, all the small objects John scattered about him, had been stored away. I would certainly not replace them to create the illusion of his presence now. "An excellent room in which to receive," I thought. "Already so many strangers have crowded in here, John and I have nothing to say to each other.' But Tatus, fearing that now the coffin had been removed I would be overcome, put his arms about my shoulder murmuring as he drew me into the room, *"Biedne dziecko* — my poor child — come now and sit down, a cup of tea will restore you, *Biedne dziecko."*

241

"Mother will cross the ocean — she is taking the first ship."

"Will she travel alone ?" He asked in astonishment. I told him she planned to come immediately to Warsaw leaving my father to go to the south of France.

"Would it not be better for you or Michael to meet her in Paris ?" Tatus suggested. On the day following the funeral, he left for Cracow. "Each of us must face this alone," he had said.

Jadwiga, my friend from the eastern province, when she saw the Warsaw paper and read of the accident, packed up her bag and came to me at once. I was so astonished to see her at the door that I gasped. She told me how the express had just left when she had arrived at the station, so she took the local for the eight hundred miles, and travelled third class for twenty hours from the Russian frontier.

"How could you ever leave your children and your poultry ?"

"If your sister needed you, would you hesitated ? You have no sister, so I came. The boys are now old enough to take care of themselves."

"But the chickens ?"

"The business is going well this autumn. I supply five hundred pieces to Lwow every week and we have other orders too. This year I have turkeys and ducks as well as chickens."

"How did you manage to get away ?"

"I only came to see how you were. If you don't need me I will return tomorrow. I can go shopping for you. I'll call up your friends. You must not sit down to a meal alone. You should not be concerned with all these arrangements." In the morning she telephoned to some about meals, others to help address the five thousand envelopes for the acknowledgment cards, other friends would make clippings from the papers I did not now care to read. Members of the family would answer the letters, I was still too stunned to write.

In the *Encyclopaedia of Economists* it was printed:

"It can be said with exactitude of the late John Kostanecki that he fell as a soldier at his post. He and his mother were killed on the 11th of November, 1937, returning from his lecture at the University of Cracow. Among the wreckage were found scattered pages of a manuscript he was preparing for the 'Economist.' He followed a path rarely chosen by scholars. After achieving a brilliant doctor's degree in law at the University of Cracow, he obtained the title of Ph.D. at the London School of Economics. He worked with the Kemmerer Mission in Warsaw, and went through banking practice in both Warsaw and New York. He worked in the League of Nations in Geneva, and undertook economic research for the Polish Ministry of Foreign Affairs, and for the Polish Legation in Vienna concerning the economic conditions in the Danubian Basin.

"Though he had chosen a longer road than most scholars, it gave him greater knowledge of world economic conditions. It was only after that he joined the staff of the University of Cracow, and became Assistant Professor in the spring of 1937. But during these years he published many articles in various reviews. Mastery of this subject gave him an ease of thought and clarity of presentation, and such a thorough mastery of theory that he could briefly evalue the facts and make deductions. The seriousness, integrity and prudence of his opinions gave entire assurance that this training, unusual in Poland, would also produce unusual results. It is difficult to say who in Poland will be able to take his place in research, or in scholastic work.

"He had the broadest human interests, with great aesthetic sensibility, and there was no field of art that did not interest him. He was fine, noble, disinterested, the most reliable of colleagues. Such a man cannot be replaced, nor can his loss be forgotten."

From The *Times* Editorial :

"He inherited from his parents unusual intelligence and a very gifted mind. He was brought up in a highly intellectual atmosphere, with a first rate education. Nature endowed him lavishly with a rich intellect and an unusually fine, honest, simple character, loyal in friendship and with a charm that won all hearts. He was not only an economist, but an author, and in art and painting a real connoisseur.

"The accident was the more horrible as his life was radiant with family happiness, and in spite of his youth he possessed an unusually large circle of devoted, faithful friends. He promised so much! Everything prophesied a fine fruitful life. Of all this nothing remains but the memory of his good, lovely, and always slightly melancholy smile."

From *The Voice of the People* Editorial :

"His life reached far beyond the average of Polish conditions and he knew how to make the best of his exceptional opportunities, having on the one hand unusual conscientious thoroughness and the faculty for diligent work, and on the other a lively understanding of everything beautiful and good. His earnest work could not but justify in even the most jealous eyes all his social success and brilliant achievements. Half a year ago he was appointed Assistant Professor of Economics at the University of Cracow. It was always an amazement that among so many temptations of life, in the noblest sense of the word, he was able without help to keep abreast of the latest scientific discoveries and plough through the most complicated and intricate theoretical dissertations. He published several important works, including 'The Discount Policy of the Bank of England' and 'The Danubian Economic Problem.' But the most valuable of his ideas was revealed in scientific discussions and conversation. The terrible and tragic death which overtook him cut off a life which seemed a blossoming flower in the sterile Polish field. All Poland is moved by the calamity which has stricken his wife and father. May the knowledge of this widefelt grief soothe their intolerable pain."

Miss "Book" came to the house every afternoon as soon as her classes were over, to help with the writing of the letters which kept coming in every day. I asked her whether she had heard over the radio of the accident and how it was that she had managed to be there within a half hour of my coming home. She told me that she had been sitting at home in conference with the other primary teachers. She had just brought them tea when they all heard a knock at the door. She went to open it. When she came out in the hall, there stood Mr. John in his new blue suit with the white pinstripe. She was so startled to see him that she said, "Oh, Mr. John, how kind of you to come and call on me !"

He did not answer but put his hand to his head and when he took it away she saw the wound in his forehead. *"Go to my wife, I beg you, and please never leave her as long as it is in your power to help her."*

When she saw the wound, she cried out, and at that he vanished. She was so terrified she ran back and told the other teachers what she had seen. Feeling compelled at once to come to me, she left them at her house and crossed the whole city. It took her three-quarters of an hour by the street car to reach my house and when she arrived, she saw the ambulance standing before the door. She waited until the driver came out and left, before daring to enter. When she saw what had happened, she had not wished to speak to me but had knelt by John's side with the others.

"You know I will do everything to help you. I have only three hours free in the afternoon but they will be yours and Andrew's."

How could I thank her for time for which she would not now let me pay and which she could so ill afford to spare. She was so frail, she needed the rest, and her days were so wearing; yet she never failed to appear.

We had not finished all the letters before my mother arrived in Paris. Michael did not wish me to travel alone and went with me to meet my mother. She spent the winter in Warsaw and in the spring, returned to America.

CHAPTER *17*

*E*VER since I had known anything of Warsaw, I had heard eulogies of the Asylum for the Blind at Piaski. It was run by a group of young Catholics as a lay organization. There were rumors that a British Ambassadress had been so deeply impressed by this organization that she decided to become a Catholic. For the first time she saw Catholicism as a far deeper and more vital force than she had imagined from watching stodgy old ladies telling their beads in church.

In the course of many conversations I had caught the names of various people who had joined Piaski. Later I noticed that they had slipped out of fashionable society. It was hinted that Zulcia had given everything to Piaski. Some one whispered that, after the death of his father, Leonek had turned over the whole of his inheritance. I also heard that Halcia was about to join them, and that Rozyczka was working for them. However, I had no real idea of what Piaski was, so I asked Halcia, a childhood friend of John's what they did there.

"We train the blind to be self supporting," she told me. "Each year our Directress visits a different country to study the best foreign methods. I couldn't really tell you about it, you would have to see it."

"I should like to," I replied vaguely, without enthusiasm.

"It's only a short drive," she urged. "If you came out after lunch you could be back for tea. The land was given by that friend of Rozyczka's."

I pictured a made-over farm house for a few blind children. "Shall we go Thursday, then?" I suggested.

246

To my surprise, as we emerged from the highroad, we came upon a substantial institution. It was dominated by a fine modern building with a large grassy turn-around that gave it a certain dignity. At one side a lane led to the old white-washed barns and chicken houses of the original farm, set down without much ceremony along a muddy farm road. Strung out along another road as it straggled into the wood, were little buildings, some of brick and some of wood, among them a small wooden chapel.

As soon as we entered the main building, Halcia and Zulcia showed me the way to the classrooms and the gymnasium and left me in the large auditorium. Asking to be excused, they immediately became absorbed in a whispered conversation with the director and several of the teachers. I was left to wander about by myself. I had never before seen so many blind, deaf and crippled children. There were altogether four hundred of them, and the sight of these poor children was in itself so unpleasant that even the most beautiful surroundings would have presented themselves in a mournful light. I was hardly even aware of the fine steel and concrete structure about me. Nor did I know anything about teaching the blind, and so I was a poor judge of the quality of the classrooms giving off the long corridors. But I could appreciate the work of feeding and clothing so many children and I was staggered to think how my friends had accomplished it.

Some of the older children were preparing a pantomime on the auditorium stage, others were making hideous noises while learning choral songs. The littlest children were climbing up and down the stairs without supervision. Each had a still smaller child by the hand and by some miracle they neither fell headlong nor collided with the toddlers descending by the opposite rail. Whenever they passed me they seemed to sense a stranger was there, and put out their hands to feel me. I had no idea how to respond to them. They made me so uncomfortable that, without waiting for my friends to reappear, I went outside.

It was one of those late May days when, in the shade, the cold wind felt more like March, though the bright sunlight seemed to burn holes through the chill air. The wind roared in the pine woods and made the weeping birch sway like a metronome. Keeping in the sun, I hurried along the path that led to the lea of the barnyard which was enclosed on four sides by cleanly whitewashed buildings. There were two small cottages along the way, and as I passed, some ancient dames came to the doorway to call a greeting. They must have felt my step, for they too were blind. In the dairy, blind boys were milking cows under the direction of the farmer, learning a self-supporting trade. But the girls? For what were they preparing?

I was leaning against a protecting wall when Leonek, a cousin of John's, appeared. He was dressed in an old sheep-skin lined leather jacket. The red braid trimming was soiled and threadbare. His head was covered in an old fur turban, and his tweed trousers had rusted in the sun.

"Did Halcia bring you out?" he asked pleasantly. "Have you seen everything?"

"Not yet. I left Halcia and Zulcia in the main building and came out here."

"Then I will show you the men's quarters and the chapel. They will show you where the women are trained," he said, and led the way at a brisk trot. He chose a more sheltered path at the edge of the wood where several white painted cottages were secluded among the trees. Going to the door of one, he said, "This is where I live, if you would care to see my room. It's at the top."

He bounded ahead up the narrow spotless stairs, clean with monastic scrupulousness. He had a small attic room, a narrow bed, a table and a shelf of books, and on the wall photographs of Rubens' *Descent from the Cross*. His "other suit" hung against the wall under a cover, and a small chest of drawers must have held all the rest of his possessions. There were no stray objects in sight.

"How neat!" was all I could find to say. The contrast of this room with others Leonek had renounced flashed through my mind : his father's palace in Rome with the portraits of Polish Kings covering the walls of eleven drawing rooms. I wondered whether he had ceased to be Chamberlain of the Pope. I knew he had left the lovely Renaissance castle in Corinthia to his sisters, and that he had offered the house on the family estate to the Polish Army as a recreation center for the soldiers stationed in the region.

I looked at Leonek, who was cut out by inheritance and training to be a Papal Chamberlain in the gorgeous trappings of the Vatican, standing before me dressed like a peasant. He had given up a promising diplomatic career to teach blind boys how to milk cows. He had not even gone into the priesthood, for fear of diverting his energies from "serving" into making a career. As Leonek led me from one to another building, he explained how one person had given the dairy farm, another the cattle. Someone else had bought the adjacent birch woods, others had built the houses and the log chapel. Leonek, I imagined, must have donated the main building with the auditorium. I knew Michael gave the larger part of his income every month to running expenses in Piaski, though he had not yet joined the group. He had tried at various times to make me understand their feeling of social obligation. I could remember certain of his phrases : "The people who have the money should take care of those who haven't." It was as simple as that. "If you haven't money, of course you have no obligation ; but if you have money, you have to do something constructive. Pretty soon there will be no private capital anyway," he would say with a grin. "Certainly better to give it away while it is still yours to give."

All these people out here felt that way, Leonek made me understand. They were all about his age, in their twenties and thirties. They had joined Piaski because they no longer felt the usual charity work everyone did, a few hours a day, was enough. They had to give their whole time, their entire energies, their complete resources to live a totally Christian life, a life of charity, humility and poverty. As I could see, this small school which they had founded to train blind adults had grown to include blind children and even deaf mutes.

249

Leonek did not have to tell me what sacrifices he and the other members of Piaski have made. All had been born into wealth and social position. Leonek had quickly risen to First Secretary of Embassy, though he was one of the few wealthy men's sons at the Polish Foreign Office that had done so. Both Zulcia and Halcia could have made brilliant marriages. They were connected to the best country gentry and handsome young men swarmed through their drawing rooms. Rozyczka's father was a literary giant and her brother the first physicist in Poland. They had not joined through any vain notions of noblesse oblige or tickling their vanity by "doing good." They gained no publicity. No one knew the day they joined or what they did. They did not even wear a romantic costume. They all dressed in plain, nondescript suits which they wore summer and winter, on all occasions.

As early as 1935, Michael had told me the next war would become a conflict between barbarianism and Christianity. Stalin and Hitler both attacked the church and were equally opposed to any religious organization except a state church.

"You will see," Leonek told me, "the church will be the only champion of the universal right to a free education — free radio and free press."

"What about Mussolini and Franco working through the church ?" I reminded him.

"When did the church actually co-operate with them ?" he asked. "Some misguided prelates may have personally sympathized with Fascism but the church never approved of it. The dictators cleverly tried to get popular support by appearing to champion the church." I must have seemed unconvinced for he urged me to read the Papal Encyclicals.

He told me the informal international organization they were establishing. Money was being collected to aid young German and Russian Catholics. Anti-Nazi publications printed in German were smuggled over the frontier. Many of my friends who obtained German visas to visit art exhibitions met secretly with young German Catholics, and provided them with funds painfully collected in Poland from persons already living on the margin of subsistence.

250

Their Catholicism had left the drawing room and gone underground in the fight against both Communism and Fascism. Hitler's repudiation of Concordats, his confiscation of Church property, was proof enough of his intentions. They were not misled by his anti-Communist talk. They also realized that if indeed the Communists reached an agreement with their Bishops, their traditional church, which worships Holy Russia, would be no substitute for a real religion.

With these political ideas I was in full agreement. Even before John died we had discussed them. What I could not understand even after visiting Piaski was the Catholic idea of humility. It was clear that the Uncle Bishop would never permit my joining the Catholic church until I understood that fundamental dogma. On the next favorable opportunity I decided to broach this topic with Mr. Savery, the British Consul, himself a convert.

* * * * * *

Usually I took a walk at three o'clock in the afternoon. Sometimes through the crowded park to the Botanic Gardens, thronged even in the coldest weather with women and children. Sometimes I would drive the car out to the great forest fortress that circled Warsaw like a close protecting wall where one could walk on the old battle trenches, now firm and smooth with grass and heather. These woods, from ancient times, had been the last defense of Warsaw. On days of icy wind or torrid heat, I would choose the shut-in forest for protection, but it was along the dykes of the Vistula that I loved best to walk.

During the ten years I lived in Warsaw, the whole outline of the city had changed. Across the river you could see the new promenade along the waterfront, and great modern dwellings, blocks of steel and concrete encased in stone, which hid the soft baroque outline of the old tile roofs. I had heard foreigners call it "Building for the Germans," but Poles closed their ears to such talk and shut it from their minds.

From the dykes, the full open dome of heaven and the

vast circle of the horizon were hardly broken by the spires of Warsaw across the river. You could follow for miles along that high mound of earth that protected the wide Vistula plain. Here Pilsudski had turned back the Bolshevik hordes in 1920, while Marshal Foch sat sulking in Warsaw because Pilsudski had not put the river between him and the enemy.

Here I learned that death is not the end but the beginning. On these plains Poles had died in every generation, fighting for Poland. Therefore, Poland lived. This was clear to everyone in Poland : "Nations only die when their people put their personal comfort before their country's welfare."

When one afternoon Mr. Savery invited me for a walk along the river, I seized the opportunity to discuss those problems which were troubling me most. "What are the Catholic ideas of meekness, charity, Free Will vs. Destiny," I began, "I can't grasp them."

"Leonek is a perfect example," Mr. Savery said.

Still I could not understand. "What does he gain by burying himself out in that school ?"

"He humbly serves God," he replied.

"Then why does he not become a priest ?" I asked.

"Being a priest is already a position, even if it 's the bottom rung of the ladder. I think he doesn't want to be distracted by even that pomp and ceremony. After his father's death, he inherited his position as Papal Chamberlain. He could have made a great career in the Church, had he wished. He preferred to serve God, by sacrificing his life to charity."

"Charity," I seized on the word. "In America social workers live for charity," I pointed out.

"That 's not real charity. It 's a job, and they make a career for themselves in it too."

"What is wrong with that ?" I asked.

"Not wrong. But it is not the same as charity. American social work is a paid profession, like school teaching. Charity cannot be paid. Unless charity means a sacrifice it is a contradiction in terms. Do American social workers feel humble before the people they serve ?"

"Why should poverty make one feel humble ?" This was a conception I could not grasp. I had always felt intensely sorry for the poor. During my childhood in Boston, while my father was director of Lincoln House, I had seen many poor families and heard of their problems. I would have gladly engaged in any heroic deed to change their lot. Because of this emotion, I had felt rather proud and superior towards my classmates at Miss Windsor's School. Now I was being told I had no conception of charity. "Do you believe the lowliest, most ignorant beggar can come as close to God as, say you or I ?"

"I think it possible."

This amazing reply, coming from Mr. Savery, who I felt had the finest intellect of any of our friends knocked all my props from under me. The cold wind buffeting the aeroplanes wheeling overhead chilled me through.

Wildly, as if in a final challenge to God himself, I cried out, "How could an omnipotent God let John die ?"

"When war comes, John will be spared all of it," he said earnestly. "Would you prefer to have him killed on a battleground ?"

"Why should God allow wars anyway ?" I demanded. "I really don't see how anyone can believe in a Supreme Being if He could not prevent war."

"It all comes down to why we are on earth. Certainly not just to eat and sleep — " Savery began.

"Or to fight wars like animals for survival," I interrupted. A flock of crows flew up from the willow thicket along the river, and cawing mournfully, settled in the high branches of the bare sycamores.

"A different kind of survival," he corrected gently, "spiritual, not animal. War brings opportunities of heroism, generosity and dying to save others, inconceivable in animals."

"So the best are killed and the cowards live on — "

"To have another chance of lifting themselves above the animal level."

"But only the worst are left to carry on. Look how France is degenerated."

"Let's not talk like Nazis," he said with feeling. "There are millions of fine individuals in France."

The aeroplanes that had been practicing acrobatics at a great height now swooped down to cross the river, frightening the flock of crows, which flew off across the meadow with a great clatter.

"But during war what happens to progress?" I asked, digging my cold hands deeper into my pockets.

"Progress!" he exclaimed. "What, historically, do you mean by progress?"

"Surely progress is the greatest good for the greatest number," I recited as if by rote.

"Good, my dear child, is not synonymous with 'goods.' Goods have a way of stifling men's souls. With all today's material wealth, do men have more security than in the past? The nineteenth century reached the peak of peace and prosperity; it also reached the height of cynicism and agnosticism, for which we will now pay a terrible price. When war comes you will believe in God. You will have no one else to turn to."

"An expensive way to learn religion!"

"Few people value anything unless they pay a high price for it," he remarked. "The price for learning about good and God will be expensive — the brotherhood of man, real Christian love — and charity will become permanent only when brutality proves a failure."

"I still don't see why a God creates evil."

"God does not create evil. He created the free man, who has an unbounded choice to do good or evil. An animal can only follow its instinct. Because men have free choice, they can make a good or bad society. God does not organize the state."

"So you believe war is in the long run beneficial?"

"Not the war, but the results of war," he replied. "It's only in war-time that small nations gain an equality with great. Promises made under war-time necessity often force useful reforms, impossible to obtain under other conditions."

Now the heavy wind, which had filled the sky with dark

clouds, chased the planes away. Hastening our pace we turned toward home.

"Perhaps all you say is right," I had to admit. I could remember John's saying, "Everything that happens to us during life is a lesson and whether it's a harder or easier existence lies in the temper of our times." I began to realize through the hard road of war, nations would finally live in peace and cease blaming God for their own shortcomings.

"Until John died," I said, "it never occurred to me that I had not complete control over my destiny. Now I realize this control was given me for only a short span of years over only a small part of my destiny. If John were only the memory he left in dying, how futile would all his versatility and erudition have been. Going over his printed articles, so many of which are lost and incapable of translation, I realize they too are unimportant as far as he is concerned."

Mr. Savery took my hand. "Oh, I'm so glad to hear you say that now. How few Poles live to an old age. Polish history is written in the blood of their young men, and Poles can bear to see them die because they are so sure of meeting them in eternity."

Across the river, Warsaw was wreathed in an ominous cloud like a black curtain. It blocked out the sun. Suddenly we both felt cold.

"Let's hurry home to tea, to hear what's happening," I urged.

"The news from Austria sounded bad this morning," he told me. "For the last three days German troops have been marching towards the frontier."

"If only you in England would stop them!"

"Everything depends on the plebiscite Schuschnigg is holding."

"You still think they will wait for the plebiscite!"

How could one answer? A heavy black pall had hung over me ever since the night of John's death, icy cold like this late spring. I felt crushed by the colossal weight of the inescapable tragedy of the general paralysis creeping over Europe.

We had hardly returned when one of our friends from the Ministry of Foreign Affairs arrived in a great state of agitation. "I didn't dare telephone you. It won't be in the papers. We have positive information the Germans crossed at Linz."

"Then it's begun." I imagined the war had now started. "Have the Austrians asked Poland for help?"

"We can't get through to Vienna, but Schuschnigg wanted to fight."

"What did the Austrian Army plan to do?"

"Hold the Germans a day or two till the Czechs and Yugoslavs reached them," Thadee replied.

"Are they mobilizing?" I asked.

"We heard that they were. Of course it's all still a secret."

We huddled together about the fire, listening in our hearts to the throbbing tread of the German armies pouring into Austria. I shivered at the thought of those lovely peaceful meadows trampled under foreign boots, and of all my friends there in mortal danger.

As if reading my thoughts, Thadee warned, "Don't telephone anyone in Vienna. The Gestapo would seize them immediately. They will know without a message that you would take them in — friends are for times like these."

"Perhaps they haven't ready cash, or sufficient supplies in the house."

"It's too late to get it to them now," Thadee insisted.

Before the guests had gone I decided to leave for Cracow. I had the bags brought up, the administrator was summoned and the car sent to the service station. As soon as Michael returned, I told him my plan to leave early the next morning. He did not believe anything would come of the Austrian crisis. "No one will fight over Austria," he protested. But he was agreed we should go to Cracow. For some time Tatus had been urging us both to come and settle the estate. Although neither Michael nor I wished to hasten the division of property, we both felt obliged to do as Tatus wished.

We telephoned Cracow. You could hear under the businesslike tone of Tatus' voice the joy in our coming. He proposed a multitude of trivialities — suitable food for the trip, warm robes and overcoats. He made us promise to bring Edward, the house-boy in case of a breakdown and to send the nursemaid away on her vacation.

Soon after we arrived in Cracow, I was alone in my room and asked Andzia how it had been in the last war.

"Somehow one managed to find an egg here, an egg there. Country women smuggled them to town. Bread was not good, for the substitute flour was bad, but we got on. But does the young lady really believe the Germans will come now?"

"What do they say at the market?"

"People talk of it," Andzia replied, "but they have no fear. Somehow we will manage. God will protect us."

"I wish you would get a few supplies."

"Flour becomes wormy if you keep it too long. The Professor does not wish it. I will make many preserves and jam. But it is not well to have stocks in the larder."

Andzia was reassuring and confident. Surely one could not foretell the future. This tragic year had proved that. Now my own sister was dying in New York, and even the greatest doctors and the best of care could not save her. One must learn to live as the Poles did, with confidence that one was fulfilling one's destiny, and make the best of each problem when it presented itself. No use standing still, immobilized with fear, or trying to hide away. It was clear that even the Tibetan steppes would be no refuge in this war. "There is no escape, whether I stay here or run away. The disaster of this war will be everywhere." As surely as I had been drawn against my will into this land, so indeed must I suffer with it. As a prelude to this suffering I had lost the three closest to me, as though it were said, "Now you must face the future unaided."

I had spent this year learning to accept my fate, and I felt that no matter what happened, nothing could hurt me. Death meant reunion. Normal life as we had known it would never exist again. I was unable to take very

257

seriously the probable loss of material possessions. Their destruction would seem the natural accompaniment of the greater loss of John. I found it difficult to attach much importance to the division of property between Michael and me, which Tatus wished accomplished in his lifetime. Only in deference to Tatus' feelings, Michael and I read and signed papers which Tatus had prepared carefully, and in great detail. My mind was out the window, in the garden; I could hear the endless drone of the second maid, Bronia, talking to Andrew, like the comforting hum of a well-running engine. Though I could not distinguish the words, I could well imagine them.

"Now, Pan Andrzej is building a railroad, a railroad to Warsaw for his daddy and mummy to ride upon. Up the hill goes the railroad, and through the tunnel it goes, to Warsaw with his daddy and mummy riding on it. Into the station the train rolls like thunder, and out of the train jumps Pan Andrzej. He crosses the station and calls for an automobile, and away he rides, off to the house of his granny and granddaddy. Now Pan Andrzej rings the bell . . ."

The church bells across the street ring for the benediction, and there is the unusual clatter of hurrying steps on the sidewalks, of gates banged shut, of rustling skirts and muffled greetings. High in the sky above us the ever circling planes guard us from German marauders. When the engines backfire, it makes us gasp. Everyone thinks, "This is war. They are firing." Then the comforting even roar of the motor whirring away brings peace once more, and an inner apology at having been frightened. What has Tatus been saying? Something about the picture collection — the great Matejko in the salon, and the Giermskis and Falats. Neither Michael nor I can conceive of a future with a salon big enough to house such pictures.

Timidly, not to hurt Tatus' feelings, Michael, said, "I think your collection of Michalowski should be left to the nation, and the other pictures too."

"Yes, do," I begged. "Just put aside small personal things for Andrew."

Tatus passed his hand over his poor tired brow. "What will you do with this furniture — the clocks and bronzes and wall hangings?"

"Everything in this room could be left to the Wawel. You know how often the director has been hinting to have them."

"I will have to think about it," Tatus said wearily. "Now, pay attention, while I read you the list of actions and hypotheks. Two thousand shares of Sukrovnia, two thousand Bank Polski, twenty-five thousand First Pozyczka Amerykanska, fifty thousand Second Pozyczka," etc., etc.

When he had finished reading, he took off his glasses and handed each of us a copy of the hand-written account.

"Please," I begged, "let's not actually divide anything just yet."

"The law exacts it."

"We can carry out the legal requirements. Still, surely Michael feels as I do. He wouldn't touch a penny of Mulka's money."

"Let's not go over that again. Since Mulka died without testament, the money goes to the next generation."

"Surely, privately, we can do as we choose."

Michael whispered, "If there is a war, then nothing matters anyway. If not, by the end of the year we'll persuade Tatus."

Was Tatus' eagerness a pose? Did he imagine we would ever actually come into this property? Surely he must see the impending disaster. To be finished with the business I was willing to agree to any project, and, knowing Tatus' scrupulous exactitude, to sign any agreement. I longed to drive out of Cracow to lie down on a soft meadow and smell the sweet herbs, to gaze across the fields towards the pink brick spires of the Gothic churches that crown the city. Andrew would run in the grass and gather the flowers, while I would try to make my mind blank in the peace of the moment.

As we came out of Tatus' room, Andzia was holding a telegram, saying, "I did not know whether I should disturb you. Is the lady's sister any better?"

In the telegram it was written that my sister had died that morning.

"Poor Madame."

"You poor darling!"

"*Moja Kochana.*"

But still I could not believe it. Michael said, "Let's walk up the Kopiec, from the steep side. The way I took Elizabeth up when she was in Cracow. We can make plans while we are walking."

When we returned it was settled that I should leave to visit my parents in America. We would find a suitable companion in Warsaw for it was nine years since I had made the trip. If no one could be found, then Michael would bring me across. Leaving Andrew in Cracow until his nurse came back from her vacation, we took the evening train to Warsaw.

There was a young couple from California on the train who were touring every country of Europe on a two weeks' trip. Could it be that we were compatriots? They made me feel so shy and embarrassed, that I huddled into my corner and let Michael do the talking. I thought, "Will all Americans seem so strange and incomprehensible? Is environment really stronger than blood?" I had completely lost the habit of being satisfied with picking up odd facts and thinking I knew something about a question. Knowledge had become a long and serious process on whose outer periphery I stood. I knew few persons with whom I would venture an opinion. All our companions had too much respect for facts to play with them, and think they knew the answers. Then there was the custom of each American battling independently for his own position. How bare and lonely a life, that is not fully shared with a large circle of friends and family! In America I might be safe from physical danger but I would be consumed with lonely anguish and sorrow.

CHAPTER *18*

I WAS to have spent the whole month of
September in Warsaw, but one morning at eight o'clock Hal-
cia telephoned. She had just heard over the radio that
Chamberlain was flying to Munich.

"Czechoslovakia will surely fight," she said, "and Poland
will support her. You must leave for the United States at
once, for today may be your last chance to travel."

"The British can't give in," we both agreed. "This means
war." However, I hesitated, being unprepared to depart
so suddenly.

"Telephone one of your friends in the Embassy !" Halcia
urged. "They will know whether the Czechs are mobilizing."

The Embassy told me to go at once. While pulling a few
clothes from my closet, I made a plan of order for the day —
tickets, visas, money — all must be obtained in five hours.
When Michael came down for breakfast, I told him what I
had learned and added, "I'm leaving for Italy on the 3:30
train this afternoon."

"You can't possibly travel without a maid," he protested.

"How could I get a passport for Wladzia ?" Our chambermaid had left her birth certificate in the country. "I'd
rather go alone than face travelling with that old governess."

"Padowski will arrange it," Michael reassured me.

This was our by-word. Our Administrator had never
failed to arrange anything yet. Agreeing, "If Padowski can
fix it by two !" I hurried out to be at the bank when it

opened at nine. Padowski went at once to the Chief of Police to ask for a passport for Wladzia. An hour and a half later, while I was still in line at Cook's, Padowski appeared, his face as completely enigmatic as always.

"What's the outcome?"

"You have only to sign a paper that you aren't taking Wladzia away to exploit her, and promise you will bring her back. I am to supply all necessary documents after you have left."

"So it's three tickets!"

The clerk informed us that the three tickets could not be given out until the appropriate visas had been stamped on our passports. We hailed a taxi and dashed first to the Italian, then to the German and lastly to the Czechoslovakian Consulates. Because of the crisis, none of these countries would grant us a visa unless we could show the permit to enter the adjoining country.

Back in the taxi, Padowski reminded me of the signed orders I must leave him, without which the estate could not be run in my absence. We agreed that he would type them up during the half hour we would have at home, that I could read them on the way to the train, and sign them at the station.

In the front hall several large heavy portmanteaux were ready. Andrew's heaviest toys and bedding occupied two, and the maid had stuffed a third with her own sheets and towels. The man at Cook's had been dubious as to whether the train would run through and had advised taking only the lightest handbags. I therefore had to empty out the bags and pack afresh though we had only twenty minutes left. The little maid had lost her head in the joyous prospect of travelling, and was running about the house telling everyone that only a fairy princess could equal her good fortune.

"Put on your suit," I commanded sternly, to bring her from her dreams. "Fetch me your uniforms, your underwear and a handbag."

I went into the drawing room and into John's study to say good-bye. I knew better than to pick up little souvenirs.

262

My throat felt stiff and hot at leaving the books, five thousand and eighty, all neatly catalogued. But even if I had been able to take them and my furniture and pictures with me, it would not have eased the pain of leaving Poland.

When John and I had played the game of "What to take first in a fire," he always chose the Madonna his grandfather had taken to Siberia, and his great-grandfather before him to the Napoleonic Wars. But a fire destroys only a few individuals, while others escape. In this war, wherever we were, the fire would come to consume us, and no one would escape.

When we reached the station, Uncle Anthony and his family were anxiously waiting apart from the other friends who had come to say good-bye, each with a few flowers or a little box of chocolates.

"How did you know I was leaving?" I asked in bewilderment. "Who told you?"

"We were so worried you would miss your train!" was all they said. "God knows when we will see each other again."

"Why did you leave the office at this hour?" I demanded, well knowing the difficulties involved.

"Could I let you leave without saying good-bye?" They repeated one after the other, urging me on to the train.

I reached Uncle Anthony and his family who clutched at me, yet pushed me aboard. "Most beloved — good-bye," was all they said. Wozteck put a basket in Andrew's hands. "Yes, for Andrew." They were standing by the compartment window, speechless, as if to imprint their last loving looks in my soul.

Padowski humbly tugged my arm. "The signatures, please."

"Read them over, Michael, to see if they are properly worded."

"Yes, surely. Yes."

"Perhaps you better sign them," Michael suggested. "If something is not in order, I will keep it until your return."

The brakemen were waving their lanterns. Michael and Padowski dashed for the door, and slowly, so smoothly that I

263

did not feel it, the train started.   Michael ran along the platform beside the car.   "Good-bye.   God bless you," he called,
as the train pulled away.   Though I was staring at the new
tunnel through which we were running, before my eyes were
the blurred and well-known faces, and I could still feel the
pressure of their hands — until Andrew's squeals of delight
as he threw the contents out of the basket broke the contact,
and life in Warsaw was over.

❋   ❋   ❋   ❋   ❋   ❋

On arriving in America, I was very much bewildered.   I
heard people speak as angrily of Mr. Chamberlain as if they
personally had been betrayed, and yet I never met anyone
who felt American should fight to save Czechoslovakia.

"The British Empire is at stake," I was told.

"Will America join in ?" I inquired.

"Why should we fight ?" was the inevitable reply.

"The British are unprepared.   If they fought and lost, the
United States would be in a desperate situation," I tried to
explain.

"Why aren't the British ready ?   They ought to have realized — "

"Are the Americans preparing ?   Do they realize ?"

I felt distinctly uncomfortable at this idle recrimination,
expecting others to do what you yourself had no intention of
doing.   When the meeting at Munich was followed by the
anti-climax of the Czechoslovakian surrender, I decided to
return to Poland forever.   The United States seemed foreign indeed.

Tatus had written me every day.   From his letters it was
clear how much he missed me.   His letters were all alike,
simple everyday things which showed how intimately our
lives were intertwined.

"My beloved Dorothy :

Nothing new at home.   Stopped in to see Mrs. Rice for a few
minutes after Mass at Bishop G's this morning.   Her children are
in the country.   Yesterday we picked twelve kilos of pears for the

winter. Andzia preserved seven litres of peaches for you. Professor N. sent me two trout from his hatcheries. It is extraordinary : after cleaning the dogs every day for a month, they still have a few fleas. Weather remains foggy. Slight frosts at night. Picked the last Richmond roses. When are you returning ?"

I returned after Christmas. A supernatural calm hung over the city. The only outward signs of preparation for war were the colored cartoons pasted up on every building. These looked like a page from the comics. In graphic picture language, the public were instructed what to do in case of attack by air. First the enemy plane dumps its bombs, while onlookers stand in the street. Second people scatter in all directions for home. Third they seize blankets from the bed, fourth they soak them in water, and fifth, nail them to the tops of the windows. Picture six shows a bomb bursting in the street, and gives the angle of inflection. Concussion destroys the upper floors ; the lower remain intact. Someone is wounded, and a shelf is shown, on which are the bottles of iodine, aspirin and bandages which every housewife should have. At the end were the instructions : "Keep off the streets. Use the lower floors of the houses."

Michael had begun taking an extensive lecture course, as he was the chief fire warden for our street. He went every evening at six, and it was always after nine when he returned. He was taught how to fight incendiary bombs with sand and shovel. He had to organize the street, and instruct assistants from each of the neighboring houses. Our janitor also went to lectures every day at the police station ; he became an assistant policeman. He was to see that everyone observed the black-out and kept the heavy wet blankets over the windows as a protection against flying glass and poison gases. It would be his duty to stand in the street and bury the incendiary bombs Michael was to toss him from the roof.

Anielka, Zulcia, Halcia and all my other women friends were attending Red Cross classes. They were instructed to set up dressing stations in their own apartments, since the hospitals would be overcrowded, dangerous targets.

During the late afternoon they dropped in for tea.

"Why did you come back?" each asked rather crossly. "Children should be kept out the city. They will only be in the way. You should take your child and leave while you can."

"I have only just returned," I protested, "I feel more at home in Warsaw than in the United States."

"If you decide to stay, you take a great responsibility, unless you can make yourself useful in some organization. This is no time for sentimental emotion."

"Even if you could be helpful, you should consider Andrew."

"Think what you could do for us in America."

"No one believes what I say in America. Poland has a very bad Press." To prove it, I pulled out a recent copy of *Life* magazine. It pictured some ragged country children playing near a duck pond against a background of old tumbledown thatched barns. It was intimated that these were houses, and suggested that most of Poland was Feudal, owned by a few rich aristocrats, and governed by a ruthless military clique.

"That's so ridiculous it's funny," they all laughed. "Anyone who can check figures should know it was not true."

"Americans read newspapers. They don't check figures." I tried to explain that no American journalist had ever spent more than a week in Poland and yet without having learned the language, or checked statistics, had written numerous articles about us.

Our conversation was interrupted by the ringing of the front door bell.

"More cups," I called to Edward as he went to answer it.

It was our family doctor, Dr. Bergson. Since John's death he had tried to help me more with good advice than with medicine.

"I learned in town you had returned. You never even telephoned."

"I've only been back three days, yet everyone is trying to get rid of me."

"We would not wish to see you leave, but you must understand how heavy the food problem will be."

"I brought back six boxes of vitamins for Andrew!"

"Think what you could do for us in America!" the doctor exclaimed.

"That is just what we have been trying to tell her," the others echoed in chorus.

"There is nothing I could do for you in America," I said desperately.

"You could tell American Jews that we Polish Jews are standing by Poland," the doctor suggested.

"I don't know what you mean."

"You will see in America," he said prophetically, "German Jews who are actually pro-German because they think of Hitler as only a transitory phenomenon in the super-German State." His tone was bitter. "Among German Jews are the most implacable enemies of Poland."

We stirred uneasily, embarrassed by this glimpse into what we imagined was a family quarrel.

"If the American Jewish bankers would back us," he went on, "we could still stop Hitler, but many of them have actually made loans to Germany."

"Then Polish Jews feel closer to Polish Gentiles than to German Jews?"

"The educated ones do, surely. As for the Orthodox I cannot speak for them. I feel really uncomfortable when I am called on a case by an orthodox Jew. They have no conception of our ideas of hygiene, and we have so many difficulties over ritualistic food and other things with them in the hospital."

Anielka, Halcia and Zulcia stood up to leave.

"May I stay?" Dr. Bergson asked. "I don't disturb you?"

"Indeed, stay for dinner," I begged.

When they had gone, he said with some embarrassment, "My girls, you know, went to Miss Landowska's school. They want to become Catholics. That is all right for them — to be like all their friends. But if I followed them, every-

267

one would say that I was making a last minute effort to escape."

It was difficult to find the right answer.

"Don't care what people think. It's what you believe," I said.

"If I had joined ten years ago, before religion became a public issue," he remarked wistfully. "Nothing is private any more. The most sacred rights — religion and democracy are jeered and spat upon by the dictators."

We sat in silence, while I thought over what he had said.

"In your innermost self do you feel more Polish or Jewish?"

"Certainly more Polish. I feel at home with Poles. Most of my patients are Polish. The free patients are Jews. My whole career is lost if Poland falls."

"Are there many who feel as you do?"

"All my acquaintances. Of Jews from Russia I have no experience . . . they keep to themselves! But Polish-Jewish professional men, intellectuals, bankers, industrialists," he said earnestly, "such Jews are solidly behind the Government. We are Poles."

Suddenly he began reciting, "*W glebinie syberyskich rud* — In deepest Siberian mines — ." He spoke as if enchanted, and as if the poem dissolved him in a trance.

I sat spellbound. . . "*Gdy sie Judaszem galaz oberwala sucha* — When the hanging Judas with the dry branch fell — "

"What is it?" I murmured, fearing to break the mood.

"Poems of Tuwim, translations of Puszkin. You don't know them? Please, then, let me send you the volume. I want you to have it from me." He pulled his watch out of his pocket, looked at it mechanically, kissed my hand and said, "I know I've stayed too long. You will pardon me? Good night."

It was after midnight when he had gone. I wandered from room to room wondering what to take with me if I should really leave. Mechanically I pulled out the drawers of John's desk and sorted the letters that had collected while

I was away. The piles of books standing on the floor, I replaced on the shelves in proper order. I was still no nearer the answer, "what to take ?" I tried sensibly to imagine myself in the two or three small rooms of a New York apartment, — a small table, a few chairs, a little rug ; the utilitarian objects that would be necessary.

CHAPTER *19*

*A*NDREW and I had been invited to spend the 3rd of May holiday with the Minister of Communications, Mr. Ulrich and his wife. We were to have taken the children for an all-day picnic at our favorite spot by the river Bug, but at the last moment the Minister fearing to be the whole day away from the telephone, invited us to lunch in his private apartment. So now Andrew and I walked down the quiet brick walk at the rear of the towering new building of the Department of the Interior. In the flower beds that bordered the walk, daffodils were still blooming and the roses, which formed garlands between the dwarf lilacs had feathery new leaves. Thick young grass glowed blue-green even in the shade. The little walled garden had a monastic, peaceful privacy in spite of the gigantic modernistic building at its side, and the Minister's door at the end of the walk was unobtrusively tucked away. The stairway up to his apartment was sheathed in wood and hung with *kilims* in the Polish manner, but his immense private office had been arranged by a decorator in harmony with the new style of the building. His fine old Empire desk and side chairs were stiffly silhouetted against the apple green velvet hangings, and a group of heavy upholstered chairs was arranged about a low glass table.

"What are they saying of Beck's address to Parliament?" he asked at once, as I came in.

"Everyone is glad of his unequivocal attitude towards Germany."

"We Poles make a cult of fearlessness," his voice was bitter.

"What else can people do?"

"Make more preparation !" he fairly bellowed.

"They are buying whatever the Government tells them to. They don't want to 'sow panic' by hoarding."

" 'Sow panic !' Does it help to leave all the art treasures for the Germans to destroy ? Why don't people build underground vaults to hide their most valued objects ?" I laughed uneasily.

"I speak in earnest. It does not add to valor that all our priceless rugs, all our ancient documents and modern libraries should be left unprotected against bombing and burning. Everyone who can leave the city should do so now and establish himself in the country."

"One cannot conceive of bombing beforehand nor feel imaginary pain. The public draws strength while it can," I said, trying to excuse my many friends engaged in usual daily occupations out of an effort not to undermine their morale by fear and brooding. Those who had lived through the last war were the most intrepid.

"It 's not for lack of appreciation of danger," I continued, thinking that because of his cabinet position the Minister was too far from the pulse of the people. "Take old Mrs. Morawska," I said, "during the last war she escaped to Kiev to be behind the fighting line only to be caught up in the Bolshevik revolution and to see many of her relatives shot."

"Just the same, those who can should leave. You should go at once."

"At once ? Surely the Germans won't begin before August. Everyone is agreed they will wait for harvest to be gathered."

"If you have decided to go, what do you gain by remaining ?"

"Countess George Potocka, (the wife of the Polish Ambassador in Washington) wants to rent my apartment for the summer."

"Splendid, only do not rent it furnished ; take everything with you."

Impossible, I thought to myself, but aloud I murmured something about expense.

"What will you do with the things you intend to leave here? Do not be as foolhardy as the Poles!"

"I couldn't hurt my family here by running out on them."

The Minister spoke harshly, "Does no one understand what war is? The Germans will take away everything when they come. This is a war of extermination — Hitler has already said so." His vehemence withered my hopes and blasted away all illusion of safety. In an instant that broad, sunny and seemingly endless plain that stretched so safely to the distant frontier shrank and narrowed before my eyes. What could I say? I felt ashamed at my childishly eager naïveté.

"Why doesn't the Government tell the truth?" I echoed.

"The public wouldn't believe us. Everyone loves the newspaper stories of unrest, of food shortage and apathetic morale in Germany, of the superiority of Polish troops. All such stories give an illusion of safety. Unfortunately, an honest warning would play into Germany's hands."

"How?"

"By discouraging resistance. I even believe the Nazi originated those stories of ersatz cannon and sabotage in factories so that the public will underestimate German strength. If Government officials would say as much, we would be accused of being pro-German."

A cold shiver went down my spine. I was one of those very people who believed that because the individual Polish soldier could endure great hardship, he would in some mysterious fashion hold back the German tanks, with his little machine gun hidden under a mud bank, until England and France attacking Germany in the rear would come to his rescue.

"The whole nation is behind the Government's preparations now and every man, woman and child will resist the invader," I pleaded. "Take Lepkowski's small brick factory. It runs three shifts daily and Sundays. His men proposed giving one day's labor if he would give one day's profit for the aviation fund."

"My dear lady, we can't buy the planes either in England or France. You heard Minister Rose that night at your house

272

just after he had come back from London. It's not even a question of a few planes. It's the question of the whole supply system. The British won't give us even the promise of supplies for fear we will become 'overbearing' and 'provoke' the German government!"

A secretary, who had placed papers on his desk several times during our conversation, now asked the Minister if he would speak on the telephone.

"Connect me here," he said.

I quickly went into the next room. Madame Ulrich who was helping the maid set the table, put the jardiniere of ferns on the table. The children's voices rang merrily from across the hall and I was impressed once more by the informality and lack of servants in this cabinet minister's apartment.

The Minister was so preoccupied during dinner, that his conversation kept shifting between reminiscences of the last war and comments upon each of several further telephone calls which interrupted the meal. He had been incarcerated, together with Pilsudski, at Magdeburg by the Germans. While he was telling us how they spent their long prison days, the telephone brought news of two new incidents at the Danzig border. A German automobilist had demanded the right to cross the Corridor without entrance visa, and had never reappeared on the opposite side. A man on foot, like several thousand other Germans that spring, had demanded a similar right, and had then disappeared into Poland without further trace. Because of the Polish-Danzig treaty, any German could cross that part of Poland at will. Had the Polish frontier guards prevented them, the German government would have made of the incident a "casus belli."

"Over a month ago we offered them an elevated express highway across Poland into East Prussia, but that is not what they want," the Minister said, "and every day of peace further undermines our position."

For the first time I realized the wheel of fate was out of control. I had imagined like everyone else that the firmness of our ministers was our protection in stopping the storm. In Austria, Holland, France and England, even many of the aristocracy had gone over to Fascism saying, "No use bucking the modern world." But in Poland I knew no one who did not hold to the old-fashioned belief that "there were things worth dying for" which is perhaps why they did not build "that little house out in the country for the day of the revolution." They were calm because they had taken the great decision to fight. They believed therefore that though Hitler might bluster and threaten, their adamant position would be their protection.

When the Minister said, as I was leaving, "Good-bye, I hope you won't put off your departure," I replied in the words I had heard repeated a hundred times, "Hitler is only bluffing; he knows the Poles will fight so he is trying to get the French and British to put pressure on Poland to give up the forts around Danzig, the way he got the forts in the Sudeten Mountains. Since we won't give in without a war, he will have to go down the Danube, and if there is a war the whole world will be in it, so there is no use in running away."

"There will be more food in America."

"But America will be in the war."

"Granted !"

"Then why leave home, friends and relatives to jump into another fire ?"

"I wouldn't advise you to go if you had no family there."

The chorus began singing in my ears, *Go away, go away, you can't be useful here. Go away, each has his part to play, you can't be useful here.*

All day long friends came to say good-bye. No sooner would my head be deep in one of the capacious trunks, in which I was packing linens and woolens, than I would be called away. As soon as I had decided to leave everyone knew it. Yet I always asked in amazement, "How did you know I was going ?"

"You are, aren't you ?" would be the reply. "Please take this letter to my uncle in America. Tell him not to worry, we will live through it."

Again the telephone bell would ring. "I called because I heard you were leaving."

"Not yet," I would say, ashamed at appearing to run away.

"Don't put it off," they would advise, as if to stiffen my will. "No one ever knows, and once you have decided — "

"I won't be going for a month at least," I would reply, putting off that horrid moment as long as possible.

"Is that prudent ?"

Then the door bell would ring. "Excuse my coming so late, I heard you were leaving and wanted to give you this scrap of material from the dress of Saint Theresa to keep you safe on your journey." My friend held me tight as if to emphasize in the all embracing power of love — the heavenly protection of Saint Theresa.

"How can I thank you ?" I muttered humbly.

"It will take no space and is better than flowers, isn't it ?" she said as gaily as if she were giving me a trinket.

"What will you do ?" I asked, appalled by the sudden realization of how vulnerable she would be. She had worked in the office of the Chief of Staff of Aviation, and the Germans would certainly try to extract information from her.

"I am waiting for mobilization, and then I am to go to a secret airport. None of us know where it is."

"And Alfred ?" I asked.

"He is in the Reserve Officers Corps, doing three months' intensive training."

"If only I could stay !" I cried out.

"Don't even consider it," she said gently. "But if you are caught in Warsaw, come to us in the country. You will be safer there and nearer the frontier."

Once more the telephone was ringing. "Hello."

"My brother tells me that you are leaving," the voice said. "Could you take a letter to my sister ? I 'll mail it to you, we are very busy preparing my son for the army."

"Will they conscript him ?" I thought the boy was far too young.

"He has volunteered, of course ; he is nearly eighteen."

"How terrible for you!" I thought, having only just lost her husband. . .

"We Polish mothers must expect to give our sons," she said firmly. "We cannot hope to have an easy, happy life." She asked for no pity and permitted no sharing of her deep felt suffering.

I was so abashed I mumbled when I said, "Good-bye."

That night voices kept me from sleeping, *"You're going, don't tarry."* . . . *"Go while you can go in peace, it's not cowardice to go when you have a child."* . . . *"This is our business."* . . . *"You've no place here."* . . . *"Go where you can be of more help!"*

I sat up in bed. It was still night. Outside I could see streaks of light shooting up into the sky where the search lights were sweeping. Overhead the solid roar of planes, broken by the familiar backfire of bombers swooping down in their night practice, magnified those voices that would not let me sleep. I crept to the window to lean my cheek on the cool glass pane. The damp summer wind was sweet with lilacs — the lilacs in Warsaw. Could spring anywhere else be half so sweet! Lilacs and lilies-of-the-valley soften the meanest courtyards.

How could I pull my heart up by the roots and go away? Other lands might shine more fair but none could hold this distilled sweetness. I closed the window to shut out the fresh night air, whose soft fragrance recalled a thousand scenes and memories. But I could not close my mind and tuck it away like a photograph album on a shelf. Memories came tumbling upon me in a nightmare jumble. . . Driving home at dawn in a horse cab snuggled under John's greatcoat to be warm. . . Dawn just breaking and myriads of sparrows chirping in the leafless trees. . . The sound of distant horse hoofs on a far-off pavement. . . The splash of water and muffled commands of the men who washed the pavements. . . A man's voice, singing "As long as I live, Poland will not die!" . . . The first spring bunch of violets and John's pale face as I brought him home upon the stretcher.

276

I ran out of my room.   Racing up the stairs, I knocked at Michael's door until I roused him to come and open it.

"What 's happened ?   What is it ?"

"I can't sleep, Michael.   I can't make up my mind to go away.   Please say you think I should stay.   Please tell me not to leave.   Please, please !"

The insistence in my voice waked Michael instantly.   I knew he would not say, "Go back to sleep, there 's a good girl, we 'll talk it over in the morning."   He would try no easy consolation, he would show no surprise at being wakened.

"Go, get in my bed.   You are cold," was what he said.

Opening his cupboard, he took out his heavy blue wool bathrobe with the thick tassels and braid in scrolls, and putting a steamer rug around his knees, he chose a comfortable chair, prepared to stay up for the rest of the night if need be.

"I can't leave," I said, "I'd rather die here if there is going to be a war."

"That 's not like you.   What about Andrew ?"

"Suppose there is no war ?"

"Then you will come back in the autumn.   But the situation looks very gloomy.   The world seems to be filled with only two kinds of people ; those moved by egoism and hatred, and those whose only concern is to avoid responsibility."

"Not here in Poland ?"

"No, the way people take it here is rather comforting."

"Everyone has kept his head."

"Because, if we are to have a war, we 'll have one.   Still, even the pleasantest way of approaching a war is pretty poor consolation.   If it comes, everything, including us, will be blown to bits rather thoroughly.   And there isn't much to look forward to since no one can believe the 1914 stories that this would be 'the last war' before the millennium. . ."   He paused.

"Then you do think war is inevitable."

"No, no.   But I do think we are in for a period of everyone preparing for war.   Everything else will be suspended. That isn't a happy prospect."

277

"They won't stop you building and doing whatever it is you do out at Piaski."

He picked up *The Bridge of San Luis Rey* which was on his bed table, and opened it saying, "Do you remember the concluding chapter ? The Abbess accepted the fact that it was of no importance whether her work went on or not. It was enough to work. She was the nurse who tends the sick who never recover. She was the priestess who perpetually renews the office before an altar to which no worshipers come. After her death her work would relapse into the indolence and indifference of her colleagues. It seemed to be sufficient for Heaven that, for awhile in Peru, a disinterested love had flowered and faded."

It was my turn to wait for him to speak.

"That's the situation in Poland. Nobody seems to want any of the things we could do. It certainly is little use building something that will in all probability be reduced to dust in the immediate future."

"That doesn't seem an adequate reason why I should leave."

"What could you do by staying here ? I only keep active now out of a kind of fear of inactivity, or something of the kind."

"Michael !"

"Still I believe that every life or death is for a purpose ; that we should push on as best we can, even if we don't know what will remain of it or what the purpose is under the circumstances. Do you remember the last words of the book : 'Love, the only survival — the only meaning.'"

"Yet you advise me to leave the country that I love, the people that I love, and the obligations I have undertaken ?"

"Try to imagine this house being blown to bits ; the city with no food nor water ; money, if you had it, could buy you nothing ! Then you would not be able to execute the most elementary of your obligations. You would not be able to take care of Andrew, much less help any of us. Take just a few things for the emergency and go to America. If war comes, it will be after harvest. If war does not come this year, return in October."

"I will do as you suggest."

"Then let us go for steamship tickets tomorrow and not put it off. If you need money, I could lend you a thousand dollars. While you are away I will attend to everything until you come back. You know I will do the best I can."

"I know you will. I won't try to thank you. Is it time enough if we take the tickets for passage in a month, so I can get in a visit to Cracow before I leave?" I asked, and standing, stretched and yawned at last.

"Do you think you can sleep now? Don't feel you must hurry," Michael said with his affectionate smile, always tinged with sadness.

* * * * * *

Once it was settled I was to leave Warsaw, I called the Countess Potocka to tell her that she could have my apartment for the summer. I would begin packing immediately, and in ten days I would leave for Cracow.

I had decided to drive down to Cracow in the Buick and leave it there, hoping that Tatus would use it while I was away. Besides, leaving Warsaw by car lacked the sense of finality of the lugubrious leaving by train; the tearful good-byes on the platform and the compartment full of flowers. The car could wait while the last-minute search about the house was in progress, and a last-minute telephone call was answered. But when we were finally ready, it was four o'clock and the trip had to be put off till the next day. The extra evening was like a reprieve. The heart-breaking farewell visits had been paid with Aunt Emily and Aunt Lola; it has been a good-bye, forever! Michael and I would spend this evening with Uncle Anthony.

We ran up the familiar stairs without waiting for the elevator. Long ago when I first came to Poland I had railed against walking down. Now I even loved running upstairs like any Pole. Though Uncle Anthony's door was opened by their sloppily dressed maid, the whole family had crowded

279

into the hall to meet us.

I remembered that first visit — the children in their very best clothes — the well-rehearsed English greeting and the hum and bustle behind closed doors. Now I was one of the family and Zosia who had recently married, quickly drew me into her own bedroom for the usual exchange of whispered confidences.

"Jas telephoned — he will be here immediately," she began. Jas, her new husband, was a geographical economist. While she showed me some linen napkins which she was about to embroider with the coats of arms of the principal Polish cities, she continued her chatter : "Oh, such good news ! Do you remember Bronia ? She was at my wedding — she married secretly during Christmas vacation while skiing in the mountains ! She's going to have a baby ! The tests from the pharmacist were positive ! She's much older than I, she will be nineteen in August. Today Wojtek received a prize for the essay he wrote on English Geography, a beautifully bound book about English Cathedrals. Mother and Wojtek can read it. When we all meet in the autumn you will see how much I have learned ! Father always says 'Do one thing at a time not to get in a jumble.' *Kochana* (dearest) — do you think I will get pregnant now ? I've waited so long. It's over four months since I was married. Mother says I must go to the country and rest all summer, but poor Jas will have to work at the Institute. If we don't get a baby we are going skiing next Christmas. You will come with us, won't you — *Kochana !*"

"Why does Dorota hide in Zosia's room," Uncle Anthony called out jovially from the dining room. "It's time she joined us."

"Dorota hasn't seen my book yet," Wojtek shouted from his room.

"*Zaras, zaras* (immediately)," I replied. "You see, I have not been polite," I told Zosia, getting up off the couch. Her room was stacked with the accumulations of the twenty years Uncle Anthony and Aunt Anita had been married. When Zosia moved into her own apartment, this room had been left exactly as it had been, the dolls and toys of her childhood pushed back to make room for the books, bric-a-brac and letters of her adolescence. Her bed was piled with sewing materials and clothes, some to be discarded, others to be mended.

Nothing had been changed in the house. There was the same untidy stack of overcoats in the hall, the same last-minute bustle over dinner, the same whispered consultations in the dining room after which Zosia, as on every other occasion, ran to ask her father for money. I watched him mechanically pull coins from his pocket which he held out for her to choose while he continued his conversation without a break.

As soon as she was gone Uncle Anthony led us to the library, and began at once questioning Michael, whom he had seen in the city, what they had said. Then he discussed the changes in the University; how this pupil had received a Rockefeller scholarship, and that one had gone to France. As in the past Uncle Anthony avoided generalities. It was hard to keep my mind on what was being said. I thought I had never seen a room that changed less in fourteen years. The old palm which had outgrown the room, had been exchanged by the Botanic Society for an identical smaller plant. But everything else stood where it had always been.

"Why do you look so sad?" Zosia asked, coming in and sitting on the arm of my chair.

"This may be the last time I sit here."

"Nonsense!" she said swiftly, "it's wicked to speak that way." She put her arms about me and gave me a warm hug. "Dorota is talking war scares," she said scornfully.

"You don't mean it!" everyone said in unison. "Now that England signed the treaty with us, the Germans won't dare."

I tried to speak patiently. "Even our own Polish Cabinet Ministers know it is inevitable. Everyone I have spoken with says we should prepare for the worst."

"I've bought just what the Government told me, a hundred pounds of sugar, fifty pounds of soap, candles and a first aid kit. What else do you advise one to do?" Aunt Anita asked seriously.

"Let's talk of more cheerful things," Zosia interrupted. "Can we count on you to meet us in Italy in September? Would you trust Jas to drive your car down? We could meet the boat at Genoa and all go back to the Lido for two weeks. Then we could drive slowly home, stopping at every village in Piedmont. We don't have to be back until the first of October." Zosia continued chattering about inconsequential matters as if she were determined to make this last evening festive. "I always think of us being at the Lido together. Remember the bicycle trip — ?"

From time to time I would surreptitiously glance at my watch, which seemed to stand still. Yet I loved this family beyond any other on earth and I knew they would all be hurt if I left before midnight. Habitually, Uncle Anthony never went to bed before two. Yet at eleven, pleading an early morning start for Cracow, I begged to be excused.

"You will promise then to come back to Italy in time for our holiday," Zosia repeated. "There won't be a stupid war! there can't be, with social conditions so bad in Germany! The Czechs ruined all the guns with sand and the shells are ersatz. Don't worry, everything will be alright and, if the Germans should march, we'll show them. That's why they don't dare! Isn't it true?"

No one dared deny what she had said, and there was silence as I stood up. It was so much easier to say good-bye if it was only for the summer as usual.

"Write me in care of Janek in July," Zosia said gaily. "We are going to Dambrowa in August, then we'll all meet in Italy during the first week of September! Is that a promise?"

"If there is peace, of course."

"Then it's a promise! Good-bye and God bless you."

It was good-bye.

I had said it so lightly. Yet Michael and I could find no light comfortable words as we walked home along the silent street; still in spite of the distant drone of planes, caught like moths in the searchlight beams which cut the sky in a dozen paths of light. Occasionally, a taxi would tear by, breaking only for a moment the deep tranquility of the sleeping city.

In the circles cut out of the pavement around the trees, pansies and newly set out geraniums smelled sweet in the gentle night air. Tubs of vines and oleanders flanked the doorways of the tobacconist open at that late hour. As we crossed the Aleja the young leaves on the tall clipped beaches looked emerald green in the arclight.

"I'm feeling morbid and sad. I've left so often before. Why should I feel worse this time? It is a comfort nothing ever happens as you imagined it."

As Michael did not reply, we walked on in silence. In nearly every house we passed lived someone I knew. The very streets emanated that warm and comfortable feeling of great familiarity. There were few outward visible changes during the fourteen years, though every year had seen new window boxes filled with flowers. Then plaster on the buildings was crumbling away. Now the scars left from the other war were neatly repaired and repainted. These were the very apartments that had been sub-divided for half a dozen families, when I had first come to Warsaw. Now no one rented rooms. The former tenants had either bought or built, or returned to the country. In spite of hard times, a sense of comfort hung over all.

Driving to Cracow, the country on either side of the newly opened pink and white cut granite highway seemed clad in holiday attire. Poland, like an altar, was decked in flowers. In every hamlet, before every crossroad shrine, every house and central square, homely bouquets of flowers were reverently placed. The many small towns through which I passed had been freshly painted during the spring cleaning. Young trees and flower beds were set out along newly paved streets. These very streets, when John and I last passed here, had been torn up to lay sewers and electric conduits.

For the past twenty years these villagers had toiled to reach a level of comfort and tidiness never dreamed of under Russian and German rule. For the first time country children everywhere wore leather shoes and dressed in white summer muslin. Babies were being rolled along the new sidewalks

283

in perambulators instead of carried in swaddling clothes on pillows. Motor trucks, crowding the highroad, drove milk to town. The women no longer carried milk on their backs. Bicyclists blocked traffic where pedestrians had thronged. Radio programs from England, Italy and Russia blared from every window. The "Palace Cinema" displayed bills from Hollywood. Well stocked shops neatly displayed provisions on white enamel counters gleaming through the brightly polished plate glass windows on either side of the street. Now all traces of the last war had been effaced.

Tears blinding my eyes made driving difficult. I thought of Michael's words, "Every life is for a purpose, we should push on as best we can even if we don't know what will remain of it, or what the purpose is under the circumstances." And I wondered, was it enough that Poland should flower for so short a time? Surely this could not be all that life had in store for these people; to have rebuilt their country, only to have it smashed again within two decades! Would the Polish example inspire other nations never to compromise for temporary gains? Would her steadfastness rally other peoples? Would she in the end become the spiritual leader her prophets had foretold?

Yet Poland stood alone. How sad it was no picturesque leader had made these people intelligible to the world at large. How many people still believed Poland was ruled by an autocratic military clique that should have been destroyed? Surely the nation's determined unity could belie this slur against her real democracy. It should be clear at last that Russia and Germany have covered their own imperialistic designs by implicating Poland. Yet many still believe Poland has German and Russian provinces and that these provinces ought to be restored. What can one individual say to correct this misconception? Surely in the end all will recognize this prevarication and abstract justice will prevail!

Poles knew they would have to die if Poland were to live. . . The enduring courage of her soldiers and her peoples, the untainted loyalty of the nation will prove how shallow its judgment has been. Surely her dauntlessness in the face of death will show the world what Poland is.

284